CONTEMPORARY
AMERICAN POETRY

CONTEMPORARY AMERICAN POETRY

SEVENTH EDITION

Edited by

A. Poulin, Jr.

State University of New York,
College at Brockport

and

Michael Waters

Salisbury University,
Maryland

HOUGHTON MIFFLIN COMPANY BOSTON NEW YORK

Senior sponsoring editor: Dean Johnson
Senior production editor: Rosemary Winfield
Senior production/design coordinator: Carol Merrigan
Senior manufacturing coordinator: Marie Barnes
Senior marketing manager: Nancy Lyman

Cover designer: Daphne Poulin-Stofer, Forward Design

Acknowledgments begin on page 671.

Printed in the U.S.A.

Library of Congress Catalog Card Number: 00-133916

ISBN: 0-618-04299-7

456789-HPC-05 04 03 02

AMERICAN POETRY

Whatever it is, it must have
A stomach that can digest
Rubber, coal, uranium, moons, poems.

Like the shark, it contains a shoe.
It must swim for miles through the desert
Uttering cries that are almost human.

—Louis Simpson

A. Poulin, Jr.

Arthur Furst

Michael Waters

Rick Maloof

in memory of A. *Poulin, Jr.*
1938–1996

for Boo and Daphne
— A. P., Jr.

for Mihaela and Kiernan
— M.W.

Contents

CONTENTS

Contemporary American Poetry:
A Chronology

The following is a listing of the poets in *Contemporary American Poetry* by year of birth. Information about each poet's life and work is found in the Notes on the Poets (page 585).

Preface

When the First Edition of *Contemporary American Poetry* appeared in 1971, it included work by twenty-two poets in its four hundred pages. Twenty-five years later, the Sixth Edition included work by sixty poets and the number of pages had doubled. The work in that First Edition spanned a quarter-century. The work in the Sixth Edition spanned a half-century, placing some strain on the *Contemporary* of the book's title and prodding the anthology toward the unwieldy. For this Seventh Edition, I've shifted the generally acknowledged, post–World War II, 1945 starting point of contemporary American poetry, never more than a convenient marker, to the more convenient though still somewhat arbitrary 1960 — the beginning of the literary decade that absorbed the lessons of Allen Ginsberg's *Howl* (1956) and Robert Lowell's *Life Studies* (1959) and hastened to replace ironic detachment and formal convention with subjectivity and irregular verse. In *Howl*, Ginsberg breathed the rowdy, democratic spirit of Whitman back into American poetry while bemoaning the nation's vast, spiritual ennui; in *Life Studies*, Lowell whispered forth the dramatic intimacies of marriage while brooding on the origins of his own soul-sickness. The work of poets who had published their first books in the 1950s — W. S. Merwin, Adrienne Rich, and James Wright, for example — underwent significant revision in the early 1960s, at least partly in response to an atmosphere now charged with the possibility of change.

It was in this atmosphere that the original editor of *Contemporary American Poetry*, A. Poulin, Jr., began to write his own poems (his first collection, *In Advent*, appeared in 1972) and to gather work toward this anthology. His selections reflected the influence of those movements and schools — Beat, Black Mountain, Black, Women's, among others — dominant at the time. Over the next five editions during the quarter-century to follow, as these influences gathered force and spread, or weakened and dispersed, or — more accurately, in most instances — commingled in fresh and unforeseen variations, especially with regard to individual poets represented in the anthology, Poulin added poets — more than three dozen — to reflect the vitality and diversity evident in our poetry. Fewer than a handful of poets in that First Edition were not included in all subsequent editions. In many ways, the Sixth Edition seemed an expanded version of that First Edition, and when it appeared in 1996 Poulin and I agreed that the next edition — this one — would incorporate the first in a series of changes necessary to the essential *freshness* of the anthology as it was originally conceived thirty years ago.

I've updated and revised, sometimes wholly, the selections, no longer needing to demonstrate the changes, now widely acknowledged, that took place in poetry between the 1950s and 1960s. I've dropped, for example, "The Drunk in the Furnace" by Merwin, "Aunt Jennifer's Tigers" by Rich, and "Saint Judas" by James Wright, in favor of more recent work ("recent" still encompassing the past forty years) that more accurately depicts the poets' achievements. For the same reason, I've retained or selected, in a few instances, some pre-1960 work — by Ginsberg and Lowell, as well as by Gwendolyn Brooks, for example. I've also had to face the unpleasant task of dropping poets from the book — often poets whose work I admire — while reducing, slightly, the number of pages of each section in order to add new poets. The anthology simply could not expand beyond the length of the previous edition.

Such changes — fifteen new poets have been included here — reflect the fact that any anthology needs to be flexible and active, edition by edition, in order to remain essential. *Contemporary American Poetry* will reshape itself in future editions as poets struggle toward defining and honing the aesthetics of the narrowly defined age. And just as previous editions of the anthology demonstrated, to some extent, Poulin's biases (though more often they reflected his remarkable generosity and catholicity of taste), this Seventh Edition reflects my own leanings and enthusiasms. Having worked with Poulin on an informal though regular basis on previous editions, I felt it incumbent on me to honor his predilections as much as possible while still pressing my own thumb, however lightly, on each page. This edition is collaborative in that many of the selections that have remained from previous editions were agreed on by both editors. Also, I've left, as much as possible, Poulin's "Notes on the Poets" intact, revising them mainly with regard to references to poems either no longer included or new to this edition. However, when Poulin quoted a brief passage in considering a poet's body of work, I've let it remain, whether or not the poem still appears in the anthology. The notes on the poets new to this edition are my own. Finally, I've not reprinted Poulin's essay, "Contemporary American Poetry: The Radical Tradition," written in 1970.

Although A. Poulin, Jr. died in 1996, the year the previous edition of this anthology appeared, his terse spirit offered lively company and judicious chiding as I gathered these poems. His presence in contemporary literature — as poet, translator, editor, and publisher — was inestimable, always generative, and his presence in my life, since 1971, has been a source of undiminished light.

I remain grateful to my wife, Mihaela, and my daughter, Kiernan, for their patience and wisdom while I prepared this edition, and also remain grateful for — and ever-astonished by — their unfathomable love . . .

. . . and Boo and Daphne, family too, this one's still for you.

Michael Waters
January 2000
Salisbury, Maryland

CONTEMPORARY
AMERICAN POETRY

Ai

THE MOTHER'S TALE

Once when I was young, Juanito,
there was a ballroom in Lima
where Hernán, your father,
danced with another woman
and I cut him across the cheek
with a pocketknife.
Oh, the pitch of the music sometimes,
the smoke and rustle of crinoline.
But what things to remember now
on your wedding day.
I pour a kettle of hot water
into the wooden tub where you are sitting.
I was young, free.
But Juanito, how free is a woman? —
born with Eve's sin between her legs,
and inside her,
Lucifer sits on a throne of abalone shells,
his staff with the head of John the Baptist
skewered on it.
And in judgment, son, in judgment he says
that women will bear the fruit of the tree
we wished so much to eat
and that fruit will devour us
generation by generation,
so my son,
you must beat Rosita often.
She must know the weight of a man's hand,
the bruises that are like the wounds of Christ.
Her blood that is black at the heart
must flow until it is as red and pure as His.
And she must be pregnant always
if not with child
then with the knowledge
that she is alive because of you.
That you can take her life
more easily than she creates it,
that suffering is her inheritance from you
and through you, from Christ,

who walked on his mother's body
to be the King of Heaven.

THE MORTICIAN'S TWELVE-YEAR-OLD SON

Lady, when you were alive
I'd see you on the streets,
the long green dress with the velvet flower
sewn dead center between your breasts
so tightly I could never get a look inside.

Now the gas lamps half-light the table,
washing the sheet that covers you with shadows.
A few strands of your dyed red hair
hang nearly to the floor,
as if all your blood had run there to hide.

I lift the sheet, rub the mole on your cheek
and it comes off black and oily on my hand.
I bend over your breasts and sing,
love, sister, is just a kiss away.
I cover each nipple with my mouth.
Tonight, just a kiss away.

TWENTY-YEAR MARRIAGE

You keep me waiting in a truck
with its one good wheel stuck in the ditch,
while you piss against the south side of a tree.
Hurry. I've got nothing on under my skirt tonight.
That still excites you, but this pickup has no windows
and the seat, one fake leather thigh,
pressed close to mine is cold.
I'm the same size, shape, make as twenty years ago,
but get inside me, start the engine;
you'll have the strength, the will to move.
I'll pull, you push, we'll tear each other in half.
Come on, baby, lay me down on my back.

Pretend you don't owe me a thing
and maybe we'll roll out of here,
leaving the past stacked up behind us;
old newspapers nobody's ever got to read again.

WHY CAN'T I LEAVE YOU?

You stand behind the old black mare,
dressed as always in that red shirt,
stained from sweat, the crying of the armpits,
that will not stop for anything,
stroking her rump, while the barley goes unplanted.
I pick up my suitcase and set it down,
as I try to leave you again.
I smooth the hair back from your forehead.
I think with your laziness and the drought too,
you'll be needing my help more than ever.
You take my hands, I nod
and go to the house to unpack,
having found another reason to stay.

I undress, then put on my white lace slip
for you to take off, because you like that
and when you come in, you pull down the straps
and I unbutton your shirt.
I know we can't give each other any more
or any less than what we have.
There is safety in that, so much
that I can never get past the packing,
the begging you to please, if I can't make you happy,
come close between my thighs
and let me laugh for you from my second mouth.

I HAVE GOT TO STOP LOVING YOU
SO I HAVE KILLED MY BLACK GOAT

His kidney floats in a bowl,
a beige, flat fish, around whom parasites, slices of lemon,

break through the surface of hot broth, then sink below,
as I bend, face down in the steam, breathing in.
I hear this will cure anything.

When I am finished, I walk up to him.
He hangs from a short wooden post,
tongue stuck out of his mouth,
tasting the hay-flavored air.
A bib of flies gather at his throat
and further down, where he is open
and bare of all his organs,
I put my hand in, stroke him once,
then taking it out, look at the sky.
The stormclouds there break open
and raindrops, yellow as black cats' eyes, come down
each a tiny river, hateful and alone.

Wishing I could get out of this alive, I hug myself.
It is hard to remember if he suffered much.

FINISHED

You force me to touch
the black, rubber flaps
of the garbage disposal
that is open like a mouth saying, ah.
You tell me it's the last thing I'll feel
before I go numb.
Is it my screaming that finally stops you,
or is it the fear
that even you are too near the edge
of this Niagara to come back from?
You jerk my hand out
and give me just enough room
to stagger around you.
I lean against the refrigerator,
not looking at you, or anything,
just staring at a space which you no longer inhabit,
that you've abandoned completely now
to footsteps receding
to the next feeding station,
where a woman will be eaten alive

after cocktails at five.
The flowers and chocolates, the kisses,
the swings and near misses of new love
will confuse her,
until you start to abuse her,
verbally at first.
As if trying to quench a thirst,
you'll drink her
in small outbursts of rage
then you'll whip out your semiautomatic,
make her undress, or listen to hours
of radio static as torture
for being amazed that the man of her dreams
is a nightmare, who only seems happy
when he's making her suffer.

The first time you hit me,
I left you, remember?
It was December. An icy rain was falling
and it froze on the roads,
so that driving was unsafe, but not as unsafe
as staying with you.
I ran outside in my nightgown,
while you yelled at me to come back.
When you came after me,
I was locked in the car.
You smashed the window with a crowbar,
but I drove off anyway.
I was back the next day
and we were on the bare mattress,
because you'd ripped up the sheets,
saying you'd teach me a lesson.
You wouldn't speak except
to tell me I needed discipline,
needed training in the fine art
of remaining still
when your fist slammed into my jaw.
You taught me how ropes could be tied
so I'd strangle myself,
how pressure could be applied to old wounds
until I cried for mercy,
until tonight, when those years
of our double exposure end
with shot after shot.

How strange it is to be unafraid.
When the police come,
I'm sitting at the table,
the cup of coffee
that I am unable to drink
as cold as your body.
I shot him, I say, he beat me.
I do not tell them how the emancipation from pain
leaves nothing in its place.

RIOT ACT, APRIL 29, 1992

I'm going out and get something.
I don't know what.
I don't care.
Whatever's out there, I'm going to get it.
Look in those shop windows at boxes
and boxes of Reeboks and Nikes
to make me fly through the air
like Michael Jordan
like Magic.
While I'm up there, I see Spike Lee.
Looks like he's flying too
straight through the glass
that separates me
from the virtual reality
I watch everyday on TV.
I know the difference between
what it is and what it isn't.
Just because I can't touch it
doesn't mean it isn't real.
All I have to do is smash the screen,
reach in and take what I want.
Break out of prison.
South Central homey's newly risen
from the night of living dead,
but this time he lives,
he gets to give the zombies
a taste of their own medicine.
Open wide and let me in,
or else I'll set your world on fire,

but you pretend that you don't hear.
You haven't heard the word is coming down
like the hammer of the gun
of this black son, locked out of the big house,
while massa looks out the window and sees only smoke.
Massa doesn't see anything else,
not because he can't,
but because he won't.
He'd rather hear me talking about mo' money,
mo' honeys and gold chains
and see me carrying my favorite things
from looted stores
than admit that underneath my Raiders' cap,
the aftermath is staring back
unblinking through the camera's lens,
courtesy of CNN,
my arms loaded with boxes of shoes
that I will sell at the swap meet
to make a few cents on the declining dollar.
And if I destroy myself
and my neighborhood
"ain't nobody's business, if I do,"
but the police are knocking hard
at my door
and before I can open it,
they break it down
and drag me in the yard.
They take me in to be processed and charged,
to await trial,
while Americans forget
the day the wealth finally trickled down
to the rest of us.

A. R. Ammons

WITH ROPES OF HEMP

With ropes of hemp
I lashed my body to the great oak
saying odes for the fiber of the oakbark
and the oakwood saying supplications
to the root mesh
deep and reticular in the full earth
through the night saying these
and early into the wild unusual dawn
chanting hysterical though quiet
watching the ropes ravel
and the body go raw
    while eternity
greater than the ravelings of a rope
waited with me patient in my experiment
Oh I said listening to the raucous
words of the nightclouds
how shadowy is the soul
how fleet with the wildness of wings

Under the grip of my bonds
I say Oh and melt beyond the ruthless coil
but return again saying odes in the night
where I stand splintered to the oak
gathering the dissentient ghosts of my spirit
into the oakheart
I in the night standing saying oaksongs
entertaining my soul to me

OPEN

Exuberance: joy to the last
pained loss
    and hunger of air:
life open, not decided on,
though decided in death:

11

      the mind cannot be
rid
while it works
   of remembered genitals
beautiful, dank, pliant,

of canyons, brush hills, pastures, streets,
   unities and divisions,
meetings,

exact remembrance of liquid buttocks,
navel, ellipse of hand,

magnified territories of going down
and rising,
the thin tracing saliva line,

   joy's configurations:

serendipity: the unexpected,
the
possible, the unembodied,
    unevented:

the sun will burst: death
is certain: the future limited
   nevertheless is
limitless: the white knotted

   groin,
the finger describing
   entrances!

the dark, warm with glowing awareness, the
hot dis-
   missals of desire
until the last last tear of pain:

until the end nothing ends, lust
forward, rushing;
   pillars of ice wet-bright in melt,
warm

with always-yielding joy: yes
　　yes
yes, the loose mouths hiss in the mornings of death.

CATALYST

Honor the maggot,
　supreme catalyst:
he spurs the rate of change:
(all scavengers are honorable: I love them
all,
will scribble hard as I can for them)

　he accelerates change
　in the changeless continuum;
where the body falls completed, he sets to work:
where the spirit attains
　indifference

he makes his residence:
in the egg on wing from mound
to mound he travels,
feeds, finds his wings,

　　after the wet-sweet of decay,
　　after the ant-sucked earth has drunk
　　the honey-fluids,
　　after
　　the veins
　lie dried to streaks of tendon
　　inside the meat-free, illuminated skull,

lofts, saws the air, copulates in a hung
rapture
of riding, holds the sweet-clear
connection
　　through dual flights, male and female,
　　soil's victory:
　　(dead cell dross transfigured
　　into gloss,

iridescence of compound eyes,
duck-neck purple of hairy abdomen)

O worm supreme,
transformer of bloated, breaking flesh
into colorless netted wings,
into the wills of sex and song, leaving
ash on odorless ground, the scent
of pinestraw
rising dominant from the striking sun!

GRACE ABOUNDING

for E.C.

What is the misery in one that turns one with gladness
to the hedge strung lucid with ice: is it that one's
misery, penetrating there as sight, meets neither

welcome nor reprimand but finds nevertheless a picture
of itself sympathetic, held as the ice-blurred stems
increased: ah, what an abundance is in the universe

when one can go for gladness to the indifferent ghastly,
feel alliances where none may ever take: find one's
misery made clear, borne, as if also, by a hedge of ice.

TRIPHAMMER BRIDGE

I wonder what to mean by *sanctuary*, if a real or
apprehended place, as of a bell rung in a gold
surround, or as of silver roads along the beaches

of clouds seas don't break or black mountains
overspill; jail: ice here's shapelier than anything,
on the eaves massive, jawed along gorge ledges, solid

in the plastic blue boat fall left water in: if I
think the bitterest thing I can think of that seems like
reality, slickened back, hard, shocked by rip-high wind:

sanctuary, sanctuary, I say it over and over and the
word's sound is the one place to dwell: that's it, just
the sound, and the imagination of the sound — a place.

EPIPHANY

Like a single drop of rain,
    the wasp strikes
the windowpane; buzzes rapidly
away, disguising

error in urgent business:
    such is the
invisible, hard as glass,
unrenderable by the senses,

not known until stricken by:
    some talk that
there is safety in the visible,
the definite, the heard and felt,

pre-stressing the rational and
    calling out with
joy, like people far from death:
how puzzled they will be when

going headlong secure in "things"
    they strike the
intangible and break, lost,
unaccustomed to transparency, to

being without body, energy
    without image:
how they will be dealt
hard realizations, opaque as death.

MARGINALS

Some of these old widow women around here are roving
loners: no matter how deep the snow or bitterly near
zero the air, they're long-gaited out in their boots

of a morning and gone: one's high hip spins outward
every step, and one's eyes set ahead just above the
trees, and one hangs over a slouchy net bag lumpy at

the bottom, suggesting she could pack up and off
in any direction without regret, unsurprised: one
leans into a leaning shoulder, sidelong, as if eyeing

the ditch, as if listening with one ear (but
I've seen her on both sides of town in a morning): I
don't know where they go, probably not out to eat,

because they often don't have their teeth in: I don't
know what they do: mostly they just go, it's the motion,
going, I think, and, going, they rise through high

lattices till motion fills with song, their heads fill
with sky, and a wind rises in them like ecstasy or
death and, their minds made up, they let the earth go.

THE ONLY WAY AROUND IS THROUGH

I've lost my ambition to be somebody:
what is there to be except
free of the need to be somebody:

the brook doesn't save itself: slate
honings, root wear, underminings,
silt-flow slopes

express to the sweetest reader former
times and ways but
the brook isn't trying mainly to stay recalled:

enough remains, bits, bunches, not to
take currency out of change: but
the brook's glassy noise this

evening (jay and robin fighting dominion
out in a bankside crabapple bush)
feels like its oldest recollection, the song

brassy, ledge-displaced, ledge-displayed
rattle-rush hard to find anything to to
repeat yet always the same: trying to

write free of writing keeps me
at it, writing my brook, not
to keep but to mumble by with.

THE CLENCHED-JAW SCHOOL

The holdout of brook-glitter in a drought,
the skittery edginess of leaves against a windy hedge row —

I sit out of the way by the brookfalls
looking in places too drab for pilgrimage
for revelations such
as the sun's surviving the all-day splintering
of running water, the

water broken, too, over and over into falls: stones hear
or say my verses:
brookbanks set out
staves of music for me:
I put the bars in, I take them out, I move them around.

Juno Germes

John Ashbery

SELF-PORTRAIT IN A CONVEX MIRROR

As Parmigianino did it, the right hand
Bigger than the head, thrust at the viewer
And swerving easily away, as though to protect
What it advertises. A few leaded panes, old beams,
Fur, pleated muslin, a coral ring run together
In a movement supporting the face, which swims
Toward and away like the hand
Except that it is in repose. It is what is
Sequestered. Vasari says, "Francesco one day set himself
To take his own portrait, looking at himself for that purpose
In a convex mirror, such as is used by barbers . . .
He accordingly caused a ball of wood to be made
By a turner, and having divided it in half and
Brought it to the size of the mirror, he set himself
With great art to copy all that he saw in the glass,"
Chiefly his reflection, of which the portrait
Is the reflection once removed.
The glass chose to reflect only what he saw
Which was enough for his purpose: his image
Glazed, embalmed, projected at a 180-degree angle.
The time of day or the density of the light
Adhering to the face keeps it
Lively and intact in a recurring wave
Of arrival. The soul establishes itself.
But how far can it swim out through the eyes
And still return safely to its nest? The surface
Of the mirror being convex, the distance increases
Significantly; that is, enough to make the point
That the soul is a captive, treated humanely, kept
In suspension, unable to advance much farther
Than your look as it intercepts the picture.
Pope Clement and his court were "stupefied"
By it, according to Vasari, and promised a commission
That never materialized. The soul has to stay where it is,
Even though restless, hearing raindrops at the pane,
The sighing of autumn leaves thrashed by the wind,
Longing to be free, outside, but it must stay
Posing in this place. It must move

19

As little as possible. This is what the portrait says.
But there is in that gaze a combination
Of tenderness, amusement and regret, so powerful
In its restraint that one cannot look for long.
The secret is too plain. The pity of it smarts,
Makes hot tears spurt: that the soul is not a soul,
Has no secret, is small, and it fits
Its hollow perfectly: its room, our moment of attention.
That is the tune but there are no words.
The words are only speculation
(From the Latin *speculum*, mirror):
They seek and cannot find the meaning of the music.
We see only postures of the dream,
Riders of the motion that swings the face
Into view under evening skies, with no
False disarray as proof of authenticity.
But it is life englobed.
One would like to stick one's hand
Out of the globe, but its dimension,
What carries it, will not allow it.
No doubt it is this, not the reflex
To hide something, which makes the hand loom large
As it retreats slightly. There is no way
To build it flat like a section of wall:
It must join the segment of a circle,
Roving back to the body of which it seems
So unlikely a part, to fence in and shore up the face
On which the effort of this condition reads
Like a pinpoint of a smile, a spark
Or star one is not sure of having seen
As darkness resumes. A perverse light whose
Imperative of subtlety dooms in advance its
Conceit to light up: unimportant but meant.
Francesco, your hand is big enough
To wreck the sphere, and too big,
One would think, to weave delicate meshes
That only argue its further detention.
(Big, but not coarse, merely on another scale,
Like a dozing whale on the sea bottom
In relation to the tiny, self-important ship
On the surface.) But your eyes proclaim
That everything is surface. The surface is what's there
And nothing can exist except what's there.
There are no recesses in the room, only alcoves,

And the window doesn't matter much, or that
Sliver of window or mirror on the right, even
As a gauge of the weather, which in French is
Le temps, the word for time, and which
Follows a course wherein changes are merely
Features of the whole. The whole is stable within
Instability, a globe like ours, resting
On a pedestal of vacuum, a ping-pong ball
Secure on its jet of water.
And just as there are no words for the surface, that is,
No words to say what it really is, that it is not
Superficial but a visible core, then there is
No way out of the problem of pathos vs. experience.
You will stay on, restive, serene in
Your gesture which is neither embrace nor warning
But which holds something of both in pure
Affirmation that doesn't affirm anything.

The balloon pops, the attention
Turns dully away. Clouds
In the puddle stir up into sawtoothed fragments.
I think of the friends
Who came to see me, of what yesterday
Was like. A peculiar slant
Of memory that intrudes on the dreaming model
In the silence of the studio as he considers
Lifting the pencil to the self-portrait.
How many people came and stayed a certain time,
Uttered light or dark speech that became part of you
Like light behind windblown fog and sand,
Filtered and influenced by it, until no part
Remains that is surely you. Those voices in the dusk
Have told you all and still the tale goes on
In the form of memories deposited in irregular
Clumps of crystals. Whose curved hand controls,
Francesco, the turning seasons and the thoughts
That peel off and fly away at breathless speeds
Like the last stubborn leaves ripped
From wet branches? I see in this only the chaos
Of your round mirror which organizes everything
Around the polestar of your eyes which are empty,
Know nothing, dream but reveal nothing.
I feel the carousel starting slowly
And going faster and faster: desk, papers, books,

Photographs of friends, the window and the trees
Merging in one neutral band that surrounds
Me on all sides, everywhere I look.
And I cannot explain the action of leveling,
Why it should all boil down to one
Uniform substance, a magma of interiors.
My guide in these matters is your self,
Firm, oblique, accepting everything with the same
Wraith of a smile, and as time speeds up so that it is soon
Much later, I can know only the straight way out,
The distance between us. Long ago
The strewn evidence meant something,
The small accidents and pleasures
Of the day as it moved gracelessly on,
A housewife doing chores. Impossible now
To restore those properties in the silver blur that is
The record of what you accomplished by sitting down
"With great art to copy all that you saw in the glass"
So as to perfect and rule out the extraneous
Forever. In the circle of your intentions certain spars
Remain that perpetuate the enchantment of self with self:
Eyebeams, muslin, coral. It doesn't matter
Because these are things as they are today
Before one's shadow ever grew
Out of the field into thoughts of tomorrow.

Tomorrow is easy, but today is uncharted,
Desolate, reluctant as any landscape
To yield what are laws of perspective
After all only to the painter's deep
Mistrust, a weak instrument though
Necessary. Of course some things
Are possible, it knows, but it doesn't know
Which ones. Some day we will try
To do as many things as are possible
And perhaps we shall succeed at a handful
Of them, but this will not have anything
To do with what is promised today, our
Landscape sweeping out from us to disappear
On the horizon. Today enough of a cover burnishes
To keep the supposition of promises together
In one piece of surface, letting one ramble
Back home from them so that these
Even stronger possibilities can remain

Whole without being tested. Actually
The skin of the bubble-chamber's as tough as
Reptile eggs; everything gets "programmed" there
In due course: more keeps getting included
Without adding to the sum, and just as one
Gets accustomed to a noise that
Kept one awake but now no longer does,
So the room contains this flow like an hourglass
Without varying in climate or quality
(Except perhaps to brighten bleakly and almost
Invisibly, in a focus sharpening toward death — more
Of this later). What should be the vacuum of a dream
Becomes continually replete as the source of dreams
Is being tapped so that this one dream
May wax, flourish like a cabbage rose,
Defying sumptuary laws, leaving us
To awake and try to begin living in what
Has now become a slum. Sydney Freedberg in his
Parmigianino says of it: "Realism in this portrait
No longer produces an objective truth, but a *bizarria*. . . .
However its distortion does not create
A feeling of disharmony. . . . The forms retain
A strong measure of ideal beauty," because
Fed by our dreams, so inconsequential until one day
We notice the hole they left. Now their importance
If not their meaning is plain. They were to nourish
A dream which includes them all, as they are
Finally reversed in the accumulating mirror.
They seemed strange because we couldn't actually see them.
And we realize this only at a point where they lapse
Like a wave breaking on a rock, giving up
Its shape in a gesture which expresses that shape.
The forms retain a strong measure of ideal beauty
As they forage in secret on our idea of distortion.
Why be unhappy with this arrangement, since
Dreams prolong us as they are absorbed?
Something like living occurs, a movement
Out of the dream into its codification.

As I start to forget it
It presents its stereotype again
But it is an unfamiliar stereotype, the face
Riding at anchor, issued from hazards, soon
To accost others, "rather angel than man" (Vasari).

JOHN ASHBERY

Perhaps an angel looks like everything
We have forgotten, I mean forgotten
Things that don't seem familiar when
We meet them again, lost beyond telling,
Which were ours once. This would be the point
Of invading the privacy of this man who
"Dabbled in alchemy, but whose wish
Here was not to examine the subtleties of art
In a detached, scientific spirit: he wished through them
To impart the sense of novelty and amazement to the spectator"
(Freedberg). Later portraits such as the Uffizi
"Gentleman," the Borghese "Young Prelate" and
The Naples "Antea" issue from Mannerist
Tensions, but here, as Freedberg points out,
The surprise, the tension are in the concept
Rather than its realization.
The consonance of the High Renaissance
Is present, though distorted by the mirror.
What is novel is the extreme care in rendering
The velleities of the rounded reflecting surface
(It is the first mirror portrait),
So that you could be fooled for a moment
Before you realize the reflection
Isn't yours. You feel then like one of those
Hoffmann characters who have been deprived
Of a reflection, except that the whole of me
Is seen to be supplanted by the strict
Otherness of the painter in his
Other room. We have surprised him
At work, but no, he has surprised us
As he works. The picture is almost finished,
The surprise almost over, as when one looks out,
Startled by a snowfall which even now is
Ending in specks and sparkles of snow.
It happened while you were inside, asleep,
And there is no reason why you should have
Been awake for it, except that the day
Is ending and it will be hard for you
To get to sleep tonight, at least until late.

The shadow of the city injects its own
Urgency: Rome where Francesco
Was at work during the Sack: his inventions
Amazed the soldiers who burst in on him;

They decided to spare his life, but he left soon after;
Vienna where the painting is today, where
I saw it with Pierre in the summer of 1959; New York
Where I am now, which is a logarithm
Of other cities. Our landscape
Is alive with filiations, shuttlings;
Business is carried on by look, gesture,
Hearsay. It is another life to the city,
The backing of the looking glass of the
Unidentified but precisely sketched studio. It wants
To siphon off the life of the studio, deflate
Its mapped space to enactments, island it.
That operation has been temporarily stalled
But something new is on the way, a new preciosity
In the wind. Can you stand it,
Francesco? Are you strong enough for it?
This wind brings what it knows not, is
Self-propelled, blind, has no notion
Of itself. It is inertia that once
Acknowledged saps all activity, secret or public:
Whispers of the word that can't be understood
But can be felt, a chill, a blight
Moving outward along the capes and peninsulas
Of your nervures and so to the archipelagoes
And to the bathed, aired secrecy of the open sea.
This is its negative side. Its positive side is
Making you notice life and the stresses
That only seemed to go away, but now,
As this new mode questions, are seen to be
Hastening out of style. If they are to become classics
They must decide which side they are on.
Their reticence has undermined
The urban scenery, made its ambiguities
Look willful and tired, the games of an old man.
What we need now is this unlikely
Challenger pounding on the gates of an amazed
Castle. Your argument, Francesco,
Had begun to grow stale as no answer
Or answers were forthcoming. If it dissolves now
Into dust, that only means its time had come
Some time ago, but look now, and listen:
It may be that another life is stocked there
In recesses no one knew of; that it,
Not we, are the change; that we are in fact it

If we could get back to it, relive some of the way
It looked, turn our faces to the globe as it sets
And still be coming out all right:
Nerves normal, breath normal. Since it is a metaphor
Made to include us, we are a part of it and
Can live in it as in fact we have done,
Only leaving our minds bare for questioning
We now see will not take place at random
But in an orderly way that means to menace
Nobody — the normal way things are done,
Like the concentric growing up of days
Around a life: correctly, if you think about it.

A breeze like the turning of a page
Brings back your face: the moment
Takes such a big bite out of the haze
Of pleasant intuition it comes after.
The locking into place is "death itself,"
As Berg said of a phrase in Mahler's Ninth;
Or, to quote Imogen in *Cymbeline*, "There cannot
Be a pinch in death more sharp than this," for,
Though only exercise or tactic, it carries
The momentum of a conviction that had been building.
Mere forgetfulness cannot remove it
Nor wishing bring it back, as long as it remains
The white precipitate of its dream
In the climate of sighs flung across our world,
A cloth over a birdcage. But it is certain that
What is beautiful seems so only in relation to a specific
Life, experienced or not, channeled into some form
Steeped in the nostalgia of a collective past.
The light sinks today with an enthusiasm
I have known elsewhere, and known why
It seemed meaningful, that others felt this way
Years ago. I go on consulting
This mirror that is no longer mine
For as much brisk vacancy as is to be
My portion this time. And the vase is always full
Because there is only just so much room
And it accommodates everything. The sample
One sees is not to be taken as
Merely that, but as everything as it
May be imagined outside time — not as a gesture
But as all, in the refined, assimilable state.

But what is this universe the porch of
As it veers in and out, back and forth,
Refusing to surround us and still the only
Thing we can see? Love once
Tipped the scales but now is shadowed, invisible,
Though mysteriously present, around somewhere.
But we know it cannot be sandwiched
Between two adjacent moments, that its windings
Lead nowhere except to further tributaries
And that these empty themselves into a vague
Sense of something that can never be known
Even though it seems likely that each of us
Knows what it is and is capable of
Communicating it to the other. But the look
Some wear as a sign makes one want to
Push forward ignoring the apparent
Naïveté of the attempt, not caring
That no one is listening, since the light
Has been lit once and for all in their eyes
And is present, unimpaired, a permanent anomaly,
Awake and silent. On the surface of it
There seems no special reason why that light
Should be focused by love, or why
The city falling with its beautiful suburbs
Into space always less clear, less defined,
Should read as the support of its progress,
The easel upon which the drama unfolded
To its own satisfaction and to the end
Of our dreaming, as we had never imagined
It would end, in worn daylight with the painted
Promise showing through as a gage, a bond.
This nondescript, never-to-be defined daytime is
The secret of where it takes place
And we can no longer return to the various
Conflicting statements gathered, lapses of memory
Of the principal witnesses. All we know
Is that we are a little early, that
Today has that special, lapidary
Todayness that the sunlight reproduces
Faithfully in casting twig-shadows on blithe
Sidewalks. No previous day would have been like this.
I used to think they were all alike,
That the present always looked the same to everybody
But this confusion drains away as one

Is always cresting into one's present.
Yet the "poetic," straw-colored space
Of the long corridor that leads back to the painting,
Its darkening opposite — is this
Some figment of "art," not to be imagined
As real, let alone special? Hasn't it too its lair
In the present we are always escaping from
And falling back into, as the waterwheel of days
Pursues its uneventful, even serene course?
I think it is trying to say it is today
And we must get out of it even as the public
Is pushing through the museum now so as to
Be out by closing time. You can't live there.
The gray glaze of the past attacks all know-how:
Secrets of wash and finish that took a lifetime
To learn and are reduced to the status of
Black-and-white illustrations in a book where colorplates
Are rare. That is, all time
Reduces to no special time. No one
Alludes to the change; to do so might
Involve calling attention to oneself
Which would augment the dread of not getting out
Before having seen the whole collection
(Except for the sculptures in the basement:
They are where they belong).
Our time gets to be veiled, compromised
By the portrait's will to endure. It hints at
Our own, which we were hoping to keep hidden.
We don't need paintings or
Doggerel written by mature poets when
The explosion is so precise, so fine.
Is there any point even in acknowledging
The existence of all that? Does it
Exist? Certainly the leisure to
Indulge stately pastimes doesn't,
Any more. Today has no margins, the event arrives
Flush with its edges, is of the same substance,
Indistinguishable. "Play" is something else;
It exists, in a society specifically
Organized as a demonstration of itself.
There is no other way, and those assholes
Who would confuse everything with their mirror games
Which seem to multiply stakes and possibilities, or
At least confuse issues by means of an investing

Aura that would corrode the architecture
Of the whole in a haze of suppressed mockery,
Are beside the point. They are out of the game,
Which doesn't exist until they are out of it.
It seems like a very hostile universe
But as the principle of each individual thing is
Hostile to, exists at the expense of all the others
As philosophers have often pointed out, at least
This thing, the mute, undivided present,
Has the justification of logic, which
In this instance isn't a bad thing
Or wouldn't be, if the way of telling
Didn't somehow intrude, twisting the end result
Into a caricature of itself. This always
Happens, as in the game where
A whispered phrase passed around the room
Ends up as something completely different.
It is the principle that makes works of art so unlike
What the artist intended. Often he finds
He has omitted the thing he started out to say
In the first place. Seduced by flowers,
Explicit pleasures, he blames himself (though
Secretly satisfied with the result), imagining
He had a say in the matter and exercised
An option of which he was hardly conscious,
Unaware that necessity circumvents such resolutions.
So as to create something new
For itself, that there is no other way,
That the history of creation proceeds according to
Stringent laws, and that things
Do get done in this way, but never the things
We set out to accomplish and wanted so desperately
To see come into being. Parmigianino
Must have realized this as he worked at his
Life-obstructing task. One is forced to read
The perfectly plausible accomplishment of a purpose
Into the smooth, perhaps even bland (but so
Enigmatic) finish. Is there anything
To be serious about beyond this otherness
That gets included in the most ordinary
Forms of daily activity, changing everything
Slightly and profoundly, and tearing the matter
Of creation, any creation, not just artistic creation
Out of our hands, to install it on some monstrous, near

Peak, too close to ignore, too far
For one to intervene? This otherness, this
"Not-being-us" is all there is to look at
In the mirror, though no one can say
How it came to be this way. A ship
Flying unknown colors has entered the harbor.
You are allowing extraneous matters
To break up your day, cloud the focus
Of the crystal ball. Its scene drifts away
Like vapor scattered on the wind. The fertile
Thought-associations that until now came
So easily, appear no more, or rarely. Their
Colorings are less intense, washed out
By autumn rains and winds, spoiled, muddied,
Given back to you because they are worthless.
Yet we are such creatures of habit that their
Implications are still around *en permanence*, confusing
Issues. To be serious only about sex
Is perhaps one way, but the sands are hissing
As they approach the beginning of the big slide
Into what happened. This past
Is now here: the painter's
Reflected face, in which we linger, receiving
Dreams and inspirations on an unassigned
Frequency, but the hues have turned metallic,
The curves and edges are not so rich. Each person
Has one big theory to explain the universe
But it doesn't tell the whole story
And in the end it is what is outside him
That matters, to him and especially to us
Who have been given no help whatever
In decoding our own man-size quotient and must rely
On second-hand knowledge. Yet I know
That no one else's taste is going to be
Any help, and might as well be ignored.
Once it seemed so perfect — gloss on the fine
Freckled skin, lips moistened as though about to part
Releasing speech, and the familiar look
Of clothes and furniture that one forgets.
This could have been our paradise: exotic
Refuge within an exhausted world, but that wasn't
In the cards, because it couldn't have been
The point. Aping naturalness may be the first step
Toward achieving an inner calm

But it is the first step only, and often
Remains a frozen gesture of welcome etched
On the air materializing behind it,
A convention. And we have really
No time for these, except to use them
For kindling. The sooner they are burnt up
The better for the roles we have to play.
Therefore I beseech you, withdraw that hand,
Offer it no longer as shield or greeting,
The shield of a greeting, Francesco:
There is room for one bullet in the chamber:
Our looking through the wrong end
Of the telescope as you fall back at a speed
Faster than that of light to flatten ultimately
Among the features of the room, an invitation
Never mailed, the "it was all a dream"
Syndrome, though the "all" tells tersely
Enough how it wasn't. Its existence
Was real, though troubled, and the ache
Of this waking dream can never drown out
The diagram still sketched on the wind,
Chosen, meant for me and materialized
In the disguising radiance of my room.
We have seen the city; it is the gibbous
Mirrored eye of an insect. All things happen
On its balcony and are resumed within,
But the action is the cold, syrupy flow
Of a pageant. One feels too confined,
Sifting the April sunlight for clues,
In the mere stillness of the ease of its
Parameter. The hand holds no chalk
And each part of the whole falls off
And cannot know it knew, except
Here and there, in cold pockets
Of remembrance, whispers out of time.

Marvin Bell

THE SELF AND THE MULBERRY

I wanted to see the self, so I looked at the mulberry.
It had no trouble accepting its limits,
yet defining and redefining a small area
so that any shape was possible, any movement.
It stayed put, but was part of all the air.
I wanted to learn to be there and not there
like the continually changing, slightly moving
mulberry, wild cherry and particularly the willow.
Like the willow, I tried to weep without tears.
Like the cherry tree, I tried to be sturdy and productive.
Like the mulberry, I tried to keep moving.
I couldn't cry right, couldn't stay or go.
I kept losing parts of myself like a soft maple.
I fell ill like the elm. That was the end
of looking in nature to find a natural self.
Let nature think itself not manly enough!
Let nature wonder at the mystery of laughter.
Let nature hypothesize man's indifference to it.
Let nature take a turn at saying what love is!

THE MYSTERY OF EMILY DICKINSON

Sometimes the weather goes on for days
but you were different. You were divine.
While the others wrote more and longer,
you wrote much more and much shorter.
I held your white dress once: 12 buttons.
In the cupola, the wasps struck glass
as hard to escape as you hit your sound
again and again asking Welcome. No one.

Except for you, it were a trifle:
This morning, not much after dawn,
in level country, not New England's,
through leftovers of summer rain I

33

went out rag-tag to the curb, only
a sleepy householder at his routine
bending to trash, when a young girl
in a white dress your size passed,

so softly!, carrying her shoes. It must be
she surprised me — her barefoot quick-step
and the earliness of the hour, your dress —
or surely I'd have spoken of it sooner.
I should have called to her, but a neighbor
wore that look you see against happiness.
I won't say anything would have happened
unless there was time, and eternity's plenty.

TREETOPS

My father moves through the South hunting duck.
It is warm, he has appeared
like a ship, surfacing, where he floats, face up,
through the ducklands. Over the tops
of trees duck will come, and he strains
not to miss seeing the first of each flock,
although it will be impossible to shoot one
from such an angle, face up like that
in a floating coffin where the lid obstructs
half a whole view, if he has a gun.
Afterlives are full of such hardships.

One meets, for example, in one's sinlessness,
high water and our faithlessness,
so the dead wonder if they are imagined
but they are not quite.

How could they know we know
when the earth shifts deceptively
to set forth ancestors to such pursuits?
My father will be asking, Is this fitting?
And I think so — I, who, with the others,
coming on the afterlife after the fact

in a dream, in a probable volume, in a
probable volume of dreams, think so.

TO AN ADOLESCENT WEEPING WILLOW

I don't know what you think you're doing,
sweeping the ground. You
do it so easily, backhanded, forehanded.
You hardly bend. Really, you sway.
What can it mean
when a thing is so easy?

I threw dirt on my father's floor.
Not dirt, but a chopped green
dirt which picked up dirt.

I pushed the pushbroom.
I oiled the wooden floor of the store.

He bent over and lifted the coal
into the coalstove. With the back of the shovel
he came down on the rat just topping the bin
and into the fire.

What do you think? — Did he sway?
Did he kiss a rock for luck?
Did he soak up water
and climb into light and turn and turn?

Did he weep and weep in the yard?

Yes, I think he did. Yes,
now I think he did.

So Willow, you come sweep my floor.
I have no store.
I have a yard. A big yard.

I have a song to weep.
I have a cry.

You who rose up from the dirt,
because I put you there
and like to walk my head in under
your earliest feathery branches —
what can it mean
when a thing is so easy?

It means you are a boy.

WHITE CLOVER

Once when the moon was out about three-quarters
and the fireflies who are the stars
of backyards
were out about three-quarters
and about three-fourths of all the lights
in the neighborhood
were on because people can be at home,
I took a not so innocent walk
out among the lawns,
navigating by the light of lights,
and there there were many hundreds of moons
on the lawns
where before there was only polite grass.
These were moons on long stems,
their long stems giving their greenness
to the center of each flower
and the light giving its whiteness to the tops
of the petals. I could say
it was light from stars
touched the tops of flowers and no doubt
something heavenly reaches what grows outdoors
and the heads of men who go hatless,
but I like to think we have a world
right here, and a life
that isn't death. So I don't say it's better
to be right here. I say this is where
many hundreds of core-green moons
gigantic to my eye
rose because men and women had sown green grass,
and flowered to my eye in man-made light,

and to some would be as fire in the body
and to others a light in the mind
over all their property.

DRAWN BY STONES, BY EARTH, BY THINGS
THAT HAVE BEEN IN THE FIRE

I can tell you about this because I have held in my hand
the little potter's sponge called an "elephant ear."
Naturally, it's only a tiny version of an ear,
but it's the thing you want to pick up out of the toolbox
when you wander into the deserted ceramics shop
down the street from the cave where the fortune-teller works.
Drawn by stones, by earth, by things that have been in the fire.

The elephant ear listens to the side of the vase
as it is pulled upwards from a dome of muddy clay.
The ear listens to the outside wall of the pot
and the hand listens to the inside wall of the pot,
and between them a city rises out of dirt and water.
Inside this city live the remains of animals,
animals who prepared for two hundred years to be clay.

Rodents make clay, and men wearing spectacles make clay,
though the papers they were signing go up in flames
and nothing more is known of these long documents
except by those angels who divine in our ashes.
Kings and queens of the jungle make clay
and royalty and politicians make clay although
their innocence stays with their clothes until unravelled.

There is a lost soldier in every ceramic bowl.
The face on the dinner plate breaks when the dish does
and lies for centuries unassembled in the soil.
These things that have the right substance to begin with,
put into the fire at temperatures that melt glass,
keep their fingerprints forever, it is said,
like inky sponges that walk away in the deep water.

SEVENS (VERSION 3):
IN THE CLOSED IRIS OF CREATION

A pair of heavy scissors lay across the sky
waiting for an affirmation,
waiting for the go-ahead of tragic love.
The sky, as always, was full of sobbing clouds
ready to rain down heavily on desire
wherever a hand opens or a leg stretches out
and life waits to begin —
the way everything, even scissors, waits to begin.
We who began in water, in clay,
in the ancient diggings of the word,
whitened by the chalk of dreams,
bloom in colors (everyone has noticed!)
blind toward scissors and clouds.
Within the sight of a pail of water,
our mothers pushed us away
for the good of our souls
into a world where the sun had burned a hole
in the name of love.
Sleep in the sewers
descends, bringing an inner life
utterly at peace behind an in-turning iris —
crawling, pre-cadaverous, fetal.
To choose between knowing the truth
or, on the other hand, orgasm and repose,
always with the patience of a cricket on guard
in case Spring should arrive in disguise,
hiding its muscular body under rags,
its footsteps muffled by the mating of vines —
to choose at all, we have to crawl
on bare knees down alleys of pumice
and plead among the red columns of silos,
in the dust of exploding grains,
with shaking hands and trembling lips
plead for a severing of knives.
If now in the blackest hole we sometimes dance
like an orphan among loaves of black bread,
and lift plain water to our lips to toast
our good luck, and if in a thicket of almonds
with a smell of oil before it turns
to bitter wine,

we laugh so hard we lose our bodies momentarily,
we are also, at the same time, absorbing
the shivering of all cities
born of this baked earth, this chaste diamond
that flowered, reluctantly, absurdly,
into an eternity of ice
and descended through the decorations of the frost
to be shipwrecked in space.
And so each morning I throw a little chalk into my coffee
in memory of the blood and bones of the universe,
and each morning I eat some sacramental bread
as a prayer
not to become one of the thieves
but to save and keep my life for whenever I may need it,
perhaps when things are going better,
when everything is or isn't sevens,
and the planet is in perpetual motion
giving regular birth to the spaces behind her.
I myself swear never to be surprised
when someone elects to stay in the womb.
True silence existed only before there was life
and was eaten in the first rain of the universe,
beaten into piles of grain and no grain
in the first silo, in the first air,
without a place to put a foot down, without an us,
all in a hole
that held (aloft? upside down?) as if in an iris
the thin tracings of the first wax,
and of the first delicate amoebic embracings,
and of the shapes to come when love
began to sever us.

John Berryman

4

Filling her compact & delicious body
with chicken páprika, she glanced at me
twice.
Fainting with interest, I hungered back
and only the fact of her husband & four other people
kept me from springing on her

or falling at her little feet and crying
'You are the hottest one for years of night
Henry's dazed eyes
have enjoyed, Brilliance.' I advanced upon
(despairing) my spumoni. — Sir Bones: is stuffed,
de world, wif feeding girls.

— Black hair, complexion Latin, jewelled eyes
downcast . . . The slob beside her   feasts . . . What wonders is
she sitting on, over there?
The restaurant buzzes. She might as well be on Mars.
Where did it all go wrong? There ought to be a law against Henry.
— Mr. Bones: there is.

14

Life, friends, is boring. We must not say so.
After all, the sky flashes, the great sea yearns,
we ourselves flash and yearn,
and moreover my mother told me as a boy
(repeatedly) 'Ever to confess you're bored
means you have no

Inner Resources.' I conclude now I have no
inner resources, because I am heavy bored.
Peoples bore me,
literature bores me, especially great literature,

41

Henry bores me, with his plights & gripes
as bad as achilles,

who loves people and valiant art, which bores me.
And the tranquil hills, & gin, look like a drag
and somehow a dog
has taken itself & its tail considerably away
into mountains or sea or sky, leaving
behind: me, wag.

26

The glories of the world struck me, made me aria, once.
— What happen then, Mr Bones?
if be you cares to say.
— Henry. Henry became interested in women's bodies,
his loins were & were the   scene of stupendous
      achievement.
Stupor. Knees, dear. Pray.

All the knobs & softnesses of, my God,
the ducking & trouble it swarm on Henry,
at one time.
— What happen then, Mr Bones?
you seems excited-like.
— Fell Henry back into   the original crime: art, rime

besides a sense of others, my God, my God,
and a jealousy for the honour (alive) of his country,
what can get more odd?
and discontent with the thriving gangs & pride.
— What happen then, Mr Bones?
— I had a most marvellous   piece of luck. I died.

29

There sat down, once, a thing on Henry's heart
só heavy, if he had a hundred years
& more, & weeping, sleepless, in all them time
Henry could not make good.

Starts again always in Henry's ears
the little cough somewhere, an odour, a chime.

And there is another thing he has in mind
like a grave Sienese face a thousand years
would fail to blur the still profiled reproach of. Ghastly,
with open eyes, he attends, blind.
All the bells say: too late. This is not for tears;
thinking.

But never did Henry, as he thought he did,
end anyone and hacks her body up
and hide the pieces, where they may be found.
He knows: he went over everyone, & nobody's missing.
Often he reckons, in the dawn, them up.
Nobody is ever missing.

47

APRIL FOOL'S DAY, OR, ST MARY OF EGYPT

— Thass a funny title, Mr Bones.
— When down she saw her feet, sweet fish, on the threshold,
she considered her fair shoulders
and all them hundreds who have held them, all
the more who to her mime thickened & maled
from the supple stage,

and seeing her feet, in a visit, side by side
paused on the sill of The Tomb, she shrank: 'No.
They are not worthy,
fondled by many' and rushed from The Crucified
back through her followers out of the city ho
across the suburbs, plucky

to dare my desert in her late daylight
of animals and sands. She fall prone.
Only wind whistled.
And forty-seven years went by like Einstein.
We celebrate her feast with our caps on,
whom God has not visited.

89

OP. POSTH. NO. 12

In a blue series towards his sleepy eyes
they slid like wonder, women tall & small,
of every shape & size,
in many languages to lisp 'We do'
to Henry almost waking. What is the night at all,
his closed eyes beckon you.

In the Marriage of the Dead, a new routine,
he gasped his crowded vows past lids shut tight
and a-many rings fumbled on.
His coffin like Grand Central to the brim
filled up & emptied with the lapse of light.
Which one will waken him?

O she must startle like a fallen gown,
content with speech like an old sacrament
in deaf ears lying down,
blazing through darkness till he feels the cold
& blindness of his hopeless tenement
while his black arms unfold.

91

OP. POSTH. NO. 14

Noises from underground made gibber some
others collected & dug Henry up
saying 'You *are* a sight.'
Chilly, he muttered for a double rum
waving the mikes away, putting a stop
to rumours, pushing his fright

off with the now accumulated taxes
accustomed in his way to solitude
and no bills.
Wives came forward, claiming a new Axis,

fearful for their insurance, though, now, glued
to disencumbered Henry's many ills.

A fortnight later, sense a single man
upon the trampled scene at 2 a.m.
insomnia-plagued, with a shovel
digging like mad, Lazarus with a plan
to get his own back, a plan, a stratagem
no newsman will unravel.

129

Thin as a sheet his mother came to him
during the screaming evenings after he did it,
touched F.J.'s dead hand.
The parlour was dark, he was the first pall-bearer in,
he gave himself a dare & then did it,
the thing was quite unplanned,

riots for Henry the unstructured dead,
his older playmate fouled, reaching for him
and never will he be free
from the older boy who died by the cottonwood
& now is to be planted, wise & slim,
as part of Henry's history.

Christ waits. That boy was good beyond his years,
he served at Mass like Henry, he never did
one extreme thing wrong
but tender his cold hand, latent with Henry's fears
to Henry's shocking touch, whereat he fled
and woke screaming, young & strong.

172

Your face broods from my table, Suicide.
Your force came on like a torrent toward the end
of agony and wrath.
You were christened in the beginning Sylvia Plath
and changed that name for Mrs Hughes and bred
and went on round the bend

till the oven seemed the proper place for you.
I brood upon your face, the geography of grief,
hooded, till I allow
again your resignation from us now
though the screams of orphaned children fix me anew.
Your torment here was brief,

long falls your exit all repeatingly,
a poor exemplum, one more suicide
to stack upon the others
till stricken Henry with his sisters & brothers
suddenly gone pauses to wonder why he
alone breasts the wronging tide.

366

Chilled in this Irish pub I wish my loves
well, well to strangers, well to all his friends,
seven or so in number,
I forgive my enemies, especially two,
races his heart, at so much magnanimity,
can it at all be true?

— Mr Bones, you on a trip outside yourself.
Has you seen a medicine man? You sound will-like,
a testament & such.
Is you going? — Oh, I suffer from a strike
& a strike & three balls: I stand up for much,
Wordsworth & that sort of thing.

The pitcher dreamed. He threw a hazy curve,
I took it in my stride & out I struck,
lonesome Henry.
These Songs are not meant to be understood, you understand.
They are only meant to terrify & comfort.
Lilac was found in his hand.

382

At Henry's bier let some thing fall out well:
enter there none who somewhat has to sell,
the music ancient & gradual,

the voices solemn but the grief subdued,
no hairy jokes but everybody's mood
subdued, subdued,

until the Dancer comes, in a short short dress
hair black & long & loose, dark dark glasses,
uptilted face,
pallor & strangeness, the music changes
to 'Give!' & 'Ow!' and how! the music changes,
she kicks a backward limb

on tiptoe, pirouettes, & she is free
to the knocking music, sails, dips, & suddenly
returns to the terrible gay
occasion hopeless & mad, she weaves, it's hell,
she flings to her head a leg, bobs, all is well,
she dances Henry away.

384

The marker slants, flowerless, day's almost done,
I stand above my father's grave with rage,
often, often before
I've made this awful pilgrimage to one
who cannot visit me, who tore his page
out: I come back for more,

I spit upon this dreadful banker's grave
who shot his heart out in a Florida dawn
O ho alas alas
When will indifference come, I moan & rave
I'd like to scrabble till I got right down
away down under the grass

and ax the casket open ha to see
just how he's taking it, which he sought so hard
we'll tear apart
the mouldering grave clothes ha & then Henry
will heft the ax once more, his final card,
and fell it on the start.

Elizabeth Bishop

THE FISH

I caught a tremendous fish
and held him beside the boat
half out of water, with my hook
fast in a corner of his mouth.
He didn't fight.
He hadn't fought at all.
He hung a grunting weight,
battered and venerable
and homely. Here and there
his brown skin hung in strips
like ancient wallpaper,
and its pattern of darker brown
was like wallpaper:
shapes like full-blown roses
stained and lost through age.
He was speckled with barnacles,
fine rosettes of lime,
and infested
with tiny white sea-lice,
and underneath two or three
rags of green weed hung down.
While his gills were breathing in
the terrible oxygen
— the frightening gills,
fresh and crisp with blood,
that can cut so badly —
I thought of the coarse white flesh
packed in like feathers,
the big bones and the little bones,
the dramatic reds and blacks
of his shiny entrails,
and the pink swim-bladder
like a big peony.
I looked into his eyes
which were far larger than mine
but shallower, and yellowed,
the irises backed and packed
with tarnished tinfoil

seen through the lenses
of old scratched isinglass.
They shifted a little, but not
to return my stare.
— It was more like the tipping
of an object toward the light.
I admired his sullen face,
the mechanism of his jaw,
and then I saw
that from his lower lip
— if you could call it a lip —
grim, wet, and weaponlike,
hung five old pieces of fish-line,
or four and a wire leader
with the swivel still attached,
with all their five big hooks
grown firmly in his mouth.
A green line, frayed at the end
where he broke it, two heavier lines,
and a fine black thread
still crimped from the strain and snap
when it broke and he got away.
Like medals with their ribbons
frayed and wavering,
a five-haired beard of wisdom
trailing from his aching jaw.
I stared and stared
and victory filled up
the little rented boat,
from the pool of bilge
where oil had spread a rainbow
around the rusted engine
to the bailer rusted orange,
the sun-cracked thwarts,
the oarlocks on their strings,
the gunnels — until everything
was rainbow, rainbow, rainbow!
And I let the fish go.

AT THE FISHHOUSES

Although it is a cold evening,
down by one of the fishhouses
an old man sits netting,
his net, in the gloaming almost invisible,
a dark purple-brown,
and his shuttle worn and polished.
The air smells so strong of codfish
it makes one's nose run and one's eyes water.
The five fishhouses have steeply peaked roofs
and narrow, cleated gangplanks slant up
to storerooms in the gables
for the wheelbarrows to be pushed up and down on.
All is silver: the heavy surface of the sea,
swelling slowly as if considering spilling over,
is opaque, but the silver of the benches,
the lobster pots, and masts, scattered
among the wild jagged rocks,
is of an apparent translucence
like the small old buildings with an emerald moss
growing on their shoreward walls.
The big fish tubs are completely lined
with layers of beautiful herring scales
and the wheelbarrows are similarly plastered
with creamy iridescent coats of mail,
with small iridescent flies crawling on them.
Up on the little slope behind the houses,
set in the sparse bright sprinkle of grass,
is an ancient wooden capstan,
cracked, with two long bleached handles
and some melancholy stains, like dried blood,
where the ironwork has rusted.
The old man accepts a Lucky Strike.
He was a friend of my grandfather.
We talk of the decline in the population
and of codfish and herring
while he waits for a herring boat to come in.
There are sequins on his vest and on his thumb.
He has scraped the scales, the principal beauty,
from unnumbered fish with that black old knife,
the blade of which is almost worn away.

Down at the water's edge, at the place
where they haul up the boats, up the long ramp
descending into the water, thin silver
tree trunks are laid horizontally
across the gray stones, down and down
at intervals of four or five feet.

Cold dark deep and absolutely clear,
element bearable to no mortal,
to fish and to seals . . . One seal particularly
I have seen here evening after evening.
He was curious about me. He was interested in music;
like me a believer in total immersion,
so I used to sing him Baptist hymns.
I also sang "A Mighty Fortress Is Our God."
He stood up in the water and regarded me
steadily, moving his head a little.
Then he would disappear, then suddenly emerge
almost in the same spot, with a sort of shrug
as if it were against his better judgment.
Cold dark deep and absolutely clear,
the clear gray icy water . . . Back, behind us,
the dignified tall firs begin.
Bluish, associating with their shadows,
a million Christmas trees stand
waiting for Christmas. The water seems suspended
above the rounded gray and blue-gray stones.
I have seen it over and over, the same sea, the same,
slightly, indifferently swinging above the stones,
icily free above the stones,
above the stones and then the world.
If you should dip your hand in,
your wrist would ache immediately,
your bones would begin to ache and your hand would burn
as if the water were a transmutation of fire
that feeds on stones and burns with a dark gray flame.
If you tasted it, it would first taste bitter,
then briny, then surely burn your tongue.
It is like what we imagine knowledge to be:
dark, salt, clear, moving, utterly free,
drawn from the cold hard mouth
of the world, derived from the rocky breasts
forever, flowing and drawn, and since
our knowledge is historical, flowing, and flown.

CAPE BRETON

Out on the high "bird islands," Ciboux and Hertford,
the razorbill auks and the silly-looking puffins all stand
with their backs to the mainland
in solemn, uneven lines along the cliff's brown grass-frayed edge,
while the few sheep pastured there go "Baaa, baaa."
(Sometimes, frightened by aeroplanes, they stampede
and fall over into the sea or onto the rocks.)
The silken water is weaving and weaving,
disappearing under the mist equally in all directions,
lifted and penetrated now and then
by one shag's dripping serpent-neck,
and somewhere the mist incorporates the pulse,
rapid but unurgent, of a motorboat.

The same mist hangs in thin layers
among the valleys and gorges of the mainland
like rotting snow-ice sucked away
almost to spirit; the ghosts of glaciers drift
among those folds and folds of fir: spruce and hackmatack —
dull, dead, deep peacock-colors,
each riser distinguished from the next
by an irregular nervous saw-tooth edge,
alike, but certain as a stereoscopic view.

The wild road clambers along the brink of the coast.
On it stand occasional small yellow bulldozers,
but without their drivers, because today is Sunday.
The little white churches have been dropped into the matted hills
like lost quartz arrowheads.
The road appears to have been abandoned.
Whatever the landscape had of meaning appears to have been
    abandoned,
unless the road is holding it back, in the interior,
where we cannot see,
where deep lakes are reputed to be,
and disused trails and mountains of rock
and miles of burnt forests standing in gray scratches
like the admirable scriptures made on stones by stones —
and these regions now have little to say for themselves
except in thousands of light song-sparrow songs floating upward

freely, dispassionately, through the mist, and meshing
in brown-wet, fine, torn fish-nets.

A small bus comes along, in up-and-down rushes,
packed with people, even to its step.
(On weekdays with groceries, spare automobile parts, and pump
    parts,
but today only two preachers extra, one carrying his frock coat
    on a hanger.)
It passes the closed roadside stand, the closed schoolhouse,
where today no flag is flying
from the rough-adzed pole topped with a white china doorknob.
It stops, and a man carrying a baby gets off,
climbs over a stile, and goes down through a small steep meadow,
which establishes its poverty in a snowfall of daisies,
to his invisible house beside the water.

The birds keep on singing, a calf bawls, the bus starts.
The thin mist follows
the white mutations of its dream;
an ancient chill is rippling the dark brooks.

IN THE WAITING ROOM

In Worcester, Massachusetts,
I went with Aunt Consuelo
to keep her dentist's appointment
and sat and waited for her
in the dentist's waiting room.
It was winter. It got dark
early. The waiting room
was full of grown-up people,
arctics and overcoats,
lamps and magazines.
My aunt was inside
what seemed like a long time
and while I waited I read
the *National Geographic*
(I could read) and carefully
studied the photographs:
the inside of a volcano,

black, and full of ashes;
then it was spilling over
in rivulets of fire.
Osa and Martin Johnson
dressed in riding breeches,
laced boots, and pith helmets.
A dead man slung on a pole
— "Long Pig," the caption said.
Babies with pointed heads
wound round and round with string;
black, naked women with necks
wound round and round with wire
like the necks of light bulbs.
Their breasts were horrifying.
I read it right straight through.
I was too shy to stop.
And then I looked at the cover:
the yellow margins, the date.

Suddenly, from inside,
came an *oh!* of pain
— Aunt Consuelo's voice —
not very loud or long,
I wasn't at all surprised;
even then I knew she was
a foolish, timid woman.
I might have been embarrassed,
but wasn't. What took me
completely by surprise
was that it was *me:*
my voice, in my mouth.
Without thinking at all
I was my foolish aunt,
I — we — were falling, falling,
our eyes glued to the cover
of the *National Geographic,*
February, 1918.

I said to myself: three days
and you'll be seven years old.
I was saying it to stop
the sensation of falling off
the round, turning world
into cold, blue-black space.

But I felt: you are an *I*,
you are an *Elizabeth*,
you are one of *them*.
Why should you be one, too?
I scarcely dared to look
to see what it was I was.
I gave a sidelong glance
— I couldn't look any higher —
at shadowy gray knees,
trousers and skirts and boots
and different pairs of hands
lying under the lamps.
I knew that nothing stranger
had ever happened, that nothing
stranger could ever happen.
Why should I be my aunt,
or me, or anyone?
What similarities —
boots, hands, the family voice
I felt in my throat, or even
the *National Geographic*
and those awful hanging breasts —
held us all together
or made us all just one?
How — I didn't know any
word for it — how "unlikely" . . .
How had I come to be here,
like them, and overhear
a cry of pain that could have
got loud and worse but hadn't?

The waiting room was bright
and too hot. It was sliding
beneath a big black wave,
another, and another.

Then I was back in it.
The War was on. Outside,
in Worcester, Massachusetts,
were night and slush and cold,
and it was still the fifth
of February, 1918.

ELIZABETH BISHOP

ONE ART

The art of losing isn't hard to master;
so many things seem filled with the intent
to be lost that their loss is no disaster.

Lose something every day. Accept the fluster
of lost door keys, the hour badly spent.
The art of losing isn't hard to master.

Then practice losing farther, losing faster:
places, and names, and where it was you meant
to travel. None of these will bring disaster.

I lost my mother's watch. And look! my last, or
next-to-last, of three loved houses went.
The art of losing isn't hard to master.

I lost two cities, lovely ones. And, vaster,
some realms I owned, two rivers, a continent.
I miss them, but it wasn't a disaster.

— Even losing you (the joking voice, a gesture
I love) I shan't have lied. It's evident
the art of losing's not too hard to master
though it may look like (*Write* it!) like disaster.

Robert Bly

AN EMPTY PLACE

The eyes are drawn to the dusty ground in fall —
pieces of crushed oyster shell
like doors into the earth made of mother-of-pearl,
slivers of glass,
a white chicken's feather that still seems excited by the warm blood,
and a corncob, all kernels gone, room after room in its endless palace . . .
this is the palace, the place of many mansions,
which Christ has gone to prepare for us.

SNOWBANKS NORTH OF THE HOUSE

Those great sweeps of snow that stop suddenly six feet from the
      house . . .
Thoughts that go so far.
The boy gets out of high school and reads no more books;
the son stops calling home.
The mother puts down her rolling pin and makes no more bread.
And the wife looks at her husband one night at a party and loves him no
      more.
The energy leaves the wine, and the minister falls leaving the church.
It will not come closer —
the one inside moves back, and the hands touch nothing, and are safe.

And the father grieves for his son, and will not leave the room where the
      coffin stands;
he turns away from his wife, and she sleeps alone.

And the sea lifts and falls all night; the moon goes on through the unat-
      tached heavens alone.
And the toe of the shoe pivots
in the dust. . . .
The man in the black coat turns, and goes back down the hill.
No one knows why he came, or why he turned away, and did not climb
      the hill.

THE RESEMBLANCE BETWEEN YOUR LIFE AND A DOG

I never intended to have this life, believe me —
It just happened. You know how dogs turn up
At a farm, and they wag but can't explain.

It's good if you can accept your life — you'll notice
Your face has become deranged trying to adjust
To it. Your face thought your life would look

Like your bedroom mirror when you were ten.
That was a clear river touched by mountain wind.
Even your parents can't believe how much you've changed.

Sparrows in winter, if you've ever held one, all feathers,
Burst out of your hand with a fiery glee.
You see them later in hedges. Teachers praise you,

But you can't quite get back to the winter sparrow.
Your life is a dog. He's been hungry for miles,
Doesn't particularly like you, but gives up, and comes in.

WARNING TO THE READER

Sometimes farm granaries become especially beautiful when all the oats or wheat are gone, and wind has swept the rough floor clean. Standing inside, we see around us, coming in through the cracks between shrunken wall boards, bands or strips of sunlight. So in a poem about imprisonment, one sees a little light.

But how many birds have died trapped in these granaries. The bird, seeing the bands of light, flutters up the walls and falls back again and again. The way out is where the rats enter and leave; but the rat's hole is low to the floor. Writers, be careful then by showing the sunlight on the walls not to promise the anxious and panicky blackbirds a way out!

I say to the reader, beware. Readers who love poems of light may sit hunched in the corner with nothing in their gizzards for four days, light failing, the eyes glazed. . . . They may end as a mound of feathers and a skull on the open boardwood floor . . .

ROBERT BLY

SIX WINTER PRIVACY POEMS

I

About four, a few flakes.
I empty the teapot out in the snow,
Feeling shoots of joy in the new cold.
By nightfall, wind,
The curtains on the south sway softly.

II

My shack has two rooms; I use one.
The lamplight falls on my chair and table,
And I fly into one of my own poems —
I can't tell you where —
As if I appeared where I am now,
In a wet field, snow falling.

III

More of the fathers are dying each day.
It is time for the sons.
Bits of darkness are gathering around them.
The darkness appears as flakes of light.

IV *On Meditation*

There is a solitude like black mud!
Sitting in this darkness singing,
I can't tell if this joy
Is from the body, or the soul, or a third place!

V *Listening to Bach*

Inside this music there is someone
Who is not well described by the names
Of Jesus, or Jehovah, or the Lord of Hosts!

VI

When I woke, a new snow had fallen.
I am alone, yet someone else is with me,
Drinking coffee, looking out at the snow.

DRIVING TO TOWN LATE TO MAIL A LETTER

It is a cold and snowy night. The main street is deserted.
The only things moving are swirls of snow.
As I lift the mailbox door, I feel its cold iron.
There is a privacy I love in this snowy night.
Driving around, I will waste more time.

ON THE OREGON COAST

For William Stafford

The waves come — the large fourth wave
Looming up, thinking, crashing down — all
Roll in so prominently that I become small
And write this in a cramped script, hard to read.

Well, all this fury, prominent or not
Is also hard to read, and the ducks don't help,
Settling down in furry water, shaking
Themselves, and then forgetting it within a minute.

Remembering the fury, it is up to us, even
Though we feel small compared to the loose
Ocean, to keep sailing and not land,
And figure out what to say to our children.

THE DEAD SEAL

1

Walking north toward the point, I come on a dead seal. From a few feet away, he looks like a brown log. The body is on its back, dead only a few hours. I stand and look at him. There's a quiver in the dead flesh: My God, he's still alive. And a shock goes through me, as if a wall of my room had fallen away.

His head is arched back, the small eyes closed; the whiskers sometimes rise and fall. He is dying. This is the oil. Here on its back is the oil that heats our houses so efficiently. Wind blows fine sand back toward the ocean. The flipper near me lies folded over the stomach, looking like an unfinished arm, lightly glazed with sand at the edges. The other flipper lies half underneath. And the seal's skin looks like an old overcoat, scratched here and there — by sharp mussel shells maybe.

I reach out and touch him. Suddenly he rears up, turns over. He gives three cries: Awaark! Awaark! Awaark! — like the cries from Christmas toys. He lunges toward me; I am terrified and leap back, though I know there can be no teeth in that jaw. He starts flopping toward the sea. But he falls over, on his face. He does not want to go back to the sea. He looks up at the sky, and he looks like an old lady who has lost her hair. He puts his chin back down on the sand, rearranges his flippers, and waits for me to go. I go.

2

The next day I go back to say goodbye. He's dead now. But he's not. He's a quarter mile farther up the shore. Today he is thinner, squatting on his stomach, head out. The ribs show more: each vertebra on the back under the coat is visible, shiny. He breathes in and out.

A wave comes in, touches his nose. He turns and looks at me — the eyes slanted; the crown of his head looks like a boy's leather jacket bending over some bicycle bars. He is taking a long time to die. The whiskers white as porcupine quills, the forehead slopes. . . . Goodbye, brother, die in the sound of the waves. Forgive us if we have killed you. Long live your race, your inner-tube race, so uncomfortable on land, so comfortable in the ocean. Be comfortable in death then, when the sand will be out of your nostrils, and you can swim in long loops through the pure death, ducking under as assassinations break above you. You don't want to be touched by me. I climb the cliff and go home the other way.

LOOKING INTO A TIDE POOL

It is a tide pool, shallow, water coming in, clear, tiny white shell-people on the bottom, asking nothing, not even directions! On the surface the noduled seaweed, lying like hands, slowly drawing back and returning, hands laid on fevered bodies, moving back and forth, as the healer sings wildly, shouting to Jesus and his dead mother.

THE YELLOW DOT

God does what she wants. She has very large
Tractors. She lives at night in the sewing room
Doing stitchery. Then chunks of land at mid-
Sea disappear. The husband knows that his wife
Is still breathing. God has arranged the open
Grave. That grave is not what we want,
But to God it's a tiny hole, and he has
The needle, draws thread through it, and soon
A nice pattern appears. The husband cries,
"Don't let her die!" But God says, "I
Need a yellow dot here, near the mailbox."

The husband is angry. But the turbulent ocean
Is like a chicken scratching for seeds. It doesn't
Mean anything, and the chicken's claws will tear
A Rembrandt drawing if you put it down.

In memory of Jane Kenyon

THE RUSSIAN

"The Russians had few doctors on the front line.
My father's job was this: after the battle
Was over, he'd walk among the men hit,
Sit down and ask: 'Would you like to die on your
Own in a few hours, or should I finish it?'
Most said, 'Don't leave me.' The two would have
A cigarette. He'd take out his small notebook —
We had no dogtags, you know — and write the man's
Name down, his wife's, his children, his address, and what
He wanted to say. When the cigarette was done,
The soldier would turn his head to the side. My father
Finished off four hundred men that way during the war.
He never went crazy. They were his people.

He came to Toronto. My father in the summers
Would stand on the lawn with a hose, watering
The grass that way. It took a long time. He'd talk
To the moon, to the wind. 'I can hear you growing' —
He'd say to the grass. 'We come and go.
We're no different from each other. We are all
Part of something. We have a home.' When I was thirteen,
I said, 'Dad, do you know they've invented sprinklers
Now?' He went on watering the grass.
'This is my life. Just shut up if you don't understand it.'"

Gwendolyn Brooks

from **A STREET IN BRONZEVILLE**

to David and Keziah Brooks

the mother

Abortions will not let you forget.
You remember the children you got that you did not get,
The damp small pulps with a little or with no hair,
The singers and workers that never handled the air.
You will never neglect or beat
Them, or silence or buy with a sweet.
You will never wind up the sucking-thumb
Or scuttle off ghosts that come.
You will never leave them, controlling your luscious sigh,
Return for a snack of them, with gobbling mother-eye.

I have heard in the voices of the wind the voices of my dim killed
     children.
I have contracted. I have eased
My dim dears at the breasts they could never suck.
I have said, Sweets, if I sinned, if I seized
Your luck
And your lives from your unfinished reach,
If I stole your births and your names,
Your straight baby tears and your games,
Your stilted or lovely loves, your tumults, your marriages, aches, and your
     deaths,
If I poisoned the beginnings of your breaths,
Believe that even in my deliberateness I was not deliberate.
Though why should I whine,
Whine that the crime was other than mine? —
Since anyhow you are dead.
Or rather, or instead,
You were never made.
But that too, I am afraid,
Is faulty: oh, what shall I say, how is the truth to be said?
You were born, you had body, you died.
It is just that you never giggled or planned or cried.

Believe me, I loved you all.
Believe me, I knew you, though faintly, and I loved, I loved you
All.

a song in the front yard

I've stayed in the front yard all my life.
I want a peek at the back
Where it's rough and untended and hungry weed grows.
A girl gets sick of a rose.

I want to go in the back yard now
And maybe down the alley,
To where the charity children play.
I want a good time today.

They do some wonderful things.
They have some wonderful fun.
My mother sneers, but I say it's fine
How they don't have to go in at quarter to nine.
My mother, she tells me that Johnnie Mac
Will grow up to be a bad woman.
That George'll be taken to Jail soon or late
(On account of last winter he sold our back gate).

But I say it's fine. Honest, I do.
And I'd like to be a bad woman, too,
And wear the brave stockings of night-black lace
And strut down the streets with paint on my face.

THE LOVERS OF THE POOR

     arrive. The Ladies from the Ladies' Betterment
        League
Arrive in the afternoon, the late light slanting
In diluted gold bars across the boulevard brag
Of proud, seamed faces with mercy and murder hinting
Here, there, interrupting, all deep and debonair,
The pink paint on the innocence of fear;
Walk in a gingerly manner up the hall.
Cutting with knives served by their softest care,

Served by their love, so barbarously fair.
Whose mothers taught: You'd better not be cruel!
You had better not throw stones upon the wrens!
Herein they kiss and coddle and assault
Anew and dearly in the innocence
With which they baffle nature. Who are full,
Sleek, tender-clad, fit, fiftyish, a-glow, all
Sweetly abortive, hinting at fat fruit,
Judge it high time that fiftyish fingers felt
Beneath the lovelier planes of enterprise.
To resurrect. To moisten with milky chill.
To be a random hitching-post or plush.
To be, for wet eyes, random and handy hem.
      Their guild is giving money to the poor.
The worthy poor. The very very worthy
And beautiful poor. Perhaps just not too swarthy?
Perhaps just not too dirty nor too dim
Nor — passionate. In truth, what they could wish
Is — something less than derelict or dull.
Not staunch enough to stab, though, gaze for gaze!
God shield them sharply from the beggar-bold!
The noxious needy ones whose battle's bald
Nonetheless for being voiceless, hits one down.
      But it's all so bad! and entirely too much for them.
The stench; the urine, cabbage, and dead beans,
Dead porridges of assorted dusty grains,
The old smoke, *heavy* diapers, and, they're told,
Something called chitterlings. The darkness. Drawn
Darkness, or dirty light. The soil that stirs.
The soil that looks the soil of centuries.
And for that matter the *general* oldness. Old
Wood. Old marble. Old tile. Old old old.
Not homekind Oldness! Not Lake Forest, Glencoe.
Nothing is sturdy, nothing is majestic,
There is no quiet drama, no rubbed glaze, no
Unkillable infirmity of such
A tasteful turn as lately they have left,
Glencoe, Lake Forest, and to which their cars
Must presently restore them. When they're done
With dullards and distortions of this fistic
Patience of the poor and put-upon.
      They've never seen such a make-do-ness as
Newspaper rugs before! In this, this "flat,"
Their hostess is gathering up the oozed, the rich

Rugs of the morning (tattered! the bespattered. . . .)
Readies to spread clean rugs for afternoon.
Here is a scene for you. The Ladies look,
In horror, behind a substantial citizeness
Whose trains clank out across her swollen heart.
Who, arms akimbo, almost fills a door.
All tumbling children, quilts dragged to the floor
And tortured thereover, potato peelings, soft-
Eyed kitten, hunched-up, haggard, to-be-hurt.
  Their League is alloting largesse to the Lost.
But to put their clean, their pretty money, to put
Their money collected from delicate rose-fingers
Tipped with their hundred flawless rose-nails seems . . .
  They own Spode, Lowestoft, candelabra,
Mantels, and hostess gowns, and sunburst clocks,
Turtle soup, Chippendale, red satin "hangings,"
Aubussons and Hattie Carnegie. They Winter
In Palm Beach; cross the Water in June; attend,
When suitable, the nice Art Institute;
Buy the right books in the best bindings; saunter
On Michigan, Easter mornings, in sun or wind.
Oh Squalor! This sick four-story hulk, this fibre
With fissures everywhere! Why, what are bringings
Of loathe-love largesse? What shall peril hungers
So old old, what shall flatter the desolate?
Tin can, blocked fire escape and chitterling
And swaggering seeking youth and the puzzled wreckage
Of the middle-passage, and urine and stale shames
And, again, the porridges of the underslung
And children children children. Heavens! That
Was a rat, surely, off there, in the shadows? Long
And long-tailed? Gray? The Ladies from the Ladies'
Betterment League agree it will be better
To achieve the outer air that rights and steadies,
To hie to a house that does not holler, to ring
Bells elsetime, better presently to cater
To no more Possibilities, to get
Away. Perhaps the money can be posted.
Perhaps they two may choose another Slum!
Some serious sooty half-unhappy home! —
Where loathe-love likelier may be invested.
  Keeping their scented bodies in the center
Of the hall as they walk down the hysterical hall,
They allow their lovely skirts to graze no wall,

Are off at what they manage of a canter,
And, resuming all the clues of what they were,
Try to avoid inhaling the laden air.

WE REAL COOL

The Pool Players.
Seven at the Golden Shovel.

We real cool. We
Left school. We

Lurk late. We
Strike straight. We

Sing sin. We
Thin gin. We

Jazz June. We
Die soon.

AN ASPECT OF LOVE, ALIVE IN THE ICE AND FIRE

LaBohem Brown

It is the morning of our love.

In a package of minutes there is this We.
How beautiful.
Merry foreigners in our morning,
we laugh, we touch each other,
are responsible props and posts.

A physical light is in the room.

Because the world is at the window
we cannot wonder very long.

You rise. Although
genial, you are in yourself again.
I observe
your direct and respectable stride.
You are direct and self-accepting as a lion
in African velvet. You are level, lean,
remote.

There is a moment in Camaraderie
when interruption is not to be understood.
I cannot bear an interruption.
This is the shining joy;
the time of not-to-end.

On the street we smile.
We go
in different directions
down the imperturbable street.

THE BEAN EATERS

They eat beans mostly, this old yellow pair.
Dinner is a casual affair.
Plain chipware on a plain and creaking wood,
Tin flatware.

Two who are Mostly Good.
Two who have lived their day,
But keep on putting on their clothes
And putting things away.

And remembering . . .
Remembering, with twinklings and twinges,
As they lean over the beans in their rented back room that is full of beads
    and receipts and dolls and cloths, tobacco crumbs, vases and fringes.

GWENDOLYN BROOKS

THE COORA FLOWER

Today I learned the *coora* flower
grows high in the mountains of Itty-go-luba Bésa.

Province Meechee.
Pop. 39.

Now I am coming home.
This, at least, is Real, and what I know.

It was restful, learning nothing necessary.
School is tiny vacation. At least you can sleep.
At least you can think of love or feeling your boy friend against you
(which is not free from grief).

But now it's Real Business.
I am Coming Home.

My mother will be screaming in an almost dirty dress.
The crack is gone. So, a Man will be in the house.

I must watch myself.
I must not dare to sleep.

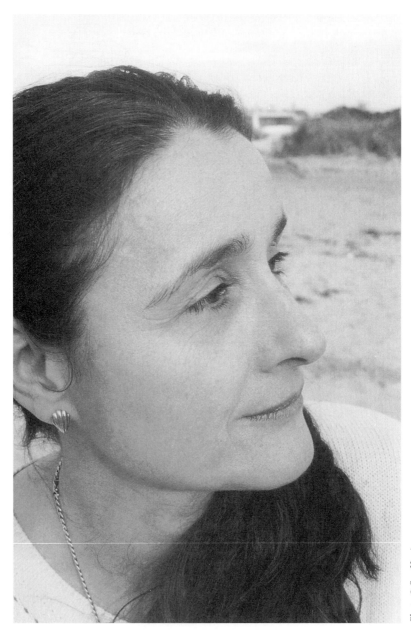

Olga Broumas

THE CHOIR

I walk and I rest while the eyes of my dead
look through my own, inaudible
hosannas greet
the panorama charged serene
and almost ultraviolet with so much witness.
Holy the sea, the palpitating membrane
divided into dazzling fields and whaledark by the sun.
Holy the dark, pierced by late revelers and dawnbirds,
the garbage truck suspended in shy light,
the oystershell and crushed clam of the driveway,
the dahlia pressed like lotus on its open palm.
Holy the handmade and created side by side,
the sapphire of their marriage,
green flies and shit and condoms in the crabshell
rinsed by the buzzing tide.
Holy the light —
the poison ivy livid in its glare,
the gypsy moths festooning the pine barrens,
the mating monarch butterflies between the chic boutiques.
The mermaid's handprint on the artificial reef. Holy the we,
cast in the mermaid's image, smooth crotch of mystery and scale,
inscrutable until divulged by god
and sex into its gender, every touch
a secret intercourse with angels as we walk
proffered and taken. Their great wings
batter the air, our retinas bloom silver spots like beacons.
Better than silicone or graphite flesh absorbs
the shock of the divine crash-landing.
I roll my eyes back, skylights brushed by plumage of detail,
the unrehearsed and minuscule, the anecdotal midnight
themes of the carbon sea where we are joined:
zinnia, tomato, garlic wreaths
crowning the compost heap.

CARITAS

Thank someone for being
that one. Walk with her
to the center of a place
and back again
singing a little song.
Burn something.
—Seneca Tribe of
Native Americans

1

Erik Satie, accused
once of formlessness, composed
a sonata titled: Composition in the Form
of a Pear. When I tell you
that it would take
more brilliance than Mozart
more melancholy precision than Brahms
to compose a sonata in the form of
your breasts, you
don't believe me. I lie
next to your infidel sleep, all night
in pain
and lonely with my silenced
pleasure. Your breasts
in their moonlit pallor
invade me, lightly, like minor
fugues. I lie
between your sappling thighs, tongue
flat on your double lips, giving
voice, giving
voice. Opulent
as a continent in the rising light, you sleep
on, indifferent
to my gushing praises. It is
as it should be. Atlantis,
Cyprus, Crete, the encircled
civilizations, serene
in their tidal basins, dolphin-
loved, didn't heed to the faint, the
riotous

praise
of the lapping sea.

2

Your knees, those pinnacles
competing with the finest
dimpled, five-
year-old chins are
dancing. Ecstatic as nuns
in their delirious habit, like
runaway needles on a multiple graph,
the first organic model of
seismographs, charting
the crest I keep you on
and on till all
the sensitive numbers on the
Richter scale ring out at
once, but
silently: a choir
of sundial alarums. You reach that place,
levitated by pleasure, the first
glimpse the melting
glacier must
have had, rounding the precipice,
of what came to be known as
Niagara Falls. After all this time,
every time,
like a finger inside
the tight-gummed,
spittle-bright, atavistic
suckle of
a newborn's fragile-lipped
mouth, I
embrace you, my heart
a four-celled embryo, swimming
a pulse, a bloodstream that becomes, month
to month, less
of a stranger's, more
intimate, her
own.

3

There are people who do not explore the in-
Sides of flowers . . .
—Sandra Hochman

With the clear
plastic speculum, transparent
and, when inserted, pink like the convex
carapace of a prawn, flashlight in hand, I
guide you
inside the small
cathedral of my cunt. The unexpected
light dazzles you. This flesh, my darling, always
invisible like the wet
side of stones, the hidden
hemisphere of the moon, startles you
with its brilliance, the little
dome a spitting
miniature of the Haghia Sophia
with its circlet of openings
to the Mediterranean sun.
A woman-made language would
have as many synonyms for pink / light-filled / holy as
the Eskimo does
for snow. Speechless, you
shift the flashlight from
hand to hand, flickering. An orgy
of candles. Lourdes in mid-August. A flurry of
audible breaths, a seething
of holiness, and
behold
a tear
forms in the single eye, carmine
and catholic. You too, my darling, are
folded, clean
round a light-filled temple, complete
with miraculous icon, shedding
her perfect tears, in touch
with the hidden hemispheres,
the dome
of our cyclops moon.

4

She's white and her shoulders sing
like a singular vein of marble
alive and kicking in the jagged hill.
Her eyes are wet heaps
of seaweed in the sullen dusk.
Eyes of shadow and latitudes. Eyes of slate,
eyes of flint, eyes the color of certain stones
prized above all by Georgia
O'Keeffe. Eyes of an agile
wilderness, wings of a desert
moth. Her handsome hands. Each
one a duchess in her splendid gardens, each
one a pastry cook at her pliable dough, each one
a midwife at her palpable labor, the referee
of our relay race.
Her belly lulls me like an immense coastline
of dunes beneath a floating gull.
Her belly lulls me in a lustrous bowl
so precious
all the Asiatic dynasties
roll in their gilded graves, tarnished
with envy. Skin like the awning of
a ceremonial tent, the cloth draped over
the bread and wine of
an ungodly marriage. Is not this love
also a tavern? Is this meal not also
a public meal? I am encircled like a pit
in the fruit's ripe stomach, an ovum in cilia-lined
amniotic space, a drunken satellite, home
at last from its dizzy orbit.
Strike
up the music, my
love will dance. The loaf
of bread held against her breasts, the blade
in her nimble fingers, her feet stamping patterns
like snakes in the circle of dust, her waist a
scorpion's, she'll
dance, dance
the bread dance, slicing
out flawless ovals from
her inexhaustible loaf.

5

Imagine
something so beautiful
your liver would swell with contraband
chemicals, laughter, the dangerous
and infectious song.
Something so fine
you'd need no alibi for
your avid enchantment. A small
thing to start with: a special hairline
on a special nape, bent
low towards you. Imagine now
how your fingertips throb. You follow
the spinal valley, dipping
its hollow core like a ladle of light
in your ministering fingers.
Intuit the face
like that of a woman's
inscribed upon the porous
tablets of the law, rich with an age,
with tenderness, various, and like a map
of recurring lives. Here the remnants of
an indefatigable anger, the jubilant
birth-yell, here the indelible
covens of pleasure, a web
of murmurs, a lace
mantilla of sighs.
Recapture
the fleshy mouth full of fissures, the tongue
on the sated lip, the residual flare
of a regal nostril, the purple shade
of an earlobe, the eyebrows meeting
squarely above the lids.
You laugh
at this like a daughter, a young
sprig of amaranth caught
in your gelding teeth, that fade-
less flower you call a pigweed, a prince's
feather, a love-
lies-bleeding. But
not this love. Laugh, lover, laugh
with me. In that side-
splitting reservoir, in the promised calm

of its heaving waters, you'll
bend, you'll see this woman's
beautiful
and familiar face.

PERPETUA

As the seed of a mole for
Generations carried across
Time on a woman's belly
Flowers one morning blackly
Exposed to poison and poison
Itself is not
Disease but mutation is one
Understanding the strong
Shaft of your clitoris I kiss
As the exposed tip of your
Heart is another

SOOTHSAYING

Two coins round my neck, warm coins, lonely
light, full moon beneath the cirrus sheet.
Without you, lonely, happy in each thing
(how beautiful the two small plants are
by the bathtub) plants, moon, light, water
enter me at will. I wear the thin
    flat coins bent for luck, one black

one yellow copper, Arabic script-raised ridges
on each cheek. They touch me, touch each other, rub
abstractions on my skin. No god, but kismet
like a virus rubs its code inside our cells.
The gypsies scrawl theirs in the dirt, twigs,
bird-claws, absentminded laws: here one slept
    with dreams; here one wished himself

child. Jade, aloe in the porcelain light. I bathe,
I glisten. Who knows why. From memory, so far
    away from you, crossed fingers, heart.

CALYPSO

I've gathered the women like talismans, one
by one. They first came for tarot card
gossip, mystified
by my hands, by offers
cut with escape. They came

undone in my studio, sailing long eyes, heavy
with smoke and wet
with the force of dream: a vagina
folding mandala-like
out of herself, in full bloom. I used them. I used

the significance
of each card to uphold the dream, soon
they came back with others. I let the bitch
twitch in my lap. I listened. I let the tea steep
till the pot was black. Soon

there was no need for cards. We would use
stills from our daily lives, every woman
a constellation of images, every
portrait each other's chart.
We came together

like months
in a lunar year, measured in nights, dividing
perfectly into female phases. Like women anywhere
living in groups we had synchronous menses. And had
no need of a wound, a puncture, to seal our bond.

MERCY

Out in the harbor breaths of smoke
are rising from the water, sea-smoke
some call it or breath of souls,

the air so cold the great salt mass
shivers and, underlit, unfurls the ghosts
transfigured in its fathoms, some

having died there, most aslant
the packed earth to this lassitude,
this liquid recollection

of god's eternal mood. All afternoon
my friend counts from her window
the swaths like larkspur in a field of land

as if she could absorb their emanations
and sorting through them find the one
so recent to my grief, which keeps,

she knows, my eyes turned from the beach.
She doesn't say this, only, have you seen
the sea-smoke on the water, a voice absorbed

by eyes and eyes by those
so close to home, so ready to resume
the lunge of a desire, rested and clear of debris

they leave, like waking angels rising
on a hint of wind, visible or unseen, a print,
a wrinkle on the water.

Lucille Clifton

[i was born with twelve fingers]

i was born with twelve fingers
like my mother and my daughter.
each of us
born wearing strange black gloves
extra baby fingers hanging over the sides of our cribs and
dipping into the milk.
somebody was afraid we would learn to cast spells
and our wonders were cut off
but they didn't understand
the powerful memory of ghosts.   now
we take what we want
with invisible fingers
and we connect
my dead mother   my live daughter   and me
through our terrible shadowy hands.

at the cemetery,
walnut grove plantation, south carolina, 1989

among the rocks
at walnut grove
your silence drumming
in my bones,
tell me your names.

nobody mentioned slaves
and yet the curious tools
shine with your fingerprints.
nobody mentioned slaves
but somebody did this work
who had no guide, no stone,
who moulders under rock.

tell me your names,
tell me your bashful names
and i will testify.

the inventory lists ten slaves
but only men were recognized.

among the rocks
at walnut grove
some of these honored dead
were dark
some of these dark
were slaves
some of these slaves
were women
some of them did this
honored work.
tell me your names
foremothers, brothers,
tell me your dishonored names.
here lies
here lies
here lies
here lies
hear

the lost baby poem

the time i dropped your almost body down
down to meet the waters under the city
and run one with the sewage to the sea
what did i know about waters rushing back
what did i know about drowning
or being drowned

you would have been born into winter
in the year of the disconnected gas
and no car   we would have made the thin
walk over genesee hill into the canada wind
to watch you slip like ice into strangers' hands
you would have fallen naked as snow into winter

if you were here i could tell you these
and some other things

if i am ever less than a mountain
for your definite brothers and sisters
let the rivers pour over my head
let the sea take me for a spiller
of seas   let black men call me stranger
always   for your never named sake

[at last we killed the roaches]

at last we killed the roaches.
mama and me. she sprayed,
i swept the ceiling and they fell
dying onto our shoulders, in our hair
covering us with red. the tribe was broken,
the cooking pots were ours again
and we were glad, such cleanliness was grace
when i was twelve. only for a few nights,
and then not much, my dreams were blood
my hands were blades and it was murder murder
all over the place.

homage to my hips

these hips are big hips
they need space to
move around in.
they don't fit into little
petty places. these hips
are free hips.
they don't like to be held back.
these hips have never been enslaved,
they go where they want to go
they do what they want to do.
these hips are mighty hips.
these hips are magic hips.

i have known them
to put a spell on a man and
spin him like a top!

wishes for sons

i wish them cramps.
i wish them a strange town
and the last tampon.
i wish them no 7-11.

i wish them one week early
and wearing a white skirt.
i wish them one week late.

later i wish them hot flashes
and clots like you
wouldn't believe.   let the
flashes come when they
meet someone special.
let the clots come
when they want to.

let them think they have accepted
arrogance in the universe,
then bring them to gynecologists
not unlike themselves.

poem to my uterus

you   uterus
you have been patient
as a sock
while i have slippered into you
my dead and living children
now
they want to cut you out
stocking i will not need

where i am going
where am i going
old girl
without you
uterus
my bloody print
my estrogen kitchen
my black bag of desire
where can i go
barefoot
without you
where can you go
without me

lumpectomy eve

all night i dream of lips
that nursed and nursed
and the lonely nipple

lost in loss and the need
to feed that turns at last
on itself   that will kill

its body for its hunger's sake
all night i hear the whispering
the soft

      love calls you to this knife
      for love   for love

all night it is the one breast
comforting the other

scar

we will learn
to live together.

i will call you
ribbon of hunger
and desire
empty pocket flap
edge of before and after.

and you
what will you call me?

woman i ride
who cannot throw me
and i will not fall off.

lorena

it lay in my palm soft and trembled
as a new bird and i thought about
authority and how it always insisted
on itself, how it was master
of the man, how it measured him, never
was ignored or denied and how it promised
there would be sweetness if it was obeyed
just like the saints do, like the angels,
and i opened the window and held out my
uncupped hand. i swear to god,
i thought it could fly

moonchild

whatever slid into my mother's room that
late june night, tapping her great belly,
summoned me out roundheaded and unsmiling.
is this the moon, my father used to grin,
cradling my head. it was the moon
but nobody knew it then.

the moon understands dark places.
the moon has secrets of her own.
she holds what light she can.

we girls were ten years old and giggling
in our hand-me-downs. we wanted breasts,
pretended that we had them, tissued
our undershirts. jay johnson is teaching
me to french kiss, ella bragged, who
is teaching you? how do you sigh; my father?

the moon remembers everything.
she rules the oceans, rivers, rain.
when i am asked whose tears these are
i always say; the moon's.

the birth of language

and adam rose
fearful in the garden
without words
for the grass
his fingers plucked
without a tongue
to name the taste
shimmering in his mouth
did they draw blood
the blades   did it become
his early lunge
toward language
did his astonishment
surround him
did he shudder
did he whisper
eve

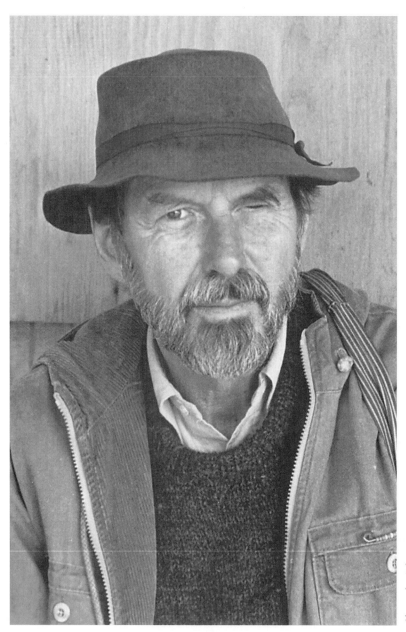

Robert Creeley

I KNOW A MAN

As I sd to my
friend, because I am
always talking, — John, I

sd, which was not his
name, the darkness sur-
rounds us, what

can we do against
it, or else, shall we &
why not, buy a goddamn big car,

drive, he sd, for
christ's sake, look
out where yr going.

AFTER LORCA

for M. Marti

The church is a business, and the rich
are the business men.
                    When they pull on the bells, the
poor come piling in and when a poor man dies, he has a
        wooden
cross, and they rush through the ceremony.

But when a rich man dies, they
drag out the Sacrament
and a golden Cross, and go *doucement, doucement*
to the cemetery.

And the poor love it
and think it's crazy.

ROBERT CREELEY

THE FIGURES

The stillness
of the wood,
the figures formed

by hands so still
they touched it
to be one

hand holding one
hand, faces
without eyes,

bodies of wooden
stone, so still
they will not move

from that quiet
action ever
again. Did the man

who made them find
a like quiet? In
the act of making them

it must have been
so still he heard the wood
and felt it with his hands

moving into
the forms
he has given to them,

one by singular
one, so quiet,
so still.

ROBERT CREELEY

THE LANGUAGE

Locate *I*
love you some-
where in

teeth and
eyes, bite
it but

take care not
to hurt, you
want so

much so
little. Words
say everything,

I
love you
again,

then what
is emptiness
for. To

fill, fill.
I heard words
and words full

of holes
aching. Speech
is a mouth.

ROBERT CREELEY

THE FLOWER

I think I grow tensions
like flowers
in a wood where
nobody goes.

Each wound is perfect,
encloses itself in a tiny
imperceptible blossom,
making pain.

Pain is a flower like that one,
like this one,
like that one,
like this one.

SOMETHING

I approach with such
a careful tremor, always
I feel the finally foolish

question of how it is,
then, supposed to be felt,
and by whom. I remember

once in a rented room on
27th street, the woman I loved
then, literally, after we

had made love on the large
bed sitting across from
a basin with two faucets, she

had to pee but was nervous,
embarrassed I suppose I
would watch her who had but

a moment ago been completely
open to me, naked, on
the same bed. Squatting, her

head reflected in the mirror,
the hair dark there, the
full of her face, the shoulders,

sat spread-legged, turned on
one faucet and shyly pissed. What
love might learn from such a sight.

THE WARNING

For love — I would
split open your head and put
a candle in
behind the eyes.

Love is dead in us
if we forget
the virtues of an amulet
and quick surprise.

THE ACT OF LOVE

for Bobbie

Whatever constitutes
the act of love,
save physical

encounter, you are
dear to me,
not value as

with banks —
but a meaning self-
sufficient, dry

ROBERT CREELEY

at times as sand,
or else the trees,
dripping with

rain. How shall
one, this so-
called person,

say it? He
loves, his mind
is occupied, his

hands move
writing words
which come

into his head.
Now here,
the day surrounds

this man
and woman
sitting a small

distance apart.
Love will not
solve it — but

draws closer,
always, makes
the moisture of their

mouths and bodies
actively
engage. If I

wanted
a dirty picture,
would it always

be of a
woman straddled?
Yes

and no, these
are true opposites,
a you and me

of non-
sense,
for our love.

Now, one
says, the wind
lifts, the sky

is very blue, the
water just
beyond me makes

its lovely sounds.
How *dear*
you are

to me, how love-
ly all your
body *is*, how

all these
senses do
commingle, so

that in your very
arms I still
can think of you.

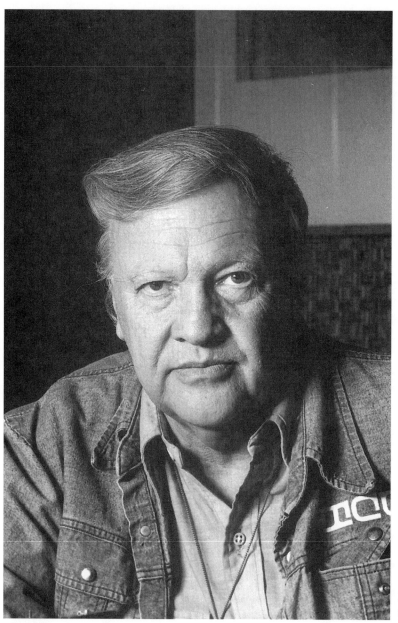

James Dickey

THE HEAVEN OF ANIMALS

Here they are. The soft eyes open.
If they have lived in a wood
It is a wood.
If they have lived on plains
It is grass rolling
Under their feet forever.

Having no souls, they have come,
Anyway, beyond their knowing.
Their instincts wholly bloom
And they rise.
The soft eyes open.

To match them, the landscape flowers,
Outdoing, desperately
Outdoing what is required:
The richest wood,
The deepest field.

For some of these,
It could not be the place
It is, without blood.
These hunt, as they have done,
But with claws and teeth grown perfect,

More deadly than they can believe.
They stalk more silently,
And crouch on the limbs of trees,
And their descent
Upon the bright backs of their prey

May take years
In a sovereign floating of joy.
And those that are hunted
Know this as their life,
Their reward: to walk

Under such trees in full knowledge
Of what is in glory above them,
And to feel no fear,
But acceptance, compliance.
Fulfilling themselves without pain

At the cycle's center,
They tremble, they walk
Under the tree,
They fall, they are torn,
They rise, they walk again.

THE SHEEP CHILD

Farm boys wild to couple
With anything   with soft-wooded trees
With mounds of earth   mounds
Of pinestraw   will keep themselves off
Animals by legends of their own:
In the hay-tunnel dark
And dung of barns, they will
Say   I have heard tell

That in a museum in Atlanta
Way back in a corner somewhere
There's this thing that's only half
Sheep   like a woolly baby
Pickled in alcohol   because
Those things can't live   his eyes
Are open   but you can't stand to look
I heard from somebody who . . .

But this is now almost all
Gone. The boys have taken
Their own true wives in the city,
The sheep are safe in the west hill
Pasture   but we who were born there
Still are not sure. Are we,
Because we remember, remembered
In the terrible dust of museums?

Merely with his eyes, the sheep-child may

Be saying   saying

    I am here, in my father's house.
    I who am half of your world, came deeply
    To my mother in the long grass
    Of the west pasture, where she stood like moonlight
    Listening for foxes. It was something like love
    From another world that seized her
    From behind, and she gave, not lifting her head
    Out of dew, without ever looking, her best
    Self to that great need. Turned loose, she dipped her face
    Farther into the chill of the earth, and in a sound
    Of sobbing   of something stumbling
    Away, began, as she must do,
    To carry me. I woke, dying,

    In the summer sun of the hillside, with my eyes
    Far more than human. I saw for a blazing moment
    The great grassy world from both sides,
    Man and beast in the round of their need,
    And the hill wind stirred in my wool,
    My hoof and my hand clasped each other,
    I ate my one meal
    Of milk, and died
    Staring. From dark grass I came straight

    To my father's house, whose dust
    Whirls up in the halls for no reason
    When no one comes   piling deep in a hellish mild corner,
    And, through my immortal waters,
    I meet the sun's grains eye
    To eye, and they fail at my closet of glass.
    Dead, I am most surely living
    In the minds of farm boys: I am he who drives
    Them like wolves from the hound bitch and calf
    And from the chaste ewe in the wind.
    They go into woods   into bean fields   they go
    Deep into their known right hands. Dreaming of me,
    They groan   they wait   they suffer
    Themselves, they marry, they raise their kind.

JAMES DICKEY

THE POISONED MAN

When the rattlesnake bit, I lay
In a dream of the country, and dreamed
Day after day of the river,

Where I sat with a jackknife and quickly
Opened my sole to the water.
Blood shed for the sake of one's life

Takes on the hid shape of the channel,
Disappearing under logs and through boulders.
The freezing river poured on

And, as it took hold of my blood,
Leapt up round the rocks and boiled over.
I felt that my heart's blood could flow

Unendingly out of the mountain,
Splitting bedrock apart upon redness,
And the current of life at my instep

Give deathlessly as a spring.
Some leaves fell from trees and whirled under.
I saw my struck bloodstream assume,

Inside the cold path of the river,
The inmost routes of a serpent
Through grass, through branches and leaves.

When I rose, the live oaks were ashen
And the wild grass was dead without flame.
Through the blasted cornfield I hobbled,

My foot tied up in my shirt,
And met my old wife in the garden,
Where she reached for a withering apple.

I lay in the country and dreamed
Of the substance and course of the river
While the different colors of fever

Like quilt patches flickered upon me.
At last I arose, with the poison
Gone out of the seam of the scar,

And brought my wife eastward and weeping,
Through the copper fields springing alive
With the promise of harvest for no one.

AT DARIEN BRIDGE

The sea here used to look
As if many convicts had built it,

Standing deep in their ankle chains,
Ankle-deep in the water, to smite

The land and break it down to salt.
I was in this bog as a child

When they were all working all day
To drive the pilings down.

I thought I saw the still sun
Strike the side of a hammer in flight

And from it a sea bird be born
To take off over the marshes.

As the gray climbs the side of my head
And cuts my brain off from the world,

I walk and wish mainly for birds,
For the one bird no one has looked for

To spring again from a flash
Of metal, perhaps from the scratched

Wedding band on my ring finger.
Recalling the chains of their feet,

I stand and look out over grasses
At the bridge they built, long abandoned,

Breaking down into water at last,
And long, like them, for freedom

Or death, or to believe again
That they worked on the ocean to give it

The unchanging, hopeless look
Out of which all miracles leap.

ADULTERY

We have all been in rooms
We cannot die in, and they are odd places, and sad.
Often Indians are standing eagle-armed on hills

In the sunrise   open wide to the Great Spirit
Or gliding in canoes   or cattle are browsing on the walls
Far away   gazing down with the eyes of our children

Not far away   or there are men driving
The last railspike, which has turned
Gold in their hands. Gigantic forepleasure lives

Among such scenes, and we are alone with it
At last. There is always some weeping
Between us   and someone is always checking

A wrist watch by the bed to see how much
Longer we have left. Nothing can come
Of this   nothing can come

Of us: of me with my grim techniques
Or you who have sealed your womb
With a ring of convulsive rubber:

Although we come together,
Nothing will come of us. But we would not give
It up, for death is beaten

By praying Indians   by distant cows   historical
Hammers   by hazardous meetings that bridge
A continent. One could never die here

Never die   never die
While crying. My lover, my dear one
I will see you next week

When I'm in town. I will call you
If I can. Please get hold of   please don't
Oh God, Please don't any more I can't bear . . . Listen:

We have done it again   we are
Still living. Sit up and smile,
God bless you. Guilt is magical.

Stephen Dobyns

BOWLERS ANONYMOUS

Here comes the woman who wears the plastic prick
hooked to a string around her waist, the man who
puts girls' panties like a beanie on his head,
the chicken molester, the lady who likes Great Danes,
the boy who likes sheep, the old fellow who likes
to watch turkeys dance on the top of a hot stove,
the bicycle-seat sniffer, grasshopper muncher,
the bubbles-in-the-bath biter — they all meet
each night at midnight and, oh lord, they bowl.
From twelve to six they take it out on the pins
as they discuss their foibles with their friends.
I'm trying to cut down, says the woman who nibbles
the tails of mice. I've thrown away my Zippo, says
the man who sticks matches between people's toes.
There is nothing that can't become a pleasure
if one lets it, and so they bowl. They think
of that oddly handsome German shepherd face
and they bowl. Their hands quiver at the thought
of jamming their fingers in a car door
and they bowl. These are the heroes, these
grocers and teachers and postmen and plumbers.
They bring snapshots of themselves and Scotch tape,
then fix their photos to the pins and they bowl.
They focus on their faces at the end of the alley
and they bowl. They see the hunger in their eyes,
the twist of anticipation in their lips, and oh
they bowl — bowl to remember, bowl to forget,
as the pins with their own bruised faces explode
from midnight to six. While in those explosions
of wood, in which each pin describes an exact arc,
they feast on those moments when the world seems to stop
and everything conspires to push some fleeting
beauty — ripening peach or blossoming rose —
to the queer brink of perfection, where it flames,
flickers, fades, and is never perfect again.

STEPHEN DOBYNS

HOW TO LIKE IT

These are the first days of fall. The wind
at evening smells of roads still to be traveled,
while the sound of leaves blowing across the lawns
is like an unsettled feeling in the blood,
the desire to get in a car and just keep driving.
A man and a dog descend their front steps.
The dog says, Let's go downtown and get crazy drunk.
Let's tip over all the trash cans we can find.
This is how dogs deal with the prospect of change.
But in his sense of the season, the man is struck
by the oppressiveness of his past, how his memories
which were shifting and fluid have grown more solid
until it seems he can see remembered faces
caught up among the dark places in the trees.
The dog says, Let's pick up some girls and just
rip off their clothes. Let's dig holes everywhere.
Above his house, the man notices wisps of cloud
crossing the face of the moon. Like in a movie,
he says to himself, a movie about a person
leaving on a journey. He looks down the street
to the hills outside of town and finds the cut
where the road heads north. He thinks of driving
on that road and the dusty smell of the car
heater, which hasn't been used since last winter.
The dog says, Let's go down to the diner and sniff
people's legs. Let's stuff ourselves on burgers.
In the man's mind, the road is empty and dark.
Pine trees press down to the edge of the shoulder,
where the eyes of animals, fixed in his headlights,
shine like small cautions against the night.
Sometimes a passing truck makes his whole car shake.
The dog says, Let's go to sleep. Let's lie down
by the fire and put our tails over our noses.
But the man wants to drive all night, crossing
one state line after another, and never stop
until the sun creeps into his rearview mirror.
Then he'll pull over and rest awhile before
starting again, and at dusk he'll crest a hill
and there, filling a valley, will be the lights
of a city entirely new to him.
But the dog says, Let's just go back inside.

Let's not do anything tonight. So they
walk back up the sidewalk to the front steps.
How is it possible to want so many things
and still want nothing. The man wants to sleep
and wants to hit his head again and again
against a wall. Why is it all so difficult?
But the dog says, Let's go make a sandwich.
Let's make the tallest sandwich anyone's ever seen.
And that's what they do and that's where the man's
wife finds him, staring into the refrigerator
as if into the place where the answers are kept —
the ones telling why you get up in the morning
and how it is possible to sleep at night,
answers to what comes next and how to like it.

HOW COULD YOU EVER BE FINE

I dreamt last night I heard someone speak your name,
two women were talking about you and I went to them
and asked about you and they gave me your number.
So I called you and we talked and you said
you were fine, and I doubted it was really you,
because how could you ever be fine? What have
twenty years done to you? Where are you now?
You had the smoothest skin, a face like a beautiful
wax figure as you moved from one messed-up man
to another. There was one who used to shoot up
Jack Daniel's, and when I told him that was stupid,
he said, That's right, I'm stupid, I'm really stupid,
somebody should kill me! Until I said it actually
wasn't so stupid just to calm him. But all those men
who hit you and abused you and how you explained
they must have been right or else they wouldn't
have done it. I was too tame, didn't stick myself
with pins or know the names for all the drugs,
and had a vague idea of what I wanted to do
next week, next year. You would listen with one
black eye swollen half shut, then go back to the guy
who had done it so he could blacken the other.
I remember you told me how your mother had said
it was your duty to love her, and you shouted, No,

and kept shouting no. And when she died you felt glad,
but years later I took you to one funeral director
after another so you could find her ashes.
You said you wanted to talk to her, a beautiful
woman telling her troubles to a cardboard box.
Then you would sprinkle her ashes into the canal
and feel something, you weren't sure what, maybe
just done with something, the sense that something
was over. But either we couldn't find the right
funeral director or the ashes were already gone,
and that night you went back to a man who beat you,
and shortly after that you slipped out of my life —
a few cards, a few phone calls, then nothing.
Right now you are either out there or you're not —
smoking a cigarette, touching a sore place, looking
from the window and letting all the old faces
drift across your mind. It is hard to think of you
dowdy and forty, the problems dealt with, a life
of some sort on track, hard to think of you making it
past twenty-five. At least in books we know the end,
know the characters died or got married, had great
success or failure. But you are out there someplace,
and your friend who shot up the Jack Daniel's,
and the guy I took the knife away from,
and the other who wanted to be a writer,
and the girl who quit school to have a baby,
and another girl who smashed the doors of my truck
on an acid trip. They are all out there, just
putting one foot in front of another, just like
the torturers are out there, and the men who worked
on firing squads, and the men who like to hit things
just to hurt them. And you are out there too,
picking your way between the paper, the tin cans,
the broken glass. You had the most wonderful smile.
On whom does it shine now, who does it welcome?
People on hard streets dragged to inevitable ends.

for S.C.

STEPHEN DOBYNS

FRAGMENTS

Now there is a slit in the blue fabric of air.
His house spins faster. He holds down books,
chairs; his life and its objects fly upward:
vanishing black specks in the indifferent sky.

The sky is a torn piece of blue paper.
He tries to repair it, but the memory
of death is like paste on his fingers
and certain days stick like dead flies.

Say the sky goes back to being the sky
and the sun continues as always. Now,
knowing what you know, how can you not see
thin cracks in the fragile blue vaults of air.

My friend, what can I give you or darkness
lift from you but fragments of language,
fragments of blue sky. You had three
beautiful daughters and one has died.

for Donald Murray

BEAUTY

The father gets a bullet in the eye, killing him
instantly. His daughter raises an arm to say stop
and gets shot in the hand. He's a grocer from Baghdad
and at that time lots of Iraqis are moving to Detroit
to open small markets in the ghetto. In a month,
three have been murdered and since it is becoming
old news your editor says only to pick up a photo
unless you can find someone half decent to talk to.

Jammed into the living room are twenty men in black,
weeping, and thirty women wailing and pulling their hair —
something not prepared for by your Episcopal upbringing.
The grocer had already given the black junkie his money

and the junkie was already out the door when he fired,
for no apparent reason, the cops said. The other daughter,
who gives you the picture, has olive skin, great dark eyes
and is so beautiful you force yourself to stare only

at the passport photo in order not to offend her.
The photo shows a young man with a thin face cheerfully
expecting to make his fortune in the black ghetto.
As you listen to the girl, the wailing surrounds you
like bits of flying glass. It was a cousin who was shot
the week before, then a good friend two weeks before that.
Who can understand it? During the riots, he told people
to take what they needed, pay when they were able.

Although the girl has little to do with your story,
she is, in a sense, the entire story. She is young,
beautiful and her father has just been shot. As you
accept the picture, her mother grabs it, presses it
to her lips. The girl gently pries her mother's fingers
from the picture and returns it. Then the sister with
the wounded hand snatches the picture and you want to
unwrap the bandages, touch your fingers to the bullet hole.

Again the girl retrieves the picture, but before she
can give it back, a third woman in black grabs it,
begins kissing it and crushing it to her bosom. You think
of the unflappable photographers on the fourth floor
unfolding the picture and trying to erase the creases,
but when the picture appears in the paper it still bears
the wrinkles of the fat woman's heart, and you feel caught
between the picture grabbing which is comic and the wailing

which is like an animal gnawing your stomach. The girl
touches your arm, asks if anything is wrong, and you say,
no, you only want to get out of there; and once back
at the paper you tell your editor of this room with fifty
screaming people, how they kept snatching the picture.
So he tells you about a kid getting drowned when he was
a reporter, but that's not the point, nor is the screaming,
nor the fact that none of this will appear in a news story

about an Iraqi grocer shot by a black drug addict,
and see, here is his picture as he looked when he first
came to our country eight years ago, so glad to get

out of Baghdad. What could be worse than Baghdad?
The point is in the sixteen-year-old daughter giving back
the picture, asking you to put it in your pocket, then
touching your arm, asking if you are all right and
would you like a glass of water? The point is she hardly

belongs to that room or any reality found in newspapers,
that she's one of the few reasons you get up in the morning,
pursue your life all day and why you soon quit the paper
to find her: beautiful Iraqi girl last seen surrounded by
wailing for the death of her father. For Christ's sake,
those fools at the paper thought you wanted to fuck her,
as if that's all you can do with something beautiful,
as if that's what it means to govern your life by it.

TENDERLY

It's not a fancy restaurant, nor is it
a dump and it's packed this Saturday night
when suddenly a man leaps onto his tabletop,
whips out his prick and begins sawing at it

with a butter knife. I can't stand it
anymore! he shouts. The waiters grab him
before he draws blood and hustle him
out the back. Soon the other diners return

to their fillets and slices of duck. How
peculiar, each, in some fashion, articulates.
Consider how the world implants a picture
in our brains. Maybe thirty people watched

this nut attack his member with a dull knife
and for each, forever after, the image pops up
a thousand times. I once saw the oddest thing —
how often does each announce this fact?

In the distant future, several at death's door
once more recollect this guy hacking at himself
and die shaking their heads. So they are linked
as a family is linked — through a single portrait.

The man's wobbly perch on the white tablecloth,
his open pants and strangled red chunk of flesh
become for each a symbol of having had precisely
enough, of slipping over the edge, of being whipped

about the chops by the finicky world, and of reacting
with a rash mutiny against the tyranny of desire.
As for the lunatic who was tossed out the back
and left to rethink his case among the trash cans,

who knows what happened to him? A short life,
most likely, additional humiliation and defeat.
But the thirty patrons wish him well. They all
have burdens to shoulder in this world and whenever

one feels the strap begin to slip, he or she thinks
of the nut dancing with his dick on the tabletop
and trudges on. At least life has spared me this,
they think. And one — a retired banker — represents

the rest when he hopes against hope that the lunatic
is parked on a topless foreign beach with a beauty
clasped in his loving arms, breathing heavily, Oh,
darling, touch me there, tenderly, one more time!

CEMETERY NIGHTS

Sweet dreams, sweet memories, sweet taste of earth:
here's how the dead pretend they're still alive —
one drags up a chair, a lamp, unwraps
the newspaper from somebody's garbage,
then sits holding the paper up to his face.
No matter if the lamp is busted and his eyes
have fallen out. Or some of the others
group together in front of the TV, chuckling
and slapping what's left of their knees.
No matter if the screen is dark. Four more
sit at a table with glasses and plates,
lift forks to their mouths and chew. No matter
if their plates are empty and they chew only air.
Two of the dead roll on the ground,

banging and rubbing their bodies together
as if in love or frenzy. No matter if their skin
breaks off, that their genitals are just a memory.

The head cemetery rat calls in all the city rats,
who pay him what rats find valuable —
the wing of a pigeon or ear of a dog.
The rats perch on tombstones and the cheap
statues of angels and, oh, they hold their bellies
and laugh, laugh until their guts half break;
while the stars give off the same cold light
that all these dead once planned their lives by,
and in someone's yard a dog barks and barks
just to see if some animal as dumb as he is
will wake from sleep and perhaps bark back.

Rita Dove

DAYSTAR

She wanted a little room for thinking:
but she saw diapers steaming on the line,
a doll slumped behind the door.

So she lugged a chair behind the garage
to sit out the children's naps.

Sometimes there were things to watch —
the pinched armor of a vanished cricket,
a floating maple leaf. Other days
she stared until she was assured
when she closed her eyes
she'd see only her own vivid blood.

She had an hour, at best, before Liza appeared
pouting from the top of the stairs.
And just *what* was mother doing
out back with the field mice? Why,

building a palace. Later
that night when Thomas rolled over and
lurched into her, she would open her eyes
and think of the place that was hers
for an hour — where
she was nothing,
pure nothing, in the middle of the day.

CRAB-BOIL

(Ft. Myers, 1962)

Why do I remember the sky
above the forbidden beach,
why only blue and the scratch,

shell on tin, of their distress?
The rest

imagination supplies:
bucket and angry pink beseeching
claws. Why does Aunt Helen
laugh before saying "Look at that —

a bunch of niggers, not
a-one get out 'fore the others pull him
back." I don't believe her —

just as I don't believe *they* won't come
and chase us back to the colored-only shore
crisp with litter and broken glass.

"When do we kill them?"
"Kill 'em? Hell, the water does *that.*
They don't feel a thing . . . no nervous system."

I decide to believe this: I'm hungry.
Dismantled, they're merely exotic,
a blushing meat. After all, she *has*
grown old in the South. If
we're kicked out now, I'm ready.

WINGFOOT LAKE

(Independence Day, 1964)

On her 36th birthday, Thomas had shown her
her first swimming pool. It had been
his favorite color, exactly — just
so much of it, the swimmers' white arms jutting
into the chevrons of high society.
She had rolled up her window
and told him to drive on, fast.

Now this *act of mercy:* four daughters
dragging her to their husbands' company picnic,
white families on one side and them
on the other, unpacking the same

squeeze bottles of Heinz, the same
waxy beef patties and Salem potato chip bags.
So he was dead for the first time
on Fourth of July — ten years ago

had been harder, waiting for something to happen,
and ten years before that, the girls
like young horses eyeing the track.
Last August she stood alone for hours
in front of the T.V. set
as a crow's wing moved slowly through
the white streets of government.
That brave swimming

scared her, like Joanna saying
Mother, we're Afro-Americans now!
What did she know about Africa?
Were there lakes like this one
with a rowboat pushed under the pier?
Or Thomas' Great Mississippi
with its sullen silks? (There was
the Nile but the Nile belonged

to God.) Where she came from
was the past, 12 miles into town
where nobody had locked their back door,
and Goodyear hadn't begun to dream of a park
under the company symbol, a white foot
sprouting two small wings.

THE BREATHING, THE ENDLESS NEWS

Every god is lonely, an exile
composed of parts: elk horn,
cloven hoof. Receptacle

for wishes, each god is empty
without us, penitent,
raking our yards into windblown piles. . . .

Children know this: they are
the trailings of gods. Their eyes
hold nothing at birth then fill slowly

with the myth of ourselves. Not so the dolls,
out for the count, each toe pouting from
the slumped-over toddler clothes:

no blossoming there. So we
give our children dolls, and
they know just what to do —

line them up and shoot them.
With every execution
doll and god grow stronger.

AFTER READING *MICKEY IN THE NIGHT KITCHEN* FOR THE THIRD TIME BEFORE BED

I'm in the milk and the milk's in me! . . . I'm Mickey!

My daughter spreads her legs
to find her vagina:
hairless, this mistaken
bit of nomenclature
is what a stranger cannot touch
without her yelling. She demands
to see mine and momentarily
we're a lopsided star
among the spilled toys,
my prodigious scallops
exposed to her neat cameo.

And yet the same glazed
tunnel, layered sequences.
She is three; that makes this
innocent. *We're pink!*
she shrieks, and bounds off.

Every month she wants
to know where it hurts

and what the wrinkled string means
between my legs. *This is good blood*
I say, but that's wrong, too.
How to tell her that it's what makes us —
black mother, cream child.
That we're in the pink
and the pink's in us.

PARSLEY

1. *The Cane Fields*

There is a parrot imitating spring
in the palace, its feathers parsley green.
Out of the swamp the cane appears

to haunt us, and we cut it down. El General
searches for a word; he is all the world
there is. Like a parrot imitating spring,

we lie down screaming as rain punches through
and we come up green. We cannot speak an R —
out of the swamp, the cane appears

and then the mountain we call in whispers *Katalina.*
The children gnaw their teeth to arrowheads.
There is a parrot imitating spring.

El General has found his word: *perejil.*
Who says it, lives. He laughs, teeth shining
out of the swamp. The cane appears

in our dreams, lashed by wind and streaming.
And we lie down. For every drop of blood
there is a parrot imitating spring.
Out of the swamp the cane appears.

2. *The Palace*

The word the general's chosen is parsley.
It is fall, when thoughts turn
to love and death; the general thinks

of his mother, how she died in the fall
and he planted her walking cane at the grave
and it flowered, each spring stolidly forming
four-star blossoms. The general

pulls on his boots, he stomps to
her room in the palace, the one without
curtains, the one with a parrot
in a brass ring. As he paces he wonders
Who can I kill today. And for a moment
the little knot of screams
is still. The parrot, who has traveled

all the way from Australia in an ivory
cage, is, coy as a widow, practising
spring. Ever since the morning
his mother collapsed in the kitchen
while baking skull-shaped candies
for the Day of the Dead, the general
has hated sweets. He orders pastries
brought up for the bird; they arrive

dusted with sugar on a bed of lace.
The knot in his throat starts to twitch;
he sees his boots the first day in battle
splashed with mud and urine
as a soldier falls at his feet amazed —
how stupid he looked! — at the sound
of artillery. *I never thought it would sing*
the soldier said, and died. Now

the general sees the fields of sugar
cane, lashed by rain and streaming.
He sees his mother's smile, the teeth
gnawed to arrowheads. He hears
the Haitians sing without R's
as they swing the great machetes:
Katalina, they sing, *Katalina,*

mi madle, mi amol en muelte. God knows
his mother was no stupid woman; she
could roll an R like a queen. Even
a parrot can roll an R! In the bare room

the bright feathers arch in a parody
of greenery, as the last pale crumbs
disappear under the blackened tongue. Someone

calls out his name in a voice
so like his mother's, a startled tear
splashes the tip of his right boot.
My mother, my love in death.
The general remembers the tiny green sprigs
men of his village wore in their capes
to honor the birth of a son. He will
order many, this time, to be killed

for a single, beautiful word.

TESTIMONIAL

Back when the earth was new
and heaven just a whisper,
back when the names of things
hadn't had time to stick;

back when the smallest breezes
melted summer into autumn,
when all the poplars quivered
sweetly in rank and file . . .

the world called, and I answered.
Each glance ignited to a gaze.
I caught my breath and called that life,
swooned between spoonfuls of lemon sorbet.

I was pirouette and flourish,
I was filigree and flame.
How could I count my blessings
when I didn't know their names?

Back when everything was still to come,
luck leaked out everywhere.
I gave my promise to the world,
and the world followed me here.

Alan Dugan

CLOSING TIME AT THE SECOND AVENUE DELI

This is the time of night of the delicatessen
when the manager is balancing
a nearly empty ketchup bottle
upside-down on a nearly full ketchup bottle
and spreading his hands slowly away
from the perfect balance like shall I say
a priest blessing the balance, the achievement
of perfect emptiness, of perfect fullness? No,
this is a kosher delicatessen. The manager
is not like. He is not like a priest,
he is not even like a rabbi, he
is not like anyone else except the manager
as he turns to watch the waitress
discussing the lamb stew with my wife,
how most people eat the whole thing,
they don't take it home in a container,
as she mops up the tables, as the
cashier shall I say balances out?
No. The computer does all that. This
is not the time for metaphors. This is the time
to turn out the lights, and yes,
imagine it, those two ketchup bottles
will stand there all night long
as acrobatic metaphors of balance,
of emptiness, of fullness perfectly contained,
of any metaphor you wish unless
the manager snaps his fingers at the door,
goes back, and separates them for the night
from that unnatural balance, and the store goes dark
as my wife says should we take a cab
or walk, the stew is starting to drip already.
Shall I say that the container can not
contain the thing contained anymore? No.
Just that the lamb stew is leaking all across town
in one place: it is leaking on the floor of the taxi-cab,
and that somebody is going to pay for this ride.

ELEGY

I know but will not tell
you, Aunt Irene, why there
are soapsuds in the whiskey:
Uncle Robert had to have
a drink while shaving. May
there be no bloodshed in your house
this morning of my father's death
and no unkept appearance
in the living, since he has
to wear the rouge and lipstick
of your ceremony, mother,
for the first and last time:
father, hello and goodbye.

MORNING SONG

Look, it's morning, and a little water gurgles in the tap.
I wake up waiting, because it's Sunday, and turn twice more
than usual in bed, before I rise to cereal and comic strips.
I have risen to the morning danger and feel proud,
and after shaving off the night's disguises, after searching
close to the bone for blood, and finding only a little,
I shall walk out bravely into the daily accident.

LOVE SONG: I AND THOU

Nothing is plumb, level, or square:
    the studs are bowed, the joists
are shaky by nature, no piece fits
    any other piece without a gap
or pinch, and bent nails
    dance all over the surfacing
like maggots. By Christ
    I am no carpenter. I built
the roof for myself, the walls

for myself, the floors
for myself, and got
    hung up in it myself. I
danced with a purple thumb
    at this house-warming, drunk
with my prime whiskey: rage.
    Oh I spat rage's nails
into the frame-up of my work:
    it held. It settled plumb,
level, solid, square and true
    for that great moment. Then
it screamed and went on through,
    skewing as wrong the other way.
God damned it. This is hell,
    but I planned it, I sawed it,
I nailed it, and I
    will live in it until it kills me.
I can nail my left palm
    to the left-hand crosspiece but
I can't do everything myself.
    I need a hand to nail the right,
a help, a love, a you, a wife.

UNTITLED POEM

Once, one of my students read a book we had.
She was doing a history assignment on
the decline and fall of the Roman Empire
and crying. When I asked her why
she said Because. All those people died.
I said that if you start to cry for the dead
you won't have much time for anything else.
Besides, after all the city people were killed
or died off, because their cultures got too high,
the barbarians kept some peasants alive
for their food value. Some barbarian raped
some peasant woman who produced
a child who ultimately produced you
and me, so there is this family continuity,
so don't cry, it's obvious, look around!
This is the reason why we Americans
are a nation of peasants and barbarians.

TO AN EX-STUDENT

Annie, your face is in fashion this year and so are your legs.
When I look at the child models in the high-fashion ads in
     The New York Times
I get a hard-on remembering our horizontal conferences at college.
I wonder what happened to you after you graduated and I got fired.
I remember saying, "Go get a modeling job, get notoriety, get around:
those of us who get around a lot tend almost inevitably to meet again,"
and you saying, "I had to wait around all day with two hundred other
     girls
for some raging fag to say, 'Look up, look down, let's see the legs, that's
     all.'"

CRITICISM OF BERGSON AND DARWIN

The primeval fish was like a squid, all mouth,
with eyes, ears, feelers, nostrils (or gills),
and ten tentacles set closely all around it.
The tentacles kept pushing food into the mouth.
The mouth was always snapping open and closed
with teeth: choppers in front, fangs at the sides,
grinders in back. Inside the mouth
a tongue was always lashing ground-up fish
and chopped-up seaweed into a rear gut.
Behind the gut there were two thrashing tails,
and between them there were two holes and a barb.
Fish bones and mash came out of one hole. The squid
put the barb into the other hole of another squid
while the other squid put its barb into
the other hole of the first squid. After a while
squid eggs came out of both of these holes,
and some of them floated ashore and became us.
What a tragedy. You lost your barb
and kept your hole. I lost my hole
and kept my barb. You get to make the babies.
Why? Why? Bergson and Darwin do not say.
Is this Creative Evolution? No. Is this
Origin of Species and Descent of Man? Yes.

SURVIVING THE HURRICANE

When the neighbor's outhouse went by
and landed upside down on my property,
unoccupied, I laughed and yelled, "It's mine,"
but what's so funny? the TV says
that many, many will get blown away
in the hurricane's uproarious humors,
and now the horizontal rain comes through
my wall, the wallpaper heaves and cries
and runs down to the floor as pulp
as the windows go out with the wind,
poof!, and the wind picks off the roof
two shingles at a time in love-me-nots,
and there is no difference inside or out:
Leaning against the wall or the wind
is the same. This wet is that wet.
There is no protection anywhere except
I go stand in the upside-down outhouse
with the crapper over my stinking head,
once it has dripped dry of its storm-borne shit,
and be the dry mummy of its sarcophagus
under the whole hurricane of the universe.
That's what's so funny: Egypt.

LAMENT FOR CELLISTS AND JACQUELINE DUPRÉ

When the beautiful cellist Jacqueline DuPré
died of multiple sclerosis at forty-two
all the cellists grieved, and one
fell on her instrument, not
as a sacrifice, but as an accident,
if there are such accidents. She was
hysterical, but there was no
damage to the tone, and it only cost
a thousand bucks to fix. Remember,
a cello is a beautiful shape of air
set in the right box and played by strings
played by strings the player plays:
the player can't get close to it the way

a violinist does, feeling the air play
the wood play the bones of his/her head
as the violinist joins the music to the brain.
That's why some cellists dance
with it like Yo Yo Ma, because it is
an outside music that they have to join
as athletes of a different air,
so when Jacqueline DuPré died young,
her muscles dying on her first,
it got to the cellists in their very art
because they're distant from their instrument:
it can't go to their heads, like violins.
With her, the music started distantly, then
it got more distant, then the distance
got to be the infinity of cello death
the way a cellist I knew would drape his tux
around his instrument before he went to sleep
after a performance in a strange town
so the cello could be the cellist through the night,
dead silent, with a black bow tie around its neck,
and he could joke away the horrors.

RISING IN FALL,

the mushrooms feel like stiff pricks made of rot.
Oh spreading glans, what
a botanical striving to butt
hogberry branches and leaves apart
to rise to fuck the sky so fast,
six inches in, up IT, with dirt
on top of each umbrella ribbed beneath,
in one night after rain. Stars,
there is life down here in the dark.
It wants you, upward, but not much.
The mushrooms die so fast
in their external manifestations that
their maggots working to be flies
make moving liquid of their blackening heads.
Oh you can see them falling downward for a week
to dirt — that's when they really live —
and then the flies take off.

How high do they get to sting us?
Not high. It's ridiculous. I ask
a woman, "Do you get the point
of all this pointless action?"
She answers, "Naturally. Yes. Idiot."

Carol Frost

CHIMERA

By the verge of the sea a man finds a gelatinous creature,
parching, thick as a shoe, its head a doubtful dark green
that leans toward him as he bends near in some dark
wonderment of his own. The sky is haunted by pure light,

the sea a rough mixture of blue, and green, and black. Suddenly
he hears the air rent with loud cries and looks to see
pelicans on the piers raising their wings then falling, changing shape
to dive into the sea. He thinks of Bosch's rebellious angels
changing shape as they are pursued out of the immaculate sky.

Who are they? Angels who accept the hideous
and monstrous. Fallen, they make up a nightmare fauna.
Say the sea is to be questioned. Below the bounds
of this estate, through rainbowed cold, the rockheaded and cored

of bone, the chimera our madness does not cease to reinvent
and which we dare not think alive, crawls in a thick ooze.
Yet even this one, torn to the plain insides and leaking dyes,
exudes a gentle unrest of the soul. Is it not good? The man pauses,
looks around — the sea undulated, sharpening and smoothing

all the grooves that history has graven on the sand —
then he puts his hands under the terrible flesh and heaves it
as far as he can back into the Atlantic, as if it were the mirror
of a lost estate, the dawn-time of the world's first season.

HOMO SAPIENS

In this lonely, varying light of dawn with the residue of desire
like mist departing, I am walking. Was it in your eyes,
where my elongated face shone, I saw for the first time —
as if all the transparent fire in these trees had become palpable —
a hunger that was not wholly animal?
The need to tremble like dogwood, feeling the rain touch down.

My strange blood rises, and I may see you, fair leaves slipping over you,
    half-hidden
in the morning. With the beasts beside a pond,
I conjure the inward sun to leap into my brain. What remains?
Wild, beautiful petals all around.
A beast's face. And something, something else.

SEXUAL JEALOUSY

Think of the queen mole who is unequivocal,
exuding a scent to keep the other females neuter
and bringing forth the colony's only babies, hairless and pink in the dark
of her tunneled chamber. She may chew a pale something, a root,
find it tasteless, drop it for the dreary others to take away, then demand
more; she must suckle the young. Of course
they all hate her and are jealous of the attention given her
by her six bedmates. In their mutual dream she is dead and her urine
no longer arrests their maturing. As irises infallibly unfold,
one of their own will feel her sex grow quickest and greatest. As they dig
together, their snouts full of soil, they hope this and are ruthless in their
    waiting.

HARM

She had only begun to get used to her body's exposures
to pain, like the insinuations behind questions: winter
asking the tree, where's your strength? — a priest asking a soul, where's
    your marrow?
Aversions, truth, invective,
it wasn't her answers which mattered, only her lying on a bed
being administered shocks until the world grew tired
of experimenting with another bit of clay and the inward liberties. So it
    seemed.
And when the intern came into the room, asking how she was
and snouting through her chest with drainage tubes, as strong a desire
as she'd ever had rose up in her. She must have gestured, or he already
    knew, because,
as if in expectation, he smiled at her and stepped out of harm's way,
    backward, for just a moment.

LAWS

She knows of doom only what all women know,
deciding not to speak of it, since speech pretends
its course can be made to bend: — someone fleeing hot and sweating
and the victors close behind, then two roads all at once in a wood.
    Which one leads
farther away? Under cover of silence
she goes along as if perhaps nothing would happen to her,
seeming to be swayed by breezes — dazed, her friends say in their con-
    cern,
after, when they've thought of it, having called or dropped by.
Once, though, late in her illness, in the heat of a morning walk,
she raises her wig and shows us this surge of white back from the fore-
    head. The tablets
Moses carried, with his guesses, in the end could not have been more
    blinding or more lawful.

NOTHING

She turned away. And her child slid toward
the ice edge of the precipice, gravity and momentum wrestling on his
    shoulders.
She could not bear to see the outcome and was starting to pretend he
    did not exist;
if his existence would come to an end. See: there is a snowy peak and
    clouds
spilling so softly they create a whirlpool of silence. She lets herself be in
    it.
She no longer hears anything. Not the wind. Not the scraping shoes. Not
    him.
How she used to fret, to brush the hair back from his eyes
so everyone could see his beauty and she could see the least shadow
of sorrow or illness. But there is nothing left to do for him.
Since the forces like acrobats keep somersaulting and playing
with him, she will not hearken or give them the pleasure of her scream.

FURY

And the whole night she had told herself to be pleasant
as she lay by the sleeping man, and she'd gladly have listened to herself,
but as the enormous dawn sneaked into their darkness
and seized them in its paws, she found herself with the old fury,
past her carefullest politeness. She saw she'd need millennia to find a
    way
to comprehend the reason for the difference between their early
    ideals —
a garden where plums and peaches grew well and tasted wild
and they were unembarrassed by genitals — and what had become of
    them.
This apple-pose. It was no good blaming God or Adam, she knew, but
    she couldn't help herself — :
Why hadn't the one spoken forthrightly and had the other caved in?
Then, hardly allowing him to fully awaken, she said her first sarcasm.
    Then another.

SCORN

She thought of no wilder delicacy than the starling eggs she fed him for
    breakfast,
and if he sat and ate like a farmhand and she hated him sometimes,
she knew it didn't matter: that whatever in the din of argument
was harshly spoken, something else was done, soothed and patted away.
When they were young the towering fierceness
of their differences had frightened her even as she longed for physical
    release.
Out of their mouths such curses; their hands huge, pointing, stabbing
    the air.
How had they *not* been wounded? And wounded they'd convalesced in
    the same rooms
and bed. When at last they knew everything without confiding — fears,
    stinks,
boiling hearts — they gave up themselves a little so that they might both
    love and scorn
each other, and they ate from each other's hands.

CAROL FROST

TO KILL A DEER

Into the changes of autumn brush
the doe walked, and the hide, head, and ears
were the tinsel browns. They made her.
I could not see her. She reappeared, stuffed with apples,
and I shot her. Into the pines she ran,
and I ran after. I might have lost her,
seeing no sign of blood or scuffle,
but felt myself part of the woods,
a woman with a doe's ears, and heard her
dying, counted her last breaths like a song
of dying, and found her dying.
I shot her again because her lungs rattled like castanets,
then poked her with the gun barrel
because her eyes were dusty and unreal.
I opened her belly and pushed the insides
like rotted fruit into a rabbit hole,
skinned her, broke her leg joints under my knee,
took the meat, smelled the half-digested smell
that was herself. Ah, I closed her eyes.
I left her refolded in some briars
with the last sun on her head
like a benediction, head tilted on its axis
of neck and barren bone; head bent
wordless over a death, though I heard
the night wind blowing through her fur,
heard riot in the emptied head.

PAPILIO

Collecting is a basic human trait. The great collectors
found the Nabokov Pug, *suvarovius* flying by the hundreds,
and the common glider, then spread their wings, medicating them
so carefully that no corruption invaded; they placed
them in beautifully carved bureaus to remember
the graceful madnesses of their flight over the white clearings,
the dark green ferns, the wildflowers, and the peculiar, crooked branches
of the thorn apple like crucifixions. Some lay their eggs near violets;
some need the salts and minerals in animal urine;

most are diurnal. The only time I held one in my hand
was when I found it in my garden, fanning itself
on a bean plant. It seemed to have muscles in its wings,
but all I could see, on closer inspection, were its veins, its curled
    proboscis,
and its horrible compound eyes, like those on the fallen preening angels
of the imagination. I like to think that its letting me pick it up
was sign of its complicated instinct for survival — in the way its eyespots
can persuade birds to peck at a dispensable part of its wings.
When I let it go, it wafted over to the barn wall.
What trick of pen or brush could capture that slightness
of flying? No wonder they are pinned to boards, romantics exaggerate
their delicacy, and modern poets dislike them. But they are not frail.
Think of their long thin hearts pumping yellow blood, their concealed
    poisons,
and their pheromones and colors which are sexual — they grow trans-
    parent
from sex. They are also territorial. Think of the rate of speed of autumn.

APPLE RIND

Someone else was afraid and spoke to me
and I couldn't answer. . . swallowing oxygen
from a tube. And then? The cool blade
freeing rind from an apple
like the first touch of day. How long
I'd been in someone's still life — the blade
hidden, dividing — and was helpless.

Perfectly drugged, I lay just shy of winter
in my own mind. My cut chest felt nothing,
no terror, no pain. And there were morphine's sweet-
and-fruit boxes piled on the white terrain
like reasons for lives and death.
The orchard was weathered to admonitory bareness
except for a few frozen apples
above a disturbance of snow — the hoofprints
of deer coming by several routes to this late harvest,
the dim haunches and various limbs
afloat on movement that can break
or double back into the gray calm of woods.

How to explain directions a mind takes
or why I told no one how much I wanted
to come back to this beautiful, stupid world.

THE ST. LOUIS ZOO

The isle is full of noises, / Sounds, and sweet air . . . sometimes voices.
— The Tempest

High, yellow, coiled and weighting the branch like an odd piece of fruit,
   a snake slept
by the gate, in the serpent house. I walked around the paths hearing

hushed air, piecemeal remarks, and the hoarse voice of the keeper
   spreading cabbage
and pellets in the elephant compound — "Hungry, are you? There's a
   girl.

How's Pearl?" — A clucking music, then silence again crept past me
on the waters of the duck pond. Birds with saffron wings in the flight
   cage

and flamingos the color of mangoes, even their webbed feet red-orange,
   made so
"by the algae they ingest," as angels are made of air — some bickered,

some were tongue-tied, some danced on one leg in the honeyed light.
I thought of autumn as leaves scattered down. Nearby, closed away

in his crude beginnings in a simulated rain forest, the gorilla pulled out
   handfuls
of grass, no Miranda to teach him to speak, though he was full of noises

and rank air after swallowing. Smooth rind and bearded husks lay about
   him.
His eyes were ingots when he looked at me.

In late-summer air thick with rose and lily, I felt the old malevolence;
the snake tonguing the air, as if to tell me of its dreaming: — birds of
   paradise

gemming a pond; the unspooling; soft comings on, soft, soft
gestures, twisted and surreptitious; the shock; the taste; the kingdom.

In something more than words, *You are the snake, snake coils in you,*
it said. Do you think anyone knows its own hunger as well as the snake?

Why am I not just someone alive? When did Spirit tear me
to see how void of blessing I was? The snake hesitated, tasting dusk's
    black honey,

to feel if it was still good. And through its swoon
it knew it. Leaf, lichen, the least refinements, and the perfection.

SIN

The tree bore the efflorescence of October apples
like the bush that burned with fire and was not consumed.

The wind blew in cold sweet gusts
and the burning taste of fresh snow came with the gradual dark

down through the goldenrod. The blue and scarlet sky
was gently losing its color,

as if from use.
The towers and telephone poles rose in the distance.

And a decline
of spirit, hearing, all senses; where the mind no longer rests,

dwells, intrigues; and Satan's quick perspective of what lies ahead
were foretold by the springing back of a bough.

— We'll never know the all of it: nature's manifesto,
the sleight-of-hand in god's light, the invisible,

visible, sinned against, absolved, no matter the enormity
of trying, and Eve's help.

But come just before sunrise and see and taste again
the apple tree coming into fire

— shadow-glyphs on the crystallized grasses,
geese surging above the loblolly pine, the smell of sap — ,

as if willingly through its long life
it held on to one unclarified passion and grew and regretted nothing.

THE UNDRESSING

They took off their clothes 1000 nights
and felt the plaster of the moon
sift over them, and the ground roll
them in its dream. Little did they know
the light and clay and their own sweat
became a skin they couldn't wash away.
Each night bonded to the next,
and they grew stiffer. They noticed this
in sunlight — there were calluses,
round tough moons on their extremities,
shadows under their eyes,
and sometimes a faint sour smell they hadn't had as children.
It worried them, but at night the animal
in their bodies overcame their reluctance
to be naked with each other,
and the mineral moon did its work.
At last when they woke up and were dead,
statues on their backs in the park,
they opened their mouths
and crawled out, pitifully soft and small,
not yet souls.

Allen Ginsberg

HOWL

for Carl Solomon

I

I saw the best minds of my generation destroyed by madness, starving
    hysterical naked,
dragging themselves through the negro streets at dawn looking for an
    angry fix,
angelheaded hipsters burning for the ancient heavenly connection to the
    starry dynamo in the machinery of night,
who poverty and tatters and hollow-eyed and high sat up smoking in the
    supernatural darkness of cold-water flats floating across the tops of
    cities contemplating jazz,
who bared their brains to Heaven under the El and saw Mohammedan
    angels staggering on tenement roofs illuminated,
who passed through universities with radiant cool eyes hallucinating
    Arkansas and Blake-light tragedy among the scholars of war,
who were expelled from the academies for crazy & publishing obscene
    odes on the windows of the skull,
who cowered in unshaven rooms in underwear, burning their money in
    wastebaskets and listening to the Terror through the wall,
who got busted in their pubic beards returning through Laredo with a
    belt of marijuana for New York,
who ate fire in paint hotels or drank turpentine in Paradise Alley, death,
    or purgatoried their torsos night after night
with dreams, with drugs, with waking nightmares, alcohol and cock and
    endless balls,
incomparable blind streets of shuddering cloud and lightning in the
    mind leaping toward poles of Canada & Paterson, illuminating all
    the motionless world of Time between,
Peyote solidities of halls, backyard green tree cemetery dawns, wine
    drunkenness over the rooftops, storefront boroughs of teahead
    joyride neon blinking traffic light, sun and moon and tree vibrations
    in the roaring winter dusks of Brooklyn, ashcan rantings and kind
    king light of mind,
who chained themselves to subways for the endless ride from Battery to
    holy Bronx on benzedrine until the noise of wheels and children

brought them down shuddering mouth-wracked and battered bleak
of brain all drained of brilliance in the drear light of Zoo,
who sank all night in submarine light of Bickford's floated out and sat
through the stale beer afternoon in desolate Fugazzi's, listening to
the crack of doom on the hydrogen jukebox,
who talked continuously seventy hours from park to pad to bar to
Bellevue to museum to the Brooklyn Bridge,
a lost battalion of platonic conversationalists jumping down the stoops
off fire escapes off windowsills off Empire State out of the moon,
yacketayakking screaming vomiting whispering facts and memories and
anecdotes and eyeball kicks and shocks of hospitals and jails and
wars,
whose intellects disgorged in total recall for seven days and nights with
brilliant eyes, meat for the Synagogue cast on the pavement,
who vanished into nowhere Zen New Jersey leaving a trail of ambiguous
picture postcards of Atlantic City Hall,
suffering Eastern sweats and Tangerian bone-grindings and migraines of
China under junk-withdrawal in Newark's bleak furnished room,
who wandered around and around at midnight in the railroad yard wondering where to go, and went, leaving no broken hearts,
who lit cigarettes in boxcars boxcars boxcars racketing through snow
toward lonesome farms in grandfather night,
who studied Plotinus Poe St. John of the Cross telepathy and bop kabal-
la because the cosmos instinctively vibrated at their feet in Kansas,
who loned it through the streets of Idaho seeking visionary indian angels
who were visionary indian angels,
who thought they were only mad when Baltimore gleamed in supernatural ecstasy,
who jumped in limousines with the Chinaman of Oklahoma on the
impulse of winter midnight streetlight smalltown rain,
who lounged hungry and lonesome through Houston seeking jazz or sex
or soup, and followed the brilliant Spaniard to converse about
America and Eternity, a hopeless task, and so took ship to Africa,
who disappeared into the volcanoes of Mexico leaving behind nothing
but the shadow of dungarees and the lava and ash of poetry scattered in fireplace Chicago,
who reappeared on the West Coast investigating the F.B.I. in beards and
shorts with big pacifist eyes sexy in their dark skin passing out
incomprehensible leaflets,
who burned cigarette holes in their arms protesting the narcotic tobacco haze of Capitalism,
who distributed Supercommunist pamphlets in Union Square weeping
and undressing while the sirens of Los Alamos wailed them down,
and wailed down Wall, and the Staten Island ferry also wailed,

who broke down crying in white gymnasiums naked and trembling
before the machinery of other skeletons,

who bit detectives in the neck and shrieked with delight in policecars for
committing no crime but their own wild cooking pederasty and
intoxication,

who howled on their knees in the subway and were dragged off the roof
waving genitals and manuscripts,

who let themselves be fucked in the ass by saintly motorcyclists, and
screamed with joy,

who blew and were blown by those human seraphim, the sailors, caress-
es of Atlantic and Caribbean love,

who balled in the morning in the evenings in rosegardens and the grass
of public parks and cemeteries scattering their semen freely to
whomever come who may,

who hiccupped endlessly trying to giggle but wound up with a sob
behind a partition in a Turkish Bath when the blonde & naked angel
came to pierce them with a sword,

who lost their loveboys to the three old shrews of fate the one eyed shrew
of the heterosexual dollar the one eyed shrew that winks out of the
womb and the one eyed shrew that does nothing but sit on her ass
and snip the intellectual golden threads of the craftsman's loom,

who copulated ecstatic and insatiate with a bottle of beer a sweetheart a
package of cigarettes a candle and fell off the bed, and continued
along the floor and down the hall and ended fainting on the wall
with a vision of ultimate cunt and come eluding the last gyzym of
consciousness,

who sweetened the snatches of a million girls trembling in the sunset,
and were red eyed in the morning but prepared to sweeten the
snatch of the sunrise, flashing buttocks under barns and naked in
the lake,

who went out whoring through Colorado in myriad stolen night-cars,
N.C., secret hero of these poems, cocksman and Adonis of Denver
— joy to the memory of his innumerable lays of girls in empty lots
& diner backyards, moviehouses' rickety rows, on mountaintops in
caves or with gaunt waitresses in familiar roadside lonely petticoat
upliftings & especially secret gas-station solipsisms of johns, &
hometown alleys too,

who faded out in vast sordid movies, were shifted in dreams, woke on a
sudden Manhattan, and picked themselves up out of basements
hungover with heartless Tokay and horrors of Third Avenue iron
dreams & stumbled to unemployment offices,

who walked all night with their shoes full of blood on the snowbank
docks waiting for a door in the East River to open to a room full of
steamheat and opium,

who created great suicidal dramas on the apartment cliff-banks of the
    Hudson under the wartime blue floodlight of the moon & their
    heads shall be crowned with laurel in oblivion,
who ate the lamb stew of the imagination or digested the crab at the
    muddy bottom of the rivers of Bowery,
who wept at the romance of the streets with their pushcarts full of
    onions and bad music,
who sat in boxes breathing in the darkness under the bridge, and rose up
    to build harpsichords in their lofts,
who coughed on the sixth floor of Harlem crowned with flame under the
    tubercular sky surrounded by orange crates of theology,
who scribbled all night rocking and rolling over lofty incantations which
    in the yellow morning were stanzas of gibberish,
who cooked rotten animals lung heart feet tail borsht & tortillas dream-
    ing of the pure vegetable kingdom,
who plunged themselves under meat trucks looking for an egg,
who threw their watches off the roof to cast their ballot for Eternity out-
    side of Time, & alarm clocks fell on their heads every day for the
    next decade,
who cut their wrists three times successively unsuccessfully, gave up and
    were forced to open antique stores where they thought they were
    growing old and cried,
who were burned alive in their innocent flannel suits on Madison
    Avenue amid blasts of leaden verse & the tanked-up clatter of the
    iron regiments of fashion & the nitroglycerine shrieks of the fairies
    of advertising & the mustard gas of sinister intelligent editors, or
    were run down by the drunken taxicabs of Absolute Reality,
who jumped off the Brooklyn Bridge this actually happened and walked
    away unknown and forgotten into the ghostly daze of Chinatown
    soup alleyways & firetrucks, not even one free beer,
who sang out of their windows in despair, fell out of the subway window,
    jumped in the filthy Passaic, leaped on negroes, cried all over the
    street, danced on broken wineglasses barefoot smashed phonograph
    records of nostalgic European 1930's German jazz finished the
    whiskey and threw up groaning into the bloody toilet, moans in their
    ears and the blast of colossal steamwhistles,
who barreled down the highways of the past journeying to each other's
    hotrod-Golgotha jail-solitude watch or Birmingham jazz incarna-
    tion,
who drove crosscountry seventytwo hours to find out if I had a vision or
    you had a vision or he had a vision to find out Eternity,
who journeyed to Denver, who died in Denver, who came back to Denver
    & waited in vain, who watched over Denver & brooded & loned in
    Denver and finally went away to find out the Time, & now Denver
    is lonesome for her heroes,

who fell on their knees in hopeless cathedrals praying for each other's
　　salvation and light and breasts, until the soul illuminated its hair for
　　a second,
who crashed through their minds in jail waiting for impossible criminals
　　with golden heads and the charm of reality in their hearts who sang
　　sweet blues to Alcatraz,
who retired to Mexico to cultivate a habit, or Rocky Mount to tender
　　Buddha or Tangiers to boys or Southern Pacific to the black loco-
　　motive or Harvard to Narcissus to Woodlawn to the daisychain or
　　grave,
who demanded sanity trials accusing the radio of hypnotism & were left
　　with their insanity & their hands & a hung jury,
who threw potato salad at CCNY lectures on Dadaism and subsequent-
　　ly presented themselves on the granite steps of the madhouse with
　　shaven heads and harlequin speech of suicide, demanding instanta-
　　neous lobotomy,
and who were given instead the concrete void of insulin metrasol elec-
　　tricity hydrotherapy psychotherapy occupational therapy pingpong
　　& amnesia,
who in humorless protest overturned only one symbolic pingpong table,
　　resting briefly in catatonia,
returning years later truly bald except for a wig of blood, and tears and
　　fingers, to the visible madman doom of the wards of the madtowns
　　of the East,
Pilgrim State's Rockland's and Greystone's foetid halls, bickering with
　　the echoes of the soul, rocking and rolling in the midnight soli-
　　tude-bench dolmen-realms of love, dream of life a nightmare, bod-
　　ies turned to stone as heavy as the moon,
with mother finally ******, and the last fantastic book flung out of the
　　tenement window, and the last door closed at 4 A.M. and the last
　　telephone slammed at the wall in reply and the last furnished room
　　emptied down to the last piece of mental furniture, a yellow paper
　　rose twisted on a wire hanger in the closet, and even that imaginary,
　　nothing but a hopeful little bit of hallucination —
ah, Carl, while you are not safe I am not safe, and now you're really in
　　the total animal soup of time —
and who therefore ran through the icy streets obsessed with a sudden
　　flash of the alchemy of the use of the ellipse the catalog the meter
　　& the vibrating plane,
who dreamt and made incarnate gaps in Time & Space through images
　　juxtaposed, and trapped the archangel of the soul between 2 visual
　　images and joined the elemental verbs and set the noun and dash
　　of consciousness together jumping with sensation of Pater Omni-
　　potens Aeterna Deus

to recreate the syntax and measure of poor human prose and stand
before you speechless and intelligent and shaking with shame,
rejected yet confessing out the soul to conform to the rhythm of
thought in his naked and endless head,

the madman bum and angel beat in Time, unknown, yet putting down
here what might be left to say in time come after death,

and rose reincarnate in the ghostly clothes of jazz in the goldhorn shadow of the band and blew the suffering of America's naked mind for
love into an eli eli lamma lamma sabacthani saxophone cry that
shivered the cities down to the last radio

with the absolute heart of the poem of life butchered out of their own
bodies good to eat a thousand years.

II

What sphinx of cement and aluminum bashed open their skulls and ate
up their brains and imagination?

Moloch! Solitude! Filth! Ugliness! Ashcans and unobtainable dollars!
Children screaming under the stairways! Boys sobbing in armies!
Old men weeping in the parks!

Moloch! Moloch! Nightmare of Moloch! Moloch the loveless! Mental
Moloch! Moloch the heavy judger of men!

Moloch the incomprehensible prison! Moloch the crossbone soulless
jailhouse and Congress of sorrows! Moloch whose buildings are
judgment! Moloch the vast stone of war! Moloch the stunned gov-
ernments!

Moloch whose mind is pure machinery! Moloch whose blood is running
money! Moloch whose fingers are ten armies! Moloch whose breast
is a cannibal dynamo! Moloch whose ear is a smoking tomb!

Moloch whose eyes are a thousand blind windows! Moloch whose sky-
scrapers stand in the long streets like endless Jehovahs! Moloch
whose factories dream and croak in the fog! Moloch whose smoke-
stacks and antennae crown the cities!

Moloch whose love is endless oil and stone! Moloch whose soul is elec-
tricity and banks! Moloch whose poverty is the specter of genius!
Moloch whose fate is a cloud of sexless hydrogen! Moloch whose
name is the Mind!

Moloch in whom I sit lonely! Moloch in whom I dream Angels! Crazy in
Moloch! Cocksucker in Moloch! Lacklove and manless in Moloch!

Moloch who entered my soul early! Moloch in whom I am a consciousness without a body! Moloch who frightened me out of my natural
ecstasy! Moloch whom I abandon! Wake up in Moloch! Light
streaming out of the sky!

Moloch! Moloch! Robot apartments! invisible suburbs! skeleton trea-
  suries! blind capitals! demonic industries! spectral nations! invinci-
  ble madhouses! granite cocks! monstrous bombs!
They broke their backs lifting Moloch to Heaven! Pavements, trees,
  radios, tons! lifting the city to Heaven which exists and is everywhere about us!
Visions! omens! hallucinations! miracles! ecstasies! gone down the
  American river!
Dreams! adorations! illuminations! religions! the whole boatload of sensitive bullshit!
Breakthroughs! over the river! flips and crucifixions! gone down the
  flood! Highs! Epiphanies! Despairs! Ten years' animal screams and
  suicides! Minds! New loves! Mad generation! down on the rocks of
  Time!
Real holy laughter in the river! They saw it all! the wild eyes! the holy
  yells! They bade farewell! They jumped off the roof! to solitude!
  waving! carrying flowers! Down to the river! into the street!

III

Carl Solomon! I'm with you in Rockland
    where you're madder than I am
I'm with you in Rockland
    where you must feel very strange
I'm with you in Rockland
    where you imitate the shade of my mother
I'm with you in Rockland
    where you've murdered your twelve secretaries
I'm with you in Rockland
    where you laugh at this invisible humor
I'm with you in Rockland
    where we are great writers on the same dreadful typewriter
I'm with you in Rockland
    where your condition has become serious and is reported on the
    radio
I'm with you in Rockland
    where the faculties of the skull no longer admit the worms of the
    senses
I'm with you in Rockland
    where you drink the tea of the breasts of the spinsters of Utica
I'm with you in Rockland
    where you pun on the bodies of your nurses the harpies of the Bronx

I'm with you in Rockland
> where you scream in a straightjacket that you're losing the game of
> the actual pingpong of the abyss

I'm with you in Rockland
> where you bang on the catatonic piano the soul is innocent and
> immortal it should never die ungodly in an armed madhouse

I'm with you in Rockland
> where fifty more shocks will never return your soul to its body again
> from its pilgrimage to a cross in the void

I'm with you in Rockland
> where you accuse your doctors of insanity and plot the Hebrew
> socialist revolution against the fascist national Golgotha

I'm with you in Rockland
> where you will split the heavens of Long Island and resurrect your
> living human Jesus from the superhuman tomb

I'm with you in Rockland
> where there are twentyfive thousand mad comrades all together
> singing the final stanzas of the Internationale

I'm with you in Rockland
> where we hug and kiss the United States under our bedsheets the
> United States that coughs all night and won't let us sleep

I'm with you in Rockland
> where we wake up electrified out of the coma by our own souls' air-
> planes roaring over the roof they've come to drop angelic bombs the
> hospital. illuminates itself imaginary walls collapse   O skinny
> legions run outside   O starry spangled shock of mercy the eternal
> war is here   O victory forget your underwear we're free

I'm with you in Rockland
> in my dreams you walk dripping from a sea-journey on the highway
> across America in tears to the door of my cottage in the Western
> night

San Francisco, 1955–56

ODE TO FAILURE

Many prophets have failed, their voices silent
ghost-shouts in basements nobody heard dusty laughter in family attics
nor glanced them on park benches weeping with relief under empty sky
Walt Whitman viva'd local losers — courage to Fat Ladies in the Freak
> Show! nervous prisoners whose mustached lips dripped sweat on
> chow lines —

Mayakovsky cried, Then die! my verse, die like the workers' rank & file
  fusilladed in Petersburg!
Prospero burned his Power books & plummeted his magic wand to the
  bottom of dragon seas
Alexander the Great failed to find more worlds to conquer!
O Failure I chant your terrifying name, accept me your 54 year old
  Prophet
epicking Eternal Flop! I join your Pantheon of mortal bards, & hasten
  this ode with high blood pressure
rushing to the top of my skull as if I wouldn't last another minute, like
  the Dying Gaul! to
You, Lord of blind Monet, deaf Beethoven, armless Venus de Milo, head-
  less Winged Victory!
I failed to sleep with every bearded rosy-cheeked boy I jacked off over
My tirades destroyed no Intellectual Unions of KGB & CIA in turtle-
  necks & underpants, their woolen suits & tweeds
I never dissolved Plutonium or dismantled the nuclear Bomb before my
  skull lost hair
I have not yet stopped the Armies of entire Mankind in their march
  toward World War III
I never got to Heaven, Nirvana, X, Whatchamacallit, I never left Earth,
I never learned to die.

Boulder, March 7 / October 10, 1980

Louise Glück

NOSTOS

There was an apple tree in the yard —
this would have been
forty years ago — behind,
only meadow. Drifts
of crocus in the damp grass.
I stood at that window:
late April. Spring
flowers in the neighbor's yard.
How many times, really, did the tree
flower on my birthday,
the exact day, not
before, not after? Substitution
of the immutable
for the shifting, the evolving.
Substitution of the image
for relentless earth. What
do I know of this place,
the role of the tree for decades
taken by a bonsai, voices
rising from the tennis courts —
Fields. Smell of the tall grass, new cut.
As one expects of a lyric poet.
We look at the world once, in childhood.
The rest is memory.

THE MIRROR

Watching you in the mirror I wonder
what it is like to be so beautiful
and why you do not love
but cut yourself, shaving
like a blind man. I think you let me stare
so you can turn against yourself
with greater violence,
needing to show me how you scrape the flesh away

155

scornfully and without hesitation
until I see you correctly,
as a man bleeding, not
the reflection I desire.

MOCK ORANGE

It is not the moon, I tell you.
It is these flowers
lighting the yard.

I hate them.
I hate them as I hate sex,
the man's mouth
sealing my mouth, the man's
paralyzing body —

and the cry that always escapes,
the low, humiliating
premise of union —

In my mind tonight
I hear the question and pursuing answer
fused in one sound
that mounts and mounts and then
is split into the old selves,
the tired antagonisms. Do you see?
We were made fools of.
And the scent of mock orange
drifts through the window.

How can I rest?
How can I be content
when there is still
that odor in the world?

THE WHITE ROSE

This is the earth? Then
I don't belong here.

LOUISE GLÜCK

Who are you in the lighted window,
shadowed now by the flickering leaves
of the wayfarer tree?
Can you survive where I won't last
beyond the first summer?

All night the slender branches of the tree
shift and rustle at the bright window.
Explain my life to me, you who make no sign,

though I call out to you in the night:
I am not like you, I have only
my body for a voice; I can't
disappear into silence —

And in the cold morning
over the dark surface of the earth
echoes of my voice drift,
whiteness steadily absorbed into darkness

as though you were making a sign after all
to convince me you too couldn't survive here

or to show me you are not the light I called to
but the blackness behind it.

MIDNIGHT

Speak to me, aching heart: what
ridiculous errand are you inventing for yourself
weeping in the dark garage
with your sack of garbage: it is not your job
to take out the garbage, it is your job
to empty the dishwasher. You are showing off again,
exactly as you did in childhood — where
is your sporting side, your famous
ironic detachment? A little moonlight hits
the broken window, a little summer moonlight, tender
murmurs from the earth with its ready sweetnesses —
is this the way you communicate
with your husband, not answering
when he calls, or is this the way the heart

behaves when it grieves: it wants to be
alone with the garbage? If I were you,
I'd think ahead. After fifteen years,
his voice could be getting tired; some night
if you don't answer, someone else will answer.

PARABLE OF FLIGHT

A flock of birds leaving the side of the mountain.
Black against the spring evening, bronze in early summer,
rising over blank lake water.

Why is the young man disturbed suddenly,
his attention slipping from his companion?
His heart is no longer wholly divided; he's trying to think
how to say this compassionately.

Now we hear the voices of the others, moving through the library
toward the veranda, the summer porch; we see them
taking their usual places on the various hammocks and chairs,
the white wood chairs of the old house, rearranging
the striped cushions.

Does it matter where the birds go? Does it even matter
what species they are?
They leave here, that's the point,
first their bodies, then their sad cries.
And from that moment, cease to exist for us.

You must learn to think of our passion that way.
Each kiss was real, then
each kiss left the face of the earth.

PARABLE OF THE GIFT

My friend gave me
a fuschia plant, expecting
much of me, in cold April

judgment not to leave it
overnight in nature, deep
pink in its plastic
basket — I have
killed my gift, exposed
flowers in a mass of leaves,
mistaking it
for part of nature with
its many stems: what
do I do with you now,
former living thing
that last night still
resembled my friend, abundant
leaves like her fluffy hair
although the leaves had
a reddish cast: I see her
climbing the stone steps in spring dusk
holding the quivering
present in her hands, with
Eric and Daphne following
close behind, each
bearing a towel of lettuce leaves:
so much, so much to celebrate
tonight, as though she were saying
here is the world, that should be
enough to make you happy.

MATINS

Forgive me if I say I love you: the powerful
are always lied to since the weak are always
driven by panic. I cannot love
what I can't conceive, and you disclose
virtually nothing: are you like the hawthorn tree,
always the same thing in the same place,
or are you more the foxglove, inconsistent, first springing up
a pink spike on the slope behind the daisies,
and the next year, purple in the rose garden? You must see
it is useless to us, this silence that promotes belief
you must be all things, the foxglove and the hawthorn tree,
the vulnerable rose and tough daisy — we are left to think

you couldn't possibly exist. Is this
what you mean us to think, does this explain
the silence of the morning,
the crickets not yet rubbing their wings, the cats
not fighting in the yard?

VESPERS

In your extended absence, you permit me
use of earth, anticipating
some return on investment. I must report
failure in my assignment, principally
regarding the tomato plants.
I think I should not be encouraged to grow
tomatoes. Or, if I am, you should withhold
the heavy rains, the cold nights that come
so often here, while other regions get
twelve weeks of summer. All this
belongs to you: on the other hand,
I planted the seeds, I watched the first shoots
like wings tearing the soil, and it was my heart
broken by the blight, the black spot so quickly
multiplying in the rows. I doubt
you a heart, in our understanding of
that term. You who do not discriminate
between the dead and the living, who are, in consequence,
immune to foreshadowing, you may not know
how much terror we bear, the spotted leaf,
the red leaves of the maple falling
even in August, in early darkness: I am responsible
for these vines.

CELESTIAL MUSIC

I have a friend who still believes in heaven.
Not a stupid person, yet with all she knows, she literally talks to god,
she thinks someone listens in heaven.
On earth, she's unusually competent.
Brave, too, able to face unpleasantness.

We found a caterpillar dying in the dirt, greedy ants crawling over it.
I'm always moved by weakness, by disaster, always eager to oppose
    vitality.
But timid, also, quick to shut my eyes.
Whereas my friend was able to watch, to let events play out
according to nature. For my sake, she intervened,
brushing a few ants off the torn thing, and set it down across the road.

My friend says I shut my eyes to god, that nothing else explains
my aversion to reality. She says I'm like the child who buries her head in
    the pillow
so as not to see, the child who tells herself
that light causes sadness —
My friend is like the mother. Patient, urging me
to wake up an adult like herself, a courageous person —
In my dreams, my friend reproaches me. We're walking
on the same road, except it's winter now;
she's telling me that when you love the world you hear celestial music:
look up, she says. When I look up, nothing.
Only clouds, snow, a white business in the trees
like brides leaping to a great height —
Then I'm afraid for her; I see her
caught in a net deliberately cast over the earth —

In reality, we sit by the side of the road, watching the sun set;
from time to time, the silence pierced by a birdcall.
It's this moment we're both trying to explain, the fact
that we're at ease with death, with solitude.
My friend draws a circle in the dirt; inside, the caterpillar doesn't move.
She's always trying to make something whole, something beautiful, an
    image
capable of life apart from her.
We're very quiet. It's peaceful sitting here, not speaking, the composi-
    tion
fixed, the road turning suddenly dark, the air
going cool, here and there the rocks shining and glittering —
it's this stillness that we both love.
The love of form is a love of endings.

Albert Goldbarth

THE TALK SHOW

*. . . in 1930, The Bell Telephone Company commissioned one of their
employees, Karl Jansky, to find out why the new car radios suffered
from static. Jansky set up radio antennae, and heard a steady hiss
coming from the direction of the Milky Way. Radio astronomy was
born thirty years later.*

—*James Burke*

A woman "heard angels." The paper says angels
sussurra'd her body, rang their praises daylong
through its reedy places, stirred her
smallest water. And elsewhere, Larry
"Dude Man" Chavez raises his #2 wrench
indifferently overhead on the C-track tightening line,
and feels something like lightning — only
there isn't lightning — beam to the wrench head,
branch down his arm, make all of his muscles
electric feathers, then exit his other arm out
its guttering candelabrum fingers and into
the frame of the Ford. It's stored

there. It happens. We all know it happens.
The cops and the hospital nightshift crew know
what a full moon means, and
if their decades of statistics don't cut diddlysquat
with you, here's someone being wheeled in
from a 3-car smashup while the universe hums
its lunar kazoo, and adrenalin everywhere dervishes.
And statistics on sunspots, and suicides.
And statistics on lines of magnetic pull,
and conception. We're the few but beautiful
units of the first day of the cosmos
densed-up over time; when the lady I love

flaps suddenly in sleep like a wire discharging, it
makes sense as much as anything — bad dreams,
zinged nerves — to simply say *we're* where
the Big Bang ripples to the limits of a continuous medium,
flickers a little, kicks. I've disappointed her
sometimes; and so, myself. I've left the house then,

163

ALBERT GOLDBARTH

while she slept, and while my neighbors slept, as if
I could walk noise out of myself
through darkness, finally dialing-in
the talk show where the blood calls with its question,
and the "sky," whatever that is, whatever portion we are
of it or once were, answers. And

I've walked past where the university's planetarium
dish-ear swivels hugely for the far
starcrackle Karl Jansky more primitively
dowsed. It happens any size; that woman? picked up
cop calls on her IUD, the paper adds, in bubble-bursting
glee. Although if angels are voices beyond us
in us, everyone's umbles are singing hosannahs
under their everyday wamble and gab. I've
slipped back into bed some nights and clasped her
till I slept, then woke to her heart
in my ear, that mysterious sound,
on earth as it is in heaven.

ANCESTORED-BACK
IS THE OVERPRESIDING SPIRIT OF THIS POEM

If only somebody would drill with a finger-long rig down
into my skull, and saw a tiny circle out of its bone,
so pools of acid antsiness and angst can steam away;
so all of the great in-gnarling, all of the bunched-up
broodiness can breathe; and so at least the day's
accumulated ephemera, its fenderbender squabbles,
its parade of petty heartache can evaporate in writhes
of sour mist — this spatting couple, for example,
in the booth across the aisle as I'm chowing on a burger
and their every more-than-whispered perturbation is,
this afternoon, a further furrow worked into my mind. . . .
You know I'm kvetching metaphorically. But literalist
Amanda Fielding, wielding a scalpel and electric drill,
bored a hole in her skull in 1970, filming that self-surgery,

and zealously thereafter promoting the benefits of this
third eye, finally "running for Parliament on a platform
of trepanation for national health." The operation

was successfully conducted in the Stone Age (72%
of the skulls we've found reveal that the patients far survived
that crisis moment), and the Chinese medico Thai Tshang Kung
(150 B.C.) was said "to cut open the skulls of the sick
and arrange their brains in order." A Roman physician's
effects from the second century A.D. include a trepanation kit
in bronze, its tooth-edged bit and driving-bow
as finely produced as any machine-tooled apparatus
a surgeon in 1996 would wish for — when the bow unfolds
it's as intricate in its simplicity as a line of true haiku.
I've read a book whose major pleasure is its breathlessness

in gasping at the ancientness of various devices,
flushing toilets(!) condoms(!) hand grenades(!) — the book
is a grove of invisible exclamation points. These
green glass beads like rain-splats on a leaf
— 4,000 years ago. Bone dice, the same. The ribbed vault
in this early Gothic church is a masterly hollowing-out
of space — but houses of *literal* ribs, of mammoth bones,
were sturdy dwellings 15,000 years ago. Rhinoplasty(!)
soccer(!) odometers(!) "Butter" (a favorite sentence)
"spread everywhere, once it was discovered." Though we don't know
poot about the urgent stirrings in our own hearts
or the dreams irrupting nightly in our own heads,
we've been diagramming stars on plaques
of tortoise plate and antler, we've made sky maps,

from before we even understood the link of sex
to birth. And if our coin-op slot machines
can be ancestored-back to that Greco-Egyptian
contrivance of Heron of Alexandria (by which
a dropped-in-place five-drachma bronze piece
starts the portioned flow of a worshiper's ablution-water) . . .
if *ancestored-back* is the overpresiding spirit
of this poem . . . we *are* the progeny of stars,
we *are* their original core-born elements
in new recombination, densed and sizzled into
sentience and soul. I can't imagine the interior tumult
driving Amanda Fielding and her followers, but
I'm not surprised our smallest human units were created
in explosion, speed, and void. My friends

are not the kind to drill their heads and rid themselves
of troubles by decanting. Even so, I've seen them consider

their restless faces in the mirror and wish for *some* release.
Our daily dole of woe is unrelenting. In this burger joint,
in the Booth of a Thousand Sorrows across the aisle,
they're arguing still. Outside, the snow provides each tree
with a clerical collar — this couple is arguing. Outside,
the setting summer sun makes each tree a flambeau
— this couple is arguing, they'll never stop, their joys
have been prodigious and their anti-joy will balance this
or more, the hands with which they make their hard points
in the air are hands of oxygen and nitrogen and argon
older than dust or salt. It's midnight. How
emphatic we can be. How long they've been at it.

REALITY ORGANIZATION

1.

4:30 a.m. with the woe adding up
in notches on your gut-wall,
guilts, indignities, whatever, there's no sleep,
you're bright, you "keep up," you know what's what, but
this isn't the time when you want to know everything's nothing

but some few subatomic elements skeetering
through emptiness, what seem the solid edges of things
are hazinesses of particle give-and-take and "really"
must look like continual maelstrom, and people you love
are whole new sets of cells each 7 years — no,

that's all fine to know but now you simply want
to walk with some dignity to the shed, and
press your forehead to the russian olive there, its trunk
unyielding, a thing not you but able to texture you,
a hardness to hold to, a firm true specific event.

2.

Zen and the Art of Computer Management Systems.
Holistic Bioengineering: A Home Cassette Series.
Alternate Consciousness and Corporation Profile — A Symposium.

By now it's no secret: scientific method,
the Newtonian / Cartesian paradigm, isn't hauling ass

and soul in happy tandem very well. And so
(as one book says) "to use an obvious example," war
we calibrate down to the leastmost ladybug's-waist-sized
chainmail link and up to megaton trajectory, we
artfully assemble, Trojan H and H-bomb, but

what makes us make war, what demanding psyche-ghosts
howl down the spiral staircase
of our genes — "we are no closer to this
understanding now than, say, in Hellenistic times." They
had *Lysistrata*. We have biofeedback and we have *Lysistrata*.

3.

We have biofeedback. We know there are levels
where light's too large to land, so "being" anything isn't
being visible or countable — levels where dream is
logic, levels where you could fall lost in the space
between your own hand and its shadow. Maybe a God,

even a God of terrible vengeance, is less frightening
than floating through physics. The God says:
Here are boundaries; this and this are real, this not.
The God says: Things actually do add up. We love
to add. The name of Allah was *26,000*

times stitched into a 16th century Turkish warship's pennant.
There are an estimated 4 *million* mummified ibises
in an Egyptian labyrinth offered unto Thoth.
We love to tally. The rosary's abacus beads.
The first worked stones are scored.

4.

It was nearly dawn when I found you. By then
you were calm. That tree had punished you or healed you
or simply been a symbol of something reliably
beyond the tormenting refinements of human confusion.
Your skin was moire from the bark — your sadness,

leached out by that contact. I led you back
into the house. Or you could have been leading me — that's
not the point. I know we can't approach the universe
as if its secrets are quantifiable, not any more. And even
so, I know we all deserve the reassurance

of weight and number, perimeter, durability. Some
days both of those opposing knowings pull, and early
sun in a slant through the basketball net
mandalas the shed — my eyes can spin in there,
electronwise, wholegalaxyclusterwise, and not be wiser.

ARGUING BARTUSIAK

*Space-time simply doesn't exist where loop lines are absent, any more than a
blanket exists between the weave of its threads.*

— Marcia Bartusiak, in a science article

The idea is, the marriage still exists
when they're at different coasts for the summer:
her job, his ailing parents. Some weeks
even fax- and phone-chat thins
to a nebular frizzle the instruments barely acknowledge.
Even so, she knows she knows she's married and
she *thinks* she knows he knows it too.
She imagines him now, he's walking through the garden
of the house in Palo Verde, in the dawnlight there
that always looks so unsoiled, so
historically uninhabited-through; and in the face
of the coffee and its seemingly prescient tentacles of steam,
he sees the day ahead, a day of salt baths
and colostomy bags, of people one loves monolithically
going grain by grain to something
a son can only sift through, shaking his head.
In a way, although the thought is shameful, she
envies him this: the lug and grunt of working
human necessities — enormous grand pianos
of human distress and their human solutions — across
the convolute rooms of a day. For her, the world is all abstraction
and the iffiness of quarkish nonevents, for her

it's less than air, since air of course is elements
imperturbable and ponderous by her standards
— she's a theoretician of quantum gravity models, and
she uses a machine the size of a shopping mall
to track the ghostly geysering of particles that exist
so far in hypothesis only. It's *beautiful,*
it's *consummatory,* labor; but some mornings
when she walks along the squabble of Atlantic water
and Jersey shore, she feels the need
to hug herself, to keep herself
from suddenly evaporating into the between-states
of her studies. Or to have *somebody*
hug her. That night, at Kelly's Reef,
as a patchwork jazz quartet is into its last set,
Mr. Silk-'n-Sip — a friend of a friend
of a friend, who's magically latched on to their party —
makes the thousand invisible signs of availability.
His hands are shapely and capable. His stories
encompass plasma physics, Van Gogh connoisseurship,
Tantric sex techniques. She's crazy
to say no, but she says no. It's 4 a.m.
and in the rumple of her by-the-month
efficiency apartment, in her sleeplessness,
she idly works the gold ring off her finger, lets the light
trace its solidity, then puffs a single
breath through its empty center. It's late,
she's sleepy at last, she
wraps herself in her blanket, and
if some of it, *somewhere* in it, isn't blanket,
she wraps herself in that too.

THE WHOLE EARTH CATALOGUE

Plate tectonics: like blackened pieces
of sweet pork crackling, the continents slide
on their underside greases. Night; outside,
the sad moon drags the sea behind, a washerwoman
her bucket. The moon
and her crimp-rimmed craters.
The maestro moon and her ever-attentive
oyster castanet orchestra. The atmosphere

of Earth weighs, oh, 5,000
million million tons but a ladybug
bears it untroubled, and

I'm stroking Skyler's back,
the rolling fold between her shoulders,
down the serial rings of the spine and
up again, just lightly, up
and down, and

70 billion neutrinos pass through our bodies
this moment and every moment
and through the lava and through the iron core.
The moon and her purely cosmetic light.
That skyhigh silversmith plating us sterling.
At the vent slits of the Mid-Atlantic Ridge
are sea worms 10 feet long
with no eyes, mouth or gut. And
there are shards of stone with
ferns inside so it looks as if Time is
waiting to be unzipped and entered. And

I'm beside Skyler, almost not touching
her eyelids and her trusting
upturned wrists, but touching them,
figure 8-ing them spiderily with my fingers.
In some Paul Klee

watercolors, as in certain Chinese landscape scrolls,
abstracted hills and sky fill space
to the edges, and it's only
on a second look we see
a minuscule man or a woman is one stroke
of deliberation dabbed in a corner,
going about its own
important business — maybe

setting up, for all we know, an easel for an afternoon
of landscape painting. Getting
the serpent of wind in the wheat
just right. The dusk
rum-coloring the chalk cliffs. Then the moon.
Anchovies gleaming like a miser's hoard
beneath the moon. The moon

and her two Martian stepsisters.
Moon in the rain forests,
moon in the arctic ice, and
mayflies stippling air, and elk
switchbacking eluding pursuing wolves, and
kelp in drift, and galaxies in drift, and

Skyler drifting to sleep, her nipples
tucked under my thumbs, and then the whorled
availability of an ear until she's under. You know
the Eskimo of Greenland voyaged with beautiful
carvings always in their canoes,
a foot long, maybe 18 inches. They look like
spinal columns of angels or troll lords, long
and knobbed and coved. They're maps
of several hundred miles of the coastline
most worth knowing. They fondled them over
and over. On nights with no moon,
in such dark there's no planet,
the eyes in their fingers knew these by heart.

Colleen McKay

Kimiko Hahn

THE SHOWER

The hot spray softens her neck muscles
as she swings her head side to side
raises an arm and spirals fingertips
from arm pit to aureola firmly firmly —
the legacy of twentieth century females,
a fact even brown rice, an underwire bra,
or low-impact aerobics cannot
cauterize. She recalls the nurse
who told a dormitory of freshmen about
self-examinations, about a farmer's wife
in Oxford, Iowa, whose breast tripled in size,
festered, stank, and still she hid
the awful message: what was meant to nourish,
what had nourished half a dozen babies,
poisoned the whole system. While soaping
beneath her breasts she remembers
an Ariyoshi novel from Japanese Lit:
the mother and daughter-in-law
in grotesque competition for the son / husband
to anesthetize and sever experimentally.
Now the left side and thoughts of nursing
at two then four in the morning.
Her own daughters are tucked
into their collective unconscious, perhaps
images of the breast, pillow-like: sweet
or so large as to suffocate. Which dream?
Which dream for me? No lumps
detected while showering she wraps
a terry cloth robe around her self,
thinks, nursing was precious and erotic, both
and it is over. What to make of these
ornaments, these empty chambers
that sting with pleasure even as
the skin begins to loosen? How to take care?
How to see these breasts as flesh
and emblem? What about her mother's breasts —

those things that finally belonged to her younger sister;
things she wanted, wanted to possess completely
like two suns emanating from her own chest.

WHEN YOU LEAVE

This sadness could only be a color
if we call it *momoiro,* Japanese

for *peach-color,* as in the first story
Mother told us: It is the color of the hero's skin

when the barren woman discovered him
inside a peach floating down the river.

And of the banner and gloves she sewed
when he left her to battle the horsemen, then found himself

torn, like fruit off a tree. Even when he met a monkey
dog and bird he could not release

the color he saw when he closed his eyes.
      In his boat
the lap of the waves against the hold

was too intimate as he leaned back to sleep.
      He wanted
to leave all thoughts of peach behind him —

the fruit that brought him to her
and she, the one who opened the color forever.

THE IZU DANCER

The story was almost too simple:
a student from Tokyo
travelling along the coast during summer break
hooks up with a dance troupe.

They move from one cheap hotel to another,
accepting him as waves accept sand and small animals.
He falls in love.
Spring buds never quivered so lightly
as his skin when he heard her drum.
Though not a difficult text
every few words I was stuck
flipping through water radicals

水　　　氵　　水

so I could resume the journey inside words
I had begun as a child, as when Kawabata wrote

雨脚が杉の密林を白く染めながら

"while the shower bleached the cedars"

I did not know
I did not want to know Japanese
so much as a way back to, say, salt
and to him in his heaven.
(Or to him, in such a rush to pick me up
he forgot his shoes, stood at my door in red woolen socks.)
Yet from the fragrance of his lines I struggled to raise:
"I thought for a moment of running out barefoot to look for her.
It was after two." from

跣で湯殿を抜け出して行ったって、どうにも出来ないのだと

思った。二時を過ぎていた。

I needed the information locked in ink —
each stroke, a signal; each kanji, a panorama.
And barbed fence.

There are over 2,000 species of fireflies,
each with its own mating signal
so as not to crossover.
If you catch one they will not burn a hole in your hand
or explode in your face.
They call out: hey baby. They say: wait up, girl.

まって

With closed eyes I imagine her thoughts:
I swept my hair up off my back,
waded in from the heat of the road,
stuffy towns and constant companions
and sat down in the surf.
The air stung with a smell of iodine.
When I returned to my towel

my legs were bright red
from the concentration of salt.
For lunch we ate squid, rice, green tea.
I wanted to lick the beads of sweat
from his temples.
The afternoon forecast a meeting,
clouds thickening offshore
but at fourteen my heart was not as willing
as my body. And too, I was afraid my body
looked funny.

The Heian poet wrote about sleeves soaked with tears.
But I know even young girls break into a sweat
in passion or terror;
a terror, as if mother left the house one morning
to buy milk and never returned.
As if you could no longer speak to her.
As if a lover said: *Goodbye.*
The season's blooms turn to fruit,
And you do see persimmons fragrant among the branches
sweat in the morning heat as the blossoms before them.
Would we run around the house looking for mother?
Would we find the suitcase gone,
drawers empty, closets
vacant, heart
lost?
But isn't everything about loss:
the pin cushion of pins, the branch
knocking against the window,
Kawabata's swiveling chair.

In time we belong to what the objects mean.
Then around 2 am the stomach sours from all the coffee.
The strokes blur into the mess of lines and noises they really are.
Though in some respects the characters are astonishingly simple:

tree 木   forest 森

woman 女   mischief; noisy; assault 姦

But the complex unfolding of a single sentence
with whole sentences modifying a noun
at the end of the line baffled, humiliated
and toughened my spirit.

I persevered in my search for the fragrance of words
in this modest story — the only Kawabata story I could read.
Where did he unearth

不自然な程美しい黒髪が私の胸に触れそうになった。

("Her hair, so rich it seemed unreal, almost brushed against my chest.")
Where did I find the hands on my shoulders, sliding down my arms
then up under my t-shirt, into my bra,
squeezing my breasts, pinching my nipples so hard
I blinked to hold back tears.
He watched my expression as a meteorologist reads delicate instruments.
If the body is a map, a weathermap, summer vacations or winter holidays
all begin here. Something a student may not realize.

Later the dancer combed the puppy's fur
with the pink comb, the one
he thought he would ask for
to prove to himself on the boat back to Tokyo
that the lengths of hair were real.
Outside this window the magnolia under the street lamp
appears as artificial as the light.

The arrangement interrupts my train of thought
as details of her life crazed him like musk.
In my search did I look for the writer
or the boy? for mother
to take me in her arms and not let go?
or father to praise the poem without:
yes, but
yes, if
yes, perhaps

The character for house is roof over pig
家
for peace, roof over woman
安
for wife, woman with a broom
婦
Then there's adulteress:
姦 婦
If I had slept with that professor
betrayal might have become real
as the magnolia in the street —
delicate, sooty and pink.

Branches open. Petals full and moist.
I wanted to cross that fence
with the passion of leaving home,
the need for certain loss
that means constructing something for oneself —
roof with pig.
To write and never discover the scent
is to signal a firefly behind the stone wall.
In looking for mother do I admit I've failed
to make these rooms home
or does she also dream of grandma sitting on the beach
her chignon unravelling in the sea breeze?
When she opens her eyes
snow covers the early blooms.
Then there he is: Kawabata pulls off a spray laden with snow
and gently carries it inside.
We enjoy the beauty of its predicament
as snow melts all over the mahogany.
Why not buckle down and learn the language cold;
why not remember

思、   field over heart means remember

If I give in to every desire
will oil spills suffocate the hemisphere,
will the ozone layer evaporate like a marriage.
Why this settling in to study
versus the constant urge to leave,
to walk in the night air free of dictionaries and parents.
The student didn't know what to say
to the little dancer, what would ease the calf-like movements
that increased her charm — ease his own breath
racing against his heart at the thought of her.
If he read her a story,
if she laughed or blushed but didn't run away
that would mean something.

The story is so clear I can dream his lines:
Stepping out of the waves
I noticed a rash spread over my legs,
the color of boiled lobster or genitals.
It embarrassed her. She turned and ran away
as if I had said something amiss.
To kiss me there.

If I saw a red Volkswagen my heart would roll like a tsunami
toward a man smoking a cigarette, leaning against the chalkboard.
Tall. Graying. In no time all lessons will be forgotten.
But not a memory of no memory.
Perhaps I did not want the language enough
or wanted something else —
— to leave a laundry-filled dormitory room
and press my whole body against the professor's doorbell
till he came downstairs and invited me inside.
Cooked me dinner. Fucked in the guest room.
Perhaps I didn't want any language. Any marriage.

Even Kawabata's snowscapes steamed in the winter light.
Is all betrayal really of father or mother?
In the kanji for mother

母

the two nipples reduce it to a primitive symbol.
I reach to touch a lover with the confidence
of a child burying into a breast;
a tangible connection but also the perfume
or stench that is language. Ah,
the irregular verbs. Oh, the conditional.
An occasional classical phrase
nestled into the vernacular.
The lullabies: should, would, could. I need
the knowledge from a peach floating downstream:
domburikokkosukkou —
of saying the right words without thinking.
When he saw her in the public bath the student was delighted
the dancer was too young to consummate his

fever   熱

He could sit beside her at dinner or the movies
finally.

  *

A waitress pours me a warmup and I look over
to catch the back of a man's neck,
his heavy black hair in a severe razor-cut style.
I imagine he is B.D. Wong
the incredibly handsome actor in M. *Butterfly*.
His moist white cotton shirt

hangs a bit off his shoulders
and he holds a cup of cappuccino in one hand
and a slim hard-cover book in the other.
I imagine he turns around to ask for —
an ashtray
and ends up at my table
talking about contemporary poetry, mutual friends
and international affairs.
But as the man gathers his belongings he turns
and instead of the aristocratic profile and rakish glow
it's an older Italian man, moustached and serious.
But briefly that fragrance!

THE OLDER CHILD

What will become her earliest memory —
the sperm whale battling the giant squid
in the dark exhibition at the museum?
looking up at 3 am
to see her sister pressed against two white breasts?
or maybe her yellow room
filled with the noise of boys in the vacant lot:
bang, boom-boom, fuckyoufuckyoufuck you.

THE GLASS BRACELETS

I know I can only speak for myself
but after reading a simple story in *The News*
wish I could speak for a ninety-four-year-old woman
who on a day of the full moon of Magha in 1907,
at age seven, was led by her parents
to the Saundatti Temple in Karnataka
and given to the Hindu goddess Yellamma:
the childish glass arm bangles broken,
a nuptual necklace given her —
wedded to the diety Dev, Murali must never
marry a mortal, has never washed or cut
her long hair, a stiff mat of gray —

her duty was forever to be fucked
by those who come to the Temple.
At onset of menstruation the child was,
and still is, auctioned for the privilege
of tearing her hymen often times
by one with syphilis or gonorrhea —
virgins believed to be a certain cure.
It is difficult for me to like men at times,
any man, when such atrocities are sanctioned
by the religious. Atrocities for male pleasure.
And I doubt a woman concocted
the legend of this goddess. I am fucking mad
and want my daughters
to never leave our small Brooklyn apartment
though I know any room can be the residence
of secrets — like that of the man in Ocala, Florida
infecting six of his fourteen children
with venereal disease, fathering his daughter's babies,
beating their faces, beating their faces. This
while the religious target abortion clinics
and rude art. Who
can believe in a god in such a world
when god is made by man for men —
I will not respect a moment of silence
in my children's public school for the sake
of semi-automatic politicians wishing to purchase votes
with their small public piety.
And if you think this is not a poem
because I've ranted without benefit of a metaphor
think again: the story of Murali
is the story of any infant female or male
until the arteries of the status quo, of the silent,
of those who silence, or those who seek
solution in prayer, of those who limit choices —
until the varicose veins of the "religiously correct"
are slit and drawn. Until then
you, reader, are the five-year-old boy,
genitals severed and flesh neatly
folded back into a tiny cunt, or
the ten-year-old girl with second-stage syphilis
now lodged in her central nervous system.
Hear me: I will not pray. I will not pray.

Donald Hall

MAPLE SYRUP

August, goldenrod blowing. We walk
into the graveyard, to find
my grandfather's grave. Ten years ago
I came here last, bringing
marigolds from the round garden
outside the kitchen.
I didn't know you then.
                         We walk
among carved names that go with photographs
on top of the piano at the farm:
Keneston, Wells, Fowler, Batchelder, Buck.
We pause at the new grave
of Grace Fenton, my grandfather's
sister. Last summer
we called on her at the nursing home,
eighty-seven, and nodding
in a blue housedress. We cannot find
my grandfather's grave.
                         Back at the house
where no one lives, we potter
and explore the back chamber
where everything comes to rest: spinning wheels,
pretty boxes, quilts,
bottles, books, albums of postcards.
Then with a flashlight we descend
firm steps to the root cellar — black,
cobwebby, huge,
with dirt floors and fieldstone walls,
and above the walls, holding the hewn
sills of the house, enormous
granite foundation stones.
Past the empty bins
for squash, apples, carrots, and potatoes,
we discover the shelves for canning, a few
pale pints
of tomato left, and — what
is this? — syrup, maple syrup
in a quart jar, syrup

my grandfather made twenty-five
years ago
for the last time.
           I remember
coming to the farm in March
in sugaring time, as a small boy.
He carried the pails of sap, sixteen-quart
buckets, dangling from each end
of a wooden yoke
that lay across his shoulders, and emptied them
into a vat in the saphouse
where fire burned day and night
for a week.
           Now the saphouse
tilts, nearly to the ground,
like someone exhausted
to the point of death, and next winter
when snow piles three feet thick
on the roofs of the cold farm,
the saphouse will shudder and slide
with the snow to the ground.
              Today
we take my grandfather's last
quart of syrup
upstairs, holding it gingerly,
and we wash off twenty-five years
of dirt, and we pull
and pry the lid up, cutting the stiff,
dried rubber gasket, and dip our fingers
in, you and I both, and taste
the sweetness, you for the first time,

the sweetness preserved, of a dead man
in the kitchen he left
when his body slid
like anyone's into the ground.

IN THE KITCHEN OF THE OLD HOUSE

    In the kitchen of the old house, late,
I was making some coffee
    and I daydreamed sleepily of old friends.

Then the dream turned. I waited.
    I walked alone all day in the town
where I was born. It was cold,
    a Saturday in January
when nothing happens. The streets
    changed as the sky grew dark around me.
The lamps in the small houses
    had tassels on them, and the black cars
at the curb were old and square.
    A ragman passed with his horse, their breaths
blooming like white peonies,
    when I turned into a darker street
and I recognized the house
    from snapshots. I felt as separate
as if the city and the house
    were closed inside a globe which I shook
to make it snow. No sooner
    did I think of snow, but snow started
to fill the heavy darkness
    around me. It reflected the glare
of the streetlight as it fell
    melting on the warmth of the sidewalk
and frozen on frozen grass.
    Then I heard out of the dark the sound
of steps on the bare cement
    in a familiar rhythm. Under
the streetlight, bent to the snow,
    hatless, younger than I, so young that
I was not born, my father
    walked home to his bride and his supper.
A shout gathered inside me
    like a cold wind, to break the rhythm,
to keep him from entering
    that heavy door — but I stood under
a tree, closed in by the snow,
    and did not shout, to tell what happened
in twenty years, in winter,
    when his early death grew inside him
like snow piling on the grass.
    He opened the door and met the young
woman who waited for him.

WHEN THE YOUNG HUSBAND

When the young husband picked up his friend's pretty wife
in the taxi one block from her townhouse for their
first lunch together, in a hotel dining room
       with a room key in his pocket,

midtown traffic gridlocked and was abruptly still.
For one moment before klaxons started honking,
a prophetic voice spoke in his mind's ear despite
       his pulse's erotic thudding:

"The misery you undertake this afternoon
will accompany you to the ends of your lives.
She knew what she did when she agreed to this lunch,
       although she will not admit it;

and you've constructed your playlet a thousand times:
cocktails, an omelet, wine; the revelation
of a room key; the elevator rising as
       the penis elevates; the skin

flushed, the door fumbled at, the handbag dropped; the first
kiss with open mouths, nakedness, swoon, thrust-and-catch;
endorphins followed by endearments; a brief nap;
       another fit; restoration

of clothes, arrangements for another encounter,
the taxi back, and the furtive kiss of goodbye.
Then, by turn: tears, treachery, anger, betrayal;
       marriages and houses destroyed;

small children abandoned and inconsolable,
their foursquare estates disestablished forever;
the unreadable advocates; the wretchedness
       of passion outworn; anguished nights

sleepless in a bare room; whiskey, meth, cocaine; new
love, essayed in loneliness with miserable
strangers, that comforts nothing but skin; hours with sons
       and daughters studious always

to maintain distrust; the daily desire to die
and the daily agony of the requirement
to survive, until only the quarrel endures."
                    Prophecy stopped; traffic started.

THE PORCELAIN COUPLE

When Jane felt well enough for me to leave her
a whole day, I drove south by the river
to empty my mother's house in Connecticut.
I hurried from room to room, cellar to attic,
looking into a crammed storeroom, then turning
to discover a chest with five full drawers.
I labeled for shipping sofas and chairs,
bedroom sets, and tables; I wrapped figurines
and fancy teacups in paper, preserving
things she had cherished — and in late years dreaded
might go for a nickel at a sale on the lawn.
Everywhere I saw shelves and tabletops
covered with glass animals and music boxes.
In closets, decades of finery hung in dead air.
I swept ashtrays and blouses into plastic sacks,
and the green-gold dress she wore to Bermuda.
At the last moment I discovered and saved
a cut-glass tumbler, stained red at the top,
Lucy 1905 scripted on the stain. In the garage
I piled bags for the dump, then drove four hours
north with my hands tight on the steering wheel,
drank a beer looking through the day's mail,
and pitched into bed with Jane who slept fitfully.
When I woke, I rose as if from a drunken sleep
after looting a city and burning its temples.
All day, while I ate lunch or counted out pills,
I noticed the objects of our twenty years:
a blue vase, a candelabrum Jane carried on her lap
from the Baja, and the small porcelain box
from France I found under the tree one Christmas
where a couple in relief stretch out asleep,
like a catafalque, on the pastel double bed
of the box's top, both wearing pretty nightcaps.

THE SHIP POUNDING

Each morning I made my way
among gangways, elevators,
and nurses' pods to Jane's room
to interrogate the grave helpers
who tended her through the night
while the ship's massive engines
kept its propellers turning.
Week after week, I sat by her bed
with black coffee and the *Globe*.
The passengers on this voyage
wore masks or cannulae
or dangled devices that dripped
chemicals into their wrists.
I believed that the ship
traveled to a harbor
of breakfast, work, and love.
I wrote: "When the infusions
are infused entirely, bone
marrow restored and lymphoblasts
remitted, I will take my wife,
bald as Michael Jordan,
back to our dog and day." Today,
months later at home, these
words turned up on my desk
as I listened in case Jane called
for help, or spoke in delirium,
ready to make the agitated
drive to Emergency again
for readmission to the huge
vessel that heaves water month
after month, without leaving
port, without moving a knot,
without arrival or destination,
its great engines pounding.

DONALD HALL

DIGGING

One midnight, after a day when lilies
lift themselves out of the ground while you watch them,
and you come into the house at dark
your fingers grubby with digging, your eyes
vague with the pleasure of digging,

let a wind raised from the South
climb through your bedroom window, lift you in its arms
— you have become as small as a seed —
and carry you out of the house, over the black garden,
spinning and fluttering,

and drop you in cracked ground.
The dirt will be cool, rough to your clasped skin
like a man you have never known.
You will die into the ground
in a dead sleep, surrendered to water.

You will wake suffering
a widening pain in your side, a breach
gapped in your tight ribs
where a green shoot struggles to lift itself upwards
through the tomb of your dead flesh

to the sun, to the air of your garden
where you will blossom
in the shape of your own self, thoughtless
with flowers, speaking
to bees, in the language of green and yellow, white and red.

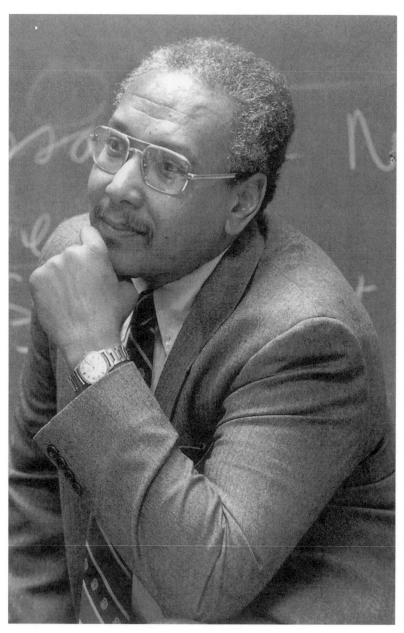

Michael S. Harper

**WE ASSUME: ON THE DEATH OF OUR SON,
REUBEN MASAI HARPER**

We assume
that in 28 hours,
lived in a collapsible isolette,
you learned to accept pure oxygen
as the natural sky;
the scant shallow breaths
that filled those hours
cannot, did not make you fly —
but dreams were there
like crooked palmprints on
the twin-thick windows of the nursery —
in the glands of your mother.

We assume
the sterile hands
drank chemicals in and out
from lungs opaque with mucus,
pumped your stomach,
eeked the bicarbonate in
crooked, green-winged veins,
out in a plastic mask;

A woman who'd lost her first son
consoled us with an angel gone ahead
to pray for our family —
gone into that sky
seeking oxygen,
gone into autopsy,
a fine brown powdered sugar,
a disposable cremation:

We assume
you did not know we loved you.

MICHAEL S. HARPER

REUBEN, REUBEN

I reach from pain
to music great enough
to bring me back,
swollenhead, madness,
lovefruit, a pickle of hate
so sour my mouth twicked
up and would not sing;
there's nothing in the beat
to hold it in
melody and turn human skin;
a brown berry gone
to rot just two days on the branch;
we've lost a son,
the music, *jazz*, comes in.

DEAR JOHN, DEAR COLTRANE

a love supreme, a love supreme
a love supreme, a love supreme
Sex fingers toes
in the marketplace
near your father's church
in Hamlet, North Carolina —
witness to this love
in this calm fallow
of these minds,
there is no substitute for pain:
genitals gone or going,
seed burned out,
you tuck the roots in the earth,
turn back, and move
by river through the swamps,
singing: *a love supreme, a love supreme;*
what does it all mean?
Loss, so great each black
woman expects your failure
in mute change, the seed gone.
You plod up into the electric city —

your song now crystal and
the blues. You pick up the horn
with some will and blow
into the freezing night:
a love supreme, a love supreme —

Dawn comes and you cook
up the thick sin 'tween
impotence and death, fuel
the tenor sax cannibal
heart, genitals and sweat
that makes you clean —
a love supreme, a love supreme —

Why you so black?
cause I am
why you so funky?
cause I am
why you so black?
cause I am
why you so sweet?
cause I am
why you so black?
cause I am
a love supreme, a love supreme:

So sick
you couldn't play *Naima,*
so flat we ached
for song you'd concealed
with your own blood,
your diseased liver gave
out its purity,
the inflated heart
pumps out, the tenor kiss,
tenor love:
a love supreme, a love supreme —
a love supreme, a love supreme —

LOVE MEDLEY: PATRICE CUCHULAIN

"Stirrups, leggings, a stainless
steel slide, a dishpan, sheet,
a thread spool, scissors,
three facemasks, smocks, paper
overshoes, a two-way mirror, dials":
the head and left arm
cruise out, almost together,
and you drop into gloves,
your own ointment
pulling your legs
binding your cord; the cheesed
surface skin, your dark
hairless complexion, the metallic room,
orchestrate and blow up your lungs,
clogged on protein and vitamins,
for the sterile whine of the delivery
room and your staff of attendants.
It is free exercise when the cord's
cut; you weigh in for the clean up
as your mother gets her local
for her stitches: boy, 6 lbs 13 oz.

As you breathe easily, your mother's
mother is tubed and strapped,
hemorrhaging slowly from her varices;
your two dead brothers who could
not breathe are berries
gone to rot at our table:
what is birth but death
with complexity: blood, veins,
machinery and love: our names.

THIS IS MY SON'S SONG: *"UNGIE, HI UNGIE"*

A two-year-old boy
is a blossom in the intensive
care aisle, small as
a ball-bearing,

round, open and smooth;
for a month, in his first
premature hours, his shaved
head made him a mohawk Indian
child, tubes the herbs
for his nest, a collapsed lung
the bulbous wing of a hawk.
Slivered into each sole
is an intravenous solution
to balance his losses
or what they take out
for the lab; the blue spot
on his spine is a birth
mark of needle readings;
the hardened thighs immune
from 70 shots of various
drugs of uneven depth; the chest
is thick with congestion: bad
air and mucus — good air and pure
oxygen; jerky pouch buffalo lungs —
It does not surprise me
when he waits patiently for his
grandmother, over her five-hour
painless operation; he has
waited in his isolette
before: the glow in his eyes
is for himself, will and love:
an exclamation of your name:
"Ungie, hi Ungie"; you are saved.

MY FATHER AT 75

He makes his own soup from scratch;
by the watch he does crossword, cleanup
and the stationary bicycle;
if allowed to he lives in the past
but the phone, news, and memoirs
tabulate and afflict him.

He was born in a small town
and still is uncomfortable

with his people;
discomforture hones standards.
He refuses to budge.

I like his attire when he flies,
pressed jacket and slacks,
a few papers, his walking shoes;
I have seen the women of the world
make passes at him directly to his face;
my mother would laugh at this:

get yourself a young Mexican,
make fire steam from my daughter's nose.

I don't ask about the neighborhood
or prospects south of the border,
but when he walks his innings at dawn
I walk with him.

      La Brea is not the tarpits
but the bottom of a hill where my brother
did a blind cutaway, with his helmet on,
on the right lane pavement,
blindsided by a woman in a Continental.

After two weeks it was him that gave the word
to unplug him. On the next street
lived a childhood friend who's disappeared;
he has the face of many abused children
anxious to please, on crack or benzedrine,
for his face is cracked by the fruit
of camouflage, and betrayal:
he did not bury his parents
or let them rest in an urn.

This is the street of weights; it is a system
of barbells and pulleys in anxious backyards;
it is the nectar of barking dogs on chains;
there are parked cars everywhere and license
plates from the Caribbean, from Quantico Bay.

We will not go on from here; we will return
to the ivy, and the digging, and when the rains
come, to watering in the early hours.

He will feed the dogs at dusk. And let them go.
Portraits of the world, which was my mother, and her children,
caress and afflict him. He has the neat
penchant of a man who contends to stay home.

STUDS

Off-color eyes that shine through lobes,
the flesh still uneaten by stickpin,
he was stuck to her; this attachment,
like string from the loops of IUD
caught him unawares, in planes
above the Earth, on plains
near the homestead, on water
which he has touched with his belt
and bow, as a lifeguard,
before he met her.
                    Yes, she could brown
in that sun, the broad shoulders
concealed in flesh for his children,
who grew beyond her; he built a shed
for her tools, the garden, the chain saw —
windows faced toward the southern estuary
where turtles called, for the pond
swelled in the porous ground,
from springs, and she was a spring.

All day he has thought of Seminoles;
all day he has dreamed of the Narragansett;
his children could fit in if the drum
were opened to shells he could use
for the dinner table, and shells
from the sea decorate the walls
of the uterus, mystery of caves
he got lost in on special dates,
January 15 for instance,
now a national holiday;
and April 23, her father's birthday,
and Shakespeare's,
where he read in a long line
at the Library of Congress

after visiting the Capitol
where Martin Luther King, Jr.
stood in consummate black stone.

Now he must ask about diamonds;
how refraction turns into bloodlines
he could choose for band music,
the territory bands
of Count Basie, without charts,
in a beat-up van,
passing for Indians,
passing in the slow lane
through the culture.

He would place her flesh there;
he would ask her to wear these,
diamond studs, in each ear,
to hear his song: to hear his name
come alive in her ears.

HERE WHERE COLTRANE IS

Soul and race
are private dominions,
memories and modal
songs, a tenor blossoming,
which would paint suffering
a clear color but is not in
this Victorian house
without oil in zero degree
weather and a forty-mile-an-hour wind;
it is all a well-knit family:
a love supreme.
Oak leaves pile up on walkway
and steps, catholic as apples
in a special mist of clear white
children who love my children.
I play "Alabama"
on a warped record player
skipping the scratches
on your faces over the fibrous

conical hairs of plastic
under the wooden floors.

Dreaming on a train from New York
to Philly, you hand out six
notes which become an anthem
to our memories of you:
oak, birch, maple,
apple, cocoa, rubber.
For this reason Martin is dead;
for this reason Malcolm is dead;
for this reason Coltrane is dead;
in the eyes of my first son are the browns
of these men and their music.

Robert Hass

THE IMAGE

The child brought blue clay from the creek
and the woman made two figures: a lady and a deer.
At that season deer came down from the mountain
and fed quietly in the redwood canyons.
The woman and the child regarded the figure of the lady,
the crude roundnesses, the grace, the coloring like shadow.
They were not sure where she came from,
except the child's fetching and the woman's hands
and the lead-blue clay of the creek
where the deer sometimes showed themselves at sundown.

MEDITATION AT LAGUNITAS

All the new thinking is about loss.
In this it resembles all the old thinking.
The idea, for example, that each particular erases
the luminous clarity of a general idea. That the clown-
faced woodpecker probing the dead sculpted trunk
of that black birch is, by his presence,
some tragic falling off from a first world
of undivided light. Or the other notion that,
because there is in this world no one thing
to which the bramble of *blackberry* corresponds,
a word is elegy to what it signifies.
We talked about it late last night and in the voice
of my friend, there was a thin wire of grief, a tone
almost querulous. After a while I understood that,
talking this way, everything dissolves: *justice,
pine, hair, woman, you* and *I.* There was a woman
I made love to and I remembered how, holding
her small shoulders in my hands sometimes,
I felt a violent wonder at her presence
like a thirst for salt, for my childhood river
with its island willows, silly music from the pleasure boat,
muddy places where we caught the little orange-silver fish

201

called *pumpkinseed*. It hardly had to do with her.
Longing, we say, because desire is full
of endless distances. I must have been the same to her.
But I remember so much, the way her hands dismantled bread,
the thing her father said that hurt her, what
she dreamed. There are moments when the body is as numinous
as words, days that are the good flesh continuing.
Such tenderness, those afternoons and evenings,
saying *blackberry, blackberry, blackberry.*

LATE SPRING

And then in mid-May the first morning of steady heat,

the morning, Leif says, when you wake up, put on shorts, and that's it for
the day,

when you pour coffee and walk outside, blinking in the sun.

Strawberries have appeared in the markets, and peaches will soon;

squid is so cheap in the fishstores you begin to consult Japanese and
Italian cookbooks for the various and ingenious ways of preparing *ika*
and *calamari;*

and because the light will enlarge your days, your dreams at night will be
as strange as the jars of octopus you saw once in a fisherman's boat under
the summer moon;

and after swimming, white wine; and the sharing of stories before dinner
is prolonged because the relations of the children in the neighborhood
have acquired village intensity and the stories take longer telling;

and there are the nights when the fog rolls in that nobody likes — hey,
fog, the Miwok sang, who lived here first, you better go home, pelican is
beating your wife —

and after dark in the first cool hour, your children sleep so heavily in their
beds exhausted from play, it is a pleasure to watch them,

Leif does not move a muscle as he lies there; no, wait; it is Luke who lies there in his eight-year-old body,

Leif is taller than you are and he isn't home; when he is, his feet will extend past the end of the mattress, and Kristin is at the corner in the dark, talking to neighborhood boys;

things change; there is no need for this dream-compelled narration; the rhythm will keep me awake, changing.

A STORY ABOUT THE BODY

The young composer, working that summer at an artist's colony, had watched her for a week. She was Japanese, a painter, almost sixty, and he thought he was in love with her. He loved her work, and her work was like the way she moved her body, used her hands, looked at him directly when she made amused and considered answers to his questions. One night, walking back from a concert, they came to her door and she turned to him and said, "I think you would like to have me. I would like that too, but I must tell you that I have had a double mastectomy," and when he didn't understand, "I've lost both my breasts." The radiance that he had carried around in his belly and chest cavity — like music — withered very quickly, and he made himself look at her when he said, "I'm sorry. I don't think I could." He walked back to his own cabin through the pines, and in the morning he found a small blue bowl on the porch outside his door. It looked to be full of rose petals, but he found when he picked it up that the rose petals were on top; the rest of the bowl — she must have swept them from the corners of her studio — was full of dead bees.

PRIVILEGE OF BEING

Many are making love. Up above, the angels
in the unshaken ether and crystal of human longing
are braiding one another's hair, which is strawberry blond
and the texture of cold rivers. They glance
down from time to time at the awkward ecstasy —
it must look to them like featherless birds

splashing in the spring puddle of a bed —
and then one woman, she is about to come,
peels back the man's shut eyelids and says,
look at me, and he does. Or is it the man
tugging the curtain rope in that dark theater?
Anyway, they do, they look at each other;
two beings with evolved eyes, rapacious,
startled, connected at the belly in an unbelievably sweet
lubricious glue, stare at each other,
and the angels are desolate. They hate it. They shudder pathetically
like lithographs of Victorian beggars
with perfect features and alabaster skin hawking rags
in the lewd alleys of the novel.
All of creation is offended by this distress.
It is like the keening sound the moon makes sometimes,
rising. The lovers especially cannot bear it,
it fills them with unspeakable sadness, so that
they close their eyes again and hold each other, each
feeling the mortal singularity of the body
they have enchanted out of death for an hour or so,
and one day, running at sunset, the woman says to the man,
I woke up feeling so sad this morning because I realized
that you could not, as much as I love you,
dear heart, cure my loneliness,
wherewith she touched his cheek to reassure him
that she did not mean to hurt him with this truth.
And the man is not hurt exactly,
he understands that life has limits, that people
die young, fail at love,
fail of their ambitions. He runs beside her, he thinks
of the sadness they have gasped and crooned their way out of
coming, clutching each other with old, invented
forms of grace and clumsy gratitude, ready
to be alone again, or dissatisfied, or merely
companionable like the couples on the summer beach
reading magazine articles about intimacy between the sexes
to themselves, and to each other,
and to the immense, illiterate, consoling angels.

from DRAGONFLIES MATING

6

This morning in the early sun,
steam rising from the pond the color of smoky topaz,
a pair of delicate, copper-red, needle-fine insects
are mating in the unopened crown of a Shasta daisy
just outside your door. The green flowerheads look like wombs
or the upright, supplicant bulbs of a vegetal pre-erection.
The insect lovers seem to be transferring the cosmos into each other
by attaching at the tail, holding utterly still, and quivering intently.

I think (on what evidence?) that they are different from us.
That they mate and are done with mating.
They don't carry all this half-mated longing up out of childhood
and then go looking for it everywhere.
And so, I think, they can't wound each other the way we do.
They don't go through life dizzy or groggy with their hunger,
kill with it, smear it on everything, though it is perhaps also true
that nothing happens to them quite like what happens to us
when the blue-backed swallow dips swiftly toward the green pond
and the pond's green and blue reflected swallow marries it a moment
in the reflected sky and the heart goes out to the end of the rope
it has been throwing into abyss after abyss, and a singing shimmers
from every color the morning has risen into.

My insect instructors have stilled, they are probably stuck together
in some bliss and minute pulse of after-longing
evolution worked out to suck the last juice of the world
into the receiver body. They can't separate probably
until it is done.

HAPPINESS

Because yesterday morning from the steamy window
we saw a pair of red foxes across the creek
eating the last windfall apples in the rain;

they looked up at us with their green eyes
long enough to symbolize the wakefulness of living things
and then went back to eating;

and because this morning
when she went into the gazebo with her black pen and yellow pad
to coax an inquisitive soul
from what she thinks of as the reluctance of matter,
I drove into town to drink tea in the cafe
and write notes in a journal; mist rose from the bay
like the luminous and indefinite aspect of intention,
and a small flock of tundra swans
for the second winter in a row were feeding on new grass
in the soaked fields — they symbolize mystery, I suppose,
they are also called whistling swans, are very white,
and their eyes are black —

and because the tea steamed in front of me,
and the notebook, turned to a new page,
was blank except for a faint blue idea of order,
I wrote: *happiness! it is December, very cold,*
we woke early this morning,
and lay in bed kissing,
our eyes squinched up like bats.

OUR LADY OF THE SNOWS

In white,
the unpainted statue of the young girl
on the side altar
made the quality of mercy seem scrupulous and calm.

When my mother was in a hospital drying out,
or drinking at a pace that would put her there soon,
I would slip in the side door,
light an aromatic candle,
and bargain for us both.
Or else I'd stare into the day-moon of that face
and, if I concentrated, fly.

Come down! come down!
she'd call, because I was so high.

Though mostly when I think of myself
at that age, I am standing at my older brother's closet
studying the shirts,
convinced that I could be absolutely transformed
by something I could borrow.
And the days churned by,
navigable sorrow.

SPRING DRAWING 2

A man says *lilacs against white houses, two sparrows, one streaked, in a thinning birch*, and can't find his way to a sentence.

In order to be respectable, Thorstein Veblen said, desperate in Palo Alto, a thing must be wasteful, i.e., "a selective adaptation of forms to the end of conspicuous waste."

So we try to throw nothing away, as Keith, making dinner for us as his grandmother had done in Jamaica, left nothing; the kitchen was as clean at the end as when he started; even the shrimp shells and carrot fronds were part of the process,

and he said, when we tried to admire him, "Listen, I should send you into the chickenyard to look for a rusty nail to add to the soup for iron."

The first temptation of Sakyamuni was desire, but he saw that it led to fulfillment and then to desire, so that one was easy.

Because I have pruned it badly in successive years, the climbing rose has sent out, among the pale pink floribunda, a few wild white roses from the rootstalk.

Suppose, before they said *silver* or *moonlight* or *wet grass*, each poet had to agree to be responsible for the innocence of all the suffering on earth,

because they learned in arithmetic, during the long school days, that if there was anything left over,

you had to carry it. The wild rose looks weightless, the floribunda are
heavy with the richness and sadness of Europe

as they imitate the dying, petal by petal, of the people who bred them.

You hear pain singing in the nerves of things; it is not a song.

The gazelle's head turned; three jackals are eating his entrails and he is
watching.

FAINT MUSIC

Maybe you need to write a poem about grace.

When everything broken is broken,
and everything dead is dead,
and the hero has looked into the mirror with complete contempt,
and the heroine has studied her face and its defects
remorselessly, and the pain they thought might,
as a token of their earnestness, release them from themselves
has lost its novelty and not released them,
and they have begun to think, kindly and distantly,
watching the others go about their days —
likes and dislikes, reasons, habits, fears —
that self-love is the one weedy stalk
of every human blossoming, and understood,
therefore, why they had been, all their lives,
in such a fury to defend it, and that no one —
except some almost inconceivable saint in his pool
of poverty and silence — can escape this violent, automatic
life's companion ever, maybe then, ordinary light,
faint music under things, a hovering like grace appears.

As in the story a friend told once about the time
he tried to kill himself. His girl had left him.
Bees in the heart, then scorpions, maggots, and then ash.
He climbed onto the jumping girder of the bridge,
the bay side, a blue, lucid afternoon.
And in the salt air he thought about the word "seafood,"
that there was something faintly ridiculous about it.

No one said "landfood." He thought it was degrading to the rainbow
      perch
he'd reeled in gleaming from the cliffs, the black rockbass,
scales like polished carbon, in beds of kelp
along the coast — and he realized that the reason for the word
was crabs, or mussels, clams. Otherwise
the restaurants could just put "fish" up on their signs,
and when he woke — he'd slept for hours, curled up
on the girder like a child — the sun was going down
and he felt a little better, and afraid. He put on the jacket
he'd used for a pillow, climbed over the railing
carefully, and drove home to an empty house.

There was a pair of her lemon yellow panties
hanging on a doorknob. He studied them. Much-washed.
A faint russet in the crotch that made him sick
with rage and grief. He knew more or less
where she was. A flat somewhere on Russian Hill.
They'd have just finished making love. She'd have tears
in her eyes and touch his jawbone gratefully. "God,"
she'd say, "you are so good for me." Winking lights,
a foggy view downhill toward the harbor and the bay.
"You're sad," he'd say. "Yes." "Thinking about Nick?"
"Yes," she'd say and cry. "I tried so hard," sobbing now,
"I really tried so hard." And then he'd hold her for a while —
Guatemalan weavings from his fieldwork on the wall —
and then they'd fuck again, and she would cry some more,
and go to sleep.
               And he, he would play that scene
once only, once and a half, and tell himself
that he was going to carry it for a very long time
and that there was nothing he could do
but carry it. He went out onto the porch, and listened
to the forest in the summer dark, madrone bark
cracking and curling as the cold came up.

It's not the story though, not the friend
leaning toward you, saying "And then I realized — ,"
which is the part of stories one never quite believes.
I had the idea that the world's so full of pain
it must sometimes make a kind of singing.
And that the sequence helps, as much as order helps —
First an ego, and then pain, and then the singing.

Robert Hayden

THOSE WINTER SUNDAYS

Sundays too my father got up early
and put his clothes on in the blueblack cold,
then with cracked hands that ached
from labor in the weekday weather made
banked fires blaze. No one ever thanked him.

I'd wake and hear the cold splintering, breaking.
When the rooms were warm, he'd call,
and slowly I would rise and dress,
fearing the chronic angers of that house,

Speaking indifferently to him,
who had driven out the cold
and polished my good shoes as well.
What did I know, what did I know
of love's austere and lonely offices?

NIGHT, DEATH, MISSISSIPPI

I

A quavering cry. Screech-owl?
Or one of them?
The old man in his reek
and gauntness laughs —

One of them, I bet —
and turns out the kitchen lamp,
limping to the porch to listen
in the windowless night.

Be there with Boy and the rest
if I was well again.

Time was. Time was.
White robes like moonlight

In the sweetgum dark.
Unbucked that one then
and him squealing bloody Jesus
as we cut it off.

Time was. A cry?
A cry all right.
He hawks and spits,
fevered as by groinfire.

Have us a bottle,
Boy and me —
he's earned him a bottle —
when he gets home.

II

Then we beat them, he said,
beat them till our arms was tired
and the big old chains
messy and red.

O Jesus burning on the lily cross

Christ, it was better
than hunting bear
which don't know why
you want him dead.

O night, rawhead and bloodybones night

You kids fetch Paw
some water now so's he
can wash that blood
off him, she said.

O night betrayed by darkness not its own

MONET'S "WATERLILIES"

(for Bill and Sonja)

Today as the news from Selma and Saigon
poisons the air like fallout,
    I come again to see
the serene great picture that I love.

Here space and time exist in light
the eye like the eye of faith believes.
    The seen, the known
dissolve in iridescence, become
illusive flesh of light
    that was not, was, forever is.

O light beheld as through refracting tears.
Here is the aura of that world
    each of us has lost.
Here is the shadow of its joy.

SOLEDAD

(And I, I am no longer of that world)
Naked, he lies in the blinded room
chainsmoking, cradled by drugs, by jazz
as never by any lover's cradling flesh.

Miles Davis coolly blows for him:
O *pena negra*, sensual Flamenco blues;
the red clay foxfire voice of Lady Day

(lady of the pure black magnolias)
sobsings her sorrow and loss and fare you well,
dryweeps the pain his treacherous jailers

have released him from for awhile.
His fears and his unfinished self
await him down in the anywhere streets.

He hides on the dark side of the moon,
takes refuge in a stained-glass cell,
flies to a clockless country of crystal.

Only the ghost of Lady Day knows where
he is. Only the music. And he swings
oh swings: beyond complete immortal now.

THE NIGHT-BLOOMING CEREUS

And so for nights
we waited, hoping to see
the heavy bud
    break into flower.

On its neck-like tube
hooking down from the edge
of the leaf-branch
    nearly to the floor,

the bud packed
tight with its miracle swayed
stiffly on breaths
    of air, moved

as though impelled
by stirrings within itself.
It repelled as much
    as it fascinated me

sometimes — snake,
eyeless bird head,
beak that would gape
    with grotesque life-squawk.

But you, my dear,
conceded less to the bizarre
than to the imminence
    of bloom. Yet we agreed

        we ought
to celebrate the blossom,
paint ourselves, dance
        in honor of

        archaic mysteries
when it appeared. Meanwhile
we waited, aware
        of rigorous design.

        Backster's
polygraph, I thought,
would have shown
        (as clearly as it had

        a philodendron's
fear) tribal sentience
in the cactus, focused
        energy of will.

        That belling of
tropic perfume — that
signalling
        not meant for us;

        the darkness
cloyed with summoning
fragrance. We dropped
        trivial tasks

        and marvelling
beheld at last the achieved
flower. Its moonlight
        petals were

        still unfold-
ing, the spike fringe of the outer
perianth recessing
        as we watched.

        Lunar presence,
foredoomed, already dying,

it charged the room
    with plangency

    older than human
cries, ancient as prayers
invoking Osiris, Krishna,
    Tezcátlipóca.

    We spoke
in whispers when
we spoke
    at all . . .

A PLAGUE OF STARLINGS (FISK CAMPUS)

Evenings I hear
the workmen fire
into the stiff
magnolia leaves,
routing the starlings
gathered noisy and
befouling there.

Their scissoring
terror like glass
coins spilling breaking
the birds explode
into mica sky
raggedly fall
to ground rigid
in clench of cold.

The spared return,
when the guns are through,
to the spoiled trees
like choiceless poor
to a dangerous
dwelling place,
chitter and quarrel
in the piercing dark
above the killed.

FREE FANTASIA: TIGER FLOWERS

(for Michael)

The sporting people
along St. Antoine —
that scufflers'
paradise of ironies —
    bet salty money
on his righteous
    hook and jab.

I was a boy then, running
(unbeknownst to Pa)
errands for Miss Jackie
and Stack-o'-Diamonds' Eula Mae.
. . . Their perfumes,
rouged Egyptian faces.
    Their pianolas jazzing.

O Creole babies,
Dixie odalisques,
speeding through cutglass
dark to see the macho angel
    trick you'd never
turn, his bluesteel prowess
    in the ring.

Hardshell believers
amen'd the wreck
as God A'mighty's
will. I'd thought
    such gaiety could not
die. Nor could our
    elegant avenger.

The Virgin Forest
by Rousseau —
its psychedelic flowers
towering, its deathless
    dark dream figure
death the leopard
    claws — I choose it
now as elegy
    for Tiger Flowers.

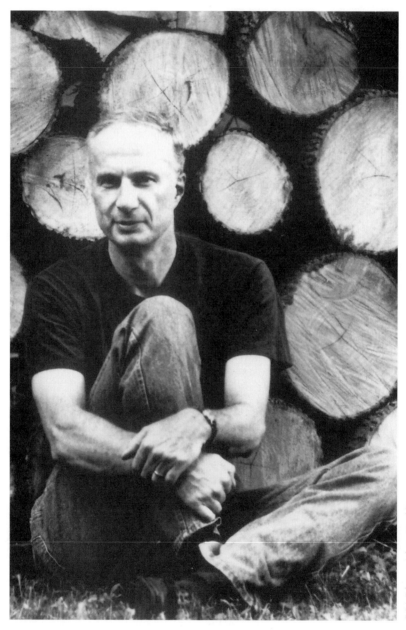

William Heyen

THE RETURN

I will touch things and things and no more thoughts.
—Robinson Jeffers

My boat slowed on the still water,
stopped in a thatch of lilies.
The moon leaned over the white lilies.

I waited for a sign, and stared
at the hooded water. On the far shore
brush broke, a deer broke cover.

I waited for a sign, and waited.
The moon lit the lilies to candles.
Their light reached down the water

to a dark flame, a fish: it hovered
under the pads, the pond held it
in its dim depths as though in amber.

Green, still, balanced in its own life,
breathing small breaths of light, this
was the world's oldest wonder, the arrow

of thought, the branch that all words
break against, the deep fire, the pure poise
of an object, the pond's presence, the pike.

THE PIGEONS

Audubon watched the flocks beat by for days,
and tried, but could not count them:
their dung fell "like melting flakes of snow,"
the air buzzed until he lost his senses.

He heard, he said, their *coo-coo*
and *kee-kee* when they courted, and saw trees
of hundreds of nests, each cradling two
"broadly elliptical pure white eggs."

Over mast, they swept in "rich deep purple
circles," then roosted so thick that high limbs
cracked, and the pigeons avalanched
down the boughs, and had not room to fly,

and died by thousands. Kentucky farmers
fed their hogs on birds
knocked out of the air with poles. No net, stone,
arrow, or bullet could miss one,

so horses drew wagons of them,
and schooners sailed cargoes of them,
and locomotives pulled freightcars of them
to the cities where they sold for one cent each.

When you touched one, its soft
feathers fell away as easily as a puff
of dandelion seeds, and its delicate breastbone seemed to return the pulse of your thumb.

WITNESS

We'd walked into the small warm shed
where spring lambs lay in straw
in the half-dark still smelling of their birth,
of ammonia, the damp grass, dung,
into this world in the middle of a field
where lambs bleating soft songs lifted
their heavy heads toward their mothers,
gentle presences within their wool clouds.
Later, outside, as I watched,
Wenzel wrapped his left arm around a sheep's neck
and struck her with the sledge in his right hand.
The dying sheep, her forehead crushed, cried out,
past pain, for her mortal life. Blood flowed
from her burst skull, over her eyes, her black nose.

Wenzel dropped her to the grass.
When I ran home, I struck my head
on a blossoming apple-bough.
Where was the dead sheep?
What did I hear?
Where is the witness now?

I was nine or ten.
Her cry was terror,
so I lay awake to hear her,
to wonder why she didn't seem to know
her next manger, her golden fields.
Her odors drifted through my screen —
the hay at the roots of her wool,
her urine, the wet graindust under her chin,
her birth fluids hot and flecked with blood.
I could hear her bleat
to her last lamb, hear her heartbeat
in the black air of my room.
Where was the dead sheep?
Why did she cry for her loss?
Where is the witness now?

Not to accept, but to awaken.
Not to understand, to cry terror, but to know
that even a billion years later, now,
we breathe the first circle of light,
and the light curves into us, into the deer's back,
the man's neck, the woman's thigh,
the cat's mouse-mossed tongue, all the ruby
berries ripening in evening air.
The dead elms and chestnuts are of it, and do not
break the curve. The jeweled flies sip it,
and do not break the curve.
Our homes inhabit, and ride the curve.
Our moon, our rivers, the furthest stars blinking blue,
the great named and nameless comets do not break the curve.
The odorous apple-blossom rain does not break the curve.
The struck ewe's broken brainpan does not break the curve.
Wenzel nor this witness breaks the curve.

In the shed's dusk where spring lambs
sang to their mothers, in my dark room
where the dead ewe's odors drifted my sleep,

and now, within these cells where her forehead blood
flows once more into recollection,
the light curves. You and I bear witness, and know this,
and as we do the light curves into this knowledge.
The struck ewe lives in this light,
in this curve of the only unbroken light.

SIMPLE TRUTHS

When a man has grown a body,
a body to carry with him
through nature for as long as he can,
when this body is taken from him
by other men and women who happen to be,
this time, in uniform,
then it is clear he has experienced
an act of barbarism,

and when a man has a wife,
a wife to love for as long as he lives,
when this wife is marked with a yellow star
and driven into a chamber she will never leave alive,
then this is murder,
so much is clear,

and when a woman has hair,
when her hair is shorn and her scalp bleeds,
when a woman has children,
children to love for as long as she lives,
when the children are taken from her,
when a man and his wife and their children
are put to death in a chamber of gas,
or with pistols at close range, or are starved,
or beaten, or injected by the thousands,
or ripped apart, by the thousands, by the millions,
it is clear that where we are
is Europe, in our century, during the years
from nineteen-hundred and thirty-five
to nineteen-hundred and forty-five
after the death of Jesus, who spoke of a different order,
but whose father, who is our father,

if he is our father,
if we must speak of him as father,
watched, and witnessed, and knew,

and when we remember,
when we touch the skin of our own bodies,
when we open our eyes into dream
or within the morning shine of sunlight
and remember what was taken
from these men, from these women,
from these children gassed and starved
and beaten and thrown against walls
and made to walk the valley
of knives and icepicks and otherwise
exterminated in ways appearing to us almost
beyond even the maniacal human imagination,
then it is clear that this is the German Reich,
during approximately ten years of our lord's time,

and when we read a book of these things,
when we hear the names of the camps,
when we see the films of the bulldozed dead
or the film of one boy struck on the head
with a club in the hands
of a German doctor who will wait
some days for the boy's skull to knit, and will enter
the time in his ledger, and then
take up the club to strike the boy again,
and wait some weeks for the boy's skull to knit,
and enter the time in his ledger again,
and strike the boy again,
and so on, until the boy, who,
at the end of the film of his life
can hardly stagger forward toward the doctor,
does die, and the doctor
enters exactly the time of the boy's death in his ledger,

when we read these things or see them,
then it is clear to us that this
happened, and within the lord's allowance, this
work of his minions, his poor
vicious dumb German victims twisted
into the swastika shapes of trees struck by lightning,
on this his earth, if he is our father,

if we must speak of him in this way,
this presence above us, within us, this
mover, this first cause, this spirit, this
curse, this bloodstream and brain-current, this
unfathomable oceanic ignorance of ourselves, this
automatic electric Aryan swerve, this

fortune that you and I were not the victims, this
luck that you and I were not the murderers, this
sense that you and I are clean and understand, this
stupidity that gives him breath, gives him life
as we kill them all, as we killed them all.

REDWINGS

Maybe you've noticed that around here
red-winged blackbirds aren't rare,
but aren't seen often, either, and then, at distance,
banking away from roads as we pass.

But one morning, I saw a hundred,
more, feeding on seed I'd scattered
under a line of pines planted
more than a hundred years before.

Almost at rest, their feathers folded close,
only yellow wingbars
break their black bodies. But when, as they did,
all at once, they lifted, that *red* . . .

I've tried for a long time, and maybe should,
to tell you how the disembodied redwings
flared and vanished.
I've lost them in every telling.

So much for me. I could die now, anyway.
Could you? We will close our eyes
and rest, in case the blackbirds, in slow motion,
assume again the flames they are, and rise.

WILLIAM HEYEN

YELLOWTHROATS

1

Very wary,
both yellowthroats
wait in the bottom branches
of silver maple: they will not drop down
to their deeply cupped nest
in the thick honey-

suckle until
certain nothing not
within the wind's movements
is moving, or watching. I know they see
me in my cabin move my pen,
blink, or look down.

2

Since that last line,
much time has passed. They're
in or near their nest now. Once in a while,
careful as they are, the honeysuckle trembles, just
a little, gives them away,
and always will,

though I might try
not to say what I might seem to.
Have you seen the female die, and then
a bloodspot fill the eye of the beautiful black-
masked male who flew to her
to shield her?

3

You don't have to:
I know why I, as now, return
that way again. But this is my new life,
each day, each line now only a rhythm, a trembling,

a prayer out from under
all that killing.

Soon, three or four
new yellowthroat hearts
will form in eggs in the hidden nest.
What will start their small hearts beating if not something
touching them that I have been
forgiven by?

4

Here, now, from past
our planet, past our solar system's edge
of the Milky Way, our immense and tiny galaxy, Li Po's
cloudy river of the sky, in everything that matters, is nameless,
and knows us, the same
holiness flows,

that which moves memory
within this cabin, that which keeps
the same returning yellowthroats alive again.
Now, evening descends with its quieting light. Now,
to see them, I close my own
quieting eyes.

BLACKBIRD SPRING

Mid-morning, walking ocean shoreline,
I found a hundred blackbirds
frozen in ice,
only their heads protruding,
black eyes open,
gleaming, most of their sharp beaks still
scissoring in mid-whistle.

Feeding, they'd been caught
in sea-spray, must be —
all males, up north early,
scarlet epaulettes aflame

a few inches under. I chipped
one bird loose with a stone,
held it in gloved hands

under the rising sun until,
until I realized, until I realized
nothing I hadn't known.
The tide retreated & would return.
Within the austere territories
these would have filled with belligerence
& song, spring had begun.

YELLOWJACKETS

How many years past was it I burned out their nest
under the melons? They'd not stung,
but worried me each time I walked among the mounds.
Gasoline, a match, the soft
concussion. I disinterred their charred comb
& found their grotesquely
fat queen exuding translucent eggs & slime from her belly.

Last night I dreamed I died in my office cubicle.
I sensed last rites, then
my corpse laid out on my desk, the space sealed off,
& over the centuries
countless more such rooms, more dead, we
colleagues together until
who knows when the resurrection might or might not be.

From each of its cells our tomb emits a faint light,
my cerements seem
to possess the half life of plutonium, or the stars. From here,
I seem to see almost
everything but cannot find my fruited acre where
yellowjackets flew between
their buried nest & one who could not live with them.

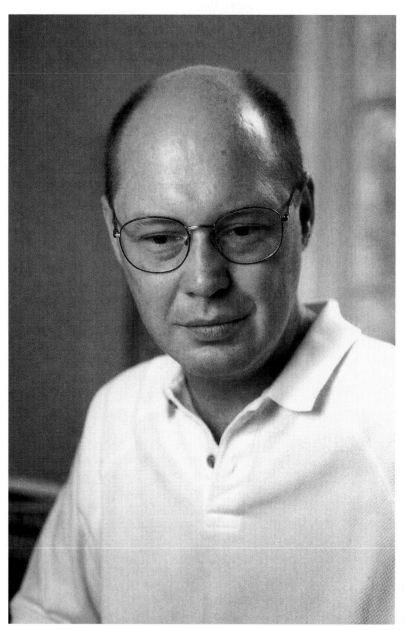

Andrew Hudgins

THE CHINABERRY

I couldn't stand still watching them forever,
but when I moved
                    the grackles covering
each branch and twig
                    sprang
                                together into flight
and for a moment in midair they held
the tree's shape,
                    the black tree
                                peeling from the green,
as if
        they were its shadow or its soul, before
they scattered,
                    circled and
                                re-formed
as grackles heading south for winter grain fields.
Oh, it
        was just a chinaberry tree,
the birds were simply grackles.
                                A miracle
made from this world and where I stood in it.
But you can't know how long
                                I stood there watching.
And you can't know how desperate I'd become
advancing
            each step on the feet of my
advancing shadow,
                    how bitter and afraid I was
matching step after step with the underworld,
my ominous, indistinct and mirror image
darkening with
                    extreme and antic nothings
the ground I walked on,
                                inexact reversals,
elongated and foreshortened parodies
of each
        foot lowering itself
                                onto its shadow.

And you can't know how I had tried to force
the moment, make it happen
                      before it happened —
not necessarily this
                though this is what I saw:
black birds deserting the tree they had become,
becoming,
        for a moment in midair,
the chinaberry's shadow for a moment
after they had ceased to be
                    the chinaberry,
then scattering:
             meaning after meaning —
birds strewn across the morning like flung gravel
until
    they found themselves again as grackles,
found each other,
           found South
                and headed there,
while I stood before
           the green, abandoned tree.

ONE THREW A DIRT CLOD AND IT RAN

One threw a dirt clod and it ran, and when it paused,
another threw a rock and it trotted out of range,
so they pursued it, lobbing rocks and sticks,
just to see it gallop, which was beautiful,
then to keep it running, but when it stumbled on barbed wire
and broke a front leg and crumpled to its knees, entangled,
one hit it with a tree limb and hit it again. It fell
and they, laughing, ran up and kicked it, jumped away,
ran off, ran back and kicked it, till they could stand beside it,
kicking. They cheered when one of them pried loose
a broken fence post. They fought for the fence post
and took turns swinging it until the tangled beast's
slack ribs stopped pumping, heaving. Gasping for breath,
they stared at one another, dropped the post, the stones, the sticks.
They nudged the huge corpse and waited for it to rise,
to rise and gallop over rutted, fenced-off fields
as if there were no ruts, no mudholes, scrub brush, wire,
so they could follow it forever, weeping and hurling stones.

ANDREW HUDGINS

HEAT LIGHTNING IN A TIME OF DROUGHT

My neighbor, drunk, stood on his lawn and yelled,
Want some! Want some! He bellowed it as cops
cuffed him, shoved him in their back seat — *Want some!* —
and drove away. Now I lie here awake,
not by choice, listening to the crickets' high
electric trill, urgent with lust. Heat lightning flashes.
The crickets will not, will not stop. I wish
that I could shut the window, pull the curtain, sleep.
But it's too hot. *Want some!* He screamed it till
I was afraid I'd made him up to scream
what I knew better than to say out loud
although it's August-hot and every move
bathes me in sweat and we are careless,
careless, careless, every one of us,
and when my neighbor screams out in his yard
like one dog howling for another dog,
I call the cops, then lie in my own sweat,
remembering the woman
who, at a party on a night this hot,
walked up to me, propped her chin on my chest,
and sighed. She was a little drunk, the love-light
unshielded in her eyes. We fell in love.
One day at supper the light fixture dropped,
exploded on the table. Glass flew around us,
a low, slow-motion blossoming of razors.
She was unhurt till I reached out my hand
— left hand — to brush glass from her face.
Two drops of blood ran down her cheek.
On TV, I'd seen a teacher dip a rose
in liquid nitrogen. When he withdrew it,
it smoked, frozen solid. He snapped one petal, frail
as isinglass, and then, against the table,
he shattered it. The whole rose blew apart.
Like us. And then one day the doorbell rang.
A salesman said, *Watch this!* He stripped my bed
and vacuumed it. The nozzle sucked up two
full, measured cups of light gray flakes. He said,
That's human skin. I stood, refusing the purchase,
stood staring at her flesh and mine commingled
inside the measuring cup, stood there and thought,
She's been gone two years, she's married, and all this time

her flesh has been in bed with me. Don't laugh.
Don't laugh. That's what the Little Moron says
when he arrives home early from a trip
and finds his wife in bed with someone else.
The man runs off. The Little Moron puts
a pistol to his own head, cocks the hammer.
His wife, in bed, sheets pulled up to her breasts,
starts laughing. *Don't you laugh!* he screams. *Don't laugh —*
you're next. It is the wisest joke I know because
the heart's a violent muscle, opening
and closing. Who knows what we might do:
by night, the craziness of dreams; by day,
the craziness of logic. Listen!
My brother told me of a man wheeled, screaming,
into the ward, a large Coke bottle rammed
up his ass. I was awed: there is no telling
what we'll do in our fierce drive to come together.
The heart keeps opening and closing like a mine
where fire still burns, a century underground,
following the veins of black coal, rearing up
to take a barn, a house, a pasture. Although
I wish that it would rain tonight, I fret
about the heat lightning that flicks and glitters
on the horizon as if it promised rain.
It can't. But I walk outside, stand on parched grass,
and watch it hungrily — all light, all dazzle —
remembering how we'd drive out past the town's light,
sit on the hood, and watch great thunderheads
huge as a state — say Delaware — sail past. Branched
lightning jagged, burst the dark from zenith to horizon.
We stared at almost nothing: some live oaks,
the waist-high corn. Slow raindrops smacked the corn,
plopped in the dirt around us, drummed the roof,
and finally reached out, tapped us on the shoulders.
We drove home in the downpour, laughed, made love
— still wet with rain — and slept. But why stop there?
Each happy memory leads me to a sad one:
the friend who helped me through my grief by drinking
all of my liquor. And when, at last, we reached
the wretched mescal, he carefully sliced off
the worm's black face, ate its white body, staggered
onto this very lawn, and racked and heaved
until I helped him up. *You're okay, John.*
You've puked it out. "No, man — you're wrong. That worm

ain't ever coming out." Heat lightning flashes.
No rain falls and no thunder cracks the heat.
No first concussion dwindles to a long
low rolling growl. I go in the house, lie down,
pray, masturbate, drift to the edge of sleep.
I wish my soul were larger than it is.

MARY MAGDALENE'S LEFT FOOT

I saw the picture in *Newsweek* or *Time*
and couldn't believe who was back in the news.
But there it sat, encased in antique gold
and pedestrian prose, apart from the rest
of her imaginably lush lost body,
which it recalls with false synecdoche.

The news is littered with the bodies of women
— whores, some — who have returned to minerals,
a pile of iron and zinc and calcium
that wouldn't even fill a shoe. We glimpse
of Mary Magdalene a golden whole
that never ached for flesh or grew hair coarse
enough to scrub mud from a traveler's foot.

But gold is meretricious flattery
for the whore who washed Christ's feet with tears,
who rubbed sweet oil into his sores, then kissed
each suppurating wound that swelled his flesh,
knowing that it was God's clear flesh beneath
its human dying. And that is more than you or I
will ever know of where we place our lips.

GRANDMOTHER'S SPIT

To wipe the sleep grains from my eyes or rub
a food smudge from my cheek, Grandmother'd lick
her rough right thumb and order me, *Come here.*
She'd clutch my arm and hold me near her face

while, with that spit-damp thumb, she scrubbed the spot.
I struggled like a kitten being licked,
then leaned into the touch, again cat-like,
helping that fierce thumb scour loose the dirt.
It smelled, her spit, of lipstick and tobacco —
breath-warm, enveloping. She'd hold me at arm's length,
peer hard into my face, and state, *You're clean.*
When she let go, I'd crouch behind the door
and, with my own spit, rub the clean spot raw.

ASHES

Bill gripped the can in both hands and dashed it upward,
casting into the March air his cousin, a man
I'd met a time or two, but now a cloud
of ash and bone grit launched above the river,
and the wind, which bloweth where it listeth, this time
amused itself to swirl the ashes overhead
and, at the moment I yawned, it slapped them back
across the clustered mourners. I sucked down
a grainy mouthful of fresh death, coughed, gagged,
and everyone surged toward me, hands outstretched.
They swatted at my dusty hair, brushed death's
gray epaulets off my shoulders and thumped my back
furiously, as if this dust were different
from other dust, and it was — or why would I
have dressed in coat and tie, and stood, head bowed,
on the soft bank of the Black Warrior, watching
huge barge trains humped with coal chug to the Gulf
while some young Baptist mumbled pieties?
I hacked death from my lungs and spat death out
and hacked up more. The mourners drummed the loose
death out of me. "I'm okay. Thanks," I said,
but they kept drumming, drumming on my back.
"Leave me alone!" I snapped, and we all glanced,
ashamed, into each other's ash-dappled faces.
We turned back to the river and its commerce,
the sermon and its commerce, the wind's new commerce,
and breathed it in and breathed it out and breathed it in.

ANDREW HUDGINS

SUPPER

We shared our supper with the flames,
or the shadow of the flames — each candle
in the light of the other casting shadows
across the table, dark flickers of a brilliant flicker,
and the grain of rubbed pine swirled with light
and shadow, shoaled and deepened in the soft
inconstancy of candlelight.
                                        With every gesture
the bright flames flinched and then corrected.
Your shrug, my laugh,
                                my nod, your tilting head
— conveyed on air — invited their response.
They bowed their heads, then snapped upright —
a ripple in the gases' fluted yellow silk,
blue silk, transparent silk. I yearned
to touch the rich untouchable fabric, and finger
the sheen beneath its scorching,
but when I reached, it leaned away
decorously, and I did not pursue it, knowing.

But the dark flames reached out, licked the meat,
licked the plate, the fork, and the knife edge.
They licked our faces and our lips — a dry unfelt tongue,
the shadow of the flame consuming nothing,
but stroking everything as if it could
grasp, hold, take, devour. How ardently it hungers
because it cannot have us.
How chaste the bright flame, because it can.

Richard Hugo

LIVING ALONE

I felt the empty cabin wasn't abandoned.
The axe, for one thing, blood still moist
on the blade. Then, warm coffee on the stove.
God, it blew outside. The owner, I said,
won't last long in this storm. By midnight
I was singing. I knew the cabin was mine.
Fifty years later, he still hadn't returned.

Moss covered the roof by then. I called
the deer by name. Alice, I liked best.
Winslow, next. Reporters came to write me up.
They called me 'animal man' in the feature
in the photogravure. The story said I led
a wonderful life out here. I said clouds
were giant toads but they quoted me wrong.

The coroner identified the bones as woman.
I denied I'd been married and the local
records backed me. Today, they are hunting all over
the world for the previous owner.
I claim the cabin by occupancy rights.
I pray each dawn. How my words climb cedars
like squirrels uttered by God.

DEGREES OF GRAY IN PHILIPSBURG

You might come here Sunday on a whim.
Say your life broke down. The last good kiss
you had was years ago. You walk these streets
laid out by the insane, past hotels
that didn't last, bars that did, the tortured try
of local drivers to accelerate their lives.
Only churches are kept up. The jail

turned 70 this year. The only prisoner
is always in, not knowing what he's done.

The principal supporting business now
is rage. Hatred of the various grays
the mountain sends, hatred of the mill,
The Silver Bill repeal, the best liked girls
who leave each year for Butte. One good
restaurant and bars can't wipe the boredom out.
The 1907 boom, eight going silver mines,
a dance floor built on springs —
all memory resolves itself in gaze,
in panoramic green you know the cattle eat
or two stacks high above the town,
two dead kilns, the huge mill in collapse
for fifty years that won't fall finally down.

Isn't this your life? That ancient kiss
still burning out your eyes? Isn't this defeat
so accurate, the church bell simply seems
a pure announcement: ring and no one comes?
Don't empty houses ring? Are magnesium
and scorn sufficient to support a town,
not just Philipsburg, but towns
of towering blondes, good jazz and booze
the world will never let you have
until the town you came from dies inside?

Say no to yourself. The old man, twenty
when the jail was built, still laughs
although his lips collapse. Someday soon,
he says, I'll go to sleep and not wake up.
You tell him no. You're talking to yourself.
The car that brought you here still runs.
The money you buy lunch with,
no matter where it's mined, is silver
and the girl who serves you food
is slender and her red hair lights the wall.

RICHARD HUGO

A MAP OF MONTANA IN ITALY

for Marjorie Carrier

On this map white. A state thick as a fist
or blunt instrument. Long roads weave and cross
red veins full of rage. Big Canada, map maker's
pink, squats on our backs, planning bad winters
for years, and Glacier Park's green with my envy
of Grizzly Bears. On the right, antelope sail
between strands of barbed wire and never
get hurt, west, I think, of Plevna, say near
Sumatra, or more west, say Shawmut,
anyway, on the right, east on the plains.
The two biggest towns are dull deposits
of men getting along, making money, driving
to church every Sunday, censoring movies and books.
The two most interesting towns, Helena, Butte,
have the good sense to fail. There's too much
schoolboy in bars — I'm tougher than you —
and too much talk about money.
Jails and police are how you dream Poland —
odd charges, bad food and forms you must fill
stating your religion. In Poland say none.
With so few Negroes and Jews we've been reduced
to hating each other, dumping our crud
in our rivers, mistreating the Indians.
Each year, 4000 move, most to the west
where ocean currents keep winter in check.
This map is white, meaning winter, ice
where you are, helping children who may be
already frozen. It's white here too
but back of me, up in the mountains where
the most ferocious animals
are obsequious wolves. No one fights
in the bars filled with pastry. There's no
prison for miles. But last night the Italians
cheered the violence in one of our westerns.

RICHARD HUGO

THE LADY IN KICKING HORSE RESERVOIR

Not my hands but green across you now.
Green tons hold you down, and ten bass curve
teasing in your hair. Summer slime
will pile deep on your breast. Four months of ice
will keep you firm. I hope each spring
to find you tangled in those pads
pulled not quite loose by the spillway pour,
stars in dead reflection off your teeth.

Lie there lily still. The spillway's closed.
Two feet down most lakes are common gray.
This lake is dark from the black blue Mission range
climbing sky like music dying Indians once wailed.
On ocean beaches, mystery fish
are offered to the moon. Your jaws go blue.
Your hands start waving every wind.
Wave to the ocean where we crushed a mile of foam.

We still love there in thundering foam
and love. Whales fall in love with gulls
and tide reclaims the Dolly skeletons
gone with a blast of aching horns to China.
Landlocked in Montana here
the end is limited by light, the final note
will trail off at the farthest point we see,
already faded, lover, where you bloat.

All girls should be nicer. Arrows rain
above us in the Indian wind. My future
should be full of windy gems, my past
will stop this roaring in my dreams.
Sorry. Sorry. Sorry. But the arrows sing:
no way to float her up. The dead sink
from dead weight. The Mission range
turns this water black late afternoons.

One boy slapped the other. Hard.
The slapped boy talked until his dignity
dissolved, screamed a single 'stop'
and went down sobbing in the company pond.
I swam for him all night. My only suit

got wet and factory hands went home.
No one cared the coward disappeared.
Morning then: cold music I had never heard.

Loners like work best on second shift.
No one liked our product and the factory closed.
Off south, the bison multiply so fast
a slaughter's mandatory every spring
and every spring the creeks get fat
and Kicking Horse fills up. My hope is vague.
The far blur of your bones in May
may be nourished by the snow.

The spillway's open and you spill out
into weather, lover down the bright canal
and mother, irrigating crops
dead Indians forgot to plant.
I'm sailing west with arrows to dissolving foam
where waves strand naked Dollys.
Their eyes are white as oriental mountains
and their tongues are teasing oil from whales.

DEATH IN THE AQUARIUM

Praise him for the place he picked.
He shot himself dead in full sight
of the red Irish lord and the rare
albino sea perch. They nosed the glass
and cried to the outside world of air
"he's bleeding" in some salt water tongue.
The flounder dozed on. The octopus
flashed one disapproving eye at the cop.

The cop found no suicide note. The cop found
no I.D. The gun could not be traced.
They questioned everyone there but the fish
who swam around those being questioned.
You'd have wanted to film it, the visitors
with no answers shaken and sad, the red
snapper behind them gasping, the misfit
rock cod proud of his bad looks

and the yellow shiners turning and turning
like beautiful words going nowhere.
What a beautiful picture.
A year later the case was filed unsolved.

And you? Me? Where should we die given
a choice? In a hothouse? Along a remote
seldom traveled dirt road? Isn't some part
of that unidentified man in us all
and wants to die where we started?
Don't we share way back a cold green past
and wouldn't we welcome dying unknown,
unnamed on the floor of the ocean,
our bones ignored by the only clock there,
that slow unrhythmic waver of kelp —
our bones giving off the phosphorus
that collects in pockets and waits,
then one night washes in glowing?
And lovers, lovers would stop making love
and stand there, each suddenly alone
amazed at that gleam riding sand.

LANGAIG

We are what we hear. A well known singer died
yesterday in Spain. Thirty-five years ago
I got fired for sneaking off to hear him. I sobbed
"sorry" at the foreman, fired days later himself.
I cast blue nylon high over water turned black
by peat and light diminished by heavy Highland low sky.
I heard music and lost my job. I've not worked hard since
on anything but words, though I fish all waters
devoted and hum old songs when I fish alone.

I hum "My Heart is Taking Lessons," a song
the dead singer sang. I hum "I Had the Words and You
in My Heart." I remember him singing that.
I hum flat and off key, but that's hardly my fault,
the lack of gift, of training. In this lake (read 'loch'
to be local) trout run black as the water though Scots
like us call them 'browns,' the old Scots, 'Loch Leven!'

I hum "Makes No Difference Now," the best recording
the dead singer made and he left lots of good records.

To relax, to slide with, ride the forces of whatever
sweeps us along, jokes well timed, phrasing under control —
that was my ideal. I didn't come close in real life.
A soft impulse was proof I was weak. I laughed
at any weak joke, still do, and believed our purpose
to lighten the day, to be tougher than fate.
In reaction to that, I believed we should give in to pathos.
Today I believe: fish hard and hum every tune
I remember hearing the dead singer sing
and leave believing in being like him to others.
Does that make us brothers? Let's be. My bobber
jitters and I know it isn't just wind. I set my line
too soon and lose the black brown. The eagle yells
from the Quirang, "Go easy. Give him time to take it."
I hum "White Christmas," though I never liked it.
Snow on mainland mountains across the minch (if you're
American read 'strait') reminds me I'm fishing
late in the season. I may be breaking Scot law.

Christ, what rain and no real Jesus in it.
No real king. No friend. What lover first inserted a tongue
in a lover's ear? And where? It must have been pre-
Peloponesian war. It must have been pre-all
language and hunger, and located song prior to lyrics.
Fishing preceded song. We know that from instinct,
not records. I've fished this loch often before
and alone with my ghosts felt free to sing.
I've got a brown on. My line is writing a song.

I'm fishing. I'm singing. My heart is not exactly
giving lessons though I've been lucky enough in rare
moments to take heart in some words, and to have
a job teaching others to sing, to locate by game
some word like 'brown' in black water, to cast
hard for that word, then wait a long time to set.
Now the reeling in, the fight, the black trout lovely
on heather, the dead singer in songs
we recover, and hum when alone, and hum wrong.

Robert Turney

David Ignatow

While my father walked through mud
in shoes borrowed from his sister,
all Kiev attended *Prince Igor* and cheered,
and while he worked in a cellar bindery
and slept on workbenches rats leapt over
at night, Dostoyevsky's *White Nights*
and *Anna Karenina* were being read avidly
amid joy, tears and protests. My father
was the silent one, walking through the streets
where the hot arguments went on about poverty
and guilt. He walked, his work bundle under arm,
from cellar to monastery, to bind holy books
and volumes of the Russian classics,
and when they had had enough of classics
and needed blood, he fled,
for his blood was real to them; only he
had worked and starved. All others were
but characters in a novel or a play,
bless Chekhov, Gogol and others for their genius,
but my father was the one who had not been
immortalized and made untouchable.
Only he was real in Russia's torment.
Only he stood for life. All else was books,
and that was the torment.

NO THEORY

No theory will stand up to a chicken's guts
being cleaned out, a hand rammed up
to pull out the wriggling entrails,
the green bile and the bloody liver;
no theory that does not grow sick
at the odor escaping.

DAVID IGNATOW

COMMUNION

In the subway I had the impulse to kill
and sat and stared straight ahead
to avoid the eyes of strangers
who might read my dread
and when finally I had the courage
to shift my gaze from the poster above
I saw to my dismay the eyes of others
turning away.

THE DREAM

Someone approaches to say his life is ruined
and to fall down at your feet
and pound his head upon the sidewalk.
Blood spreads in a puddle.
And you, in a weak voice, plead
with those nearby for help;
your life takes on his desperation.
He keeps pounding his head.
It is you who are fated;
and you fall down beside him.
It is then you are awakened,
the body gone, the blood washed from the ground,
the stores lit up with their goods.

FOR ONE MOMENT

You take the dollar
and hand it to the fellow beside you
who turns and gives it to the next one
down the line. The world being round,
you stand waiting, smoking and lifting
a cup of coffee to your lips, talking
of seasonal weather and hinting
at problems. The dollar returns,

the coffee spills to the ground
in your hurry. You have the money
in one hand, a cup in the other,
a cigarette in your mouth,
and for one moment have forgotten
what it is you have to do,
your hair grey, your legs weakened
from long standing.

THE INHERITANCE

I never thought your harsh voice would be silenced,
your contracted, vicious face relaxed and calm,
the big nose standing out magisterially,
and the once small, sharp, puckered mouth
lengthened into a soft, sad curve,
reminding me of your mother's photograph.
I kissed your cold forehead with my fingertips
first touched to my lips in farewell,
and as I lingered to study your face
the lid was slammed down by attendants
to get them on with their job. Later
I wept, and my wife too was impatient with me,
knowing you well. Nevertheless, I wept.
You gave me smiles and made me work
at your machines. It was you taught me
the necessity for freedom.
I am going to sell your shop,
you to be remembered in my lines.

SELF-EMPLOYED

(For Harvey Shapiro)

I stand and listen, head bowed,
to my inner complaint.
Persons passing by think
I am searching for a lost coin.
You're fired, I yell inside

after an especially bad episode.
I'm letting you go without notice
or terminal pay. You just lost
another chance to make good.
But then I watch myself standing at the exit,
depressed and about to leave,
and wave myself back in wearily,
for who else could I get in my place
to do the job in dark, airless conditions?

MOVING PICTURE

When two take gas
by mutual consent
and the cops come in
when the walls are broken down
and the doctor pays respects
by closing the books
and the neighbors stand about
sniffing and afraid
and the papers run a brief
under a whiskey ad
and the news is read
eating ice cream or a fruit
and the paper is used
to wrap peelings
and the garbage man
dumps the barrel
into the truck
and the paper flares
in the furnace and sinks back
charred and is scooped up
for mud flats and pressed down
by steam rollers for hard ground
and a house on it
for two to enter.

DAVID IGNATOW

EACH DAY

Cynthia Matz, with my finger in your cunt
and you sliding back and forth on it,
protesting at the late hour and tiredness
and me with kidneys straining to capacity
with piss I had no chance to release
all night, we got up from the park bench
and walked you home. I left you
at the door, you said something
dispiriting about taking a chance
and settling on me. I had left Janette
to chase after you running out
of the ice cream parlor where the three
of us had sat — I had felt so sorry
and so guilty to have you find me
with her in the street. You and I
had gone to shows together,
you needed me to talk to and I was glad.
The talk always was about him
whom you still loved and he had jilted
you for someone else. I'm sorry, Cynthia,
that it had to end this way between us too,
I did not return the next day,
after leaving you at the door.
I did not return the following day either.
I went with Janette in whom I felt
nothing standing in the way,
while with you it would have been
each day to listen to your sadness
at having been betrayed by him.
I was not to be trusted either,
I too wanted love pure and simple.

MY NATIVE LAND

I pledge allegiance to the lips of the vagina,
I swear by it and kiss its flag.
I live in that country and would be buried there,
proud of its passivity. In such a place

I could live forever but since I must die
I would let my praise live on
for I am strange to myself,
seeing that I come from between two lips
and a beard, farther in a land
pink, tender, wet and lacking air,
close-clinging,
making me breathless
as I grow in it and die of pleasure.

Hardly like America.

from TREAD THE DARK

A prominent poet receives a national award for the perfect form of his poems.

Hello, drug addict, can you become a poem of perfect form?
Hello, Mafia, can you become a poem of perfect form?
Hello, schizoid person, can you become a poem of perfect form?
Hello, raped girl, can you become a poem of perfect form?
Hello, dead, napalmed man, can you become a poem of perfect form?
Hello, incinerated Jew, can you become a poem of perfect form?
If you can't, then you don't deserve to live.
You're dead, don't exist,
we want clean earth; get out, get going, get lost.
We have built a house for ourselves called the Perfect Form
and we're trying to live in it, and if you can't take
your napalmed body and your drug addicted brain
and make them into a poem of perfect form then you don't belong
here. Go somewhere else. Go to Vietnam where all
the imperfect bodies are and stay there and don't come back
to this country where only the poem of perfect form is wanted.
That's all we live in; you're a foreigner and we don't want you.
You're a kook and we hate you. You're a shit
and we wipe you off the face of the earth.
If you can't make yourself a poem of perfect form
then you have no right to be in this country.
You're here without a passport. You've lost your citizenship
rights. You're an alien, you're a spy.
You're somebody we hate.

Hello, poem of perfect form, we're home again to you
and we're going to snuggle up to you.
You give us so much comfort and pleasure.
We can run our hands over your darling self
and feel every bit of you, it's so sensuous and delicious;
it's so distracting from those bastards outside
who want to disturb us with their imperfect poems.
Fuck me, poem of perfect form.
Let me fuck you. We'll fuck each other.
We have each other, right, so let's do all the nasty
things we dream about and we'll have fun and nobody else
will know about it but you and me and me and me and me and you.
Wow. I don't want to hear another word
except your groans and sighs.

NOTES FOR A LECTURE

I will teach you to become American, my students:
take a turn at being enigmatic, to yourselves especially.
You work at a job and write poetry at night.
You write about working. Married,
you write about love.

I speak of kisses and mean quarrels,
the kiss brings the quarrel to mind,
of differences for their own sakes.
Did I ever think, going to bed,
a woman beside me would be no more uplifting
than a five-dollar raise? Since then
I've been uplifted in bed a hundred times
and but once raised in pay,
and that once has not been forgotten.

Take a broken whiskey bottle,
set it on top of your head
and dance. You have a costume,
you have meaning.

Donald Justice

How fashionably sad those early poems are!
On their clipped lawns and hedges the snows fall.
Rains beat against the tarpaulins of their porches,
Where, Sunday mornings, the bored children sprawl,
Reading the comics before their parents rise.
— The rhymes, the meters, how they paralyze!

Who walks out through their streets tonight?
No one. You know these small towns, how all traffic stops
At ten, the corner streetlamps gathering moths,
And mute, pale mannequins waiting in dark shops,
Undressed, and ready for the dreams of men.
— Now the long silence. Now the beginning again.

FIRST DEATH

June 12, 1933

I saw my grandmother grow weak.
When she died, I kissed her cheek.

I remember the new taste —
Powder mixed with a drying paste.

Down the hallway, on its table,
Lay the family's great Bible.

In the dark, by lamplight stirred,
The Void grew pregnant with the Word.

In black ink they wrote it down.
The older ink was turning brown.

From the woods there came a cry,
The hoot owl asking who not why.

253

The men sat silent on the porch,
Each lighted pipe a friendly torch

Against the unknown and the known.
But the child knew himself alone.

June 13, 1933

The morning sun rose up and stuck.
Sunflower strove with hollyhock.

I ran the worn path past the sty.
Nothing was hidden from God's eye.

The barn door creaked. I walked among
Chaff and wrinkled cakes of dung.

In the dim light I read the dates
On the dusty license plates

Nailed to the wall as souvenirs.
I breathed the dust in of the years.

I circled the abandoned Ford
Before I tried the running board.

At the wheel I felt the heat
Press upward through the springless seat.

And when I touched the silent horn,
Small mice scattered through the corn.

June 14, 1933

I remember the soprano
Fanning herself at the piano,

And the preacher looming large
Above me in his dark blue serge.

My shoes brought in a smell of clay
To mingle with the faint sachet

Of flowers sweating in their vases.
A stranger showed us to our places.

The stiff fan stirred in mother's hand.
Air moved, but only when she fanned.

I wondered how could all her grief
Be squeezed into one small handkerchief.

There was a buzzing on the sill.
It stopped, and everything was still.

We bowed our heads, we closed our eyes
To the mercy of the flies.

CHILDREN WALKING HOME FROM SCHOOL
THROUGH GOOD NEIGHBORHOOD

They are like figures held in some glass ball,
One of those in which, when shaken, snowstorms occur;
But this one is not yet shaken.
    And they go unaccompanied still,
Out along this walkway between two worlds,
This almost swaying bridge.
    October sunlight checkers their path;
It frets their cheeks and bare arms now with shadow
Almost too pure to signify itself.
And they progress slowly, somewhat lingeringly,
Independent, yet moving all together,
Like polyphonic voices that crisscross
In short-lived harmonies.

    Today, a few stragglers.
One, a girl, stands there with hands spaced out, so —
A gesture in a story. Someone's school notebook spills,
And they bend down to gather up the loose pages.
(Bright sweaters knotted at the waist; solemn expressions.)
Not that they would shrink or hold back from what may come,
For now they all at once run to meet it, a little swirl of colors,
Like the leaves already blazing and falling farther north.

DONALD JUSTICE

PSALM AND LAMENT

Hialeah, Florida
in memory of my mother (1897–1974)

The clocks are sorry, the clocks are very sad.
One stops, one goes on striking the wrong hours.

And the grass burns terribly in the sun,
The grass turns yellow secretly at the roots.

Now suddenly the yard chairs look empty, the sky looks empty,
The sky looks vast and empty.

Out on Red Road the traffic continues; everything continues.
Nor does memory sleep; it goes on.

Out spring the butterflies of recollection,
And I think that for the first time I understand

The beautiful ordinary light of this patio
And even perhaps the dark rich earth of a heart.

(The bedclothes, they say, had been pulled down.
I will not describe it. I do not want to describe it.

No, but the sheets were drenched and twisted.
They were the very handkerchiefs of grief.)

Let summer come now with its schoolboy trumpets and fountains.
But the years are gone, the years are finally over.

And there is only
This long desolation of flower-bordered sidewalks

That runs to the corner, turns, and goes on,
That disappears and goes on

Into the black oblivion of a neighborhood and a world
Without billboards or yesterdays.

Sometimes a sad moon comes and waters the roof tiles.
But the years are gone. There are no more years.

DONALD JUSTICE

ABSENCES

It's snowing this afternoon and there are no flowers.
There is only this sound of falling, quiet and remote,
Like the memory of scales descending the white keys
Of a childhood piano — outside the window, palms!
And the heavy head of the cereus, inclining,
Soon to let down its white or yellow-white.

Now, only these poor snow-flowers in a heap,
Like the memory of a white dress cast down . . .
So much has fallen.
               And I, who have listened for a step
All afternoon, hear it now, but already falling away,
Already in memory. And the terrible scales descending
On the silent piano; the snow; and the absent flowers abounding.

MEN AT FORTY

    Men at forty
    Learn to close softly
    The doors to rooms they will not be
    Coming back to.

    At rest on a stair landing,
    They feel it
    Moving beneath them now like the deck of a ship,
    Though the swell is gentle.

    And deep in mirrors
    They rediscover
    The face of the boy as he practices tying
    His father's tie there in secret

    And the face of that father,
    Still warm with the mystery of lather.
    They are more fathers than sons themselves now.
    Something is filling them, something

That is like the twilight sound
Of the crickets, immense,
Filling the woods at the foot of the slope
Behind their mortgaged houses.

VARIATIONS ON A TEXT BY VALLEJO

Me moriré en Paris con aguacero . . .

I will die in Miami in the sun,
On a day when the sun is very bright,
A day like the days I remember, a day like other days,
A day that nobody knows or remembers yet,
And the sun will be bright then on the dark glasses of strangers
And in the eyes of a few friends from my childhood
And of the surviving cousins by the graveside,
While the diggers, standing apart, in the still shade of the palms,
Rest on their shovels, and smoke,
Speaking in Spanish softly, out of respect.

I think it will be on a Sunday like today,
Except that the sun will be out, the rain will have stopped,
And the wind that today made all the little shrubs kneel down;
And I think it will be a Sunday because today,
When I took out this paper and began to write,
Never before had anything looked so blank,
My life, these words, the paper, the gray Sunday;
And my dog, quivering under a table because of the storm,
Looked up at me, not understanding,
And my son read on without speaking, and my wife slept.

Donald Justice is dead. One Sunday the sun came out,
It shone on the bay, it shone on the white buildings,
The cars moved down the street slowly as always, so many,
Some with their headlights on in spite of the sun,
And after a while the diggers with their shovels
Walked back to the graveside through the sunlight,
And one of them put his blade into the earth
To lift a few clods of dirt, the black marl of Miami,
And scattered the dirt, and spat,
Turning away abruptly, out of respect.

IN MEMORY OF THE UNKNOWN POET,
ROBERT BOARDMAN VAUGHN

*But the essential advantage for a poet is not, to have a beautiful world with
which to deal: it is to be able to see beneath both beauty and ugliness; to see
the boredom, and the horror, and the glory.*

— T. S. Eliot

It was his story. It would always be his story.
It followed him; it overtook him finally —
The boredom, and the horror, and the glory.

Probably at the end he was not yet sorry,
Even as the boots were brutalizing him in the alley.
It was his story It would always be his story.

Blown on a blue horn, full of sound and fury,
But signifying, O signifying magnificently
The boredom, and the horror, and the glory.

I picture the snow as falling without hurry
To cover the cobbles and the toppled ashcans completely.
It was his story. It would always be his story.

Lately he had wandered between St. Mark's Place and the Bowery,
Already half a spirit, mumbling and muttering sadly.
O the boredom, and the horror, and the glory.

All done now. But I remember the fiery
Hypnotic eye and the raised voice blazing with poetry.
It was his story and would always be his story —
The boredom, and the horror, and the glory.

Maud Kinnell

Galway Kinnell

BLACKBERRY EATING

I love to go out in late September
among the fat, overripe, icy, black blackberries
to eat blackberries for breakfast,
the stalks very prickly, a penalty
they earn for knowing the black art
of blackberry-making; and as I stand among them
lifting the stalks to my mouth, the ripest berries
fall almost unbidden to my tongue,
as words sometimes do, certain peculiar words
like *strengths* or *squinched*,
many-lettered, one-syllabled lumps,
which I squeeze, squinch open, and splurge well
in the silent, startled, icy, black language
of blackberry-eating in late September.

TELEPHONING IN MEXICAN SUNLIGHT

Talking with my beloved in New York
I stood at the outdoor public telephone
in Mexican sunlight, in my purple shirt.
Someone had called it a man/woman
shirt. The phrase irked me. But then
I remembered that Rainer Maria
Rilke, who until he was seven wore
dresses and had long yellow hair,
wrote that the girl he almost was
"made her bed in my ear" and "slept me the world."
I thought, OK this shirt will clothe the other in me.
As we fell into long-distance love talk
a squeaky chittering started up all around,
and every few seconds came a sudden loud
buzzing. I half expected to find
the insulation on the telephone line
laid open under the pressure of our talk
leaking low-frequency noises.

But a few yards away a dozen hummingbirds,
gorgets going drab or blazing
according as the sun struck them,
stood on their tail rudders in a circle
around my head, transfixed
by the flower-likeness of the shirt.
And perhaps also by a flush rising into my face,
for a word — one with a thick sound,
as if a porous vowel had sat soaking up
saliva while waiting to get spoken,
possibly the name of some flower
that hummingbirds love, perhaps
"honeysuckle" or "hollyhock"
or "phlox" — just then shocked me
with its suddenness, and this time
apparently did burst the insulation,
letting the word sound in the open
where all could hear, for these tiny, irascible,
nectar-addicted puritans jumped back
all at once, fast, as if the air gasped.

THE BEAR

1

In late winter
I sometimes glimpse bits of steam
coming up from
some fault in the old snow
and bend close and see it is lung-colored
and put down my nose
and know
the chilly, enduring odor of bear.

2

I take a wolf's rib and whittle
it sharp at both ends
and coil it up

and freeze it in blubber and place it out
on the fairway of the bears.

And when it has vanished
I move out on the bear tracks,
roaming in circles
until I come to the first, tentative, dark
splash on the earth.

And I set out
running, following the splashes
of blood wandering over the world.
At the cut, gashed resting places
I stop and rest,
at the crawl-marks
where he lay out on his belly
to overpass some stretch of bauchy ice
I lie out
dragging myself forward with bear-knives in my fists.

3

On the third day I begin to starve,
at nightfall I bend down as I knew I would
at a turd sopped in blood,
and hesitate, and pick it up,
and thrust it in my mouth, and gnash it down,
and rise
and go on running.

4

On the seventh day,
living by now on bear blood alone,
I can see his upturned carcass far out ahead, a scraggled,
steamy hulk,
the heavy fur riffling in the wind.

I come up to him
and stare at the narrow-spaced, petty eyes,
the dismayed
face laid back on the shoulder, the nostrils

flared, catching
perhaps the first taint of me as he
died.

I hack
a ravine in his thigh, and eat and drink,
and tear him down his whole length
and open him and climb in
and close him up after me, against the wind,
and sleep.

5

And dream
of lumbering flatfooted
over the tundra,
stabbed twice from within,
splattering a trail behind me,
splattering it out no matter which way I lurch,
no matter which parabola of bear-transcendence,
which dance of solitude I attempt,
which gravity-clutched leap,
which trudge, which groan.

6

Until one day I totter and fall —
fall on this
stomach that has tried so hard to keep up,
to digest the blood as it leaked in,
to break up
and digest the bone itself: and now the breeze
blows over me, blows off
the hideous belches of ill-digested bear blood
and rotted stomach
and the ordinary, wretched odor of bear,

blows across
my sore, lolled tongue a song
or screech, until I think I must rise up
and dance. And I lie still.

7

I awaken I think. Marshlights
reappear, geese
come trailing again up the flyway.
In her ravine under old snow the dam-bear
lies, licking
lumps of smeared fur
and drizzly eyes into shapes
with her tongue. And one
hairy-soled trudge stuck out before me,
the next groaned out,
the next,
the next,
the rest of my days I spend
wandering: wondering
what, anyway,
was that sticky infusion, that rank flavor of blood, that poetry, by which
    I lived?

THE FUNDAMENTAL PROJECT OF TECHNOLOGY

"A flash! A white flash sparkled!"
            — Tatsuichiro Akizuki, *Concentric Circles of Death*

Under glass: glass dishes which changed
in color; pieces of transformed beer bottles;
a household iron; bundles of wire become solid
lumps of iron; a pair of pliers; a ring of skull-
bone fused to the inside of a helmet; a pair of eyeglasses
taken off the eyes of an eyewitness, without glass,
which vanished, when a white flash sparkled.

An old man, possibly a soldier back then,
now reduced down to one who soon will die,
sucks at the cigarette dangling from his lip, peers
at the uniform, scorched, of some tiniest schoolboy,
sighs out bluish mists of his own ashes over
a pressed tin lunch box well crushed back then when
the word *future* first learned, in a white flash, to jerk tears.

On the bridge outside, in navy black, a group
of schoolchildren line up, hold it, grin at a flash-pop,
scatter like pigeons across grass, see a stranger, cry
hello! hello! hello! and soon *goodbye! goodbye!*
having pecked up the greetings that fell half unspoken
and the going-sayings that those who went the day
it happened a white flash sparkled did not get to say.

If all a city's faces were to shrink back all at once
from their skulls, would a new sound come into existence,
audible above moans eaves extract from wind that smoothes
the grass on graves, or raspings heart's-blood greases still,
or wails infants trill born already skillful at the grandpa's rattle,
or infra-screams bitter-knowledge's speechlessness
memorized, at that white flash, inside closed-forever mouths?

To de-animalize human mentality, to purge it of obsolete
evolutionary characteristics, in particular of death,
which foreknowledge terrorizes the contents of skulls with,
is the fundamental project of technology; however,
pseudologica fantastica's mechanisms require:
to establish deathlessness it is necessary to eliminate
those who die; a task attempted, when a white flash sparkled.

Unlike the trees of home, which continually evaporate
along the skyline, the trees here have been enticed down
toward world-eternity. No one knows which gods they enshrine.
Does it matter? Awareness of ignorance is as devout
as knowledge of knowledge. Or more so. Even though not knowing,
sometimes we weep, from surplus of gratitude, even though
    knowing,
twice already on earth sparkled a flash, a white flash.

The children go away. By nature they do. And by memory,
in scorched uniforms, holding tiny crushed lunch tins.
All the ecstasy-groans of each night call them back, satori
their ghostliness back into the ashes, in the momentary shrines,
the thankfulness of arms, from which they will go
again and again, until the day flashes and no one lives
to look back and say, a flash, a white flash sparkled.

FLOWER OF FIVE BLOSSOMS

Flower of five blossoms
I have brought you with me here
because you might not still be blossoming when I go back,
and because you might not blossom again.
I watched each of your buds swell up,
like water collected on a child's lid, about to plop,
or the catch in a throat that turns into a sob,
or in a tenor's throat, on some nights into a hundred sobs.
But as the buds
became these blossoms,
I am trying to learn: time suffered
is not necessarily time destroyed.
Outside, snow falls down in big pieces, like petals,
while in here, fire blossoms
out of wood and goes up in flames,
which are not *things dying* but just the *dying*.
Above them on the mantelpiece,
how calm your blossoms appear, austere and orderly, like the faces of
        singers,
but singing in silence, like the child
half-hidden by the pew, who dares only to think the hymns.
Phalaenopsis, sensual Orchidaceae,
sometimes, out of the corner of the eye, your blossoms perched on their
        twigs seem true to your name, "moth-like,"
and there, in the salep risen out of the pot of chipped bark, is the origin
        of your family name, ὄρχις, "testicle."
A few minutes ago, I put on a sonata by Brahms
("Brahms," nearly the sound dwelling on you forms in my mouth)
and I was standing at the mantelpiece
just as the slowest passage began, that moment
when the bow rests nearly immobile on the strings
— as mouths might, on mouths, in stillest kissing,
when a lip could be lying against a tooth in the other mouth, one can't
        say —
the bow's tremblings at what is about to happen
all that shakes any sound out of the strings at all,
and I turned and saw
what everyone else maybe sees at once:
that in each blossom
the calyx's middle petal curves up
and flows over the mons veneris and spreads across the belly,

and the petal on either side rises over the thigh, one edge following the
    ridge of the pelvic bone, which is prominent, for she lies on her
    back,
and the two petals that are set back hold the roundness of her buttocks,
and at the center, in the little crown,
the clitoris leans, above
the vestibule opening into the center of being;
and I wanted to lean close,
without sound, with my lips
touching lightly one of your blossoms,
and find there, like a kiss that has a soft lick in it, like "blossoms,"
the name of this place and speak it.
That's what two keep trying to do,
over and over, at night,
singing,
sometimes together, sometimes alone —
but in a little while they forget, and think they haven't found it,
and what is mute and wet waits again to be sung.
As the sonata ends,
your blossoms fall more profoundly still
— their lavender streaks suddenly empty, like staff-lines before any notes
    have been entered —
have a portion of death in them,
and watch,
intent, unblinking,
like the white, hooded faces of cobras
risen up to mesmerize, or to fling themselves forward into the deadly
    kiss;
though each wears the headdress of Mary.
Or am I myself the spellbinder and the killer?
Alone here, I often find myself thinking of women —
and now your blossoms could stand for five of them —
any five, if I were to try to name them —
one could be she to whom I was married for many years,
or she who merely exchanged a few words with me, across a table, under
    the noise of the conversation of the others,
or that pale, laughing beauty I hugged at the dancing lessons, when we
    were fifteen,
and another could be the woman whose strict intelligence I revere,
    whom I kiss on the forehead, a quarter inch away from the brain, the
    way Plato kissed,
and then the fifth blossom would be my mother, risen up at my bedside,
    wanting to please, but having, the next day or another, to crush —
strange,

for I began by speaking of sexual resemblance,
but not strange, for it was as a sexual creature she seized me into exis-
    tence,
it was through her vagina, trespassed by a man one way, transpierced by
    three babies the other,
I was dragged out alive, into the dead
of winter — a day
perhaps like this day, sixty years later, when out there earth
draws down on top of herself yet another of her freezing sleeping clothes,
but underneath is awakening . . .
besoming . . . blowsining . . . blissamous . . .
and in here, at the mantelpiece,
bending close to you, praying to you almost, standing almost in flames,
I wonder
what can come of these minutes,
each a hard inner tumbling, as when a key nearly won't turn,
or the note of a piano, clattered or stroked, ringing.
Everyone knows
everything sings and dies.
But it could be, too, everything dies and sings,
and a life is the interlude
when, still humming, we can look up, gawk about, imagine whatever, say
    it,
topple back into singing.
Oh first our voice be done, and then, before and afterwards and all
    around it, that singing.

Carolyn Kizer

THRALL

The room is sparsely furnished:
A chair, a table and a father.

He sits in the chair by the window.
There are books on the table.
The time is always just past lunch.

You tiptoe past as he eats his apple
And reads. He looks up, angry.
He has heard your asthmatic breathing.

He will read for years without looking up
Until your childhood is over:

Smells, untidiness and boring questions;
Blood, from the first skinned knees
To the first stained thighs;
The foolish tears of adolescent love.

One day he looks up, pleased
At the finished product.
Now he is ready to love you!

So he coaxes you in the voice reserved
For reading Keats. You agree to everything.

Drilled in silence and duty,
You will give him no cause for reproach.
He will boast of you to strangers.

When the afternoon is older
Shadows in a smaller room
Fall on the bed, the books, the father.

You read aloud to him
"La Belle Dame sans Merci."

271

You feed him his medicine.
You tell him you love him.

You wait for his eyes to close at last
So you may write this poem.

THE INTRUDER

My mother — preferring the strange to the tame:
Dove-note, bone marrow, deer dung,
Frog's belly distended with finny young,
Leaf-mould wilderness, hare-bell, toadstool,
Odd, small snakes roving through the leaves,
Metallic beetles rambling over stones: all
Wild and natural! — flashed out her instinctive love, and quick, she
Picked up the fluttering, bleeding bat the cat laid at her feet,
And held the little horror to the mirror, where
He gazed on himself, and shrieked like an old screen door far off.

Depended from her pinched thumb, each wing
Came clattering down like a small black shutter.
Still tranquil, she began, "It's rather sweet. . . ."
The soft mouse body, the hard feral glint
In the caught eyes. Then we saw,
And recoiled: lice, pallid, yellow,
Nested within the wing-pits, cosily sucked and snoozed.
The thing dropped from her hands, and with its thud,
Swiftly, the cat, with a clean careful mouth
Closed on the soiled webs, growling, took them out to the back stoop.

But still, dark blood, a sticky puddle on the floor
Remained, of all my mother's tender, wounding passion
For a whole wild, lost, betrayed and secret life
Among its dens and burrows, its clean stones,
Whose denizens can turn upon the world
With spitting tongue, an odor, talon, claw,
To sting or soil benevolence, alien
As our clumsy traps, our random scatter of shot.
She swept to the kitchen. Turning on the tap,
She washed and washed the pity from her hands.

CAROLYN KIZER

A WIDOW IN WINTERTIME

Last night a baby gargled in the throes
Of a fatal spasm. My children are all grown
Past infant strangles; so, reassured, I knew
Some other baby perished in the snow.
But no. The cat was making love again.

Later, I went down and let her in.
She hung her tail, flagging from her sins.
Though she'd eaten, I forked out another dinner,
Being myself hungry all ways, and thin
From metaphysic famines she knows nothing of,

The feckless beast! Even so, resemblances
Were on my mind: female and feline, though
She preens herself from satisfaction, and does
Not mind lying even in snow. She is
Lofty and bedraggled, without need to choose.

As an ex-animal, I look fondly on
Her excesses and simplicities, and would not return
To them; taking no marks for what I have become,
Merely that my nine lives peal in my ears again
And again, ring in these austerities.

These arbitrary disciplines of mine,
Most of them trivial: like covering
The children on my way to bed, and trying
To live well enough alone, and not to dream
Of grappling in the snow, claws plunged in fur,

Or waken in a caterwaul of dying.

from PRO FEMINA

ONE

From Sappho to myself, consider the fate of women.
How unwomanly to discuss it! Like a noose or an albatross necktie

The clinical sobriquet hangs us: cod-piece coveters.
Never mind these epithets; I myself have collected some honeys.
Juvenal set us apart in denouncing our vices
Which had grown, in part, from having been set apart:
Women abused their spouses, cuckolded them, even plotted
To poison them. Sensing, behind the violence of his manner —
"Think I'm crazy or drunk?" — his emotional stake in us,
As we forgive Strindberg and Nietzsche, we forgive all those
Who cannot forget us. *We are* hyenas. Yes, we admit it.

While men have politely debated free will, we have howled for it,
Howl still, pacing the centuries, tragedy heroines.
Some who sat quietly in the corner with their embroidery
Were Defarges, stabbing the wool with the names of their ancient
Oppressors, who ruled by the divine right of the male —
I'm impatient of interruptions! I'm aware there were millions
Of mutes for every Saint Joan or sainted Jane Austen,
Who, vague-eyed and acquiescent, worshiped God as a man.
I'm not concerned with those cabbageheads, not truly feminine
But neutered by labor. I mean real women, like *you* and like *me*.

Freed in fact, not in custom, lifted from furrow and scullery,
Not obliged, now, to be the pot for the annual chicken,
Have we begun to arrive in time? With our well-known
Respect for life because it hurts so much to come out with it;
Disdainful of "sovereignty," "national honor" and other abstractions;
We can say, like the ancient Chinese to successive waves of invaders,
"Relax, and let us absorb you. You can learn temperance
In a more temperate climate." Give us just a few decades
Of grace, to encourage the fine art of acquiescence
And we might save the race. Meanwhile, observe our creative chaos,
Flux, efflorescence — whatever you care to call it!

SEMELE RECYCLED

After you left me forever
I was broken into pieces,
and all the pieces flung into the river.
Then the legs crawled ashore
and aimlessly wandered the dusty cow-track.
They became, for awhile, a simple roadside shrine:

A tiny table set up between the thighs
held a dusty candle, weed and fieldflower chains
placed reverently there by children and old women.
My knees were hung with tin triangular medals
to cure all forms of hysterical disease.

After I died forever in the river,
my torso floated, bloated in the stream,
catching on logs or stones among the eddies.
White water foamed around it, then dislodged it;
after a whirlwind trip it bumped ashore.
A grizzled old man who scavenged along the banks
had already rescued my arms and put them by,
knowing everything has its uses, sooner or later.

When he found my torso, he called it his canoe,
and, using my arms as paddles,
he rowed me up and down the scummy river.
When catfish nibbled my fingers he scooped them up,
and blessed his re-usable bait.
Clumsy but serviceable, that canoe!
The trail of blood that was its wake
attracted the carp and eels, and the river turtle,
easily landed, dazed by my tasty red.

A young lad found my head among the rushes
and placed it on a dry stone.
He carefully combed my hair with a bit of shell
and set small offering before it
which the birds and rats obligingly stole at night,
so it seemed I ate.
And the breeze wound through my mouth and empty sockets
so my lungs would sigh, and my dead tongue mutter.
Attached to my throat like a sacred necklace
was a circlet of small snails.
Soon the villagers came to consult my oracular head
with its waterweed crown.
Seers found occupation, interpreting sighs,
and their papyrus rolls accumulated.

Meanwhile, young boys retrieved my eyes
they used for marbles in a simple game
— till somebody's pretty sister snatched at them
and set them, for luck, in her bridal diadem.

CAROLYN KIZER

Poor girl! When her future groom caught sight of her,
all eyes, he crossed himself in horror,
and stumbled away in haste
through her dowered meadows.

When then of my heart and organs,
my sacred slit
which loved you best of all?
They were caught in a fisherman's net
and tossed at night into a pen for swine.
But they shone so by moonlight that the sows stampeded,
trampled each other in fear, to get away.
And the fisherman's wife, who had 13 living children
and was contemptuous of holy love,
raked the rest of me onto the compost heap.

Then in their various places and helpful functions,
the altar, oracle, offal, canoe and oars
learned the wild rumor of your return.
The altar leapt up, and ran to the canoe,
scattering candle grease and wilted grasses.
Arms sprang to their sockets, blind hands with nibbled nails
groped their way, aided by loud lamentation,
to the bed of the bride, snatched up those unlucky eyes
from her discarded veil and diadem,
and rammed them home. O what a bright day it was!
This empty body danced on the river bank.
Hollow, it called and searched among the fields
for those parts that steamed and simmered in the sun,
and never would have found them.

But then your great voice rang out under the skies
my name! — and all those private names
for the parts and places that had loved you best.
And they stirred in their nest of hay and dung.
The distraught old ladies chasing their lost altar,
and the seers pursuing my skull, their lost employment,
and the tumbling boys, who wanted the magic marbles,
and the runaway groom, and the fisherman's 13 children
set up such a clamor, with their cries of "Miracle!"
that our two bodies met like a thunderclap
in mid-day; right at the corner of that wretched field
with its broken fenceposts and startled, skinny cattle.

We fell in a heap on the compost heap
and all our loving parts made love at once,
while the bystanders cheered and prayed and hid their eyes
and then went decently about their business.

And here it is, moonlight again; we've bathed in the river
and are sweet and wholesome once more.
We kneel side-by-side in the sand;
we worship each other in whispers.
But the inner parts remember fermenting hay,
the comfortable odor of dung, the animal incense,
and passion, its bloody labor,
its birth and rebirth and decay.

Bill Knott

POEM TO POETRY

Poetry,
you are an electric,
a magic, field — like the space
between a sleepwalker's outheld arms . . .

POEM

I am the only one who can say
"I have never been in anyone's dreams"
Your nakedness: the sound when I break an apple in half

SLEEP

We brush the other, invisible moon.
Its caves come out and carry us inside.

POEM

The wind blows a piece of paper to my feet.
I pick it up.
It is not a petition for my death.

BILL KNOTT

DEATH

Going to sleep, I cross my hands on my chest.
They will place my hands like this.
It will look as though I am flying into myself.

DEATH

Perfume opens its eyes of you.
I shall be the shepherd of your hair.
A dawn made of all the air I ever breathed.

GOODBYE

If you are still alive when you read this,
close your eyes. I am
under their lids, growing black.

HAIR POEM

Hair is heaven's water flowing eerily over us
Often a someone drifts off down their long hair and is lost

THE CLOSET

(. . . *after my Mother's death*)

Here not long enough after the hospital happened
I find her closet lying empty and stop my play
And go in and crane up at three blackwire hangers
Which quiver, airy, released. They appear to enjoy

Their new distance, cognizance born of the absence
Of anything else. The closet has been cleaned out
Full-flush as surgeries where the hangers could be
Amiable scalpels though they just as well would be

Themselves, in basements, glovelessly scraping uteri
But, here, pure, transfigured heavenward, they're
Birds, whose wingspans expand by excluding me. Their
Range is enlarged by loss. They'd leave buzzards

Measly as moths: and the hatshelf is even higher!
As the sky over a prairie, an undotted desert where
Nothing can swoop sudden, crumple in secret. I've fled
At ambush, tag, age: six, must I face this, can

I have my hide-and-seek hole back now please, the
Clothes, the thicket of shoes, where is it? Only
The hangers are at home here. Come heir to this
Rare element, fluent, their skeletal grace sings

Of the ease with which they let go the dress, slip,
Housecoat or blouse, so absolvingly. Free, they fly
Trim, triangular, augurs leapt ahead from some geometric
God who soars stripped (of flesh, it is said): catnip

To a brat placated by model airplane kits kids
My size lack motorskills for, I wind up all glue-scabbed,
Pawing goo-goo fingernails, glaze skins fun to peer in as
Frost-i-glass doors. . . But the closet has no windows.

Opaque or sheer: I must shut my eyes, shrink within
To peep into this wall. Soliciting sleep I'll dream
Mother spilled and cold, unpillowed, the operating-
Table cracked to goad delivery: its stirrups slack,

Its forceps closed: by it I'll see mobs of obstetrical
Personnel kneel proud, congratulatory, cooing
And oohing and hold the dead infant up to the dead
Woman's face as if for approval, the prompted

Beholding, tears, a zoomshot kiss. White-masked
Doctors and nurses patting each other on the back,

Which is how in the Old West a hangman, if
He was good, could gauge the heft of his intended . . .

Awake, the hangers are sharper, knife-'n'-slice, I jump
Gropelessly to catch them to twist them clear,
Mis-shape them whole, sail them across the small air
Space of the closet. I shall find room enough here

By excluding myself; by excluding myself, I'll grow.

POEM

Night, in whose death did your ennui take refuge?
The women all lay their kerchiefs on the water, and stepped back.

POEM

I am one man, worshipping silk knees,
picking myself from between my teeth,
I write these lines to cripple the dead,
to come up halt before the living:

I am one man, I run my hand over
your body, I touch the secret vibes
of the earth, I breathe your
heartbeat, Naomi, and always

I am one man alone at night. I fill my hands
with your dark hair
and offer it to the hollows of your face. I am one man, searching,
alone at night
like a beacon of ashes. . . .

BILL KNOTT

POEM (THE STARFISH ONE)

Each evening the sea casts starfish up on the beach, —
scattering, stranding them. They die at dawn, leaving
black hungers in the sun.
                              We slept there that summer, we
fucked in their radiant evolutions up to our body. Ringed
by starfish gasping for their element,
                                        we joined to create
ours. All night they inhaled the sweat from our thrusting
limbs, and lived.
                    Often she cried out: Your hand! — It was
a starfish, caressing her with my low fire.

THE SCULPTURE

(for Star Black)

We stood there nude embracing while the sculptor
Poked and packed some sort of glop between us
Molding fast all the voids the gaps that lay
Where we'd tried most to hold each other close

Under the merge of your breasts and my chest
There remained a space above the place our
Bellies met but soon that clay or plaster
Of paris or state of the art polymer

Filled every hollow which we long to fit
Then we were told to kiss hug hug harder
And then our heat would help to harden it

We stood there fused more ways than lovers know
Before the sculptor tore us away
Forced us to look at what had made us so whole

BILL KNOTT

POEM

Once I had to leave you so
I arranged for earth-tremors at night
So in your sleep you'd think I was stroking you

RIGOR VITUS

I walk
On human stilts.
To my right lower leg a man is locked rigid
To the left a woman, lifelessly strapped.

I have to heave them up,
Heft them out and but they're so heavy heavy as head
Seems all my strength
just take the begin step

All my past to broach a future. And on top of that
They're not even dead,
Those ole hypocrites.
They perk up when they want to, they please and pleasure themselves,

It's terrible. The one consolation:
When they make love,
To someone who's far or close enough away appears it appears then
Like I'm dancing.

ANOTHER FIRST KISS: TO —

A first kiss can occur anywhere, two pairs
Of lips might meet in a cannibal's oven,
Or on the shore of a nightclub at ebb;
Preferably the latter. Except, of course,

There are no more nightclubs, or cannibals,
As such: I mean the first kiss is passé,

BILL KNOTT

Archaic, obsolete. Pre-Global Village,
It rests in wrinkles, in blinking memories . . .

Ours came in bed, but after we'd undressed;
Preceded by hugs. And so the question
Of using the tongue — that old hesitation —
Didn't apply. We plunged right in. At

Our age you get naked and then you neck,
The opposite of how it was done young.
But the hunger is still there. The thirst
Is like in a bar, when they yell out Last Round.

Note:
Line 13. "Our age" — the lovers are 53 and 61.

POEM

The way the world is not
Astonished at you
It doesn't blink a leaf
Leads me to grop
That beauty is natural, unremarkable
And not to be spoken of
Except in the course of things
The course of singing and worksharing
The course of squeezes and neighbors
The course of you tying back your raving hair to go out
And the course of course of me
Astonished at you
The way the world is not

Mandy Sayer

Yusef Komunyakaa

AUDACITY OF THE LOWER GODS

I know salt marshes that move along like one big
trembling wing. I've noticed insects
shiny as gold in a blues singer's teeth
& more keenly calibrated than a railroad watch,
but at heart I'm another breed.

The audacity of the lower gods —
whatever we name we own.
Diversiloba, we say, unfolding poison oak.
Lovers go untouched as we lean from bay windows
with telescopes trained on a yellow sky.

I'd rather let the flowers
keep doing what they do best.
Unblessing each petal,
letting go a year's worth of white
death notes, busily unnaming themselves.

BLACKBERRIES

They left my hands like a printer's
Or thief's before a police blotter
& pulled me into early morning's
Terrestrial sweetness, so thick
The damp ground was consecrated
Where they fell among a garland of thorns.

Although I could smell old lime-covered
History, at ten I'd still hold out my hands
& berries fell into them. Eating from one
& filling a half gallon with the other,
I ate the mythology & dreamt
Of pies & cobbler, almost

Needful as forgiveness. My bird dog Spot
Eyed blue jays & thrashers. The mud frogs
In rich blackness, hid from daylight.
An hour later, beside City Limits Road
I balanced a gleaming can in each hand,
Limboed between worlds, repeating *one dollar.*

The big blue car made me sweat.
Wintertime crawled out of the windows.
When I leaned closer I saw the boy
& girl my age, in the wide back seat
Smirking, & it was then I remembered my fingers
Burning with thorns among berries too ripe to touch.

WORK

I won't look at her.
My body's been one
Solid motion from sunrise,
Leaning into the lawnmower's
Roar through pine needles
& crabgrass. Tiger-colored
Bumblebees nudge pale blossoms
Till they sway like silent bells
Calling. But I won't look.
Her husband's outside Oxford,
Mississippi, bidding on miles
Of timber. I wonder if he's buying
Faulkner's ghost, if he might run
Into Colonel Sartoris
Along some dusty road.
Their teenage daughter & son sped off
An hour ago in a red Corvette
For the tennis courts,
& the cook, Roberta,
Only works a half day
Saturdays. This antebellum house
Looms behind oak & pine
Like a secret, as quail
Flash through branches.
I won't look at her. Nude

On a hammock among elephant ears
& ferns, a pitcher of lemonade
Sweating like our skin.
Afternoon burns on the pool
Till everything's blue,
Till I hear Johnny Mathis
Beside her like a whisper.
I work all the quick hooks
Of light, the same unbroken
Rhythm my father taught me
Years ago: *Always give
A man a good day's labor.*
I won't look. The engine
Pulls me like a dare.
Scent of honeysuckle
Sings black sap through mystery,
Taboo, law, creed, what kills
A fire that is its own heart
Burning open the mouth.
But I won't look
At the insinuation of buds
Tipped with cinnabar.
I'm here, as if I never left,
Stopped in this garden,
Drawn to some Lotus-eater. Pollen
Explodes, but I only smell
Gasoline & oil on my hands,
& can't say why there's this bed
Of crushed narcissus
As if gods wrestled here.

IN THE BACKGROUND OF SILENCE

First, worms begin with a man's mind.
Then they eat away his left shoe
to answer his final question.
His heart turns into a gold thimble of ashes,
his bones remind bees of honeycomb,
he falls back into himself like dirt into a hole,
his soul fits into a matchbox
in the shirt pocket
of his brother's well-tailored uniform.

Not even a stray dog dares to stir in the plaza,
after the muzzle flash,
after black coffee & Benzedrine,
after the sign of the cross a hundred times,
after sorrow's skirt drops to the floor,
after the soldier pulls off his spit-shined boots
& crawls into bed with the prettiest woman in town.

TU DO STREET

Music divides the evening.
I close my eyes & can see
men drawing lines in the dust.
America pushes through the membrane
of mist & smoke, & I'm a small boy
again in Bogalusa. *White Only*
signs & Hank Snow. But tonight
I walk into a place where bar girls
fade like tropical birds. When
I order a beer, the mama-san
behind the counter acts as if she
can't understand, while her eyes
skirt each white face, as Hank Williams
calls from the psychedelic jukebox.
We have played Judas where
only machine-gun fire brings us
together. Down the street
black GIs hold to their turf also.
An off-limits sign pulls me
deeper into alleys, as I look
for a softness behind these voices
wounded by their beauty & war.
Back in the bush at Dak To
& Khe Sanh, we fought
the brothers of these women
we now run to hold in our arms.
There's more than a nation
inside us, as black & white
soldiers touch the same lovers
minutes apart, tasting
each other's breath,

without knowing these rooms
run into each other like tunnels
leading to the underworld.

THANKS

Thanks for the tree
between me & a sniper's bullet.
I don't know what made the grass
sway seconds before the Viet Cong
raised his soundless rifle.
Some voice always followed,
telling me which foot
to put down first.
Thanks for deflecting the ricochet
against that anarchy of dusk.
I was back in San Francisco
wrapped up in a woman's wild colors,
causing some dark bird's love call
to be shattered by daylight
when my hands reached up
& pulled a branch away
from my face. Thanks
for the vague white flower
that pointed to the gleaming metal
reflecting how it is to be broken
like mist over the grass,
as we played some deadly
game for blind gods.
What made me spot the monarch
writhing on a single thread
tied to a farmer's gate,
holding the day together
like an unfingered guitar string,
is beyond me. Maybe the hills
grew weary & leaned a little in the heat.
Again, thanks for the dud
hand grenade tossed at my feet
outside Chu Lai. I'm still
falling through its silence.
I don't know why the intrepid

sun touched the bayonet,
but I know that something
stood among those lost trees
& moved only when I moved.

BOYS IN DRESSES

We were The Hottentot Venus
Draped in our mothers' dresses,
Wearing rouge & lipstick,
Pillows tucked under floral
& print cloth, the first day of spring,
As we balanced on high heels.
Women sat in a circle talking
About men; the girls off
Somewhere else, in other houses.
We felt the last kisses
Our mothers would give us
On the mouth. Medusa
Wound around our necks
As we wore out the day's
Cantillations. They gazed at us
& looked into their own eyes
Before the water broke, remembering
How we firstborn boys loved
Them from within, cleaved
Like silver on the backs of mirrors.
Would we grow into merciful
Men, less lead in our gloves?
That afternoon lives in the republic
Of our bones, when we were girlish
Women in a hermetic council
Of milky coffee & teacakes.
Dragonflies nudged window screens.
When we stepped out
Wearing an ecstasy of hues,
Faceless wolf whistles
& catcalls heated the air.
Azaleas buzzed as we went
House to house. Soon we'd be
Responsible for the chambered

Rapture honeycombed in flesh
& would mourn something lost.
It was harder than running
Naked down a double line
Of boys in those patriarchal woods,
Belts singing against our skin.

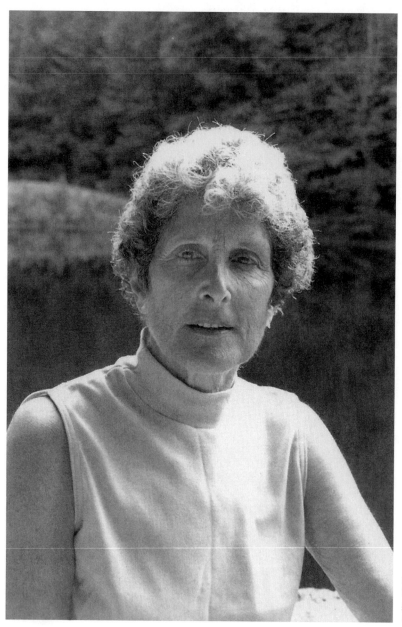

Maxine Kumin

MORNING SWIM

Into my empty head there come
a cotton beach, a dock wherefrom

I set out, oily and nude
through mist, in chilly solitude.

There was no line, no roof or floor
to tell the water from the air.

Night fog thick as terry cloth
closed me in its fuzzy growth.

I hung my bathrobe on two pegs.
I took the lake between my legs.

Invaded and invader, I
went overhand on that flat sky.

Fish twitched beneath me, quick and tame.
In their green zone they sang my name

and in the rhythm of the swim
I hummed a two-four-time slow hymn.

I hummed *Abide with Me*. The beat
rose in the fine thrash of my feet,

rose in the bubbles I put out
slantwise, trailing through my mouth.

My bones drank water; water fell
through all my doors. I was the well

that fed the lake that met my sea
in which I sang *Abide with Me*.

TO SWIM, TO BELIEVE

Centre College, Danville, Kentucky

The beautiful excess of Jesus on the waters
is with me now in the Boles Natatorium.
This bud of me exults, giving witness:

these flippers that rose up to be arms.
These strings drawn to be fingers.
Legs plumped to make my useful fork.

Each time I tear this seam to enter,
all that I carry is taken from me,
shucked in the dive.

Lovers, children, even words go under.
Matters of dogma spin off in the freestyle
earning that mid-pool spurt, like faith.

Where have I come from? Where am I going?
What do I translate, gliding back and forth
erasing my own stitch marks in this lane?

Christ on the lake was not thinking
where the next heel-toe went.
God did him a dangerous favor

whereas Peter, the thinker, sank.

The secret is in the relenting,
the partnership. I let my body work

accepting the dangerous favor
from this king-size pool of waters.
Together I am supplicant. I am bride.

HEAVEN AS ANUS

In the Defense Department there is a shop
where scientists sew the eyelids of rabbits open
lest they blink in the scorch of a nuclear drop

and elsewhere dolphins are being taught to defuse
bombs in the mock-up of a harbor and monkeys
learn to perform the simple tasks of draftees.

It is done with electric shocks. Some mice
who have failed their time tests in the maze
now go to the wire unbidden for their jolts.

Implanting electrodes yields rich results:
alley cats turn from predators into prey.
Show them a sparrow and they cower

while the whitewall labs fill up with the feces of fear
where calves whose hearts have been done away
with walk and bleat on plastic pumps.

And what is any of this to the godhead,
these squeals, whines, writhings, unexpected jumps,
whose children burn alive, booby-trap the dead,
lop ears and testicles, core and disembowel?

It all ends at the hole. No words may enter
the house of excrement. We will meet there
as the sphincter of the good Lord opens wide
and He takes us all inside.

THE EXCREMENT POEM

It is done by us all, as God disposes, from
the least cast of worm to what must have been
in the case of the brontosaur, say, spoor
of considerable heft, something awesome.

We eat, we evacuate, survivors that we are.
I think these things each morning with shovel
and rake, drawing the risen brown buns
toward me, fresh from the horse oven, as it were,

or culling the alfalfa-green ones, expelled
in a state of ooze, through the sawdust bed
to take a serviceable form, as putty does,
so as to lift out entire from the stall.

And wheeling to it, storming up the slope,
I think of the angle of repose the manure
pile assumes, how sparrows come to pick
the redelivered grain, how inky-cap

coprinus mushrooms spring up in a downpour.
I think of what drops from us and must then
be moved to make way for the next and next.
However much we stain the world, spatter

it with our leavings, make stenches, defile
the great formal oceans with what leaks down,
trundling off today's last barrowful,
I honor shit for saying: We go on.

THE GRACE OF GELDINGS IN RIPE PASTURES

Glutted, half asleep, browsing in
timothy grown so tall I see them
as through a pale-green stage scrim

they circle, nose to rump,
a trio of trained elephants.
It begins to rain, as promised.

Bit by bit they soak up drops
like laundry dampened to be ironed.
Runnels bedeck them. Their sides

drip like the ribs of very broad
umbrellas. And still they graze
and grazing, one by one let down

their immense, indolent penises
to drench the everlasting grass
with the rich nitrogen

that repeats them.

MAXINE KUMIN

WOODCHUCKS

Gassing the woodchucks didn't turn out right.
The knockout bomb from the Feed and Grain Exchange
was featured as merciful, quick at the bone
and the case we had against them was airtight,
both exits shoehorned shut with puddingstone,
but they had a sub-sub-basement out of range.

Next morning they turned up again, no worse
for the cyanide than we for our cigarettes
and state-store Scotch, all of us up to scratch.
They brought down the marigolds as a matter of course
and then took over the vegetable patch
nipping the broccoli shoots, beheading the carrots.

The food from our mouths, I said, righteously thrilling
to the feel of the .22, the bullets' neat noses.
I, a lapsed pacifist fallen from grace
puffed with Darwinian pieties for killing,
now drew a bead on the littlest woodchuck's face.
He died down in the everbearing roses.

Ten minutes later I dropped the mother. She
flipflopped in the air and fell, her needle teeth
still hooked in a leaf of early Swiss chard.
Another baby next. O one-two-three
the murderer inside me rose up hard,
the hawkeye killer came on stage forthwith.

There's one chuck left. Old wily fellow, he keeps
me cocked and ready day after day after day.
All night I hunt his humped-up form. I dream
I sight along the barrel in my sleep.
If only they'd all consented to die unseen
gassed underground the quiet Nazi way.

IN THE PEA PATCH

These as they clack in the wind
saying castanets, saying dance with me,

saying do me, dangle their intricate
nuggety scrota

and these with the light shining through
call up a woman in a gauzy dress
young, with tendrils of hair at her neck,
leaning in a summer doorway

and as the bloom of the lime-green pod
rubs away under the polishing thumb
in the interior
sweet for the taking, nine little fetuses
nod their cloned heads.

IN THE PARK

You have forty-nine days between
death and rebirth if you're a Buddhist.
Even the smallest soul could swim
the English Channel in that time
or climb, like a ten-month-old child,
every step of the Washington Monument
to travel across, up, down, over or through
— you won't know till you get there which to do.

He laid on me for a few seconds
said Roscoe Black, who lived to tell
about his skirmish with a grizzly bear
in Glacier Park. *He laid on me*
not doing anything. I could feel
his heart beating against my heart.
Never mind *lie* and *lay,* the whole world
confuses them. For Roscoe Black you might say
all forty-nine days flew by.

I was raised on the Old Testament.
In it God talks to Moses, Noah,
Samuel, and they answer.
People confer with angels. Certain
animals converse with humans.
It's a simple world, full of crossovers.

Heaven's an airy Somewhere, and God
has a nasty temper when provoked,
but if there's a Hell, little is made of it.
No longtailed Devil, no eternal fire,
and no choosing what to come back as.
When the grizzly bear appears, he lies/lays down
on atheist and zealot. In the pitch-dark
each of us waits for him in Glacier Park.

NURTURE

From a documentary on marsupials I learn
that a pillowcase makes a fine
substitute pouch for an orphaned kangaroo.

I am drawn to such dramas of animal rescue.
They are warm in the throat. I suffer, the critic proclaims,
from an overabundance of maternal genes.

Bring me your fallen fledgling, your bummer lamb,
lead the abused, the starvelings, into my barn.
Advise the hunted deer to leap into my corn.

And had there been a wild child —
filthy and fierce as a ferret, he is called
in one nineteenth-century account —

a wild child to love, it is safe to assume,
given my fireside inked with paw prints,
there would have been room.

Think of the language we two, same and not-same,
might have constructed from sign,
scratch, grimace, grunt, vowel:

Laughter our first noun, and our long verb, howl.

Stanley Kunitz

THE LAYERS

I have walked through many lives,
some of them my own,
and I am not who I was,
though some principle of being
abides, from which I struggle
not to stray.
When I look behind,
as I am compelled to look
before I can gather strength
to proceed on my journey,
I see the milestones dwindling
toward the horizon
and the slow fires trailing
from the abandoned camp-sites,
over which scavenger angels
wheel on heavy wings.
Oh, I have made myself a tribe
out of my true affections,
and my tribe is scattered!
How shall the heart be reconciled
to its feast of losses?
In a rising wind
the manic dust of my friends,
those who fell along the way,
bitterly stings my face.
Yet I turn, I turn,
exulting somewhat,
with my will intact to go
wherever I need to go,
and every stone on the road
precious to me.
In my darkest night,
when the moon was covered
and I roamed through wreckage,
a nimbus-clouded voice
directed me:
"Live in the layers,
not on the litter."

Though I lack the art
to decipher it,
no doubt the next chapter
in my book of transformations
is already written.
I am not done with my changes.

ROBIN REDBREAST

It was the dingiest bird
you ever saw, all the color
washed from him, as if
he had been standing in the rain,
friendless and stiff and cold,
since Eden went wrong.
In the house marked For Sale,
where nobody made a sound,
in the room where I lived
with an empty page, I had heard
the squawking of the jays
under the wild persimmons
tormenting him.
So I scooped him up
after they knocked him down,
in league with that ounce of heart
pounding in my palm,
that dumb beak gaping.
Poor thing! Poor foolish life!
without sense enough to stop
running in desperate circles,
needing my lucky help
to toss him back into his element.
But when I held him high,
fear clutched my hand,
for through the hole in his head,
cut whistle-clean . . .
through the old dried wound
between his eyes
where the hunter's brand
had tunneled out his wits . . .
I caught the cold flash of the blue
unappeasable sky.

STANLEY KUNITZ

THE WELLFLEET WHALE

1

You have your language too,
    an eerie medley of clicks
       and hoots and trills,
location-notes and love calls,
    whistles and grunts. Occasionally,
       it's like furniture being smashed,
or the creaking of a mossy door,
    sounds that all melt into a liquid
       song with endless variations,
as if to compensate
    for the vast loneliness of the sea.
       Sometimes a disembodied voice
breaks in as if from distant reefs,
    and it's as much as one can bear
       to listen to its long mournful cry,
a sorrow without name, both more
    and less than human. It drags
       across the ear like a record
running down.

2

No wind. No waves. No clouds.
    Only the whisper of the tide,
       as it withdrew, stroking the shore,
a lazy drift of gulls overhead,
    and tiny points of light
       bubbling in the channel.
It was the tag-end of summer.
    From the harbor's mouth
       you coasted into sight,
flashing news of your advent,
    the crescent of your dorsal fin
       clipping the diamonded surface.
We cheered at the sign of your greatness
    when the black barrel of your head
       erupted, ramming the water,
and you flowered for us
    in the jet of your spouting.

3

All afternoon you swam
    tirelessly round the bay,
        with such an easy motion,
the slightest downbeat of your tail,
    an almost imperceptible
        undulation of your flippers,
you seemed like something poured,
    not driven; you seemed
        to marry grace with power.
And when you bounded into air,
    slapping your flukes,
        we thrilled to look upon
pure energy incarnate
    as nobility of form.
        You seemed to ask of us
not sympathy, or love,
    or understanding,
        but awe and wonder.

That night we watched you
    swimming in the moon.
        Your back was molten silver.
We guessed your silent passage
    by the phosphorescence in your wake.
        At dawn we found you stranded on the rocks.

4

There came a boy and a man
    and yet other men running, and two
        schoolgirls in yellow halters
and a housewife bedecked
    with curlers, and whole families in beach
        buggies with assorted yelping dogs.
The tide was almost out.
    We could walk around you,
        as you heaved deeper into the shoal,
crushed by your own weight,
    collapsing into yourself,
        your flippers and your flukes

quivering, your blowhole
    spasmodically bubbling, roaring.
        In the pit of your gaping mouth
you bared your fringework of baleen,
    a thicket of horned bristles.
        When the Curator of Mammals
arrived from Boston
    to take samples of your blood
        you were already oozing from below.
Somebody had carved his initials
    in your flank. Hunters of souvenirs
        had peeled off strips of your skin,
a membrane thin as paper.
    You were blistered and cracked by the sun.
        The gulls had been pecking at you.
The sound you made was a hoarse and fitful bleating.

What drew us to the magnet of your dying?
    You made a bond between us,
        the keepers of the nightfall watch,
who gathered in a ring around you,
    boozing in the bonfire light.
        Toward dawn we shared with you
your hour of desolation,
    the huge lingering passion
        of your unearthly outcry,
as you swung your blind head
    toward us and laboriously opened
        a bloodshot, glistening eye,
in which we swam with terror and recognition.

5

Voyager, chief of the pelagic world,
    you brought with you the myth
        of another country, dimly remembered,
where flying reptiles
    lumbered over the steaming marshes
        and trumpeting thunder lizards
wallowed in the reeds.
    While empires rose and fell on land,
        your nation breasted the open main,

rocked in the consoling rhythm
    of the tides. Which ancestor first plunged
        head-down through zones of colored twilight
to scour the bottom of the dark?
    You ranged the North Atlantic track
        from Port-of-Spain to Baffin Bay,
edging between the ice-floes
    through the fat of summer,
        lob-tailing, breaching, sounding,
grazing in the pastures of the sea
    on krill-rich orange plankton
        crackling with life.
You prowled down the continental shelf,
    guided by the sun and stars
        and the taste of alluvial silt
on your way southward
    to the warm lagoons,
        the tropic of desire,
where the lovers lie belly to belly
    in the rub and nuzzle of their sporting;
        and you turned, like a god in exile,
out of your wide primeval element,
    delivered to the mercy of time.

    Master of the whale-roads,
let the white wings of the gulls
    spread out their cover.
        You have become like us,
disgraced and mortal.

THE ABDUCTION

    Some things I do not profess
    to understand, perhaps
    not wanting to, including
    whatever it was they did
    with you or you with them
    that timeless summer day
    when you stumbled out of the wood,
    distracted, with your white blouse torn
    and a bloodstain on your skirt.

STANLEY KUNITZ

"Do you believe?" you asked.
Between us, through the years,
from bits, from broken clues,
we pieced enough together
to make the story real:
how you encountered on the path
a pack of sleek, grey hounds,
trailed by a dumbshow retinue
in leather shrouds; and how
you were led, through leafy ways,
into the presence of a royal stag,
flaming in his chestnut coat,
who kneeled on a swale of moss
before you; and how you were borne
aloft in triumph through the green,
stretched on his rack of budding horn,
till suddenly you found yourself alone
in a trampled clearing.

That was a long time ago,
almost another age, but even now,
when I hold you in my arms,
I wonder where you are.
Sometimes I wake to hear
the engines of the night thrumming
outside the east bay window
on the lawn spreading to the rose garden.
You lie beside me in elegant repose,
a hint of transport hovering on your lips,
indifferent to the harsh green flares
that swivel through the room,
searchlights controlled by unseen hands.
Out there is childhood country,
bleached faces peering in
with coals for eyes.
Our lives are spinning out
from world to world;
the shapes of things
are shifting in the wind.
What do we know
beyond the rapture and the dread?

TOUCH ME

Summer is late, my heart.
Words plucked out of the air
some forty years ago
when I was wild with love
and torn almost in two
scatter like leaves this night
of whistling wind and rain.
It is my heart that's late,
it is my song that's flown.
Outdoors all afternoon
under a gunmetal sky
staking my garden down,
I kneeled to the crickets trilling
underfoot as if about
to burst from their crusty shells;
and like a child again
marveled to hear so clear
and brave a music pour
from such a small machine.
What makes the engine go?
Desire, desire, desire.
The longing for the dance
stirs in the buried life.
One season only,
                           and it's done.
So let the battered old willow
thrash against the windowpanes
and the house timbers creak.
Darling, do you remember
the man you married? Touch me,
remind me who I am.

THE LONG BOAT

When his boat snapped loose
from its moorings, under
the screaking of the gulls,
he tried at first to wave

to his dear ones on shore,
but in the rolling fog
they had already lost their faces.
Too tired even to choose
between jumping and calling,
somehow he felt absolved and free
of his burdens, those mottoes
stamped on his name-tag:
conscience, ambition, and all
that caring.
He was content to lie down
with the family ghosts
in the slop of his cradle,
buffeted by the storm,
endlessly drifting.
Peace! Peace!
To be rocked by the Infinite!
As if it didn't matter
which way was home;
as if he didn't know
he loved the earth so much
he wanted to stay forever.

Li-Young Lee

THE GIFT

To pull the metal splinter from my palm
my father recited a story in a low voice.
I watched his lovely face and not the blade.
Before the story ended, he'd removed
the iron sliver I thought I'd die from.

I can't remember the tale,
but hear his voice still, a well
of dark water, a prayer.
And I recall his hands,
two measures of tenderness
he laid against my face,
the flames of discipline
he raised above my head.

Had you entered that afternoon
you would have thought you saw a man
planting something in a boy's palm,
a silver tear, a tiny flame.
Had you followed that boy
you would have arrived here,
where I bend over my wife's right hand.

Look how I shave her thumbnail down
so carefully she feels no pain.
Watch as I lift the splinter out.
I was seven when my father
took my hand like this,
and I did not hold that shard
between my fingers and think,
Metal that will bury me,
christen it Little Assassin,
Ore Going Deep for My Heart.
And I did not lift up my wound and cry,
Death visited here!
I did what a child does
when he's given something to keep.
I kissed my father.

PERSIMMONS

In sixth grade Mrs. Walker
slapped the back of my head
and made me stand in the corner
for not knowing the difference
between *persimmon* and *precision.*
How to choose

persimmons. This is precision.
Ripe ones are soft and brown-spotted.
Sniff the bottoms. The sweet one
will be fragrant. How to eat:
put the knife away, lay down newspaper.
Peel the skin tenderly, not to tear the meat.
Chew the skin, suck it,
and swallow. Now, eat
the meat of the fruit,
so sweet,
all of it, to the heart.

Donna undresses, her stomach is white.
In the yard, dewy and shivering
with crickets, we lie naked,
face-up, face-down.
I teach her Chinese.
Crickets: *chiu chiu.* Dew: I've forgotten.
Naked: I've forgotten.
Ni, wo: you and me.
I part her legs,
remember to tell her
she is beautiful as the moon.

Other words
that got me into trouble were
fight and *fright, wren* and *yarn.*
Fight was what I did when I was frightened,
fright was what I felt when I was fighting.
Wrens are small, plain birds,
yarn is what one knits with.
Wrens are soft as yarn.
My mother made birds out of yarn.

I loved to watch her tie the stuff;
a bird, a rabbit, a wee man.

Mrs. Walker brought a persimmon to class
and cut it up
so everyone could taste
a *Chinese apple*. Knowing
it wasn't ripe or sweet, I didn't eat
but watched the other faces.

My mother said every persimmon has a sun
inside, something golden, glowing,
warm as my face.

Once, in the cellar, I found two wrapped in newspaper,
forgotten and not yet ripe.
I took them and set both on my bedroom windowsill,
where each morning a cardinal
sang, *The sun, the sun.*

Finally understanding
he was going blind,
my father sat up all one night
waiting for a song, a ghost.
I gave him the persimmons,
swelled, heavy as sadness,
and sweet as love.

This year, in the muddy lighting
of my parents' cellar, I rummage, looking
for something I lost.
My father sits on the tired, wooden stairs,
black cane between his knees,
hand over hand, gripping the handle.
He's so happy that I've come home.
I ask how his eyes are, a stupid question.
All gone, he answers.

Under some blankets, I find a box.
Inside the box I find three scrolls.
I sit beside him and untie
three paintings by my father:
Hibiscus leaf and a white flower.

Two cats preening.
Two persimmons, so full they want to drop from the cloth.

He raises both hands to touch the cloth,
asks, *Which is this?*

This is persimmons, Father.

Oh, the feel of the wolftail on the silk,
the strength, the tense
precision in the wrist.
I painted them hundreds of times
eyes closed. These I painted blind.
Some things never leave a person:
scent of the hair of one you love,
the texture of persimmons,
in your palm, the ripe weight.

EATING ALONE

I've pulled the last of the year's young onions.
The garden is bare now. The ground is cold,
brown and old. What is left of the day flames
in the maples at the corner of my
eye. I turn, a cardinal vanishes.
By the cellar door, I wash the onions,
then drink from the icy metal spigot.

Once, years back, I walked beside my father
among the windfall pears. I can't recall
our words. We may have strolled in silence. But
I still see him bend that way — left hand braced
on knee, creaky — to lift and hold to my
eye a rotten pear. In it, a hornet
spun crazily, glazed in slow, glistening juice.

It was my father I saw this morning
waving to me from the trees. I almost
called to him, until I came close enough
to see the shovel, leaning where I had
left it, in the flickering, deep green shade.

White rice steaming, almost done. Sweet green peas
fried in onions. Shrimp braised in sesame
oil and garlic. And my own loneliness.
What more could I, a young man, want.

EATING TOGETHER

In the steamer is the trout
seasoned with slivers of ginger,
two sprigs of green onion, and sesame oil.
We shall eat it with rice for lunch,
brothers, sister, my mother who will
taste the sweetest meat of the head,
holding it between her fingers
deftly, the way my father did
weeks ago. Then he lay down
to sleep like a snow-covered road
winding through pines older than him,
without any travelers, and lonely for no one.

MY INDIGO

It's late. I've come
to find the flower which blossoms
like a saint dying upside down.
The rose won't do, nor the iris.
I've come to find the moody one, the shy one,
downcast, grave, and isolated.
Now, blackness gathers in the grass,
and I am on my hands and knees.
What is its name?

Little sister, my indigo,
my secret, vaginal and sweet,
you unfurl yourself shamelessly
toward the ground. You burn. You live
a while in two worlds
at once.

THIS ROOM AND EVERYTHING IN IT

Lie still now
while I prepare for my future,
certain hard days ahead,
when I'll need what I know so clearly this moment.

I am making use
of the one thing I learned
of all the things my father tried to teach me:
the art of memory.

I am letting this room
and everything in it
stand for my ideas about love
and its difficulties.

I'll let your love-cries,
those spacious notes
of a moment ago,
stand for distance.

Your scent,
that scent
of spice and a wound,
I'll let stand for mystery.

Your sunken belly
is the daily cup
of milk I drank
as a boy before morning prayer.

The sun on the face
of the wall
is God, the face
I can't see, my soul,

and so on, each thing
standing for a separate idea,
and those ideas forming the constellation
of my greater idea.
And one day, when I need
to tell myself something intelligent
about love,

I'll close my eyes
and recall this room and everything in it:
My body is estrangement.
This desire, perfection.
Your closed eyes my extinction.
Now I've forgotten my
idea. The book
on the windowsill, riffled by wind . . .
the even-numbered pages are
the past, the odd-
numbered pages, the future.
The sun is
God, your body is milk . . .

useless, useless . . .
your cries are song, my body's not me . . .
no good . . . my idea
has evaporated . . . your hair is time, your thighs are song . . .
it had something to do
with death . . . it had something
to do with love.

YOU MUST SING

He sings in his father's arms, sings his father
to sleep, all the while seeing how on that face
grown suddenly strange, wasting to shadow,
time moves. Stern time. Sweet time. Because his father

asked, he sings; because they are wholly lost.
How else, in immaculate noon, will each find
each, who are so close now? So close and lost.
His voice stands at windows, runs everywhere.

Was death giant? O, how will he find his
father? They are so close. Was death a guest?
By which door did it come? All the day's doors
are closed. He must go out of those hours, that house,

the enfolding limbs, go burdened to learn:
you must sing to be found; when found, you must sing.

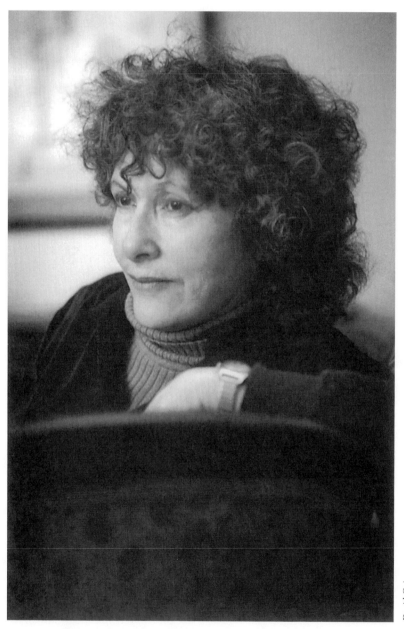

Denise Levertov

THE ACOLYTE

The large kitchen is almost dark.
Across the plain of even, diffused light,
copper pans on the wall and the window geranium
tend separate campfires.
Herbs dangle their Spanish moss from rafters.

At the table, floury hands
kneading dough, feet planted
steady on flagstones,
a woman ponders the loaves-to-be.
Yeast and flour, water and salt,
have met in the huge bowl.

It's not
the baked and cooled and cut
bread she's thinking of,
but the way
the dough rises and has a life of its own,

not the oven she's thinking of
but the way
the sour smell changes
to fragrance.

She wants to put
a silver rose or a bell of diamonds
into each loaf;
she wants

to bake a curse into one loaf,
into another, the words that break
evil spells and release
transformed heroes into their selves;
she wants to make
bread that is more than bread.

THE POEM UNWRITTEN

For weeks the poem of your body,
of my hands upon your body
    stroking, sweeping, in the rite
    of worship, going
    their way of wonder down
    from neck-pulse to breast-hair to level
    belly to cock —
for weeks that poem, that prayer,
unwritten.

    The poem unwritten, the act
left in the mind, undone. The years
a forest of giant stones, of fossil stumps,
blocking the altar.

1970

OUR BODIES

    Our bodies, still young under
    the engraved anxiety of our
    faces, and innocently

    more expressive than faces:
    nipples, navel, and pubic hair
    make anyway a

    sort of face: or taking
    the rounded shadows at
    breast, buttock, balls,

    the plump of my belly, the
    hollow of your
    groin, as a constellation,

    how it leans from earth to
    dawn in a gesture of
    play and

wise compassion —
nothing like this
comes to pass
in eyes or wistful
mouths.
                    I have

a line or groove I love
runs down
my body from breastbone
to waist. It speaks of
eagerness, of
distance.
                    Your long back,
the sand color and
how the bones show, say

what sky after sunset
almost white
over a deep woods to which

rooks are homing, says.

THE MUTES

Those groans men use
passing a woman on the street
or on the steps of the subway

to tell her she is a female
and their flesh knows it,

are they a sort of tune,
an ugly enough song, sung
by a bird with a slit tongue

but meant for music?

Or are they the muffled roaring
of deafmutes trapped in a building that is
slowly filling with smoke?

Perhaps both.

Such men most often
look as if groan were all they could do,
yet a woman, in spite of herself,

knows it's a tribute:
if she were lacking all grace
they'd pass her in silence:

so it's not only to say she's
a warm hole. It's a word

in grief-language, nothing to do with
primitive, not an ur-language;
language stricken, sickened, cast down

in decrepitude. She wants to
throw the tribute away, dis-
gusted, and can't,

it goes on buzzing in her ear,
it changes the pace of her walk,
the torn posters in echoing corridors

spell it out, it
quakes and gnashes as the train comes in.
Her pulse sullenly

had picked up speed,
but the cars slow down and
jar to a stop while her understanding

keeps on translating:
'Life after life after life goes by

without poetry,
without seemliness,
without love.'

DENISE LEVERTOV

WEDDING-RING

My wedding-ring lies in a basket
as if at the bottom of a well.
Nothing will come to fish it back up
and onto my finger again.
                       It lies
among keys to abandoned houses,
nails waiting to be needed and hammered
into some wall,
telephone numbers with no names attached,
idle paperclips.
                  It can't be given away
for fear of bringing ill-luck.
                  It can't be sold
for the marriage was good in its own
time, though that time is gone.
                  Could some artificer
beat into it bright stones, transform it
into a dazzling circlet no one could take
for solemn betrothal or to make promises
living will not let them keep? Change it
into a simple gift I could give in friendship?

WHERE IS THE ANGEL?

Where is the angel for me to wrestle?
No driving snow in the glass bubble,
but mild September.

Outside, the stark shadows
menace, and fling their huge arms about
unheard. I breathe

a tepid air, the blur
of asters, of brown fern and gold-dust
seems to murmur,

and that's what I hear, only that.
Such clear walls of curved glass:
I see the violent gesticulations

and feel — no, not nothing. But in this
gentle haze, nothing commensurate.
It is pleasant in here. History

mouths, volume turned off. A band of iron,
like they put round a split tree,
circles my heart. In here

it is pleasant, but when I open
my mouth to speak, I too
am soundless. Where is the angel

to wrestle with me and wound
not my thigh but my throat,
so curses and blessings flow storming out

and the glass shatters, and the iron sunders?

LIFE AT WAR

The disasters numb within us
caught in the chest, rolling
in the brain like pebbles. The feeling
resembles lumps of raw dough

weighing down a child's stomach on baking day.
Or Rilke said it, 'My heart . . .
Could I say of it, it overflows
with bitterness . . . but no, as though

its contents were simply balled into
formless lumps, thus
do I carry it about.'
The same war

continues.
We have breathed the grits of it in, all our lives,
our lungs are pocked with it,
the mucous membrane of our dreams
coated with it, the imagination
filmed over with the gray filth of it:

the knowledge that humankind,

delicate Man, whose flesh
responds to a caress, whose eyes
are flowers that perceive the stars,

whose music excels the music of birds,
whose laughter matches the laughter of dogs,
whose understanding manifests designs
fairer than the spider's most intricate web,

still turns without surprise, with mere regret
to the scheduled breaking open of breasts whose milk
runs out over the entrails of still-alive babies,
transformation of witnessing eyes to pulp-fragments,
implosion of skinned penises into carcass-gullays.

We are the humans, men who can make;
whose language imagines *mercy*,
lovingkindness; we have believed one another
mirrored forms of a God we felt as good —

who do these acts, who convince ourselves
it is necessary; these acts are done
to our own flesh; burned human flesh
is smelling in Viet Nam as I write.

Yes, this is the knowledge that jostles for space
in our bodies along with all we
go on knowing of joy, of love;

our nerve filaments twitch with its presence
day and night,
nothing we say has not the husky phlegm of it in the saying,
nothing we do has the quickness, the sureness,
the deep intelligence living at peace would have.

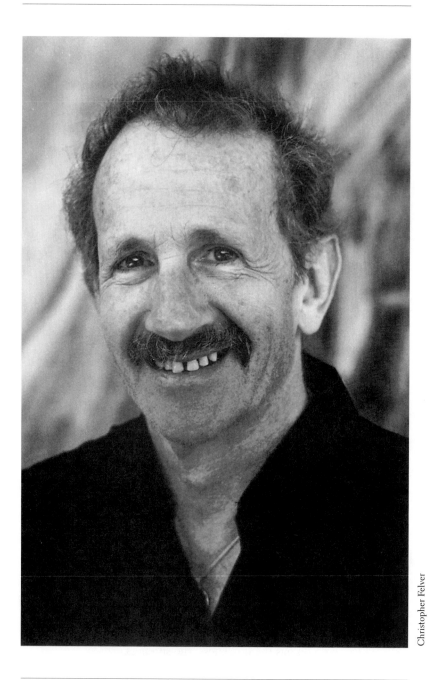

Philip Levine

THE SIMPLE TRUTH

I bought a dollar and a half's worth of small red potatoes,
took them home, boiled them in their jackets
and ate them for dinner with a little butter and salt.
Then I walked through the dried fields
on the edge of town. In middle June the light
hung on in the dark furrows at my feet,
and in the mountain oaks overhead the birds
were gathering for the night, the jays and mockers
squawking back and forth, the finches still darting
into the dusty light. The woman who sold me
the potatoes was from Poland; she was someone
out of my childhood in a pink spangled sweater and sunglasses
praising the perfection of all her fruits and vegetables
at the road-side stand and urging me to taste
even the pale, raw sweet corn trucked all the way,
she swore, from New Jersey. "Eat, eat," she said,
"Even if you don't I'll say you did."
                                    Some things
you know all your life. They are so simple and true
they must be said without elegance, meter and rhyme,
they must be laid on the table beside the salt shaker,
the glass of water, the absence of light gathering
in the shadows of picture frames, they must be
naked and alone, they must stand for themselves.
My friend Henri and I arrived at this together in 1965
before I went away, before he began to kill himself,
and the two of us to betray our love. Can you taste
what I'm saying? It is onions or potatoes, a pinch
of simple salt, the wealth of melting butter, it is obvious,
it stays in the back of your throat like a truth
you never uttered because the time was always wrong,
it stays there for the rest of your life, unspoken,
made of that dirt we call earth, the metal we call salt,
in a form we have no words for, and you live on it.

ON THE BIRTH OF GOOD & EVIL
DURING THE LONG WINTER OF '28

When the streetcar stalled on Joy Road,
the conductor finished his coffee, puffed
into his overcoat, and went to phone in.
The Hungarian punch press operator wakened
alone, 7000 miles from home, pulled down
his orange cap and set out. If he saw
the winter birds scuffling in the cinders,
if he felt this was the dawn of a new day,
he didn't let on. Where the sidewalks
were unshovelled, he stamped on, raising
his galoshes a little higher with each step.
I came as close as I dared and could hear
only the little gasps as the cold entered
the stained refectory of the breath.
I could see by the way the blue tears squeezed
from the dark of the eyes, by the way
his moustache first dampened and then froze,
that as he turned down Dexter Boulevard,
he considered the hosts of the dead,
and nearest among them, his mother-in-law,
who darkened his table for twenty-seven years
and bruised his wakings. He considered how
before she went off in the winter of '27
she had knitted this cap, knitted so slowly
that Christmas came and went, and now he could
forgive her at last for the twin wool lappets
that closed perfectly on a tiny metal snap
beneath the chin and for making all of it orange.

ANIMALS ARE PASSING FROM OUR LIVES

It's wonderful how I jog
on four honed-down ivory toes
my massive buttocks slipping
like oiled parts with each light step.

I'm to market. I can smell
the sour, grooved block, I can smell
the blade that opens the hole
and the pudgy white fingers

that shake out the intestines
like a hankie. In my dreams
the snouts drool on the marble,
suffering children, suffering flies,

suffering the consumers
who won't meet their steady eyes
for fear they could see. The boy
who drives me along believes

that any moment I'll fall
on my side and drum my toes
like a typewriter or squeal
and shit like a new housewife

discovering television,
or that I'll turn like a beast
cleverly to hook his teeth
with my teeth. No. Not this pig.

YOU CAN HAVE IT

My brother comes home from work
and climbs the stairs to our room.
I can hear the bed groan and his shoes drop
one by one. You can have it, he says.

The moonlight streams in the window
and his unshaven face is whitened
like the face of the moon. He will sleep
long after noon and waken to find me gone.

Thirty years will pass before I remember
that moment when suddenly I knew each man

has one brother who dies when he sleeps
and sleeps when he rises to face this life,

and that together they are only one man
sharing a heart that always labors, hands
yellowed and cracked, a mouth that gasps
for breath and asks, Am I gonna make it?

All night at the ice plant he had fed
the chute its silvery blocks, and then I
stacked cases of orange soda for the children
of Kentucky, one gray boxcar at a time

with always two more waiting. We were twenty
for such a short time and always in
the wrong clothes, crusted with dirt
and sweat. I think now we were never twenty.

In 1948 in the city of Detroit, founded
by de la Mothe Cadillac for the distant purposes
of Henry Ford, no one wakened or died,
no one walked the streets or stoked a furnace,

for there was no such year, and now
that year has fallen off all the old newspapers,
calendars, doctors' appointments, bonds,
wedding certificates, drivers licenses.

The city slept. The snow turned to ice.
The ice to standing pools or rivers
racing in the gutters. Then bright grass rose
between the thousands of cracked squares,

and that grass died. I give you back 1948.
I give you all the years from then
to the coming one. Give me back the moon
with its frail light falling across a face.

Give me back my young brother, hard
and furious, with wide shoulders and a curse
for God and burning eyes that look upon
all creation and say, You can have it.

PHILIP LEVINE

WHAT WORK IS

We stand in the rain in a long line
waiting at Ford Highland Park. For work.
You know what work is — if you're
old enough to read this you know what
work is, although you may not do it.
Forget you. This is about waiting,
shifting from one foot to another.
Feeling the light rain falling like mist
into your hair, blurring your vision
until you think you see your own brother
ahead of you, maybe ten places.
You rub your glasses with your fingers,
and of course it's someone else's brother,
narrower across the shoulders than
yours but with the same sad slouch, the grin
that does not hide the stubbornness,
the sad refusal to give in to
rain, to the hours wasted waiting,
to the knowledge that somewhere ahead
a man is waiting who will say, "No,
we're not hiring today," for any
reason he wants. You love your brother,
now suddenly you can hardly stand
the love flooding you for your brother,
who's not beside you or behind or
ahead because he's home trying to
sleep off a miserable night shift
at Cadillac so he can get up
before noon to study his German.
Works eight hours a night so he can sing
Wagner, the opera you hate most,
the worst music ever invented.
How long has it been since you told him
you loved him, held his wide shoulders,
opened your eyes wide and said those words,
and maybe kissed his cheek? You've never
done something so simple, so obvious,
not because you're too young or too dumb,
not because you're jealous or even mean
or incapable of crying in
the presence of another man, no,
just because you don't know what work is.

PHILIP LEVINE

I WAS BORN IN LUCERNE

Everyone says otherwise. They take me
to a flat on Pingree in Detroit
and say, Up there, the second floor. I say,
No, in a small Italian hotel overlooking
the lake. No doctor, no nurse. Just
a beautiful single woman who preferred
to remain that way and raise me to
the proper height, weight, and level of audacity.
They show me a slip of paper that says,
"Ford Hospital, Dr. Smear, male," and all
the rest of the clichés I could have lived by.
All that afternoon my mother held me close
to her side and watched the slow fog lift
and the water and sky blue all at once,
then darken to a deeper blue that turned
black at last, as I faced the longest night
of my life with tight fists and closed eyes
beside a woman of independence and courage
who sang the peasant songs of her region.
Later she recited the names of small mountain
villages like a litany that would protect
us against the rise of darkness and the fall
of hundreds of desperate men no longer
willing to pull in the fields or the factories
of Torino for a few lire and a Thank You.
She told me of those men, my uncles
and cousins, with names like water pouring
from stone jugs. Primo, Grunwald,
Carlo Finzi, Mario Antonio Todesco, Beniamino
Levi, my grandfather. They would die,
she said, as my father had died, because all
of these lands of ours were angered. No one
remembered the simple beauty of a clear dawn
and how snow fell covering the streets
littered with lies. Toward dawn she rose
and watched the light graying the still waters
and held me to the window and bobbed me up
and down until I awakened a moment to
see the golden sun splashed upon the eye
of the world. You wonder why I am
impossible, why I stand in the bus station

in Toledo baying No! No! and hurling
the luggage of strangers every which way,
why I refuse to climb ladders or descend into
cellars of coal dust and dead mice or eat
like a good boy or change my dirty clothes
no matter who complains. Look in my eyes!
They have stared into the burning eyes of earth,
molten metals, the first sun, a woman's face,
they have seen the snow covering it all
and a new day breaking over the mother sea.
I breathed the truth. I was born in Lucerne.

THEY FEED THEY LION

Out of burlap sacks, out of bearing butter,
Out of black bean and wet slate bread,
Out of the acids of rage, the candor of tar,
Out of creosote, gasoline, drive shafts, wooden dollies,
They Lion grow.
         Out of the gray hills
Of industrial barns, out of rain, out of bus ride,
West Virginia to Kiss My Ass, out of buried aunties,
Mothers hardening like pounded stumps, out of stumps,
Out of the bones' need to sharpen and the muscles' to stretch,
They Lion grow.
         Earth is eating trees, fence posts,
Gutted cars, earth is calling in her little ones,
"Come home, Come home!" From pig balls,
From the ferocity of pig driven to holiness,
From the furred ear and the full jowl come
The repose of the hung belly, from the purpose
They Lion grow.
         From the sweet glues of the trotters
Come the sweet kinks of the fist, from the full flower
Of the hams the thorax of caves,
From "Bow Down" come "Rise Up,"
Come they Lion from the reeds of shovels,
The grained arm that pulls the hands,
They Lion grow.
         From my five arms and all my hands,
From all my white sins forgiven, they feed,

From my car passing under the stars,
They Lion, from my children inherit,
From the oak turned to a wall, they Lion,
From they sack and they belly opened
And all that was hidden burning on the oil-stained earth
They feed they Lion and he comes.

ON MY OWN

Yes, I only got here on my own.
Nothing miraculous. An old woman
opened her door expecting the milk,
and there I was, seven years old, with
a bulging suitcase of wet cardboard
and my hair plastered down and stiff
in the cold. She didn't say, "Come in,"
she didn't say anything. Her luck
had always been bad, so she stood
to one side and let me pass, trailing
the unmistakable aroma of badger
which she mistook for my underwear,
and so she looked upward, not
to heaven but to the cracked ceiling
her husband had promised to mend,
and she sighed for the first time
in my life that sigh which would tell
me what was for dinner. I found my room
and spread my things on the sagging bed:
the bright ties and candy-striped shirts,
the knife to cut bread, the stuffed weasel
to guard the window, the silver spoon
to turn my tea, the pack of cigarettes
for the life ahead, and at last
the little collection of worn-out books
from which I would choose my only name —
Morgan the Pirate, Jack Dempsey, the Prince
of Wales. I chose Abraham Plain
and went off to school wearing a cap
that said "Ford" in the right script.
The teachers were soft-spoken women
smelling like washed babies and the students

PHILIP LEVINE

fierce as lost dogs, but they all hushed
in wonder when I named the 400 angels
of death, the planets sighted and unsighted,
the moment at which creation would turn
to burned feathers and blow every which way
in the winds of shock. I sat down
and the room grew quiet and warm. My eyes
asked me to close them. I did, and so
I discovered the beauty of sleep and that
to get ahead I need only say I was there,
and everything would open as the darkness
in my silent head opened onto seascapes
at the other end of the world, waves
breaking into mountains of froth, the sand
running back to become the salt savor
of the infinite. Mrs. Tarbox woke me
for lunch — a tiny container of milk
and chocolate cookies in the shape of Michigan.
Of course I went home at 3:30, with
the bells ringing behind me and four stars
in my notebook and drinking companions
on each arm. If you had been there
in your yellow harness and bright hat
directing traffic you would never
have noticed me — my clothes shabby
and my eyes bright — ; to you I'd have been
just an ordinary kid. Sure, now you
know, now it's obvious, what with the light
of the Lord streaming through the nine
windows of my soul and the music of rain
following in my wake and the ordinary air
on fire every blessed day I waken the world.

John Logan

THREE MOVES

Three moves in six months and I remain
the same.
Two homes made two friends.
The third leaves me with myself again.
(We hardly speak.)
Here I am with tame ducks
and my neighbors' boats,
only this electric heat
against the April damp.
I have a friend named Frank —
The only one who ever dares to call
and ask me, "How's your soul?"
I hadn't thought about it for a while,
and was ashamed to say I didn't know.
I have no priest for now.
Who
will forgive me then. Will you?
Tame birds and my neighbors' boats.
The ducks honk about the floats . . .
They walk dead drunk onto the land and grounds,
iridescent blue and black and green and brown.
They live on swill
our aged houseboats spill.
But still they are beautiful.
Look! The duck with its unlikely beak
has stopped to pick
and pull
at the potted daffodil.
Then again they sway home
to dream
bright gardens of fish in the early night.
Oh these ducks are all right.
They will survive.
But I am sorry I do not often see them climb.
Poor sons-a-bitching ducks.
You're all fucked up.
What do you do that for?
Why don't you hover near the sun anymore?

Afraid you'll melt?
These foolish ducks lack a sense of guilt,
and so all their multi-thousand-mile range
is too short for the hope of change.

Seattle, April 1965

SPRING OF THE THIEF

But if I look the ice is gone from the lake
and the altered air
no longer fills with the small
terrible bodies of the snow.
Only once these late winter weeks
the dying flakes
fell instead as manna or as wedding rice
blooming in the light
about the bronze Christ
and the Thieves. There these three
still hang, more than man-
sized and heavier than life
on a hill over the lake
where I walk
this Third Sunday of Lent.
I come from Mass
melancholy at its ancient story
of the unclean ghost
a man thought he'd lost.
It came back into his well-swept house
and at the final state that man
was worse than he began.
Yet again today
there is the faintest edge of green
to trees about St. Joseph's Lake.
Ah God if our confessions show contempt
because we let them free us of our guilt
to sin again
forgive us still . . . before the leaves . . .
before the leaves have formed
you can glimpse the Christ and Thieves
on top of the hill. One of them was saved.

That day the snow had seemed to drop like grace
upon the four of us,
or like the peace of intercourse,
suddenly I wanted to confess —
or simply talk.
I paid a visit to the mammoth Sacred Heart
Church, and found it shut.
Who locked him out or in?
The name of God is changing in our time.
What is his winter name?
Where was his winter home?
Oh I've kept my love to myself before.
Even those ducks weave down the shore
together, drunk with hope
for the April water. One spring festival
near here I stripped and strolled
through a rain filled field.
Spread eagled on the soaking earth
I let the rain
move its audible little hands
gently on my skin . . . let the dark rain
raise up my love.
But why? I was alone
and no one saw how ardent I grew.
And when I rolled naked in the snow one night
as St. Francis with his Brother Ass
or a hard bodied Finn
I was alone. Underneath
the howling January moon
I knelt and dug my fist
full of the cold winter sand
and rubbed and
hid my manhood under it.
Washed up at some ancient or half-heroic shore
I was ashamed that I was naked there.
Before Nausicaä and the saints. Before myself.
But who took off my coat? Who put it on?
Who drove me home?
Blessed be sin if it teaches men shame.
Yet because of it we cannot talk
and I am separated from myself.
So what is all this reveling in snow and rain?
Or in the summer sun when the heavy gold
body weeps with joy or grief or love?

When we speak of God, is it God we speak of?
Perhaps his winter home
is in that field where I rolled or ran . . .
this hill where once the snow
fell serene as rain.
Oh I have walked around the lake
when I was not alone —
sometimes with my wife have seen these swans
dip down their necks
graceful as a girl, showering white and wet!
I've seen their heads delicately turn.
Have gone sailing with my quiet, older son.
And once on a morning walk
a student who had just come back
in fall found a perfect hickory shell
among the bronze and red
leaves and purple flowers of the time
and put its white bread into my hand.
Ekelöf said there is a freshness
nothing can destroy in us —
not even we ourselves.
Perhaps that
Freshness is the changed name of God.
Where all the monsters also hide
I bear him in the ocean of my blood
and in the pulp of my enormous head.
He lives beneath the unkempt potter's grass
of my belly and chest.
I feel his terrible, aged heart
moving under mine . . . can see the shadows
of the gorgeous light
that plays at the edges of his giant eye . . .
or tell the faint press and hum
of his eternal pool of sperm.
Like sandalwood! *Like sandalwood*
the righteous man
perfumes the axe that falls on him.
The cords of elm, of cedar oak and pine
will pile again in fall.
The ribs and pockets of the barns will swell.
Winds and fires in the field rage
and again burn out each
of the ancient roots.
Again at last the late November snow

will fill those fields, change this hill,
throw these figures in relief
and raining on them
will transform
the bronze Christ's brow and cheek,
the white face and thigh of the thief.

March–April, 1962

MIDDLE-AGED MIDWESTERNER
AT WAIKIKI AGAIN

The surfers beautiful as men
                              can be
ride the warm
                blue green
                              swells
and the white sand is alive with girls.
Outriggers (double boats) ride the waves back in
as the native warriors did.
I tried to swim and tried to look,
but ended up just going back:
a huge, perfect black
man at the beach
somehow drove me away a block
to St. Augustine's Church.
The bodies were giv-
                        ing me a fit
and I have come to seek the momentary calm
we find sometimes in the musk of Christ
(when he was awake
                      and sweat-
ing blood
            as others slept,
or like a furious bouncer
hustling out the money changers).
The bodies of Mary and Christ
both still live, we're told. They're alive
and thus
must have dealt with the stress
of that long time

of turning on
to being young.
I speak of teens.
                    Fifteen and ten
years ago when I first confessed,
it was in this same church built then
as a gigantic shed
where the strange Hawaiian birds
(I forgot their names — no matter)
flew in and out of the high wood-
en rafters
like the whimsical winds of grace,
and grace gives back to sight
what beauty is —
                    as
that loveliness at the beach.
Now the church
                    has been rebuilt
in pointed stone across the street
from a much
                    higher new hotel
where at lunch
                    I almost spilled
and found I could not eat
the purple orchid in my drink.

POEM FOR MY BROTHER

Blue's my older brother's color. Mine is brown, you see.
So today I bought this ring
of gold and lapis lazuli flecked with a bright bronze.
His blue is the light hue of his eyes. Brown's the color
of our dead mother's long hair,
which fell so beautifully about her young shoulders
in the picture, and of my own eyes (I can't tell hers).
I loved my brother, but never quite knew what to think.
For example, he would beat
me up as soon as the folks
left the house, and I would cry big, loud feminine tears.
He was good at sports and played football, and so instead
I was in the marching band.

My brother stole rubbers from the store and smoked cigars
and pipes, which made me sick. But
once we swam together in
the Nishnabotna River
near home, naked, our blue overalls piled together
by the water, their copper
buttons like the bronze glints in my ring. I remember
once when I was very young
I looked deep into a pool
of blue water — we had no mirror — and I was so
amazed I looked over my shoulder, for I did not
imagine it was me, caught
in that cerulean sky.
Thinking it was someone other, I tell you I confused myself with my brother!
Nothing goes with gold, but I can see in this rich blue
stone the meeting of our clothes like the touching of hands
when he taught me to hold my fishing pole well and wound
up the reel for me. You know
blue's the last of the primary colors to be named.
Why, some primitive societies still have no word
for it except "dark." It's associated with black:
in the night my brother and I
would play at games that neither of us could understand.
But this is not a confession; it is a question.
We've moved apart and don't write,
and our children don't even know their own cousin!
So, I would have you know I
want this ring to *engage* us
in reconciliation.
Blue's the color of the heart.
I won't live forever. Is it too late now to be
a brother to my brother?
Let the golden snake bend round
again to touch itself and
all at once burst into azure!

Robert Lowell

MEMORIES OF WEST STREET AND LEPKE

Only teaching on Tuesdays, book-worming
in pajamas fresh from the washer each morning,
I hog a whole house on Boston's
"hardly passionate Marlborough Street,"
where even the man
scavenging filth in the back alley trash cans,
has two children, a beach wagon, a helpmate,
and is a "young Republican."
I have a nine months' daughter,
young enough to be my granddaughter.
Like the sun she rises in her flame-flamingo infants' wear.

These are the tranquillized *Fifties*,
and I am forty. Ought I to regret my seedtime?
I was a fire-breathing Catholic C.O.,
and made my manic statement,
telling off the state and president, and then
sat waiting sentence in the bull pen
beside a Negro boy with curlicues
of marijuana in his hair.

Given a year,
I walked on the roof of the West Street Jail, a short
enclosure like my school soccer court,
and saw the Hudson River once a day
through sooty clothesline entanglements
and bleaching khaki tenements.
Strolling, I yammered metaphysics with Abramowitz,
a jaundice-yellow ("it's really tan")
and fly-weight pacifist,
so vegetarian,
he wore rope shoes and preferred fallen fruit.
He tried to convert Bioff and Brown,
the Hollywood pimps, to his diet.
Hairy, muscular, suburban,
wearing chocolate double-breasted suits,
they blew their tops and beat him black and blue.

347

I was so out of things, I'd never heard
of the Jehovah's Witnesses.
"Are you a C.O.?" I asked a fellow jailbird.
"No," he answered, "I'm a J.W."
He taught me the "hospital tuck,"
and pointed out the T-shirted back
of *Murder Incorporated's* Czar Lepke,
there piling towels on a rack,
or dawdling off to his little segregated cell full
of things forbidden the common man:
a portable radio, a dresser, two toy American
flags tied together with a ribbon of Easter palm.
Flabby, bald, lobotomized,
he drifted in a sheepish calm,
where no agonizing reappraisal
jarred his concentration on the electric chair —
hanging like an oasis in his air
of lost connections. . . .

"TO SPEAK OF WOE THAT IS IN MARRIAGE"

*It is the future generation that presses into being by means of these
exuberant feelings and supersensible soap bubbles of ours.*

— Schopenhauer

"The hot night makes us keep our bedroom windows open.
Our magnolia blossoms. Life begins to happen.
My hopped up husband drops his home disputes,
and hits the streets to cruise for prostitutes,
free-lancing out along the razor's edge.
This screwball might kill his wife, then take the pledge.
Oh the monotonous meanness of his lust. . . .
It's the injustice . . . he is so unjust —
whiskey-blind, swaggering home at five.
My only thought is how to keep alive.
What makes him tick? Each night now I tie
ten dollars and his car key to my thigh. . . .
Gored by the climacteric of his want,
he stalls above me like an elephant."

ROBERT LOWELL

SKUNK HOUR

[for Elizabeth Bishop]

Nautilus Island's hermit
heiress still lives through winter in her Spartan cottage;
her sheep still graze above the sea.
Her son's a bishop. Her farmer
is first selectman in our village;
she's in her dotage.

Thirsting for
the hierarchic privacy
of Queen Victoria's century,
she buys up all
the eyesores facing her shore,
and lets them fall.

The season's ill —
we've lost our summer millionaire,
who seemed to leap from an L. L. Bean
catalogue. His nine-knot yawl
was auctioned off to lobstermen.
A red fox stain covers Blue Hill.

And now our fairy
decorator brightens his shop for fall;
his fishnet's filled with orange cork,
orange, his cobbler's bench and awl;
there is no money in his work,
he'd rather marry.

One dark night,
my Tudor Ford climbed the hill's skull;
I watched for love-cars. Lights turned down,
they lay together, hull to hull,
where the graveyard shelves on the town. . . .
My mind's not right.

A car radio bleats,
"Love, O careless Love. . . ." I hear
my ill-spirit sob in each blood cell,
as if my hand were at its throat. . . .

I myself am hell;
nobody's here —

only skunks, that search
in the moonlight for a bite to eat.
They march on their soles up Main Street:
white stripes, moonstruck eyes' red fire
under the chalk-dry and spar spire
of the Trinitarian Church.

I stand on top
of our back steps and breathe the rich air —
a mother skunk with her column of kittens swills the garbage pail.
She jabs her wedge-head in a cup
of sour cream, drops her ostrich tail,
and will not scare.

EYE AND TOOTH

My whole eye was sunset red,
the old cut cornea throbbed,
I saw things darkly,
as through an unwashed goldfish globe.

I lay all day on my bed.
I chain-smoked through the night,
learning to flinch
at the flash of the matchlight.

Outside, the summer rain,
a simmer of rot and renewal,
fell in pinpricks.
Even new life is fuel.

My eyes throb.
Nothing can dislodge
the house with my first tooth
noosed in a knot to the doorknob.

Nothing can dislodge
the triangular blotch

of rot on the red roof,
a cedar hedge, or the shade of a hedge.

No ease from the eye
of the sharp-shinned hawk in the birdbook there,
with reddish-brown buffalo hair
on its shanks, one ascetic talon

clasping the abstract imperial sky.
It says:
an eye for an eye,
a tooth for a tooth.

No ease for the boy at the keyhole,
his telescope,
when the women's white bodies flashed
in the bathroom. Young, my eyes began to fail.

Nothing! No oil
for the eye, nothing to pour
on those waters or flames.
I am tired. Everyone's tired of my turmoil.

FOR THE UNION DEAD

"Relinquunt Omnia Servare Rem Publicam."

The old South Boston Aquarium stands
in a Sahara of snow now. Its broken windows are boarded.
The bronze weathervane cod has lost half its scales.
The airy tanks are dry.

Once my nose crawled like a snail on the glass;
my hand tingled
to burst the bubbles
drifting from the noses of the cowed, compliant fish.

My hand draws back. I often sigh still
for the dark downward and vegetating kingdom
of the fish and reptile. One morning last March,
I pressed against the new barbed and galvanized

fence on the Boston Common. Behind their cage,
yellow dinosaur steamshovels were grunting
as they cropped up tons of mush and grass
to gouge their underworld garage.

Parking spaces luxuriate like civic
sandpiles in the heart of Boston.
A girdle of orange, Puritan-pumpkin colored girders
braces the tingling Statehouse,

shaking over the excavations, as it faces Colonel Shaw
and his bell-cheeked Negro infantry
on St. Gaudens' shaking Civil War relief,
propped by a plank splint against the garage's earthquake.

Two months after marching through Boston,
half the regiment was dead;
at the dedication,
William James could almost hear the bronze Negroes breathe.

Their monument sticks like a fishbone
in the city's throat.
Its Colonel is as lean
as a compass-needle.

He has an angry wrenlike vigilance,
a greyhound's gentle tautness;
he seems to wince at pleasure,
and suffocate for privacy.

He is out of bounds now. He rejoices in man's lovely,
peculiar power to choose life and die —
when he leads his black soldiers to death,
he cannot bend his back.

On a thousand small town New England greens,
the old white churches hold their air
of sparse, sincere rebellion; frayed flags
quilt the graveyards of the Grand Army of the Republic.

The stone statues of the abstract Union Soldier
grow slimmer and younger each year —
wasp-waisted, they doze over muskets
and muse through their sideburns . . .

ROBERT LOWELL

Shaw's father wanted no monument
except the ditch,
where his son's body was thrown
and lost with his "niggers."

The ditch is nearer.
There are no statues for the last war here;
on Boylston Street, a commercial photograph
shows Hiroshima boiling

over a Mosler Safe, the "Rock of Ages"
that survived the blast. Space is nearer.
When I crouch to my television set,
the drained faces of Negro school-children rise like balloons.

Colonel Shaw
is riding on his bubble,
he waits
for the blessèd break.

The Aquarium is gone. Everywhere,
giant finned cars nose forward like fish;
a savage servility
slides by on grease.

Star Black

William Matthews

MEN AT MY FATHER'S FUNERAL

The ones his age who shook my hand
on their way out sent fear along
my arm like heroin. These weren't
men mute about their feelings,
or what's a body language for?

And I, the glib one, who'd stood
with my back to my father's body
and praised the heart that attacked him?
I'd made my stab at elegy,
the flesh made word: the very spit

in my mouth was sour with ruth
and eloquence. What could be worse?
Silence, the anthem of my father's
new country. And thus this babble,
like a dial tone, from our bodies.

HOUSEWORK

How precise it seems, like a dollhouse,
and look: the tiniest socks ever knit
are crumpled on a chair in your bedroom.
And how still, like the air inside a church
or basketball. How you could have lived
your boyhood here is hard to know,

unless the blandishing lilacs
and slant rain stippling the lamplight
sustained you, and the friendship of dogs,
and the secrecy that flourishes in vacant lots.
For who would sleep, like a cat in a drawer,
in this house memory is always dusting,

unless it be you? I'd hear you on the stairs,
an avalanche of sneakers, and then the sift
of your absence and then I'd begin to rub
the house like a lantern until you came back
and grew up to be me, wondering how to sleep
in this lie of memory unless it be made clean.

IN MEMORY OF THE UTAH STARS

Each of them must have terrified
his parents by being so big, obsessive
and exact so young, already gone
and leaving, like a big tipper,
that huge changeling's body in his place.
The prince of bone spurs and bad knees.

The year I first saw them play
Malone was a high school freshman,
already too big for any bed,
14, a natural resource.
You have to learn not to
apologize, a form of vanity.
You flare up in the lane, exotic
anywhere else. You roll the ball
off fingers twice as long as your
girlfriend's. Great touch for a big man,
says some jerk. Now they're defunct
and Moses Malone, boy wonder at 19,
rises at 20 from the St. Louis bench,
his pet of a body grown sullen
as fast as it grew up.

Something in you remembers every
time the ball left your fingertips
wrong and nothing the ball
can do in the air will change that.
You watch it set, stupid moon,
the way you watch yourself
in a recurring dream.
You never lose your touch
or forget how taxed bodies

go at the same pace they owe,
how brutally well the universe
works to be beautiful,
how we metabolize loss
as fast as we have to.

PISSING OFF THE BACK OF THE BOAT
INTO THE NIVERNAIS CANAL

It's so cold my cock is furled
like a nutmeat and cold,
for all its warm aspirations
and traffic of urine. 37
years old and it takes me a second
to find it, the poor pink slug,
so far from the brash volunteer
of the boudoir. I arc a few
finishing stutters into the water.
Already they're converted,
opaque and chill. How com-
modious the dark universe is,
and companionable the stars.
How drunk I am. I shake
my shriveled nozzle and three
drops lurk out like syllables
from before there were languages. Snug
in my pants it will leak a whole sentence
in Latin. How like a lock-keeper's
life a penis biography would be,
bucolic and dull. What the penis
knows of sex is only arithmetic.
The tongue can kiss and tell.
But the imagination has,
as usual, most of the fun.
It makes discriminations,
bad jokes. It knows itself
to be tragic and thereby silly.
And it can tell a dull story well,
drop by reluctant drop.
What it can't do is be a body
nor survive time's acid work

on the body it enlivens,
I think as I try not to pitch
my wine-dulled body and wary
imagination with it into the inky
canal by the small force
of tugging my zipper up.
How much damage to themselves
the body and imagination
can absorb, I think as I drizzle
to sleep, and how much
the imagination makes
of its body of work
a place to recover itself.

MOVING AGAIN

At night the mountains look like huge
dim hens. In a few geological eras
new mountains may
shatter the earth's shell
and poke up like stone wings.
Each part must serve for a whole.
I bring my sons to the base
of the foothills and we go up.
From a scruff of ponderosa
pines we startle gaudy swerves
of magpies that settle in our rising
wake. Then there's a blooming
prickly pear. "Jesus, Dad, what's that?"
Willy asks. It's like a yellow tulip
grafted to a cactus: it's a beautiful
wound the cactus puts out
to bear fruit and be healed.
If I lived with my sons
all year I'd be less sentimental
about them. We go up
to the mesa top and look down
at our new hometown. The thin air
warps in the melting light
like the aura before a migraine.

WILLIAM MATTHEWS

The boys are tired. A tiny magpie
fluffs into a pine far below
and farther down in the valley
of child support and lights
people are opening drawers.
One of them finds a yellowing
patch of newsprint with a phone
number penciled on it
from Illinois, from before they moved, before
Nicky was born. Memory
is our root system.
"Verna," he says to himself
because his wife's in another room,
"whose number do you suppose this is?"

GRIEF

E detto l'ho perché doler ti debbia!
    — *Inferno, xxiv, 151*

Snow coming in parallel to the street,
a cab spinning its tires (a rising whine
like a domestic argument, and then
the words get said that never get forgot),

slush and backed-up runoff waters at each
corner, clogged buses smelling of wet wool . . .
The acrid anger of the homeless swells
like wet rice. *This slop is where I live, bitch,*

a sogged panhandler shrieks to whom it may
concern. But none of us slows down for scorn;
there's someone's misery in all we earn.
But like a bur in a dog's coat his rage

has borrowed legs. We bring it home. It lives
like kin among the angers of the house,
and leaves the same sharp zinc taste in the mouth:
And I have told you this to make you grieve.

WILLIAM MATTHEWS

THE CLOISTER

The last light of a July evening drained
into the streets below. My love and I had hard
things to say and hear, and we sat over
wine, faltering, picking our words carefully.

The afternoon before I had lain across
my bed and my cat leapt up to lie
alongside me, purring and slowly
growing dozy. By this ritual I could

clear some clutter from my baroque brain.
And into that brief vacancy the image
of a horse cantered, coming straight to me,
and I knew it brought hard talk and hurt

and fear. How did we do? A medium job,
which is well above average. But because
she had opened her heart to me as far
as she did, I saw her fierce privacy,

like a gnarled, luxuriant tree all hung
with disappointments, and I knew
that to love her I must love the tree
and the nothing it cares for me.

ONIONS

How easily happiness begins by
dicing onions. A lump of sweet butter
slithers and swirls across the floor
of the sauté pan, especially if its
errant path crosses a tiny slick
of olive oil. Then a tumble of onions.

This could mean soup or risotto
or chutney (from the Sanskrit
chatni, to lick). Slowly the onions
go limp and then nacreous

WILLIAM MATTHEWS

and then what cookbooks call clear,
though if they were eyes you could see

clearly the cataracts in them.
It's true it can make you weep
to peel them, to unfurl and to tease
from the taut ball first the brittle,
caramel-colored and decrepit
papery outside layer, the least

recent the reticent onion
wrapped around its growing body,
for there's nothing to an onion
but skin, and it's true you can go on
weeping as you go on in, through
the moist middle skins, the sweetest

and thickest, and you can go on
in to the core, to the bud-like,
acrid, fibrous skins densely
clustered there, stalky and in-
complete, and these are the most
pungent, like the nuggets of nightmare

and rage and murmury animal
comfort that infant humans secrete.
This is the best domestic perfume.
You sit down to eat with a rumor
of onions still on your twice-washed
hands and lift to your mouth a hint

of a story about loam and usual
endurance. It's there when you clean up
and rinse the wine glasses and make
a joke, and you leave the minutest
whiff of it on the light switch,
later, when you climb the stairs.

James Merrill

THE OCTOPUS

There are many monsters that a glassen surface
Restrains. And none more sinister
Than vision asleep in the eye's tight translucence.
Rarely it seeks now to unloose
Its diamonds. Having divined how drab a prison
The purest mortal tissue is,
Rarely it wakes. Unless, coaxed out by lusters
Extraordinary, like the octopus
From the gloom of its tank half-swimming half-drifting
Toward anything fair, a handkerchief
Or child's face dreaming near the glass, the writher
Advances in a godlike wreath
Of its own wrath. Chilled by such fragile reeling
A hundred blows of a boot-heel
Shall not quell, the dreamer wakes and hungers.
Percussive pulses, drum or gong,
Build in his skull their loud entrancement,
Volutions of a Hindu dance.
His hands move clumsily in the first conventional
Gestures of assent.
He is willing to undergo the volition and fervor
Of many fleshlike arms, observe
These in their holiness of indirection
Destroy, adore, evolve, reject —
Till on glass rigid with his own seizure
At length the sucking jewels freeze.

LABORATORY POEM

Charles used to watch Naomi, taking heart
And a steel saw, open up turtles, live.
While she swore they felt nothing, he would gag
At blood, at the blind twitching, even after
The murky dawn of entrails cleared, revealing
Contours he knew, egg-yellows like lamps paling.

363

Well then. She carried off the beating heart
To the kymograph and rigged it there, a rag
In fitful wind, now made to strain, now stopped
By her solutions tonic or malign
Alternately in which it would be steeped.
What the heart bore, she noted on a chart,

For work did not stop only with the heart.
He thought of certain human hearts, their climb
Through violence into exquisite disciplines
Of which, as it now appeared, they all expired.
Soon she would fetch another and start over,
Easy in the presence of her lover.

CHARLES ON FIRE

Another evening we sprawled about discussing
Appearances. And it was the consensus
That while uncommon physical good looks
Continued to launch one, as before, in life
(Among its vaporous eddies and false calms),
Still, as one of us said into his beard,
"Without your intellectual and spiritual
Values, man, you are sunk." No one but squared
The shoulders of his own unloveliness.
Long-suffering Charles, having cooked and served the meal,
Now brought out little tumblers finely etched
He filled with amber liquor and then passed.
"Say," said the same young man, "in Paris, France,
They do it this way" — bounding to his feet
And touching a lit match to our host's full glass.
A blue flame, gentle, beautiful, came, went
Above the surface. In a hush that fell
We heard the vessel crack. The contents drained
As who should step down from a crystal coach.
Steward of spirits, Charles's glistening hand
All at once gloved itself in eeriness.
The moment passed. He made two quick sweeps and
Was flesh again. "It couldn't matter less,"
He said, but with a shocked, unconscious glance
Into the mirror. Finding nothing changed,
He filled a fresh glass and sank down among us.

JAMES MERRILL

THE MAD SCENE

Again last night I dreamed the dream called Laundry.
In it, the sheets and towels of a life we were going to share,
The milk-stiff bibs, the shroud, each rag to be ever
Trampled or soiled, bled on or groped for blindly,
Came swooning out of an enormous willow hamper
Onto moon-marbly boards. We had just met. I watched
From outer darkness. I had dressed myself in clothes
Of a new fiber that never stains or wrinkles, never
Wears thin. The opera house sparkled with tiers
And tiers of eyes, like mine enlarged by belladonna,
Trained inward. There I saw the cloud-clot, gust by gust,
Form, and the lightning bite, and the roan mane unloosen.
Fingers were running in panic over the flute's nine gates.
Why did I flinch? I loved you. And in the downpour laughed
To have us wrung white, gnarled together, one
Topmost mordent of wisteria,
As the lean tree burst into grief.

THE KIMONO

When I returned from lovers' lane
My hair was white as snow.
Joy, incomprehension, pain
I'd seen like seasons come and go.
How I got home again
Frozen half dead, perhaps you know.

You hide a smile and quote a text:
Desires ungratified
Persist from one life to the next.
Hearths we strip ourselves beside
Long, long ago were x'd
On blueprints of "consuming pride."

Times out of mind, the bubble-gleam
To our charred level drew
April back. A sudden beam . . .
— Keep talking while I change into

The pattern of a stream
Bordered with rushes white on blue.

MY FATHER'S IRISH SETTERS

Always throughout his life
(The parts of it I knew)
Two or three would be racing
Up stairs and down hallways,
Whining to take us walking,
Or caked with dirt, resigning
Keen ears to bouts of talk —
Until his third, last wife
Put down her little foot.
That splendid, thoroughbred
Lineage was penned
Safely out of earshot:
Fed, of course, and watered,
But never let out to run.
"Dear God," the new wife simpered,
Tossing her little head,
"Suppose they got run over —
Wouldn't *that* be the end?"

Each time I visited
(Once or twice a year)
I'd slip out, giving my word
Not to get carried away.
At the dogs' first sight of me
Far off — of anyone —
Began a joyous barking,
A russet-and-rapid-as-flame
Leaping, then whimpering lickings
Of face and hands through wire.
Like fire, like fountains leaping
With love and loyalty,
Put, were they, in safekeeping
By love, or for love's sake?
Dear heart, to love's own shame.
But loyalty transferred

Leaves famously slim pickings,
And no one's left to blame.

Divorced again, my father
(Hair white, face deeply scored)
Looked round and heaved a sigh.
The setters were nowhere.
Fleet muzzle, soulful eye
Dead lo! these forty winters?
Not so. Tonight in perfect
Lamplit stillness begin
With updraft from the worksheet,
Leaping and tongues, far-shining
Hearths of our hinterland:
Dour chieftain, maiden pining
Away for that lost music,
Her harpist's wild red hair. . . .
Dear clan of Ginger and Finn,
As I go through your motions
(As they go through me, rather)
Love follows, pen in hand.

A DOWNWARD LOOK

Seen from above, the sky
Is deep. Clouds float down there,

Foam on a long, luxurious bath.
Their shadows over limbs submerged in "air,"

Over protuberances, faults,
A delta thicket, glide. On high, the love

That drew the bath and scattered it with salts

Still radiates new projects old as day,
And hardly registers the tug

When, far beneath, a wrinkled, baby hand
Happens upon the plug.

b o d y

Look closely at the letters. Can you see,
entering (stage right), then floating full,
then heading off — so soon —
how like a little kohl-rimmed moon
o plots her course from *b* to *d*

— as *y*, unanswered, knocks at the stage door?
Looked at too long, words fail,
phase out. Ask, now that *body* shines
no longer, by what light you learn these lines
and what the *b* and *d* stood for.

AN UPWARD LOOK

O heart green acre   sown with salt
by the departing   occupier

lay down your gallant   spears of wheat
Salt of the earth   each stellar pinch

flung in blind   defiance backwards
now takes its toll   Up from his quieted

quarry the lover   colder and wiser
hauling himself   finds the world turning

toys triumphs   toxins into
this vast facility   the living come
dearest to die in   How did it happen

In bright alternation   minutely mirrored
within the thinking   of each and every

mortal creature   halves of a clue
approach the earthlights   Morning star

evening star   salt of the sky
First the grave   dissolving into dawn

then the crucial   recrystallizing
from inmost depths   of clear dark blue

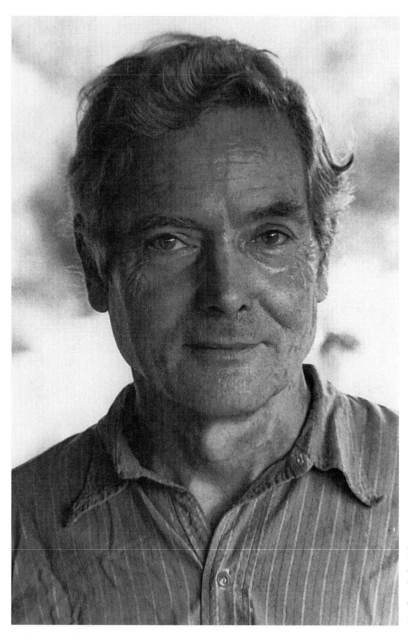

W. S. Merwin

THE POEM

Coming late, as always,
I try to remember what I almost heard.
The light avoids my eye.

How many times have I heard the locks close
And the lark take the keys
And hang them in heaven.

HOW WE ARE SPARED

At midsummer before dawn an orange light returns to the mountains
Like a great weight and the small birds cry out
And bear it up

FOR THE ANNIVERSARY OF MY DEATH

Every year without knowing it I have passed the day
When the last fires will wave to me
And the silence will set out
Tireless traveller
Like the beam of a lightless star

Then I will no longer
Find myself in life as in a strange garment
Surprised at the earth
And the love of one woman
And the shamelessness of men
As today writing after three days of rain
Hearing the wren sing and the falling cease
And bowing not knowing to what

DEAD HAND

Temptations still nest in it like basilisks.
Hang it up till the rings fall.

THE CHAFF

Those who cannot love the heavens or the earth
beaten from the heavens and the earth
eat each other
those who cannot love each other
beaten from each other
eat themselves
those who cannot love themselves
beaten from themselves
eat a terrible bread
kneaded in the morning shrouded all day
baked in the dark
whose sweet smell brings the chaff flying like empty hands
through the turning sky night after night
calling with voices of young birds
to its wheat

FIELD MUSHROOMS

I never gave a thought to them at first
with their white heads
cut into slices
under a water of plastic on a blue
section of carpet
or even hanging in a scale
like the piled ruins of a foot

I was shown that when the right time came
you could overturn a dry cow pat
by the edge of a long green swamp
late on a cold

autumn afternoon
as the sun was going down
and there underneath
the real white heads were still growing

I went on finding them
always at evening
coming to recognize a depth
in the shade of oaks and chestnuts
a quickening in the moss year after year
a suggestion of burning
signs of something already there in its own place
a texture of flesh
scarcely born
full of the knowledge of darkness

THE ROSE BEETLE

It is said that you came from China
but you never saw China
you eat up the leaves here

your ancestors travelled blind in eggs
you arrive just after dark from underground
with a clicking whir in the first night
knowing by the smell what leaves to eat here
where you have wakened for the first time

the strawberry leaves foreign as you
the beans the orchid tree the eggplant
the old leaves of the heliconia the banana some palms
and the roses from everywhere but here
and the hibiscus from here the abutilons
the royal ilima

in the night you turn them into lace
into an arid net
into sky

like the sky long ago over China

W. S. MERWIN

REMEMBERING A BOATMAN

After sundown yellow sky beyond shadow mountains
range upon range in long twilight under few distant clouds
darkening pastures run into the bays
birds are already asleep high on unlit roan cliffs
straw light still flickers on the water
between two headlands in short summer
at last a long boat rowed by one man standing
appears slowly from behind a headland on the right
and starts across
too far away to hear the sounds of the wood
or see colors
a few times the wake turns up light
then I forget him for years

FOG-HORN

Surely that moan is not the thing
That men thought they were making, when they
Put it there, for their own necessities.
That throat does not call to anything human
But to something men had forgotten,
That stirs under fog. Who wounded that beast
Incurably, or from whose pasture
Was it lost, full grown, and time closed round it
With no way back? Who tethered its tongue
So that its voice could never come
To speak out in the light of clear day,
But only when the shifting blindness
Descends and is acknowledged among us,
As though from under a floor it is heard,
Or as though from behind a wall, always
Nearer than we had remembered? If it
Was we that gave tongue to this cry
What does it bespeak in us, repeating
And repeating, insisting on something
That we never meant? We only put it there
To give warning of something we dare not
Ignore, lest we should come upon it

W. S. MERWIN

Too suddenly, recognize it too late,
As our cries were swallowed up and all hands lost.

ST VINCENT'S

Thinking of rain clouds that rose over the city
on the first day of the year

in the same month
I consider that I have lived daily and with
eyes open and ears to hear
these years across from St Vincent's Hospital
above whose roof those clouds rose

its bricks by day a French red under
cross facing south
blown-up neo-classic facades the tall
dark openings between columns at
the dawn of history
exploded into many windows
in a mortised face

inside it the ambulances have unloaded
after sirens' howling nearer through traffic on
Seventh Avenue long
ago I learned not to hear them
even when the sirens stop

they turn to back in
few passers-by stay to look
and neither do I

at night two long blue
windows and one short one on the top floor
burn all night
many nights when most of the others are out
on what floor do they have
anything

I have seen the building drift moonlit through geraniums
late at night when trucks were few

W. S. MERWIN

moon just past the full
upper windows parts of the sky
as long as I looked
I watched it at Christmas and New Year
early in the morning I have seen the nurses ray out through
arterial streets
in the evening have noticed internes blocks away
on doorsteps one foot in the door

I have come upon the men in gloves taking out
the garbage at all hours
piling up mountains of
plastic bags white strata with green intermingled and
black
I have seen one pile
catch fire and studied the cloud
at the ends of the jets of the hoses
the fire engines as near as that
red beacons and
machine-throb heard by the whole body
I have noticed molded containers stacked outside
a delivery entrance on Twelfth Street
whether meals from a meal factory made up with those
mummified for long journeys by plane
or specimens for laboratory
examination sealed at the prescribed temperatures
either way closed delivery

and approached faces staring from above
crutches or tubular clamps
out for tentative walks
have paused for turtling wheel-chairs
heard visitors talking in wind on each corner
while the lights changed and
hot dogs were handed over at the curb
in the middle of afternoon
mustard ketchup onions and relish
and police smelling of ether and laundry
were going back

and I have known them all less than the papers of our days
smoke rises from the chimneys do they have an incinerator
what for

how warm do they believe they have to maintain the air
in there
several of the windows appear
to be made of tin
but it may be the light reflected
I have imagined bees coming and going
on those sills though I have never seen them

who was St Vincent

WHEN YOU GO AWAY

for Dido

When you go away the wind clicks around to the north
The painters work all day but at sundown the paint falls
Showing the black walls
The clock goes back to striking the same hour
That has no place in the years

And at night wrapped in the bed of ashes
In one breath I wake
It is the time when the beards of the dead get their growth
I remember that I am falling
That I am the reason
And that my words are the garment of what I shall never be
Like the tucked sleeve of a one-armed boy

Marilyn Nelson

Marilyn Nelson

I DECIDE NOT TO HAVE CHILDREN

Dawn, the gulls weep for the Jews,
and up through my muddy blood
my lost sister rises like a drowned puppy.
I'd forgotten how far away
I'd sent her, wonder how it was
in that wet country,
her skin melting back into mine.
There were nights
I almost recognized her face,
like an old rose pressed under glass.
Sometimes she made
a knock in the pipes
faint as a heartbeat
and backed away again.

In some small room of myself
she has shrunk
to the size of a sparrow
since the night the soldiers came
and searched through my dreams
in their angry uniforms.
I find her there, halfway to sleep,
a sister smaller than a hare
in the blind appendix
behind my eyes.

I'd forgotten how much I cared
and she comes holding out
her fat brown fists,
the flowers of mourning
already twisted in her hair.
Her faint body made a light
that warmed the whole house.

MAMA'S MURDERS

Her leg flies open like a dictionary dropped,
the white fat sickens her till her blood
fills the wound, and I, dumb with terror,
run away from the gully gaudy with broken glass
while my sister's scream shrinks to child size
at my cowardly back. A white door opens
as my fists blur on the wood.
The white lady who takes me in
has no age, has no face, only a voice
from somewhere else that asks my mother's name
over the rip of clean sheets.
Jennifer comes alone up the forbidden trail,
leaving bloody footprints in the snow.

Five-fifty on a wet October morning.
I'm awake now, still running home to get Mama,
confession still cold on my tongue.
I sit up in the dark. I count my murders.
        My brother died, a brown leaf
        against a wire fence.
        My father never got to say goodbye.
        The boy who gave his mouth to me
        saw death in a rear-view mirror,
        turned around to meet it, met it.

Because I daydreamed about how beautiful I'd be
with tears in my eyes.
Because I didn't throw myself over a grenade.
Because of my stupid fault.
How many more have I watched,
helpless, pulled over the falls?

I might have saved them,
might have torn off my senior prom gown
and dived into the torrent.
In front of my horrified eyes
they went over without a sound
like a herd of stampeding cattle
crazy with thirst.
Bloody boys, broken women,
thin children.
I might have saved them.

As dawn colors the sky
with sad gray radiance
I count the day I ran to tell Mama
we broke Jamie Crowl's arm on the seesaw,
the day I ran to tell Mama I made Jennifer
take the dangerous shortcut from school,
the day I ran to tell Mama my voodoo had worked.

I remember how she fed me Cheerios
while the news announced in a cold white voice
the numbers of the dead.
How she watched me pore over photographs
of mountains of eyeglasses, mountains of shoes,
then sent me out to play
in the twilight under the streetlamps;
how Junebugs felt heavy and horrible
under my flying feet.

I hear my baby waking up,
trying out my new name like a chant.
Before I face his wonderful eyes
I slip into my raggedy robe
and wash my hands and face.

In the mirror I look like Mama.
I lean closer and look into her eyes:
In their black pupils, I see my grandmother,
her mother, diminishing generations
of the dead, all of them Mama.

I, too, have given my child
to the murderous world.
I go to him, pick him up,
feel in my chest like warm liquid
hundreds of generations of Mama's forgiveness.

WOMEN'S LOCKER ROOM

The splat of bare feet on wet tile
breaks the incredible luck
of my being alone in here.
I snatch a stingy towel

and sidle into the shower. I'm already soaped
by the time a white hand turns the neighboring knob.
I recognize the arm as one that flashed
for many rapid laps while I dogpaddled at the shallow end.
I dart an appraising glance: She arches down
to wash her lifted heel, and is beautiful.
As she straightens, I look into her eyes.

For an instant I remember human sacrifice:
The female explorer led skyward,
her blond tresses loose on her neck;
the drums of our pulses grew louder;
I raised the obsidian knife.
Violets bloomed in the clefts of the stairs.

I could freeze her name in an ice cube,
bottle the dirt from her footsteps
with potent graveyard dust.
I could gather the combings from her hairbrush
to burn with her fingernail clippings,
I could feed her Iago powder.
Childhood taunts, branded ears,
a thousand insults swirl through my memory
like headlines in a city vacant lot.

I jump, grimace, divide like an amoeba
into twin rages that stomp around
with their lips stuck out,
then come suddenly face to face.
They see each other and know that they
are mean mamas.
Then I bust out laughing
and let the woman live.

AS SIMPLE AS THAT

Talk about Bosnia led to the Hutu and Tutsi, two
peoples at each other's throats since time began,
the Tutsi lording it over Hutu vassals without shedding
their blood until the Germans turned Tutsi nobles

into bootlickers who took orders and handed them down,
then the Belgians converted the Tutsi court to bureaucratic,
authoritarian tyrants, and then with independence
came Hutu rebellion and years of periodic massacres,
thousands slaughtered, rivers clogged with the dead.

Abba Jacob said:
There was a man, Miringi, who used to cook for us
on the farm when I was a boy.
When he left us he bought a tiny bark boat
and fished the river. His wife sold the fish
at the village market. About ten years later I saw him
riding a bicycle with a cardboard box tied on in back.
I stopped to say hello, and asked Miringi how he was.
"Not too well," he replied. It seemed his brother
had been in a fight, and had been beheaded
with a cane-cutting knife. Miringi was on his way
to the magistrate's office to report the murder.
His brother's head was in the box.

Abba Jacob said:
Frightening, the atrocities we commit and bear.
I know I'm capable of horrors. I feel it sometimes:
the power, not the will. But as long as I remain
in communion with Christ through prayer,
love holds me back.

BOYS IN THE PARK

Chicago, 1967

In town to do good works, filled with our own
virtue, five of us joined a game of catch
with boys who looked like the boys who'd teased
us at recess, who called girls dumb, yanked pigtails,
burped, and were generally as annoying as younger
brothers. But, barely chest-high, these were a swarm
of fingerling piranhas, of little proto
rapists in t-shirts and sneakers, racing around us
with knowing hands, then running off
down the parkslope, tossing the ball,

laughing, children of our people, leaving us
to our shame.

Yes, they had poverty, futility,
unequal opportunity, childhood
neglect and abuse; they had hopelessness,
the past and future an unrelieved sentence
of humiliation and meaningless;
they had understandable grievances
against a society which treats some
with unjust contempt. (In yesterday's news
a samaritan walked six blocks to buy
gas for three people stranded in their car.
They threw it on him and tossed a lit match.
He was black, they were white, one was pregnant.)
And we had been sheltered by white-collar
fathers who insisted on A's, mothers
who read Langston Hughes aloud at bedtime.
Innocent as midwest hicktown white girls,
we had love, homes, hope. We had all the luck.
But is virtue the flip side of blessing?
Is malevolence excused by despair?

Engulfed in a stormcloud of boys, I looked down
on twenty close-shorn heads. In an instant I remembered
Dr. King's voice from the pulpit:
Freedom, hands rose under my skirt;
equality, my breasts were pinched.
The day before, I'd knelt on a sidewalk
singing, and a woman pushing a stroller
had called me a cocksucking nigger whore.
Justice I willed myself *peace* to unknow
conscience the evil I saw *dignity*
pinpricked in her *faith* blue *humanity* eyes.
They were boys, just boys, nine or ten years old.

MINOR MIRACLE

Which reminds me of another knock-on-wood
memory. I was cycling with a male friend,
through a small midwestern town. We came to a 4-way

stop and stopped, chatting. As we started again,
a rusty old pick-up truck, ignoring the stop sign,
hurricaned past scant inches from our front wheels.
My partner called, "Hey, that was a 4-way stop!"
The truck driver, stringy blond hair a long fringe
under his brand-name beer cap, looked back and yelled,
        "You fucking niggers!"
And sped off.
My friend and I looked at each other and shook our heads.
We remounted our bikes and headed out of town.
We were pedaling through a clear blue afternoon
between two fields of almost-ripened wheat
bordered by cornflowers and Queen Anne's lace
when we heard an unmuffled motor, a honk-honking.
We stopped, closed ranks, made fists.
It was the same truck. It pulled over.
A tall, very much in shape young white guy slid out:
greasy jeans, homemade finger tattoos, probably
a Marine Corps boot-camp footlockerful
of martial arts techniques.

"What did you say back there!" he shouted.
My friend said, "I said it was a 4-way stop.
You went through it."
"And what did I say?" the white guy asked.
"You said: 'You fucking niggers.'"
The afternoon froze.

"Well," said the white guy,
shoving his hands into his pockets
and pushing dirt around with the pointed toe of his boot,
"I just want to say I'm sorry."
He climbed back into his truck
and drove away.

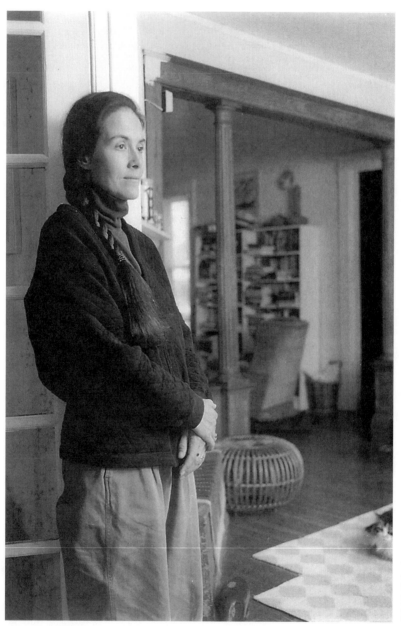

Naomi Shihab Nye

VOCABULARY OF DEARNESS

How a single word
may shimmer and rise
off the page, a wafer of
syllabic light, a bulb
of glowing meaning,
whatever the word,
try "tempestuous" or "suffer,"
any word you have held
or traded so it lives a new life
the size of two worlds.
Say you carried it
up a hill and it helped you
move. Without this
the days would be thin sticks
thrown down in a clutter of leaves,
and where is the rake?

STEPS

A man letters the sign for his grocery in Arabic and English.
Paint dries more quickly in English.
The thick swoops and curls of Arabic letters stay moist
and glistening till tomorrow when the children show up
jingling their dimes.

They have learned the currency of the New World,
carrying wishes for gum and candies shaped like fish.
They float through the streets, diving deep to the bottom,
nosing rich layers of crusted shell.

One of these children will tell a story that keeps her people
alive. We don't know yet which one she is.
Girl in the red sweater dangling a book bag,
sister with eyes pinned to the barrel of pumpkin seeds.
They are lettering the sidewalk with their steps.

They are separate and together and a little bit late.
Carrying a creased note, "Don't forget."
Who wrote it? They've already forgotten.
A purple fish sticks to the back of the throat.
Their long laughs are boats they will ride and ride,
making the shadows that cross each other's smiles.

ARABIC

(Jordan, 1992)

The man with laughing eyes stopped smiling
to say, "Until you speak Arabic —
— you will not understand pain."

Something to do with the back of the head,
an Arab carries sorrow in the back of the head
that only language cracks, the thrum of stones

weeping, grating hinge on an old metal gate.
"Once you know," he whispered, "you can enter the room
whenever you need to. Music you heard from a distance,

the slapped drum of a stranger's wedding,
wells up inside your skin, inside rain, a thousand
pulsing tongues. You are changed."

Outside, the snow had finally stopped.
In a land where snow rarely falls,
we had felt our days grow white and still.

I thought pain had no tongue. Or every tongue
at once, supreme translator, sieve. I admit my
shame. To live on the brink of Arabic, tugging

its rich threads without understanding
how to weave the rug . . . I have no gift.
The sound, but not the sense.

I kept looking over his shoulder for someone else
to talk to, recalling my dying friend who only scrawled
I can't write. What good would any grammar have been

to her then? I touched his arm, held it hard,
which sometimes you don't do in the Middle East, and said,
I'll work on it, feeling sad

for his good strict heart, but later in the slick street
hailed a taxi by shouting *Pain!* and it stopped
in every language and opened its doors.

THE SMALL VASES FROM HEBRON

Tip their mouths open to the sky.
Turquoise, amber,
the deep green with fluted handle,
pitcher the size of two thumbs,
tiny lip and graceful waist.

Here we place the smallest flower
which could have lived invisibly
in loose soil beside the road,
sprig of succulent rosemary,
bowing mint.

They grow deeper in the center of the table.

Here we entrust the small life,
thread, fragment, breath.
And it bends. It waits all day.
As the bread cools and the children
open their gray copybooks
to shape the letter that looks like
a chimney rising out of a house.

And what do the headlines say?

Nothing of the smaller petal
perfectly arranged inside the larger petal
or the way tinted glass filters light.
Men and boys, praying when they died,
fall out of their skins.
The whole alphabet of living,
heads and tails of words,

sentences, the way they said,
"Ya'Allah!" when astonished,
or "ya'ani" for "I mean" —
a crushed glass under the feet
still shines.
But the child of Hebron sleeps
with the thud of her brothers falling
and the long sorrow of the color red.

THE SHAPES OF MOUTHS AT PARTIES

A mouth like a hammer
pounding out its own tale.
Sometimes I float among the mouths
carrying my own like an unpicked plum.
The man who tells about crashing in an airplane
does not need my "Oh really?" for his story to go on.
As if we were standing at some coast,
things continue without our help,
the predictable waves, the smooth-backed shells,
and the mouths like jellyfish swelling . . .
As if the mouth were the opening
most suited to knowledge and communication,
more than the weightless eye,
landing carefully on each occupied chair,
the fluent nose, vibrantly awake
before the mouth names what it is eating,
or the hand, the articulate hand,
which comes undressed to every party,
opens easily to receive wine or cake,
and secretly converses with the rug, the dog, the air.

MORNING PAPER, SOCIETY PAGE

I can never see fashion models,
lean angular cheeks, strutting hips
and blooming hair, without thinking of
the skulls at the catacombs in Lima, Peru.

How we climbed down from blurred markets
to find a thousand unnamed friends smiling at us
as if they too could advertise
a coming style.

WHAT BRINGS US OUT

Something about pumpkins caused
the man who had not spoken in three years
to lean forward, cough, open his mouth.
How the room heaved into silence,
his words enormous in that air:
"I won't . . . be . . . afraid . . .
of my . . . father . . . anymore."
And what silence followed,
as if each heart had spoken
its most secret terror,
had combed the tangled clump
for the hardest line
and pulled it, intact,
from the mass.

I bless that man forever
for his courage, his voice
which started with one thing
and went to many, opening up and up
to the rim of the world.
So much silence had given him
a wisdom which held us all at bay,
amazed. Sometimes when I see
mountains of pumpkins by the roadside,
or watermelons, a hill of autumn gourds
piled lavishly on crates, I think
perhaps this one, or that, were it to
strike someone right,
this curl of hardened stalk,
this pleated skin . . .
or, on an old bureau drawer,
the vegetable-like roundness of a glass knob
that the baby turns and turns
emerging, later, from a complicated dream . . .

the huge navigational face of a radio
which never worked while I was alive
but gave me more to go on than most sounds:
how what brings us out may be
small as that black arrow, swinging
the wide arc, the numbers where silent voices lived,
how fast you had to turn to make it move.

THE LAST DAY OF AUGUST

A man in a lawn chair
with a book on his lap

realizes pears are falling
from the tree right beside him.

Each makes a round,
full sound in the grass.

Perhaps the stem takes an hour
to loosen and let go.

This man who has recently written words
to his father forty years in the birthing:

I was always afraid of you.
When would you explode next?

has sudden reverence for the pears.
If a dark bruise rises,

if ants inhabit the juicy crack,
or the body remains firm, unscarred,

remains secret till tomorrow . . .
By then the letter to his father

may be lying open on a table.
We gather pears in baskets, sacks.

What will we do with everything
that has been given us? Ginger pears, pear pies,

fingers weighing flesh.
Which will be perfect under the skin?

It is hard not to love the pile of peelings
growing on the counter next to the knife.

THE TRAVELING ONION

*It is believed that the onion originally came from India. In
Egypt it was an object of worship — why I haven't been able
to find out. From Egypt the onion entered Greece and on to
Italy, thence into all of Europe.*

— *Better Living Cookbook*

When I think how far the onion has traveled
just to enter my stew today, I could kneel and praise
all small forgotten miracles,
crackly paper peeling on the drainboard,
pearly layers in smooth agreement,
the way knife enters onion
and onion falls apart on the chopping block,
a history revealed.

And I would never scold the onion
for causing tears.
It is right that tears fall
for something small and forgotten.
How at meal, we sit to eat,
commenting on texture of meat or herbal aroma
but never on the translucence of onion,
now limp, now divided,
or its traditionally honorable career:
For the sake of others,
disappear.

Renate Ponsold

Frank O'Hara

WHY I AM NOT A PAINTER

I am not a painter, I am a poet.
Why? I think I would rather be
a painter, but I am not. Well,

for instance, Mike Goldberg
is starting a painting. I drop in.
"Sit down and have a drink" he
says. I drink; we drink. I look up.
"You have SARDINES in it."
"Yes, it needed something there."
"Oh." I go and the days go by
and I drop in again. The painting is
going on, and I go, and the days
go by. I drop in. The painting is
finished. "Where's SARDINES?"
All that's left is just
letters, "It was too much," Mike says.

But me? One day I am thinking of
a color: orange. I write a line
about orange. Pretty soon it is a
whole page of words, not lines.
Then another page. There should be
so much more, not of orange, of
words, of how terrible orange is
and life. Days go by. It is even in
prose, I am a real poet. My poem
is finished and I haven't mentioned
orange yet. It's twelve poems, I call
it ORANGES. And one day in a gallery
I see Mike's painting, called SARDINES.

FRANK O'HARA

POEM

I don't know as I get what D. H. Lawrence is driving at
when he writes of lust springing from the bowels
or do I
it could be the bowels of the earth
to lie flat on the earth in spring, summer or winter is sexy
you feel it stirring deep down slowly up to you
and sometimes it gives you a little nudge in the crotch
that's very sexy
and when someone looks sort of raggedy and dirty like Paulette Goddard
in *Modern Times* it's exciting, it isn't usual or attractive
perhaps D.H.L. is thinking of the darkness
certainly the crotch is light
and I suppose
any part of us that can only be seen by others
is a dark part
I feel that about the small of my back, too and the nape of my neck
they are dark
they are erotic zones as in the tropics
whereas Paris is straightforward and bright about it all
a coal miner has kind of a sexy occupation
though I'm sure it's painful down there
but so is lust
of light we can never have enough
but how would we find it
unless the darkness urged us on and into it
and I am dark
except when now and then it all comes clear
and I can see myself
as others luckily sometimes see me
in a good light

PERSONAL POEM

Now when I walk around at lunchtime
I have only two charms in my pocket
an old Roman coin Mike Kanemitsu gave me
and a bolt-head that broke off a packing case
when I was in Madrid the others never

brought me too much luck though they did
help keep me in New York against coercion
but now I'm happy for a time and interested

I walk through the luminous humidity
passing the House of Seagram with its wet
and its loungers and the construction to
the left that closed the sidewalk if
I ever get to be a construction worker
I'd like to have a silver hat please
and get to Moriarty's where I wait for
LeRoi and hear who wants to be a mover and
shaker the last five years my batting average
is .016 that's that, and LeRoi comes in
and tells me Miles Davis was clubbed 12
times last night outside BIRDLAND by a cop
a lady asks us for a nickel for a terrible
disease but we don't give her one we
don't like terrible diseases, then

we go eat some fish and some ale it's
cool but crowded we don't like Lionel Trilling
we decide, we like Don Allen we don't like
Henry James so much we like Herman Melville
we don't want to be in the poets' walk in
San Francisco even we just want to be rich
and walk on girders in our silver hats
I wonder if one person out of the 8,000,000 is
thinking of me as I shake hands with LeRoi
and buy a strap for my wristwatch and go
back to work happy at the thought possibly so

STEPS

How funny you are today New York
like Ginger Rogers in *Swingtime*
and St. Bridget's steeple leaning a little to the left

here I have just jumped out of a bed full of V-days
(I got tired of D-days) and blue you there still
accepts me foolish and free

all I want is a room up there
and you in it
and even the traffic halt so thick is a way
for people to rub up against each other
and when their surgical appliances lock
they stay together
for the rest of the day (what a day)
I go by to check a slide and I say
that painting's not so blue

where's Lana Turner
she's out eating
and Garbo's backstage at the Met
everyone's taking their coat off
so they can show a rib-cage to the rib-watchers
and the park's full of dancers with their tights and shoes
in little bags
who are often mistaken for worker-outers at the West Side Y
why not
the Pittsburgh Pirates shout because they won
and in a sense we're all winning
we're alive

the apartment was vacated by a gay couple
who moved to the country for fun
they moved a day too soon
even the stabbings are helping the population explosion
though in the wrong country
and all those liars have left the UN
the Seagram Building's no longer rivalled in interest
not that we need liquor (we just like it)

and the little box is out on the sidewalk
next to the delicatessen
so the old man can sit on it and drink beer
and get knocked off it by his wife later in the day
while the sun is still shining

oh god it's wonderful
to get out of bed
and drink too much coffee
and smoke too many cigarettes
and love you so much

POEM

Lana Turner has collapsed!
I was trotting along and suddenly
it started raining and snowing
and you said it was hailing
but hailing hits you on the head
hard so it was really snowing and
raining and I was in such a hurry
to meet you but the traffic
was acting exactly like the sky
and suddenly I see a headline
LANA TURNER HAS COLLAPSED!
there is no snow in Hollywood
there is no rain in California
I have been to lots of parties
and acted perfectly disgraceful
but I never actually collapsed
oh Lana Turner we love you get up

FOR GRACE, AFTER A PARTY

You do not always know what I am feeling.
Last night in the warm spring air while I was
blazing my tirade against someone who doesn't
interest
          me, it was love for you that set me
afire,
          and isn't it odd? for in rooms full of
strangers my most tender feelings
                              writhe and
bear the fruit of screaming. Put out your hand,
isn't there
          an ashtray, suddenly, there? beside
the bed? And someone you love enters the room
and says wouldn't
                    you like the eggs a little
different today?
                    And when they arrive they are
just plain scrambled eggs and the warm weather
is holding.

FRANK O'HARA

THE DAY LADY DIED

It is 12:20 in New York a Friday
three days after Bastille day, yes
it is 1959 and I go get a shoeshine
because I will get off the 4:19 in Easthampton
at 7:15 and then go straight to dinner
and I don't know the people who will feed me

I walk up the muggy street beginning to sun
and have a hamburger and a malted and buy
an ugly NEW WORLD WRITING to see what the poets
in Ghana are doing these days
                              I go on to the bank
and Miss Stillwagon (first name Linda I once heard)
doesn't even look up my balance for once in her life
and in the GOLDEN GRIFFIN I get a little Verlaine
for Patsy with drawings by Bonnard although I do
think of Hesiod, trans. Richmond Lattimore or
Brendan Behan's new play or *Le Balcon* or *Les Nègres*
of Genet, but I don't, I stick with Verlaine
after practically going to sleep with quandariness

and for Mike I just stroll into the PARK LANE
Liquor Store and ask for a bottle of Strega and
then I go back where I came from to 6th Avenue
and the tobacconist in the Ziegfeld Theatre and
casually ask for a carton of Gauloises and a carton
of Picayunes, and a NEW YORK POST with her face on it

and I am sweating a lot by now and thinking of
leaning on the john door in the 5 SPOT
while she whispered a song along the keyboard
to Mal Waldron and everyone and I stopped breathing

GETTING UP AHEAD OF SOMEONE (SUN)

I cough a lot (sinus?) so I
get up and have some tea with cognac

it is dawn
        the light flows evenly along the lawn
in chilly Southampton and I smoke
and hours and hours go by I read
van Vechten's *Spider Boy* then a short
story by Patsy Southgate and a poem
by myself it is cold and I shiver a little
in white shorts the day begun
so oddly not tired not nervous I
am for once truly awake letting it all
start slowly as I watch instead of
grabbing on late as usual
                where did it go
                it's not really awake yet
                I will wait

and the house wakes up and goes
to get the dog in Sag Harbor I make
myself a bourbon and commence
to write one of my "I do this I do that"
poems in a sketch pad
                it is tomorrow
though only six hours have gone by
each day's light has more significance these days

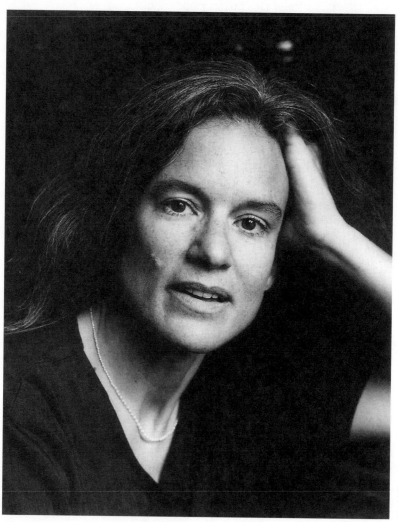

David Bartolomi

Sharon Olds

MONARCHS

All morning, as I sit thinking of you,
the Monarchs are passing. Seven stories up,
to the left of the river, they are making their way
south, their wings the dark red of
your hands like butchers' hands, the raised
veins of their wings like your scars.
I could scarcely feel your massive rough
palms on me, your touch was so light,
the delicate chapped scrape of an insect's leg
across my breast. No one had ever
touched me before. I didn't know enough to
open my legs, but felt your thighs,
feathered with red-gold hairs,
                    opening
between my legs like a
pair of wings.
The hinged print of my blood on your thigh —
a winged creature pinned there —
and then you left, as you were to leave
over and over, the butterflies moving
in masses past my window, floating
south to their transformation, crossing over
borders in the night, the diffuse blood-red
cloud of them, my body under yours,
the beauty and silence of the great migrations.

A WOMAN IN HEAT WIPING HERSELF

High in the inner regions of my body
this gloss is spun, high up
under the overhanging ledge where the
light pours down on the cliff night and day.
No workers stand around in the
camaraderie of workers,
no one lays the color down on the

lip of the braid, there is only the light,
bands and folds of light, and the clean
sand at the edge, the working surface — there is
no one around for miles, no one hungry,
no one being fed. Just as in the side of the
lamb no one is tending the hole where the
light pours out, no one is folding or
carding while the gold grease of the floss
flows through the follicle, beading and rippling back and
curving forward in solemn spillage.
Things done with no reference to the human.
Most things are done with no reference to the human
even if they happen inside us, in our
body that is far beyond our powers, that we could
never invent. Deep in my sex, the
glittering threads are thrown outward and thrown outward
the way the sea lifts up the whole edge of its body,
the rim, the slit where once or twice in a lifetime
you can look through and see the other world —
it is this world, without us,
this earth and our bodies
without us watching.

EARLY IMAGES OF HEAVEN

It amazed me that the shapes of penises,
their sizes, and angles, everything about them
was the way I would have designed them if I had
invented them. The skin, the way the skin
thickens and thins, its suppleness,
the way the head barely fits in the throat,
its mouth almost touching the valve of the stomach —
and the hair, which lifts, or crinkles, delicate
and free — I could not get over all this,
the passion for it as intense in me
as if it were made to my order, or my
desire made to its order — as if I had
known it before I was born, as if
I remembered coming through it, like God
the Father all around me.

SHARON OLDS

THE POPE'S PENIS

It hangs deep in his robes, a delicate
clapper at the center of a bell.
It moves when he moves, a ghostly fish in a
halo of silver seaweed, the hair
swaying in the dark and the heat — and at night,
while his eyes sleep, it stands up
in praise of God.

THE ELDER SISTER

When I look at my elder sister now
I think how she had to go first, down through the
birth canal, to force her way
head-first through the tiny channel,
the pressure of Mother's muscles on her brain,
the tight walls scraping her skin.
Her face is still narrow from it, the long
hollow cheeks of a Crusader on a tomb,
and her inky eyes have the look of someone who has
been in prison a long time and
knows they can send her back. I look at her
body and think how her breasts were the first to
rise, slowly, like swans on a pond.
By the time mine came along, they were just
two more birds in the flock, and when the hair
rose on the white mound of her flesh, like
threads of water out of the ground, it was the
first time, but when mine came
they knew about it. I used to think
only in terms of her harshness, sitting and
pissing on me in bed, but now I
see I had her before me always
like a shield. I look at her wrinkles, her clenched
jaws, her frown-lines — I see they are
the dents on my shield, the blows that did not reach me.
She protected me, not as a mother
protects a child, with love, but as a

hostage protects the one who makes her
escape as I made my escape, with my sister's
body held in front of me.

THE LIFTING

Suddenly my father lifted up his nightie, I
turned my head away but he cried out
Shar!, my nickname, so I turned and looked.
He was sitting in the high cranked-up hospital bed with the
gown up, around his neck,
to show me the weight he had lost. I looked
where his solid ruddy stomach had been
and I saw the skin fallen into loose
soft hairy rippled folds
lying in a pool of folds
down at the base of his abdomen,
the gaunt torso of a big man
who will die soon. Right away
I saw how much his hips are like mine,
the long, white angles, and then
how much his pelvis is shaped like my daughter's,
a chambered whelk-shell hollowed out,
I saw the folds of skin like something
poured, a thick batter, I saw
his rueful smile, the cast-up eyes as he
shows me his old body, he knows
I will be interested, he knows I will find him
appealing. If anyone had told me I would sit
by him and he would pull up his nightie and I would look
at him, his naked body, the thick
bud of his glans, his penis in all that
dark hair, look at him
in affection and uneasy wonder
I would not have believed it. But now I can still
see the tiny snowflakes, white and
night-blue, on the cotton of the gown as it
rises the way we were promised at death it would rise,
the veils would fall from our eyes, we would know everything.

SHARON OLDS

THE GLASS

I think of it with wonder now,
the glass of mucus that stood on the table
next to my father all weekend. The cancer is
growing fast in his throat now,
and as it grows it sends out pus like the
sun sending out solar flares, those
pouring tongues of fire. So my father has to
gargle, hack, cough, and spit a
mouth full of thick stuff
into the glass every ten minutes or so,
scraping the glass up his lower lip to
get the last bit off his skin, then he
sets the glass down on the table and it
sits there, shiny and faintly
gold like a glass of beer foam, he
gurgles and reaches for it again and
gets the heavy sputum out,
full of bubbles and moving around like yeast — he is
like some god producing dark food from his own mouth.
He himself can eat nothing anymore,
just a swallow of milk sometimes,
cut with water, and even then it
can't always get past the tumor,
and the next time the saliva comes up it's
chalkish and ropey, he has to roll it a
long time in his throat like a ball of
clay to form it and get it up and dis-
gorge the elliptical globule into the cup —
and the wonder to me is that it did not disgust me,
that glass of phlegm that stood there all day and
filled slowly with compound globes and then I'd
empty it and it would fill again and
shimmer there on the table until the
room seemed to turn around it
in an orderly way, like a model of the solar system
turning around the gold sun,
my father like the dark earth that
used to be the center of the universe, now
turning with the rest of us
around his death — bright glass of
spit on the table, these last mouthfuls of his life.

SHARON OLDS

MAY 1968

When the Dean said we could not cross campus
until the students gave up the buildings,
we lay down, in the street,
we said the cops will enter this gate
over us. Lying back on the cobbles,
I saw the buildings of New York City
from dirt level, they soared up
and stopped, chopped off — above them, the sky,
the night air over the island.
The mounted police moved, near us,
while we sang, and then I began to count,
12, 13, 14, 15,
I counted again, 15, 16, one
month since the day on that deserted beach,
17, 18, my mouth fell open,
my hair on the street,
if my period did not come tonight
I was pregnant. I could see the sole of a cop's
shoe, the gelding's belly, its genitals —
if they took me to Women's Detention and did
the exam on me, the speculum,
the fingers — I gazed into the horse's tail
like a comet-train. All week, I had
thought about getting arrested, half-longed
to give myself away. On the tar —
one brain in my head, another,
in the making, near the base of my tail —
I looked at the steel arc of the horse's
shoe, the curve of its belly, the cop's
nightstick, the buildings streaming up
away from the earth. I knew I should get up
and leave, but I lay there looking at the space
above us, until it turned deep blue and then
ashy, colorless, *Give me this one
night*, I thought, *and I'll give this child
the rest of my life*, the horses' heads,
this time, drooping, dipping, until
they slept in a circle around my body and my daughter.

SHARON OLDS

GOOD WILL

Sorting clothes, I find our son's old
jeans, the dirt worn so deeply in
they are almost tan, worked as a palimpsest,
the nub down to a flat gloss,
the metal of the rivets soured to ochre,
the back pockets curved like shields,
their stitching is like water far from land,
a long continuous swell. *Lee,*
the pants say in auric print,
LEE, they say in letters branded
in leather on the waistband, like the voice of a boy's
pants, the snap's rattle, the rough
descending and ascending scale of the zipper,
the coin-slot pocket inside the front pocket.
He had waited inside me so many years, his
egg in my side before I was born,
and he sprang fresh in his father that morning,
I had seen it long ago in science,
I shake out the jeans, and there are the knees
exploded, the white threads hanging
outside the body, the frail, torn,
blue knee open, singing of the boy.

Carl Phillips

BLUE

As through marble or the lining of
certain fish split open and scooped
clean, this is the blue vein
that rides, where the flesh is even
whiter than the rest of her, the splayed
thighs mother forgets, busy struggling
for command over bones: her own,
those of the chaise longue, all
equally uncooperative, and there's
the wind, too. This is her hair, gone
from white to blue in the air.

This is the black, shot with blue, of my dark
daddy's knuckles, that do not change, ever.
Which is to say they are no more pale
in anger than at rest, or when, as
I imagine them now, they follow
the same two fingers he has always used
to make the rim of every empty blue
glass in the house sing.
Always, the same
blue-to-black sorrow
no black surface can entirely hide.

Under the night, somewhere
between the white that is nothing so much as
blue, and the black that is, finally, nothing,
I am the man neither of you remembers.
Shielding, in the half-dark,
the blue eyes I sometimes forget
I don't have. Pulling my own stoop-
shouldered kind of blues across paper.
Apparently misinformed about the rumored
stuff of dreams: everywhere I inquired,
I was told look for blue.

411

CARL PHILLIPS

GLADS

Three, at the most four days later,
they're dying, knuckled
over at whichever flower has bloomed

largest. The way everything beautiful
finally breaks because of, from it.
As if this were necessary. The reason,

maybe, why the loveliest things are always
also the most ruined:
a man's aging breast falling until,

naturally, brassieres come to mind;
or why, given any crumbled wall, nobody
thinks to ask where did they go to,

bring them back, all those
missing pieces.
The difference between a cock at plain

rest, for once longing to put itself
nowhere special,
and one that, just done thirsting,

collapses, curls slowly back in on
itself.
In Renaissance Italy,

when depicting the saints and Christ
in mid-torment was all the rage,
the painters chose for their backdrops

the most unremarkable buildings,
landscapes stranded in neutral, people
doing the dull things they still do —

plowing, benchwarming a small hill,
idly swinging a staff at livestock,
or at nothing, gone fishing.

The idea was to throw up into relief,
in its rawest form, sheer affliction.
The motto was

No distractions from suffering, hence
the skies: in general, clear
or just clearing, washed of anything

like rescue birds hope clouds mercy.

OUR LADY

In the final hour, our lady — Of
the electric rosary, Of the highway,
by then Of the snows mostly — was

the man he'd always been really,
though, yes, we'd sometimes forgotten.
Still, even while he lay fanning,

as one might any spent flame, where
it was hot, between his legs, and
saying it didn't much matter anymore

about dying, what came of having
come too often, perhaps, to what in
the end had fallen short of divine

always, he said that more than the
bare-chested dancers and all-conquering
bass-line that had marked his every

sudden, strobe-lit appearance, at
precisely the same moment, in all of
the city's best clubs; more than

the just-heated towels and the water
he'd called holy in those windowless,
too thinly-walled, now all but

abandoned bath-houses, he regretted
the fine gowns that he'd made, just
by wearing them, famous; and then,

half, it seemed, to remind us, half
himself, he recreated the old shrug,
slowly raising from his hospital

robe — not green, he insisted, but
two shades, maybe three, shy of
turquoise — one shoulder to show

the words still tattooed there:
Adore me; for a moment, it was
possible to see it, the once

extraordinary beauty, the heated
grace for which we'd all of us,
once, so eagerly sought him.

AS FROM A QUIVER OF ARROWS

What do we do with the body, do we
burn it, do we set it in dirt or in
stone, do we wrap it in balm, honey,
oil, and then gauze and tip it onto
and trust it to a raft and to water?

What will happen to the memory of his
body, if one of us doesn't hurry now
and write it down fast? Will it be
salt or late light that it melts like?
Floss, rubber gloves, a chewed cap

to a pen elsewhere — how are we to
regard his effects, do we throw them
or use them away, do we say they are
relics and so treat them like relics?
Does his soiled linen count? If so,

would we be wrong then, to wash it?
There are no instructions whether it

should go to where are those with no
linen, or whether by night we should
memorially wear it ourselves, by day

reflect upon it folded, shelved, empty.
Here, on the floor behind his bed is
a bent photo — why? Were the two of
them lovers? Does it mean, where we
found it, that he forgot it or lost it

or intended a safekeeping? Should we
attempt to make contact? What if this
other man too is dead? Or alive, but
doesn't want to remember, is human?
Is it okay to be human, and fall away

from oblation and memory, if we forget,
and can't sometimes help it and sometimes
it is all that we want? How long, in
dawns or new cocks, does that take?
What if it is rest and nothing else that

we want? Is it a findable thing, small?
In what hole is it hidden? is it, maybe,
a country? Will a guide be required who
will say to us how? Do we fly? Do we
swim? What will I do now, with my hands?

LUNA MOTH

No eye that sees could fail to remark you:
like any leaf the rain leaves fixed to and
flat against the barn's gray shingle. But

what leaf, this time of year, is so pale,
the pale of leaves when they've lost just
enough green to become the green that *means*

loss and more loss, approaching? Give up
the flesh enough times, and whatever is lost
gets forgotten: that was the thought that I

woke to, those words in my head. I rose,
I did not dress, I left no particular body
sleeping and, stepping into the hour, I saw

you, strange sign, at once transparent and
impossible to entirely see through, and how
still: the still of being unmoved, and then

the still of no longer being able to be
moved. If I think of a heart, his, as I've
found it. . . . If I think of, increasingly, my

own. . . . If I look at you now, as from above,
and see the diva when she is caught in mid-
triumph, arms half-raised, the body as if

set at last free of the green sheath that has —
how many nights? — held her, it is not
without remembering another I once saw:

like you, except that something, a bird, some
wild and necessary hunger, had gotten to it;
and like the diva, but now broken, splayed

and torn, the green torn piecemeal from her.
I remember the hands, and — how small they
seemed, bringing the small ripped thing to me.

TOYS

Seeing them like this,
arranged according to size,
sectioned off by color,

I think it's not so much their being
made mostly for men, nor anything in
their being man-made; it's what

they are made *of* disturbs me: rubber
and urethane, plastic aiming for
the plastic of flesh,

and just missing. Growing up, I was
told once that, somewhere in the Vatican,
there's a room still, where —

ordered and numbered, as if
awaiting recall — lie all the phalluses
of stone, granite, tufa, fine marble,

that were removed from pagan statues
for lacking what any leaf, it seems,
can provide: some decorum.

I've never seen them, but their beauty,
I imagine, is twofold: what they're
made of, for one — what, in cracking,

suggests more than just the body that
came first, but the peril,
the vulnerability

that is all the flesh means to say,
singing; then, what even these
imitations before me — lesser somehow

but, to the eye and to touch, finally
more accurate, in being true
to an absurdity that is always there

in the real thing — even these seem
like wanting to tell about beauty,
that it also comes this way, in parts.

PARABLE

There was a saint once,
he had but to ring across
water a small bell, all

manner of fish
rose, as answer, he was
that holy, persuasive,

both, or the fish
perhaps merely
hungry, their bodies

a-shimmer with
that hope especially that
hunger brings, whatever

the reason, the fish
coming unassigned, in
schools coming

into the saint's hand and,
instead of getting,
becoming food.

I have thought, since, of
your body — as I first came
to know it, how it still

can be, with mine,
sometimes. I think on
that immediate and last gesture

of the fish leaving water
for flesh, for guarantee
they will die, and I cannot

rest on what to call it.
Not generosity, or
a blindness, trust, brute

stupidity. Not the soul
distracted from its natural
prayer, which is attention,

for in the story they are
paying attention. They
lose themselves eyes open.

LUCK

What we shall not perhaps get over, we
do get past, until — innocent,
with art for once

not in mind, *How did I get here,*
we ask one day, our gaze
relinquishing one space for the next

in which, not far from where
in the uncut grass we're sitting
four men arc the unsaid

between them with the thrown
shoes of horses, luck briefly as a thing
of heft made to shape through

air a path invisible, but there. . . .
Because we are flesh, because
who doesn't, someway, require touch,

it is the unsubstantial — that which can
neither know touch nor be known
by it — that most bewilders,

even if the four men at
play, if asked, presumably,
would not say so, anymore

than would the fifth man, busy
mowing the field's far
edge, behind me,

his slow, relentless pace promising
long hours before the sorrow
of seeing him go and,

later still, the sorrow
going, until eventually the difficulty
only is this: there was some.

Sylvia Plath

STILLBORN

These poems do not live: it's a sad diagnosis.
They grew their toes and fingers well enough,
Their little foreheads bulged with concentration.
If they missed out on walking about like people
It wasn't for any lack of mother-love.

O I cannot understand what happened to them!
They are proper in shape and number and every part.
They sit so nicely in the pickling fluid!
They smile and smile and smile and smile at me.
And still the lungs won't fill and the heart won't start.

They are not pigs, they are not even fish,
Though they have a piggy and a fishy air —
It would be better if they were alive, and that's what they were.
But they are dead, and their mother near dead with distraction,
And they stupidly stare, and do not speak of her.

CROSSING THE WATER

Black lake, black boat, two black, cut-paper people.
Where do the black trees go that drink here?
Their shadows must cover Canada.

A little light is filtering from the water flowers.
Their leaves do not wish us to hurry:
They are round and flat and full of dark advice.

Cold worlds shake from the oar.
The spirit of blackness is in us, it is in the fishes.
A snag is lifting a valedictory, pale hand;

Stars open among the lilies.
Are you not blinded by such expressionless sirens?
This is the silence of astounded souls.

421

DADDY

You do not do, you do not do
Any more, black shoe
In which I have lived like a foot
For thirty years, poor and white,
Barely daring to breathe or Achoo.

Daddy, I have had to kill you.
You died before I had time ———
Marble-heavy, a bag full of God,
Ghastly statue with one gray toe
Big as a Frisco seal

And a head in the freakish Atlantic
Where it pours bean green over blue
In the waters off beautiful Nauset.
I used to pray to recover you.
Ach, du.

In the German tongue, in the Polish town
Scraped flat by the roller
Of wars, wars, wars.
But the name of the town is common.
My Polack friend

Says there are a dozen or two.
So I never could tell where you
Put your foot, your root,
I never could talk to you.
The tongue stuck in my jaw.

It stuck in a barb wire snare.
Ich, ich, ich, ich,
I could hardly speak.
I thought every German was you.
And the language obscene

An engine, an engine
Chuffing me off like a Jew.
A Jew to Dachau, Auschwitz, Belsen.
I began to talk like a Jew.
I think I may well be a Jew.

The snows of the Tyrol, the clear beer of Vienna
Are not very pure or true.
With my gipsy ancestress and my weird luck

And my Taroc pack and my Taroc pack
I may be a bit of a Jew.

I have always been scared of *you*,
With your Luftwaffe, your gobbledygoo.
And your neat mustache
And your Aryan eye, bright blue.
Panzer-man, panzer-man, O You ——

Not God but a swastika
So black no sky could squeak through.
Every woman adores a Fascist,
The boot in the face, the brute
Brute heart of a brute like you.

You stand at the blackboard, daddy,
In the picture I have of you,
A cleft in your chin instead of your foot
But no less a devil for that, no not
Any less the black man who

Bit my pretty red heart in two.
I was ten when they buried you.
At twenty I tried to die
And get back, back, back to you.
I thought even the bones would do.

But they pulled me out of the sack,
And they stuck me together with glue.
And then I knew what to do.
I made a model of you,
A man in black with a Meinkampf look

And a love of the rack and the screw.
And I said I do, I do.
So daddy, I'm finally through.
The black telephone's off at the root,
The voices just can't worm through.

If I've killed one man, I've killed two ——
The vampire who said he was you
And drank my blood for a year,
Seven years, if you want to know.
Daddy, you can lie back now.

There's a stake in your fat black heart
And the villagers never liked you.
They are dancing and stamping on you.

They always *knew* it was you.
Daddy, daddy, you bastard, I'm through.

CUT

For Susan O'Neill Roe

What a thrill ——
My thumb instead of an onion.
The top quite gone
Except for a sort of a hinge

Of skin,
A flap like a hat,
Dead white.
Then that red plush.

Little pilgrim,
The Indian's axed your scalp.
Your turkey wattle
Carpet rolls

Straight from the heart.
I step on it,
Clutching my bottle
Of pink fizz.

A celebration, this is.
Out of a gap
A million soldiers run,
Redcoats, every one.

Whose side are they on?
O my
Homunculus, I am ill.
I have taken a pill to kill

The thin
Papery feeling.
Saboteur,
Kamikaze man ——

The stain on your
Gauze Ku Klux Klan

Babushka
Darkens and tarnishes and when

The balled
Pulp of your heart
Confronts its small
Mill of silence

How you jump ——
Trepanned veteran,
Dirty girl,
Thumb stump.

LADY LAZARUS

I have done it again.
One year in every ten
I manage it ——

A sort of walking miracle, my skin
Bright as a Nazi lampshade,
My right foot

A paperweight,
My face a featureless, fine
Jew linen.

Peel off the napkin
O my enemy.
Do I terrify? ——

The nose, the eye pits, the full set of teeth?
The sour breath
Will vanish in a day.

Soon, soon the flesh
The grave cave ate will be
At home on me

And I a smiling woman.
I am only thirty.
And like the cat I have nine times to die.

This is Number Three.
What a trash
To annihilate each decade.

What a million filaments.
The peanut-crunching crowd
Shoves in to see

Them unwrap me hand and foot ——
The big strip tease.
Gentlemen, ladies

These are my hands
My knees.
I may be skin and bone,

Nevertheless, I am the same, identical woman.
The first time it happened I was ten.
It was an accident.

The second time I meant
To last it out and not come back at all.
I rocked shut

As a seashell.
They had to call and call
And pick the worms off me like sticky pearls.

Dying
Is an art, like everything else.
I do it exceptionally well.

I do it so it feels like hell.
I do it so it feels real.
I guess you could say I've a call.

It's easy enough to do it in a cell.
It's easy enough to do it and stay put.
It's the theatrical

Comeback in broad day
To the same place, the same face, the same brute
Amused shout:

'A miracle!'
That knocks me out.
There is a charge

For the eyeing of my scars, there is a charge
For the hearing of my heart ——
It really goes.

And there is a charge, a very large charge
For a word or a touch
Or a bit of blood

Or a piece of my hair or my clothes.
So, so, Herr Doktor.
So, Herr Enemy.

I am your opus,
I am your valuable,
The pure gold baby

That melts to a shriek.
I turn and burn.
Do not think I underestimate your great concern.

Ash, ash —
You poke and stir.
Flesh, bone, there is nothing there ——

A cake of soap,
A wedding ring,
A gold filling.

Herr God, Herr Lucifer
Beware
Beware.

Out of the ash
I rise with my red hair
And I eat men like air.

Adrienne Rich

POWER

Living   in the earth-deposits   of our history

Today a backhoe divulged   out of a crumbling flank of earth
one bottle   amber   perfect   a hundred-year-old
cure for fever   or melancholy   a tonic
for living on this earth   in the winters of this climate

Today I was reading about Marie Curie:
she must have known she suffered   from radiation sickness
her body bombarded for years   by the element
she had purified
It seems she denied to the end
the source of the cataracts on her eyes
the cracked and suppurating skin   of her finger-ends
till she could no longer hold   a test-tube or a pencil

She died   a famous woman   denying
her wounds
denying
her wounds   came   from the same source as her power

PLANETARIUM

Thinking of Caroline Herschel (1750–1848)
astronomer, sister of William; and others.

A woman in the shape of a monster
a monster in the shape of a woman
the skies are full of them

a woman   'in the snow
among the Clocks and instruments
or measuring the ground with poles'

in her 98 years to discover
8 comets

she whom the moon ruled
like us
levitating into the night sky
riding the polished lenses

Galaxies of women, there
doing penance for impetuousness
ribs chilled
in those spaces   of the mind

An eye,

        'virile, precise and absolutely certain'
        from the mad webs of Uranusborg

                   encountering the NOVA

every impulse of light exploding
from the core
as life flies out of us

        Tycho whispering at last
        'Let me not seem to have lived in vain'

What we see, we see
and seeing is changing

the light that shrivels a mountain
and leaves a man alive

Heartbeat of the pulsar
heart sweating through my body

The radio impulse
pouring in from Taurus

        I am bombarded yet   I stand

I have been standing all my life in the
direct path of a battery of signals
the most accurately transmitted most
untranslatable language in the universe
I am a galactic cloud so deep   so invo-
luted that a light wave could take 15

years to travel through me   And has
taken   I am an instrument in the shape
of a woman trying to translate pulsations
into images   for the relief of the body
and the reconstruction of the mind.

DIVING INTO THE WRECK

First having read the book of myths,
and loaded the camera,
and checked the edge of the knife-blade,
I put on
the body-armor of black rubber
the absurd flippers
the grave and awkward mask.
I am having to do this
not like Cousteau with his
assiduous team
aboard the sun-flooded schooner
but here alone.

There is a ladder.
The ladder is always there
hanging innocently
close to the side of the schooner.
We know what it is for,
we who have used it.
Otherwise
it's a piece of maritime floss
some sundry equipment.

I go down.
Rung after rung and still
the oxygen immerses me
the blue light
the clear atoms
of our human air.
I go down.
My flippers cripple me,
I crawl like an insect down the ladder
and there is no one

to tell me when the ocean
will begin.

First the air is blue and then
it is bluer and then green and then
black I am blacking out and yet
my mask is powerful
it pumps my blood with power
the sea is another story
the sea is not a question of power
I have to learn alone
to turn my body without force
in the deep element.

And now: it is easy to forget
what I came for
among so many who have always
lived here
swaying their crenellated fans
between the reefs
and besides
you breathe differently down here.

I came to explore the wreck.
The words are purposes.
The words are maps.
I came to see the damage that was done
and the treasures that prevail.
I stroke the beam of my lamp
slowly along the flank
of something more permanent
than fish or weed

the thing I came for:
the wreck and not the story of the wreck
the thing itself and not the myth
the drowned face always staring
toward the sun
the evidence of damage
worn by salt and sway into this threadbare beauty
the ribs of the disaster
curving their assertion
among the tentative haunters.

This is the place.
And I am here, the mermaid whose dark hair
streams black, the merman in his armored body
We circle silently
about the wreck
we dive into the hold.
I am she: I am he

whose drowned face sleeps with open eyes
whose breasts still bear the stress
whose silver, copper, vermeil cargo lies
obscurely inside barrels
half-wedged and left to rot
we are the half-destroyed instruments
that once held to a course
the water-eaten log
the fouled compass

We are, I am, you are
by cowardice or courage
the one who find our way
back to this scene
carrying a knife, a camera
a book of myths
in which
our names do not appear.

SPLITTINGS

1

My body opens over San Francisco like the daylight raining down   each pore crying the change of light
I am not with her   I have been waking off and on
all night to that pain   not simply absence but
the presence of the past   destructive
to living here and now   Yet if I could instruct
myself, if we could learn to learn from pain
even as it grasps us   if the mind, the mind that lives
in this body could refuse   to let itself be crushed

in that grasp   it would loosen   Pain would have to stand
off from me and listen   its dark breath still on me
but the mind could begin to speak to pain
and pain would have to answer:

We are older now
we have met before   these are my hands before your eyes
my figure blotting out   all that is not mine
I am the pain of division   creator of divisions
it is I who blot your lover from you
and not the time-zones nor the miles
It is not separation calls me forth   but I
who am separation   And remember
I have no existence   apart from you

2

I believe I am choosing something new
not to suffer uselessly   yet still to feel
Does the infant memorize the body of the mother
and create her in absence?   or simply cry
primordial loneliness?   does the bed of the stream
once diverted   mourning   remember wetness?
But we, we live so much in these
configurations of the past   I choose
to separate her   from my past we have not shared
I choose not to suffer uselessly
to detect primordial pain as it stalks toward me
flashing its bleak torch in my eyes   blotting out
her particular being   the details of her love
I will not be divided   from her or from myself
by myths of separation
while her mind and body in Manhattan are more with me
than the smell of eucalyptus coolly burning   on these hills

3

The world tells me I am its creature
I am raked by eyes   brushed by hands
I want to crawl into her for refuge   lay my head
in the space   between her breast and shoulder
abnegating power for love

as women have done   or hiding
from power in her love   like a man
I refuse these givens   the splitting
between love and action   I am choosing
not to suffer uselessly   and not to use her
I choose to love   this time   for once
with all my intelligence

from AN ATLAS OF THE DIFFICULT WORLD

XIII (Dedications)

I know you are reading this poem
late, before leaving your office
of the one intense yellow lamp-spot and the darkening window
in the lassitude of a building faded to quiet
long after rush-hour.   I know you are reading this poem
standing up in a bookstore far from the ocean
on a grey day of early spring, faint flakes driven
across the plains' enormous spaces around you.
I know you are reading this poem
in a room where too much has happened for you to bear
where the bedclothes lie in stagnant coils on the bed
and the open valise speaks of flight
but you cannot leave yet.   I know you are reading this poem
as the underground train loses momentum and before running up the
        stairs
toward a new kind of love
your life has never allowed.
I know you are reading this poem by the light
of the television screen where soundless images jerk and slide
while you wait for the newscast from the *intifada.*
I know you are reading this poem in a waiting-room
of eyes met and unmeeting, of identity with strangers.
I know you are reading this poem by fluorescent light
in the boredom and fatigue of the young who are counted out,
count themselves out, at too early an age.   I know
you are reading this poem through your failing sight, the thick
lens enlarging these letters beyond all meaning yet you read on
because even the alphabet is precious.
I know you are reading this poem as you pace beside the stove
warming milk, a crying child on your shoulder, a book in your hand

because life is short and you too are thirsty.
I know you are reading this poem which is not in your language
guessing at some words while others keep you reading
and I want to know which words they are.
I know you are reading this poem listening for something, torn between
    bitterness and hope
turning back once again to the task you cannot refuse.
I know you are reading this poem because there is nothing else left to
    read
there where you have landed, stripped as you are.

THE NOVEL

All winter you went to bed early, drugging yourself on *War and Peace*
Prince Andrei's cold eyes taking in the sky from the battlefield
were your eyes, you went walking wrapped in his wound
like a padded coat against the winds from the two rivers
You went walking in the streets as if you were ordinary
as if you hadn't been pulling with your raw mittened hand
on the slight strand that held your tattered mind
blown like an old stocking from a wire
on the wind between two rivers.
                          All winter you asked nothing
of that book though it lay heavy on your knees
you asked only for a shed skin, many skins in which to walk
you were old woman, child, commander
you watched Natasha grow into a neutered thing
you felt your heart go still while your eyes swept the pages
you felt the pages thickening to the left and on the right-
hand growing few, you knew the end was coming
you knew beyond the ending lay
your own, unwritten life

ONE LIFE

A woman walking in a walker on the cliffs
recalls great bodily joys, much pain.
Nothing in her is apt to say

ADRIENNE RICH

My heart aches, though she read those words
in a battered college text, this morning
as the sun rose. It is all too
mixed, the heart too mixed with laughter
raucousing the grief, her life
too mixed, she shakes her heavy
silvered hair at all the fixed
declarations of baggage. I should be dead and I'm alive
don't ask me how; I don't eat like I should
and still I like how the drop of vodka
hits the tongue. I was a worker and a mother,
that means a worker and a worker
but for one you don't pay union dues
or get a pension; for the other
the men ran the union, we ran the home.
It was terrible and good, we had more than half a life,
I had four lives at least, one out of marriage
when I kicked up all the dust I could
before I knew what I was doing.
One life with the girls on the line during the war,
yes, painting our legs and jitterbugging together
one life with a husband, not the worst,
one with your children, none of it just what you'd thought.
None of it what it could have been, if we'd known.
We took what we could.
But even this is a life, I'm reading a lot of books
I never read, my daughter brought home from school,
plays where you can almost hear them talking,
Romantic poets, Isaac Babel. A lot of lives
worse and better than what I knew. I'm walking again.
My heart doesn't ache; sometimes though it rages.

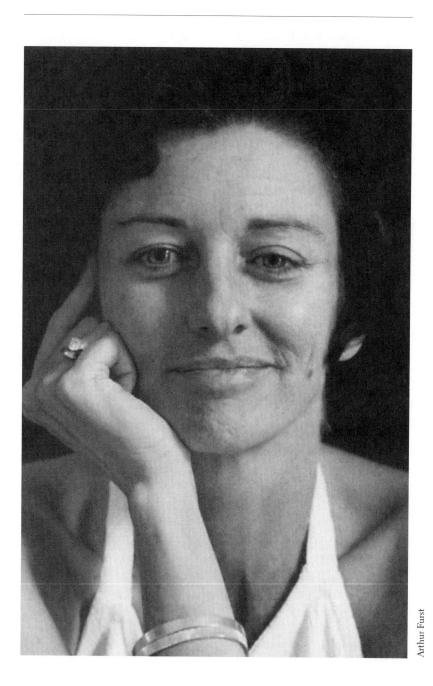

Anne Sexton

HER KIND

I have gone out, a possessed witch,
haunting the black air, braver at night;
dreaming evil, I have done my hitch
over the plain houses, light by light:
lonely thing, twelve-fingered, out of mind.
A woman like that is not a woman, quite.
I have been her kind.

I have found the warm caves in the woods,
filled them with skillets, carvings, shelves,
closets, silks, innumerable goods;
fixed the suppers for the worms and the elves:
whining, rearranging the disaligned.
A woman like that is misunderstood.
I have been her kind.

I have ridden in your cart, driver,
waved my nude arms at villages going by,
learning the last bright routes, survivor
where your flames still bite my thigh
and my ribs crack where your wheels wind.
A woman like that is not ashamed to die.
I have been her kind.

WITH MERCY FOR THE GREEDY

For my friend, Ruth, who urges me to make an
appointment for the Sacrament of Confession

Concerning your letter in which you ask
me to call a priest and in which you ask
me to wear The Cross that you enclose;
your own cross,
your dog-bitten cross,
no larger than a thumb,
small and wooden, no thorns, this rose —

I pray to its shadow,
that gray place
where it lies on your letter . . . deep, deep.
I detest my sins and I try to believe
in The Cross. I touch its tender hips, its dark jawed face,
its solid neck, its brown sleep.

True. There is
a beautiful Jesus.
He is frozen to his bones like a chunk of beef.
How desperately he wanted to pull his arms in!
How desperately I touch his vertical and horizontal axes!
But I can't. Need is not quite belief.

All morning long
I have worn
your cross, hung with package string around my throat.
It tapped me lightly as a child's heart might,
tapping secondhand, softly waiting to be born.
Ruth, I cherish the letter you wrote.

My friend, my friend, I was born
doing reference work in sin, and born
confessing it. This is what poems are:
with mercy
for the greedy,
they are the tongue's wrangle,
the world's pottage, the rat's star.

TO A FRIEND WHOSE WORK HAS COME TO TRIUMPH

Consider Icarus, pasting those sticky wings on,
testing that strange little tug at his shoulder blade,
and think of that first flawless moment over the lawn
of the labyrinth. Think of the difference it made!
There below are the trees, as awkward as camels;
and here are the shocked starlings pumping past
and think of innocent Icarus who is doing quite well:
larger than a sail, over the fog and the blast
of the plushy ocean, he goes. Admire his wings!

Feel the fire at his neck and see how casually
he glances up and is caught, wondrously tunneling
into that hot eye. Who cares that he fell back to the sea?
See him acclaiming the sun and come plunging down
while his sensible daddy goes straight into town.

THE ABORTION

Somebody who should have been born
is gone.

Just as the earth puckered its mouth,
each bud puffing out from its knot,
I changed my shoes, and then drove south.

Up past the Blue Mountains, where
Pennsylvania humps on endlessly,
wearing, like a crayoned cat, its green hair,

its roads sunken in like a gray washboard;
where, in truth, the ground cracks evilly,
a dark socket from which the coal has poured,

Somebody who should have been born
is gone.

the grass as bristly and stout as chives,
and me wondering when the ground would break,
and me wondering how anything fragile survives;

up in Pennsylvania, I met a little man,
not Rumpelstiltskin, at all, at all . . .
he took the fullness that love began.

Returning north, even the sky grew thin
like a high window looking nowhere.
The road was as flat as a sheet of tin.

Somebody who should have been born
is gone.

Yes, woman, such logic will lead
to loss without death. Or say what you meant,
you coward . . . this baby that I bleed.

MAN AND WIFE

To speke of wo
that is in mariage . . .

We are not lovers.
We do not even know each other.
We look alike
but we have nothing to say.
We are like pigeons . . .

that pair who came to the suburbs
by mistake,
forsaking Boston where they bumped
their small heads against a blind wall,
having worn out the fruit stalls in the North End,
the amethyst windows of Louisburg Square,
the seats on the Common
And the traffic that kept stamping
and stamping.

Now there is green rain for everyone
as common as eyewash.
Now they are together
like strangers in a two-seater outhouse,
eating and squatting together.
They have teeth and knees
but they do not speak.
A soldier is forced to stay with a soldier
because they share the same dirt
and the same blows.

They are exiles
soiled by the same sweat and the drunkard's dream.
As it is they can only hang on,
their red claws wound like bracelets

around the same limb.
Even their song is not a sure thing.
It is not a language;
it is a kind of breathing.
They are two asthmatics
whose breath sobs in and out
through a small fuzzy pipe.

Like them
we neither talk nor clear our throats.
Oh darling,
we gasp in unison beside our window pane,
drunk on the drunkard's dream.
Like them
we can only hang on.

But they would pierce our heart
if they could only fly the distance.

IN CELEBRATION OF MY UTERUS

Everyone in me is a bird.
I am beating all my wings.
They wanted to cut you out
but they will not.
They said you were immeasurably empty
but you are not.
They said you were sick unto dying
but they were wrong.
You are singing like a school girl.
You are not torn.

Sweet weight,
in celebration of the woman I am
and of the soul of the woman I am
and of the central creature and its delight
I sing for you. I dare to live.
Hello, spirit. Hello, cup.
Fasten, cover. Cover that does contain.
Hello to the soil of the fields.
Welcome, roots.

Each cell has a life.
There is enough here to please a nation.
It is enough that the populace own these goods.
Any person, any commonwealth would say of it,
"It is good this year that we may plant again
and think forward to a harvest.
A blight had been forecast and has been cast out."
Many women are singing together of this:
one is in a shoe factory cursing the machine,
one is at the aquarium tending a seal,
one is dull at the wheel of her Ford,
one is at the toll gate collecting,
one is tying the cord of a calf in Arizona,
one is straddling a cello in Russia,
one is shifting pots on the stove in Egypt,
one is painting her bedroom walls moon color,
one is dying but remembering a breakfast,
one is stretching on her mat in Thailand,
one is wiping the ass of her child,
one is staring out the window of a train
in the middle of Wyoming and one is
anywhere and some are everywhere and all
seem to be singing, although some can not
sing a note.

Sweet weight,
in celebration of the woman I am
let me carry a ten-foot scarf,
let me drum for the nineteen-year-olds,
let me carry bowls for the offering
(if that is my part).
Let me study the cardiovascular tissue,
let me examine the angular distance of meteors,
let me suck on the stems of flowers
(if that is my part).
Let me make certain tribal figures
(if that is my part).
For this thing the body needs
let me sing
for the supper,
for the kissing,
for the correct
yes.

ANNE SEXTON

THE FURY OF COCKS

There they are
drooping over the breakfast plates,
angel-like,
folding in their sad wing,
animal sad,
and only the night before
there they were
playing the banjo.
Once more the day's light comes
with its immense sun,
its mother trucks,
its engines of amputation.
Whereas last night
the cock knew its way home,
as stiff as a hammer,
battering in with all
its awful power.
That theater.
Today it is tender,
a small bird,
as soft as a baby's hand.
She is the house.
He is the steeple.
When they fuck they are God.
When they break away they are God.
When they snore they are God.
In the morning they butter the toast.
They don't say much.
They are still God.
All the cocks of the world are God,
blooming, blooming, blooming
into the sweet blood of woman.

Charles Simic

CHARLES SIMIC

Charles Simic is a sentence.
A sentence has a beginning and an end.

Is he a simple or compound sentence?
It depends on the weather,
It depends on the stars above.

What is the subject of the sentence?
The subject is your beloved Charles Simic.

How many verbs are there in the sentence?
Eating, sleeping and fucking are some of its verbs.

What is the object of the sentence?
The object, my little ones,
Is not yet in sight.

And who is writing this awkward sentence?
A blackmailer, a girl in love,
And an applicant for a job.

Will they end with a period or a question mark?
They'll end with an exclamation point and an ink spot.

POEM WITHOUT A TITLE

I say to the lead
Why did you let yourself
Be cast into a bullet?
Have you forgotten the alchemists?
Have you given up hope
Of turning into gold?

Nobody answers.
Lead. Bullet.

447

With names like that
The sleep is deep and long.

FEBRUARY

The one who lights the wood stove
Gets up in the dark.

How cold the iron is to the hand
Groping to open the flue,
The hand that will draw back
At the roar of the wind outside.

The wood that no longer smells of the woods;
The wood that smells of rats and mice —
And the matches which are always so loud
In the glacial stillness.

By its flare you'll see her squat;
Gaunt, wide-eyed;
Her lips saying the stark headlines
Going up in flames.

POEM

Every morning I forget how it is.
I watch the smoke mount
In great strides above the city.
I belong to no one.

Then, I remember my shoes,
How I have to put them on,
How bending over to tie them up
I will look into the earth.

CHARLES SIMIC

STONE

Go inside a stone
That would be my way.
Let somebody else become a dove
Or gnash with a tiger's tooth.
I am happy to be a stone.

From the outside the stone is a riddle:
No one knows how to answer it.
Yet within, it must be cool and quiet
Even though a cow steps on it full weight,
Even though a child throws it in a river;
The stone sinks, slow, unperturbed
To the river bottom
Where the fishes come to knock on it
And listen.

I have seen sparks fly out
When two stones are rubbed,
So perhaps it is not dark inside after all;
Perhaps there is a moon shining
From somewhere, as though behind a hill —
Just enough light to make out
The strange writings, the star-charts
On the inner walls.

FORK

This strange thing must have crept
Right out of hell.
It resembles a bird's foot
Worn around the cannibal's neck.

As you hold it in your hand,
As you stab with it into a piece of meat,
It is possible to imagine the rest of the bird:
Its head which like your fist
Is large, bald, beakless and blind.

SOLITUDE

There now, where the first crumb
Falls from the table
You think no one hears it
As it hits the floor

But somewhere already
The ants are putting on
Their Quakers' hats
And setting out to visit you.

FEAR

Fear passes from man to man
Unknowing,
As one leaf passes its shudder
To another.

All at once the whole tree is trembling
And there is no sign of the wind.

THE LITTLE PINS OF MEMORY

There was a child's Sunday suit
Pinned to a tailor's dummy
In a dusty store window.
The store looked closed for years.

I lost my way there once
In a Sunday kind of quiet,
Sunday kind of afternoon light
On a street of red-brick tenements.

How do you like that?
I said to no one.
How do you like that?
I said it again today upon waking.

That street went on forever
And all along I could feel the pins
In my back, prickling
The dark and heavy cloth.

CLASSIC BALLROOM DANCES

Grandmothers who wring the necks
Of chickens; old nuns
With names like Theresa, Marianne,
Who pull schoolboys by the ear;

The intricate steps of pickpockets
Working the crowd of the curious
At the scene of an accident; the slow shuffle
Of the evangelist with a sandwich-board;

The hesitation of the early morning customer
Peeking through the window-grille
Of a pawnshop; the weave of a little kid
Who is walking to school with eyes closed;

And the ancient lovers, cheek to cheek,
On the dancefloor of the Union Hall,
Where they also hold charity raffles
On rainy Monday nights of an eternal November.

THE OLD WORLD

for Dan and Jeanne

I believe in the soul; so far
It hasn't made much difference.
I remember an afternoon in Sicily.
The ruins of some temple.
Columns fallen in the grass like naked lovers.

The olives and goat cheese tasted delicious
And so did the wine
With which I toasted the coming night,

The darting swallows,
The Saracen wind and moon.

It got darker. There was something
Long before there were words:
The evening meal of shepherds . . .
A fleeting whiteness among the trees . . .
Eternity eavesdropping on time.

The goddess going to bathe in the sea.
She must not be followed.
These rocks, these cypress trees,
May be her old lovers.
Oh to be one of them, the wine whispered to me.

ENTERTAINING THE CANARY

Yellow feathers,
Is it true
You chirp to the cop
On the beat?

Desist. Turn your
Nervous gaze
At the open bathroom door
Where I'm soaping

My love's back
And putting my chin on her shoulder
So I can do the same for her
Breasts and crotch.

Sing. Flutter your wings
As if you were applauding,
Or I'll throw her black slip
Over your gilded cage.

errata

Where it says snow
read teeth-marks of a virgin
Where it says knife read
you passed through my bones
like a police-whistle
Where it says table read horse
Where it says horse read my migrant's bundle
Apples are to remain apples
Each time a hat appears
think of Isaac Newton
reading the Old Testament
Remove all periods
They are scars made by words
I couldn't bring myself to say
Put a finger over each sunrise
it will blind you otherwise
That damn ant is still stirring
Will there be time left to list
all errors to replace
all hands guns owls plates
all cigars ponds woods and reach
that beer-bottle my greatest mistake
the word I allowed to be written
when I should have shouted
her name

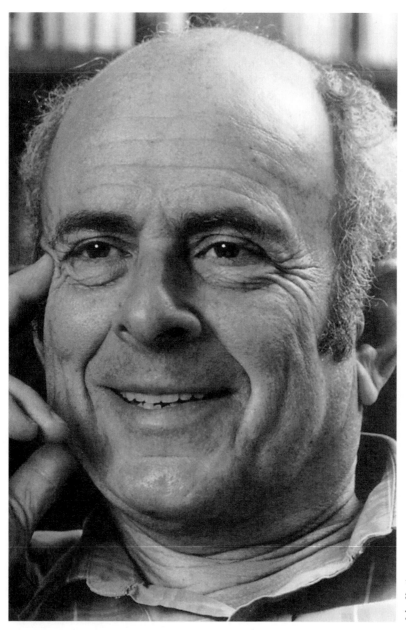

John Keating

Louis Simpson

WORKING LATE

A light is on in my father's study.
"Still up?" he says, and we are silent,
looking at the harbor lights,
listening to the surf
and the creak of coconut boughs.

He is working late on cases.
No impassioned speech! He argues from evidence,
actually pacing out and measuring,
while the fans revolving on the ceiling
winnow the true from the false.

Once he passed a brass curtain rod
through a head made out of plaster
and showed the jury the angle of fire —
where the murderer must have stood.
For years, all through my childhood,
if I opened a closet . . . bang!
There would be the dead man's head
with a black hole in the forehead.

All the arguing in the world
will not stay the moon.
She has come all the way from Russia
to gaze for a while in a mango tree
and light the wall of a veranda,
before resuming her interrupted journey
beyond the harbor and the lighthouse
at Port Royal, turning away
from land to the open sea.

Yet, nothing in nature changes, from that day to this,
she is still the mother of us all.
I can see the drifting offshore lights,
black posts where the pelicans brood.

And the light that used to shine
at night in my father's study
now shines as late in mine.

DINNER AT THE SEA-VIEW INN

1

Peter said, "I'd like some air."

"That's a good idea," said Marie's father.
"Why don't you young people go for a walk?"

Marie glanced at her mother.
Something passed between them. A warning.

2

When Peter and Marie walked through the dining room
everyone stared.
                    I just think so,
he reminded himself, and said,
"Fitzgerald says that nobody thinks about us
as much as we think they do."

"Who's he?" said Marie. "Another of your favorite authors?"

3

She wanted to know where he was taking her.

"I just had to get out of there.
Wouldn't it be great to hire a taxi
and just keep going?"

               "Why?" said Marie.

"It's a wonderful night."

"I'd rather have my own car," said Marie.

4

"I'm getting cold," said Marie.
"How much further are we going?"

"All right," he said.

And they walked back.

"When I was a child," said Peter,
"I used to think that the waves were cavalry . . .
the way they come in, curling over."

She said, "Is that what you were in,
the calvary?"

He laughed. "Calvary? For Christ's sake . . ."

5

"Did you have a good walk?" said Marie's father.

Marie said something to her mother.

Shortly after, Mr. Shulman ordered the car,
and they all drove back to New York.

They let Peter out in front of his building
on West Eighty-fourth Street, saying goodnight.
All but Marie . . . She still sat stiffly,
unsmiling. She had been offended.

6

Everything was just as he'd left it . . .
the convertible couch,
the reading lamp and chair,
and the stand with the typewriter.

He undressed and went to bed,
and turned out the light.

Lying in bed, hands clasped beneath his head,
listening . . .

to the stopping and starting of traffic
in the street five floors below.
And the opening of the elevator,
and the sound of feet going down the corridor.

RIVERSIDE DRIVE

I have been staring at a sentence
for fifteen minutes. The mind
was not made for social science.

I take my overcoat and go.

Night has fallen on Riverside Drive . . .
the sign for Spry shining
across the Hudson: "Spry for Frying ****
for Baking."

I am thinking of Rilke
and "Who if I cried would hear me
among the angelic orders?"

It seems that we are here to say
names like "Spry" and "Riverside Drive" . . .
to carry the names of places
and things with us, into the night

glimmering with stars and constellations.

THE CABIN

A woodpile and a fence,
grass, a hedge, a screen of trees . . .
I wish I had romantic neighbors
to talk about, like the lady

459

LOUIS SIMPSON

Yeats speaks of. When she was offended
by a farmer, her serving man
ran out with the garden shears
and brought her the farmer's ears
in a little covered dish.

I have no man to serve me,
but once, offended by the lout
who lives across the street,
I quarreled with him, loudly.
When his wife put her head out
and said, "Peter, I don't like your language,"
I replied, on the moment's thought,
"And I don't like your face."
We haven't been troubled by them since.

Yeats created Hanrahan,
the mighty lecher. What
lust-driven, legendary man
shall I summon? Where we live
there are no legends, only gossip.
Yet the great matter of Troy
that ended with a whole town burning
began with an inch of skin
between a woman's skirt and stocking.

I give you my friend Roger
who recently left Denise
and is living with Diane
in a motel in Florida.
Watching daytime television . . .
Mosquitoes and tractor trailers
keeping him awake, making his heart race,
like a clashing of shields
and swords, and flights of arrows.

QUIET DESPERATION

At the post office he sees Joe McInnes.
Joe says, "We're having some people over.
It'll be informal. Come as you are."

She is in the middle
of preparing dinner. Tonight
she is trying an experiment:
Hal Burgonyaual — Fish-Potato Casserole.
She has cooked and drained the potatoes
and cut the fish in pieces.
Now she has to "mash potatoes,
add butter and hot milk," et cetera.

He relays Joe's invitation.
"No," she says, "not on your life.
Muriel McInnes is no friend of mine."

It appears that she told Muriel
that the Goldins live above their means,
and Muriel told Mary Goldin.

He listens carefully, to get things right.
The feud between the Andersons and the Kellys
began with Ruth Anderson calling Mike Kelly
a reckless driver. Finally
the Andersons had to sell their house and move.

Social life is no joke.
It can be the only life there is.

*

In the living room the battle of Iwo Jima
is in progress, watched by his son.
Men are dying on the beach,
pinned down by a machine gun.

The marine carrying the satchel charge
falls. Then Sergeant Stryker
picks up the charge and starts running.

Now you are with the enemy machine gun
firing out of the pillbox
as Stryker comes running,
bullets at his heels kicking up dust.
He makes it to the base of the pillbox,
lights the charge, raises up,
and heaves it through the opening.

The pillbox explodes . . .
the NCO's wave, "Move out!"

And he rises to his feet.
He's seen the movie. Stryker gets killed
just as they're raising the flag.

         *

A feeling of pressure . . .
There is something that needs to be done
immediately.
         But there is nothing,
only himself. His life is passing,
and afterwards there will be eternity,
silence, and infinite space.

He thinks, "Firewood!" —
and goes to the basement,
takes the Swede-saw off the wall,
and goes outside, to the woodpile.

He carries an armful to the sawhorse
and saws the logs into smaller pieces.
In twenty minutes he has a pile of firewood
cut just the right length.
He carries the cut logs into the house
and arranges them in a neat pile
next to the fireplace.

Then looks around for something else to do,
to relieve the feeling of pressure.

The dog!
He will take the dog for a walk.

         *

They make a futile procession . . .
he commanding her to "Heel!" —
she dragging back or straining ahead.

The leaves are turning yellow.
Between the trunks of the trees

the cove is blue, with ripples.
The swans — this year there are seven —
are sailing line astern.

But when you come closer
the rocks above the shore are littered
with daggers of broken glass
where the boys sat on summer nights
and broke beer bottles afterwards.

And the beach is littered, with cans,
containers, heaps of garbage,
newspaper wadded against the sea-wall.
Someone has even dumped a mattress . . .
a definite success!
Some daring guy, some Stryker
in the pickup speeding away.

He cannot bear the sun
going over and going down . . .
the trees and houses vanishing
in quiet every day.

IN THE SUBURBS

There's no way out.
You were born to waste your life.
You were born to this middleclass life

As others before you
Were born to walk in procession
To the temple, singing.

PHYSICAL UNIVERSE

He woke at five and, unable
to go back to sleep,
went downstairs.

LOUIS SIMPSON

A book was lying on the table
where his son had done his homework.
He took it into the kitchen,
made coffee, poured himself a cup,
and settled down to read.

"There was a local eddy in the swirling gas
of the primordial galaxy,
and a cloud was formed, the protosun,
as wide as the present solar system.

"This contracted. Some of the gas
formed a diffuse, spherical nebula,
a thin disk, that cooled and flattened.
Pulled one way by its own gravity,
the other way by the sun,
it broke, forming smaller clouds,
the protoplanets. Earth
was 2,000 times as wide as it is now."

The earth was without form, and void,
and darkness was upon the face of the deep.

*

"Then the sun began to shine,
dispelling the gases and vapors,
shrinking the planets, melting earth,
separating iron and silicate
to form the core and mantle.
Continents appeared . . ."

history, civilization,
the discovery of America
and the settling of Green Harbor,
bringing us to Tuesday, the seventh of July.

Tuesday, the day they pick up the garbage!
He leapt into action,
took the garbage bag out of its container,
tied it with a twist of wire,
and carried it out to the toolshed,
taking care not to let the screen door slam,
and put it in the large garbage can

that was three-quarters full.
He kept it in the toolshed so the raccoons
couldn't get at it.

He carried the can out to the road,
then went back into the house
and walked around, picking up newspapers
and fliers for: "Thompson Seedless Grapes,
California's finest sweet eating";

"Scott Bathroom Tissue";

"Legislative report from Senator Ken LaValle."

He put all this paper in a box,
and emptied the waste baskets in the two
downstairs bathrooms,
and the basket in the study.

He carried the box out to the road,
taking care not to let the screen door slam,
and placed the box next to the garbage.

Now let the garbage men come!

*

He went back upstairs.
Mary said, "Did you put out the garbage?"
But her eyes were closed.
She was sleeping, yet could speak in her sleep,
ask a question, even answer one.

"Yes," he said, and climbed into bed.
She turned around to face him,
with her eyes still closed.

He thought, perhaps she's an oracle,
speaking from the Collective Unconscious.
He said to her, "Do you agree with Darwin
that people and monkeys have a common ancestor?
Or should we stick to the Bible?"

LOUIS SIMPSON

She said, "Did you take out the garbage?"

"Yes," he said, for the second time.
Then thought about it. Her answer
had something in it of the sublime.
Like a *koan* . . . the kind of irrelevance
a Zen master says to the disciple
who is asking riddles of the universe.

He put his arm around her,
and she continued to breathe evenly
from the depths of sleep.

Arthur Furst

W. D. Snodgrass

VIEWING THE BODY

Flowers like a gangster's funeral;
    Eyeshadow like a whore.
They all say isn't she beautiful.
    She, who never wore

Lipstick or such a dress,
    Never got taken out,
Was scarcely looked at, much less
    Wanted or talked about;

Who, gray as a mouse, crept
    The dark halls at her mother's
Or snuggled, soft, and slept
    Alone in the dim bedcovers.

Today at last she holds
    All eyes and a place of honor
Till the obscene red folds
    Of satin close down on her.

from HEART'S NEEDLE

9

I get numb and go in
though the dry ground will not hold
    the few dry swirls of snow
and it must not be very cold.
A friend asks how you've been
    and I don't know

or see much right to ask.
Or what use it could be to know.
    In three months since you came
the leaves have fallen and the snow;

467

your pictures pinned above my desk
        seem much the same.

    Somehow I come to find
myself upstairs in the third floor
        museum's halls,
walking to kill my time once more
among the enduring and resigned
        stuffed animals,

        where, through a century's
caprice, displacement and
        known treachery between
its wars, they hear some old command
and in their peaceable kingdoms freeze
        to this still scene,

    Nature Morte. Here
by the door, its guardian,
        the patchwork dodo stands
where you and your stepsister ran
laughing and pointing. Here, last year,
        you pulled my hands

        and had your first, worst quarrel,
so toys were put up on your shelves.
        Here in the first glass cage
the little bobcats arch themselves,
still practicing their snarl
        of constant rage.

    The bison, here, immense,
shoves at his calf, brow to brow,
        and looks it in the eye
to see what is it thinking now.
I forced you to obedience;
        I don't know why.

        Still the lean lioness
beyond them, on her jutting ledge
        of shale and desert shrub,
stands watching always at the edge,
stands hard and tanned and envious
        above her cub;

with horns locked in tall heather,
two great Olympian Elk stand bound,
   fixed in their lasting hate
till hunger brings them both to ground.
Whom equal weakness binds together
   none shall separate.

   Yet separate in the ocean
of broken ice, the white bear reels
   beyond the leathery groups
of scattered, drab Arctic seals
arrested here in violent motion
   like Napoleon's troops.

   Our states have stood so long
at war, shaken with hate and dread,
   they are paralyzed at bay;
once we were out of reach, we said,
we would grow reasonable and strong.
   Some other day.

   Like the cold men of Rome,
we have won costly fields to sow
   in salt, our only seed.
Nothing but injury will grow.
I write you only the bitter poems
   that you can't read.

   Onan who would not breed
a child to take his brother's bread
   and be his brother's birth,
rose up and left his lawful bed,
went out and spilled his seed
   in the cold earth.

   I stand by the unborn,
by putty-colored children curled
   in jars of alcohol,
that waken to no other world,
unchanging, where no eye shall mourn.
   I see the caul

   that wrapped a kitten, dead.
I see the branching, doubled throat

of a two-headed foal;
I see the hydrocephalic goat;
here is the curled and swollen head,
    there, the burst skull;

    skin of a limbless calf;
a horse's foetus, mummified;
    mounted and joined forever,
the Siamese twin dogs that ride
belly to belly, half and half,
    that none shall sever.

    I walk among the growths,
by gangrenous tissue, goiter, cysts,
    by fistulas and cancers,
where the malignancy man loathes
is held suspended and persists.
    And I don't know the answers.

    The window's turning white.
The world moves like a diseased heart
    packed with ice and snow.
Three months now we have been apart
less than a mile. I cannot fight
    or let you go.

"AFTER EXPERIENCE TAUGHT ME . . ."

After experience taught me that all the ordinary
Surroundings of social life are futile and vain;

    I'm going to show you something very
    Ugly: someday, it might save your life.

Seeing that none of the things I feared contain
In themselves anything either good or bad

    What if you get caught without a knife;
    Nothing — even a loop of piano wire;

Excepting only in the effect they had
Upon my mind, I resolved to inquire

> Take the first two fingers of this hand;
> Fork them out — kind of a "V for Victory" —

Whether there might be something whose discovery
Would grant me supreme, unending happiness.

> And jam them into the eyes of your enemy.
> You have to do this hard. Very hard. Then press

No virtue can be thought to have priority
Over this endeavor to preserve one's being.

> Both fingers down around the cheekbone
> And setting your foot high into the chest

No man can desire to act rightly, to be blessed,
To live rightly, without simultaneously

> You must call up every strength you own
> And you can rip off the whole facial mask.

Wishing to be, to act, to live. He must ask
First, in other words, to actually exist.

> And you, whiner, who wastes your time
>   Dawdling over the remorseless earth,
> What evil, what unspeakable crime
>   Have you made your life worth?

OLD APPLE TREES

Like battered old millhands, they stand in the orchard —
Like drunk legionnaires, heaving themselves up,
Lurching to attention. Not one of them wobbles
The same way as another. Uniforms won't fit them —
All those cramps, humps, bulges. Here, a limb's gone;
There, rain and corruption have eaten the whole core.
They've all grown too tall, too thick, or too something.
Like men bent too long over desks, engines, benches,
Or bent under mailsacks, under loss.
They've seen too much history and bad weather, grown

Around rocks, into high winds, diseases, grown
Too long to be willful, too long to be changed.

Oh, I could replant, bulldoze the lot,
Get nursery stock, all the latest ornamentals,
Make the whole place look like a suburb,
Each limb sleek as a teeny bopper's — pink
To the very crotch — each trunk smoothed, ideal
As the fantasy life of an adman.
We might just own the Arboreal Muscle Beach:
Each tree disguised as its neighbor. Or each disguised
As if not its neighbor — each doing its own thing
Like executives' children.

                                        At least I could prune,
At least I should trim the dead wood; fill holes
Where rain collects and decay starts. Well, I should;
I should. There's a red squirrel nests here someplace.
I live in the hope of hearing one saw-whet owl.
Then, too, they're right about Spring. Bees hum
Through these branches like lascivious intentions. The white
Petals drift down, sift across the ground; this air's so rich
No man should come here except on a working pass;
No man should leave here without going to confession.
All Fall, apples nearly crack the boughs;
They hang here red as candles in the
White oncoming snow.

Tonight we'll drive down to the bad part of town
To the New Hungarian Bar or the Klub Polski,
To the Old Hellas where we'll eat the new spring lamb;
Drink good *mavrodaphne*, say, at the Laikon Bar,
Send drinks to the dancers, those meatcutters and laborers
Who move in their native dances, the archaic forms.
Maybe we'll still find our old crone selling chestnuts,
Whose toothless gums can spit out fifteen languages,
Who turns, there, late at night, in the center of the floor,
Her ancient dry hips wheeling their slow, slow *tsamikos*;
We'll stomp under the tables, whistle, we'll all hiss
Till even the belly dancer leaves, disgraced.

We'll drive back, lushed and vacant, in the first dawn;
Out of the light gray mists may rise our flowering
Orchard, the rough trunks holding their formations

Like elders of Colonus, the old men of Thebes
Tossing their white hair, almost whispering,
Soon, each one of us will be taken
By dark powers under this ground
That drove us here, that warped us.
Not one of us got it his own way.
Nothing like any one of us
Will be seen again, forever.
Each of us held some noble shape in mind.
It seemed better that we kept alive.

LOVE LAMP

There's our candle, on the bedstand still,
That served, warm nights, for lovelight
And the rays of its glass panels played
On our entangled legs and shoulders
Like some sailor's red and blue tattoos
Or as cathedral stained glass alters
Congregated flesh to things less
Carnal, tinged by its enfolding glow.

What could that frail lamp seem
To prowlers outside — the fox, say, the owl,
Or to some smaller creature, shrieking,
Pierced in the clutch of tooth and claw
That interrupted love's enactments?
Our glancing flashlight, though, showed
Only scattered grey fur, some broken
Feathers, bloodstained, on the lawn.

Scuttling back to bed, a little
Chilled from the wet grass, we scratched
A match restoring our small gleam
To see there, sinking in soft wax,
The wings and swimming dark limbs
Of that moth — still there, hardened
By the years like amber. While I remember
The scathing fire-points of his eyes.

Christopher Felver

Gary Snyder

"ONE SHOULD NOT TALK TO A SKILLED HUNTER ABOUT WHAT IS FORBIDDEN BY THE BUDDHA"

—Hsiang-yen

A gray fox, female, nine pounds three ounces.
39 5/8" long with tail.
Peeling skin back (Kai
reminded us to chant the *Shingyo* first)
cold pelt. crinkle; and musky smell
mixed with dead-body odor starting.

Stomach content: a whole ground squirrel well chewed
plus one lizard foot
and somewhere from inside the ground squirrel
a bit of aluminum foil.

The secret.
and the secret hidden deep in that.

BUBBS CREEK HAIRCUT

High ceilinged and the double mirrors, the
    calendar a splendid alpine scene — scab barber —
in stained white barber gown, alone, sat down, old man
a summer fog gray San Francisco day
I walked right in. On Howard Street
               haircut a dollar twenty-five.
Just clip it close as it will go.
    "Now why you want your hair cut back like that."
    — Well I'm going to the Sierras for a while
Bubbs Creek and on across to upper Kern.
        He wriggled clippers
"Well I been up there, I built the cabin
    up at Cedar Grove. In nineteen five."
        Old haircut smell.

Next door, Goodwill
          where I came out.
A search for sweater and a stroll
          in the board & concrete room of
          unfixed junk downstairs —
all emblems of the past — too close —
          heaped up in chilly dust and bare-bulb glare
of tables, wheelchairs, battered trunks & lamps
& pots that boiled up coffee nineteen ten, things
swimming on their own & finally freed
               from human need. Or?
          Waiting a final flicker of desire
to tote them out once more. Some freakish use.
The Master of the limbo drag-legged watches
               making prices
          to the people seldom buy.
The sag-asst rocker has to make it now. Alone.

          A few days later drove with Locke
down San Joaquin, us barefoot in the heat
stopping for beer and melon on the way
          the Giant Orange,
rubber shreds of cast truck retreads on the pebble
shoulder, highway 99.
          Sierras marked by cumulus in the east.
Car coughing in the groves,   six thousand feet
down to Kings River Canyon; camped at Cedar Grove.
          Hard granite canyon walls that
          leave no scree.

Once tried a haircut at the Barber College too —
sat half an hour before they told me
          white men use the other side.
Goodwill, St. Vincent de Paul,
          Salvation Army up the coast
for mackinaws and boots and heavy socks
          — Seattle has the best for logger gear
once found a pair of good tricouni boots
          at the under-the-public market store,
          Mark Tobey's scene,
               torn down I hear —
and Filson jacket with a birdblood stain.

A.G. and me got winter clothes for almost nothing
    at Lake Union, telling the old gal
      we was on our way
to work the winter out up in B.C.
          hitchhiking home the
green hat got a ride (of that more later).

Hiking up Bubbs Creek saw the trail crew tent
in a scraggly grove of creekside lodgepole pine
      talked to the guy, he says

"If you see McCool on the other trail crew over there
tell him Moorehead says to go to hell."
Late snow that summer. Crossing the scarred bare
      shed of Forester Pass
   the winding rock-braced switchbacks
dive in snowbanks, we climb on where
      pack trains have to dig or wait.
A half-iced-over lake, twelve thousand feet
      its sterile boulder bank
but filled with leaping trout:
      reflections wobble in the
mingling circles always spreading out
    the crazy web of wavelets makes sense
    seen from high above.
A deva world of sorts — it's high
      — a view that few men see, a point
   bare sunlight
   on the spaces
empty sky
      molding to fit the shape of what ice left
of fire-thrust, or of tilted, twisted, faulted
      cast-out from this lava belly globe.

The boulder in my mind's eye is a chair.
      . . . why was the man drag-legged?
King of Hell
   or is it a paradise of sorts, thus freed
from acting out the function some
      creator / carpenter
thrust on a thing to think he made, himself,
   an object always "chair"?
     Sinister ritual histories.
   Is the Mountain God a gimp?

The halting metrics   and the ritual limp,
        Good   Will?

Daughter of mountains, stooped
    moon breast Parvati

        mountain thunder speaks
        hair tingling static as the lightning lashes
        is neither word of love nor wisdom;
        though this be danger: hence thee fear.
                Some flowing girl
        whose slippery dance
        en trances Shiva
                  — the valley spirit / Anahita,
                      Sarasvati,
        dark and female gate of all the world
        water that cuts back quartzflake sand
                soft is the dance that melts the
        mat-haired mountain sitter
                    to leap in fire
        & make of sand a tree
            of tree a board, of board (ideas!)
            somebody's rocking chair.
        A room of empty sun of peaks and ridges
        a universe of junk, all left alone.

The hat I always take on mountains:
When we came back down through Oregon
        (three years before)
at nightfall in the Siskiyou few cars pass.

A big truck stopped a hundred yards above
    "Siskiyou Stoneware" on the side
the driver said
he recognized my old green hat.
I'd had a ride
        with him two years before
a whole state north
        when hitching down to Portland
            from Warm Springs.

Allen in the rear on straw
forgot salami and we went on south
all night — in many cars — to Berkeley in the dawn.

Upper Kern River country now after nine days walk
it finally rain.
     We ran on that other trail crew
setting up new camp in the drizzly pine
cussing & slapping bugs, four days from road,
we saw McCool, & he said tell that Moorehead
     kiss my ass.

We squatted smoking by the fire.
     "I'll never get a green hat now"
the foreman says fifty mosquitoes sitting on the brim

        they must like green.
& two more days of thundershower and cold
     (on Whitney hair on end
     hail stinging bare legs in the blast of wind
     but yodel off the summit echoes clean)

     all this comes after:

purity of the mountains and goodwills.
The diamond drill of racing icemelt waters
     and bumming trucks & watching

buildings raze
     the garbage acres burning at the Bay
     the girl who was the skid-row
cripple's daughter —

     out of the memory of smoking pine
the lotion and the spittoon glitter rises
chair turns and in the double mirror waver
the old man cranks me down and cracks a chuckle

     "Your Bubbs Creek haircut, boy."

HAY FOR THE HORSES

He had driven half the night
From far down San Joaquin
Through Mariposa, up the

Dangerous mountain roads,
And pulled in at eight a.m.
With his big truckload of hay
    behind the barn.
With winch and ropes and hooks
We stacked the bales up clean
To splintery redwood rafters
High in the dark, flecks of alfalfa
Whirling through shingle-cracks of light,
Itch of haydust in the
    sweaty shirt and shoes.
At lunchtime under Black oak
Out in the hot corral,
— The old mare nosing lunchpails,
Grasshoppers crackling in the weeds —
"I'm sixty-eight" he said,
"I first bucked hay when I was seventeen.
I thought, that day I started,
I sure would hate to do this all my life.
And dammit, that's just what
I've gone and done."

THE BATH

Washing Kai in the sauna,
The kerosene lantern set on a box
    outside the ground-level window,
Lights up the edge of the iron stove and the
    washtub down on the slab
Steaming air and crackle of waterdrops
    brushed by on the pile of rocks on top
He stands in warm water
Soap all over the smooth of his thigh and stomach
    "Gary don't soap my hair!"
    — his eye-sting fear —
    the soapy hand feeling
    through and around the globes and curves of his body
    up in the crotch,
And washing-tickling out the scrotum, little anus,
    his penis curving up and getting hard
    as I pull back skin and try to wash it

Laughing and jumping, flinging arms around,
    I squat all naked too,
               is this our body?

Sweating and panting in the stove-steam hot-stone
    cedar-planking wooden bucket water-splashing
    kerosene lantern-flicker wind-in-the-pines-out
    sierra forest ridges night —
Masa comes in, letting fresh cool air
    sweep down from the door
    a deep sweet breath
And she tips him over gripping neatly, one knee down
    her hair falling hiding one whole side of
    shoulder, breast, and belly,
Washes deftly Kai's head-hair
    as he gets mad and yells —
The body of my lady, the winding valley spine,
    the space between the thighs I reach through,
    cup her curving vulva arch and hold it from behind,
    a soapy tickle   a hand of grail
The gates of Awe
That open back a turning double-mirror world of
    wombs in wombs, in rings,
    that start in music,
               is this our body?

The hidden place of seed
The veins net flow across the ribs, that gathers
    milk and peaks up in a nipple — fits
    our mouth —
The sucking milk from this our body sends through
    jolts of light; the son, the father,
    sharing mother's joy
That brings a softness to the flower of the awesome
    open curling lotus gate I cup and kiss
As Kai laughs at his mother's breast he now is weaned
    from, we
    wash each other,
               this our body

Kai's little scrotum up close to his groin,
    the seed still tucked away, that moved from us to him
In flows that lifted with the same joys forces
    as his nursing Masa later,
    playing with her breast,

Or me within her,
Or him emerging,

                    this is our body:

Clean, and rinsed, and sweating more, we stretch
        out on the redwood benches hearts all beating
Quiet to the simmer of the stove,
        the scent of cedar
And then turn over,
        murmuring gossip of the grasses,
        talking firewood,
Wondering how Gen's napping, how to bring him in
        soon wash him too —
These boys who love their mother
        who loves men, who passes on
        her sons to other women;

The cloud across the sky. The windy pines.
        the trickle gurgle in the swampy meadow

    this is our body.

Fire inside and boiling water on the stove
We sigh and slide ourselves down from the benches
        wrap the babies, step outside,

black night & all the stars.

Pour cold water on the back and thighs
Go in the house — stand steaming by the center fire
Kai scampers on the sheepskin
Gen standing hanging on and shouting,

"Bao! bao! bao! bao! bao!"

This is our body. Drawn up crosslegged by the flames
        drinking icy water
        hugging babies, kissing bellies,

Laughing on the Great Earth

Come out from the bath.

GARY SNYDER

AXE HANDLES

One afternoon the last week in April
Showing Kai how to throw a hatchet
One-half turn and it sticks in a stump.
He recalls the hatchet-head
Without a handle, in the shop
And go gets it, and wants it for his own.
A broken-off axe handle behind the door
Is long enough for a hatchet,
We cut it to length and take it
With the hatchet head
And working hatchet, to the wood block.
There I begin to shape the old handle
With the hatchet, and the phrase
First learned from Ezra Pound
Rings in my ears!
"When making an axe handle
            the pattern is not far off."
And I say this to Kai
"Look: We'll shape the handle
By checking the handle
Of the axe we cut with — "
And he sees. And I hear it again:
It's in Lu Ji's *Wên Fu*, fourth century
A.D. "Essay on Literature" — in the
Preface: "In making the handle
Of an axe
By cutting wood with an axe
The model is indeed near at hand."
My teacher Shih-hsiang Chen
Translated that and taught it years ago
And I see: Pound was an axe,
Chen was an axe, I am an axe
And my son a handle, soon
To be shaping again, model
And tool, craft of culture,
How we go on.

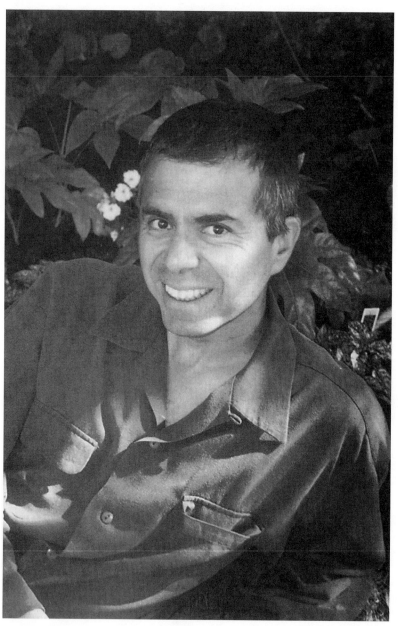

Carolyn Soto

Gary Soto

BLACK HAIR

At eight I was brilliant with my body.
In July, that ring of heat
We all jumped through, I sat in the bleachers
Of Romain Playground, in the lengthening
Shade that rose from our dirty feet.
The game before us was more than baseball.
It was a figure — Hector Moreno
Quick and hard with turned muscles,
His crouch the one I assumed before an altar
Of worn baseball cards, in my room.

I came here because I was Mexican, a stick
Of brown light in love with those
Who could do it — the triple and hard slide,
The gloves eating balls into double plays.
What could I do with 50 pounds, my shyness,
My black torch of hair, about to go out?
Father was dead, his face no longer
Hanging over the table or our sleep,
And mother was the terror of mouths
Twisting hurt by butter knives.

In the bleachers I was brilliant with my body,
Waving players in and stomping my feet,
Growing sweaty in the presence of white shirts.
I chewed sunflower seeds. I drank water
And bit my arm through the late innings.
When Hector lined balls into deep
Center, in my mind I rounded the bases
With him, my face flared, my hair lifting
Beautifully, because we were coming home
To the arms of brown people.

ENVYING THE CHILDREN OF SAN FRANCISCO

At a city square
Children laugh in the red
Sweaters of Catholics,
As they walk home between trucks
And sunlight angled off buildings that end in points.
I'm holding an apple, among shoppers
Clutching bags big enough to sleep in,
And the air is warm for October —
Torn pieces of paper
Scuttling like roaches, a burst at a time.

The children are blond,
Shiny, and careful at the lights —
The sister with her brother's hand.
They cross looking
At their watches, and I cross too.
I want to know where
They're going, what door they'll push
Open and call home —
The TV coming on,
Milk, a cookie for each hand.

As a kid I wanted to live
In the city, in a building that rose above it all,
The gray streets burst open, a rattle
Of jackhammers. I wanted to
Stare down from the eighteenth floor, and let things go —
My homework for one, a paper plane
With a half-drawn heart and a girl's name.
I wanted to say that I ate
And slept, ate and slept in a building
That faced other buildings, a sliver of sea
Blue in the distance.

I wanted to hear voices
Behind walls, the *click-click* of a poodle
Strolling to his bowl — a violin like fingers
Running down a blackboard.
I wanted to warm my hands at a teakettle
And comb my hair in an elevator, my mouth
Still rolling with cereal, as I started off

For school, a row of pens in my shirt pocket.
Back home at the window
I wanted it to be December —
Flags and honking cars,
A Santa Claus with his pot, a single red
Balloon let go and racing skyward,
And the tiny mothers who would come around
Buildings, disappear, and come around again,
Hugging bags for all they were worth to children.

ORANGES

The first time I walked
With a girl, I was twelve,
Cold, and weighted down
With two oranges in my jacket.
December. Frost cracking
Beneath my steps, my breath
Before me, then gone,
As I walked toward
Her house, the one whose
Porch light burned yellow
Night and day, in any weather.
A dog barked at me, until
She came out pulling
At her gloves, face bright
With rouge. I smiled,
Touched her shoulder, and led
Her down the street, across
A used car lot and a line
Of newly planted trees,
Until we were breathing
Before a drugstore. We
Entered, the tiny bell
Bringing a saleslady
Down a narrow aisle of goods.
I turned to the candies
Tiered like bleachers,
And asked what she wanted —
Light in her eyes, a smile
Starting at the corners

Of her mouth. I fingered
A nickel in my pocket,
And when she lifted a chocolate
That cost a dime,
I didn't say anything.
I took the nickel from
My pocket, then an orange,
And set them quietly on
The counter. When I looked up,
The lady's eyes met mine,
And held them, knowing
Very well what it was all
About.

Outside,
A few cars hissing past,
Fog hanging like old
Coats between the trees.
I took my girl's hand
in mine for two blocks,
Then released it to let
Her unwrap the chocolate.
I peeled my orange
That was so bright against
The gray of December
That, from some distance,
Someone might have thought
I was making a fire in my hands.

MEXICANS BEGIN JOGGING

At the factory I worked
In the fleck of rubber, under the press
Of an oven yellow with flame,
Until the border patrol opened
Their vans and my boss waved for us to run.
"Over the fence, Soto," he shouted,
And I shouted that I was American.
"No time for lies," he said, and pressed
A dollar in my palm, hurrying me
Through the back door.

Since I was on his time, I ran
And became the wag to a short tail of Mexicans —
Ran past the amazed crowds that lined
The street and blurred like photographs, in rain.
I ran from that industrial road to the soft
Houses where people paled at the turn of an autumn sky.
What could I do but yell *vivas*
To baseball, milkshakes, and those sociologists
Who would clock me
As I jog into the next century
On the power of a great, silly grin.

THE TALE OF SUNLIGHT

Listen, nephew.
When I opened the cantina
At noon
A triangle of sunlight
Was stretched out
On the floor
Like a rug
Like a tired cat.
It flared in
From the window
Through a small hole
Shaped like a yawn.
Strange I thought
And placed my hand
Before the opening,
But the sunlight
Did not vanish.
I pulled back
The shutters
And the room glowed,
But this pyramid
Of whiteness
Was simply brighter.
The sunlight around it
Appeared soiled
Like the bed sheet
Of a borracho.

Amazed, I locked the door,
Closed the windows.
Workers, in from
The fields, knocked
To be let in,
Children peeked
Through the shutters,
But I remained silent.
I poured a beer,
At a table
Shuffled a pack
Of old cards,
And watched it
Cross the floor,
Hang on the wall
Like a portrait
Like a calendar
Without numbers.
When a fly settled
In the sunlight
And disappeared
In a wreath of smoke,
I tapped it with the broom,
Spat on it.
The broom vanished.
The spit sizzled.
It is the truth, little one.
I stood eye to blank eye
And by misfortune
This finger
This pink stump
Entered the sunlight,
Snapped off
With a dry sneeze,
And fell to the floor
As a gift
To the ants
Who know me
For what I gave.

FAILING IN THE PRESENCE OF ANTS

We live to some purpose, daughter.
Across the park, among
The trees that give the eye
Something to do, let's spread
A blanket on the ground
And examine the ants, loose
Thread to an old coat.
Perhaps they are more human than we are.
They live for the female,
Rescue their hurt, and fall earthward
For their small cause. And
Us? We live for our bellies,
The big O of our mouths.
Give me, give me, they say,
And many people, whole countries,
May go under because we desire TV
And chilled drinks, clothes
That hang well on our bodies —
Desire sofas and angled lamps,
Hair the sea may envy
On a slow day.
It is hurtful to sweep
Ants into a frenzy, blow
Chemicals into their eyes —
Those austere marchers who will lift
Their heads to rumor — seed,
Wafer of leaf, dropped apple —
And start off, over this
And that, between sloppy feet
And staggered chairs, for no
Purpose other than it might be good.

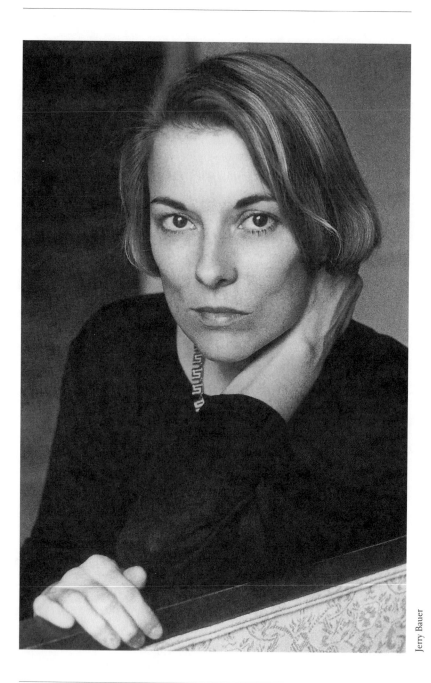

Elizabeth Spires

THE BEDS

London

Each day, I take the lift from the sublet down to the ground floor.
Out on the street, I pass the shop that sells the beds,
the sumptuous beds, made up each morning anew, afresh,
by smiling clerks who please their own moods,
doing the beds up one day in flaming sunrise and sunset tones,
and the next, in shades of white on white, with satin piping,
pillowcases expertly threaded with ribbons and bows,
like a bride's too-delicate underclothes.
And yet, nobody sleeps in the beds, makes love in the beds.
They wait, like a young girl with too much imagination,
to be taken away for a weekend in the country,
to a great house where lovers flirt and scheme
in preliminary maneuvering, but know, in the end,
what beds are for. Know, no matter what they do,
all will be plumped and tucked and smoothed,
all made as it was, by knowing maids the morning after.

The anxious clerks stare out at the soiled street,
the racing cars and taxis, the passersby, waiting for money
to stop, walk in the door, and ask to buy a bed.
There are circles under their eyes,
as if they've been sleeping badly.
Beds must make way for other beds,
pillows for other pillows, new sheets, new lives!
The seconds tick on the big clock
a block from the bed shop, the minute hand moves
with a jerk, and suddenly whole hours have flown, the day vanishes,
pulled by an unseen hand through a small hole in the sky
somewhere in the darkening East End.

Night falls so quickly on this street of Dream Merchandise!
Now all of us reverse ourselves and change direction
to come home to well-intentioned stews with husbands and wives,
yesterday's leftovers made to stretch so economically,
my heels on the sidewalk clicking in silver tones
like the small change in my pocket falling end over end over end,
all that remains of a day's hard buying.

Already the new moon is backlighting the city's towers and spires,
illuminating shadowy shop windows up and down Fulham Road.
It drapes itself casually across the beds,
like the misplaced towel or bathrobe
of a woman who has just stepped out for the evening,
wearing new evening clothes, made up so carefully
she can't be recognized, who secretly knows
she will not be coming back until morning
to sleep, if she sleeps then,
in the perfect bed of her own making.

SUNDAY AFTERNOON AT FULHAM PALACE

Putney Bridge, London

A Sunday afternoon in late September, one of the last
good weekends before the long dark, old couples
taking the air along the Thames, sunning themselves,
their arms and legs so pale, *exposed*,
eyes closed against the slanting autumn light,
while the young press forward, carry us
along in the crowd to the fair at Fulham Palace
where a few people have already spread blankets and tablecloths
for the picnics they've brought, laughing and talking
as they wait for the music to begin at three o'clock.
Inside the palace gates, a man inflates
a room-size, brightly painted rubber castle,
the children impatiently waiting for walls and turrets to go up,
the spongy floor they like to jump on.
The palace is empty. The Bishop gone.
Now overfed goldfish swim slowly round and round
in the crumbling courtyard fountain, and farther on,
a white peacock stands still as a statue,
still as a stone, whether in pride or sorrow
at being the last of its kind here I don't know.
A low door opens into the Bishop's walled garden, but once
inside nothing miraculous or forbidden tempts us,
just a few flowers and herbs among weeds
(unlike those illuminated scenes in books of hours),
the past passing away too quickly to catch or recognize.

Out on the other side, we pick our way

among booths put up for the day,
one woman, predictably, passing out pamphlets
on nuclear winter and cruise missiles, as if she could stop it alone.
The Fulham Band takes its place on the platform,
the conductor announcing as the overture
"Those Magnificent Men in Their Flying Machines,"
the crossed shadow of coincidence, of airplanes from Gatwick
passing over at two-minute intervals, touching us
for a moment before they fly into the day's
unplanned pattern of connections, the music
attracting more of a crowd, men, women, and children
making their entrances like extras in a movie,
in pairs, in families, no one alone that I can see
except one girl, no more than ten,
lagging behind the others, lost completely
in a vivid, invisible daydream until her mother finds her,
brings her back with a touch on the arm,
and the daughter says, unbelievably,
"I was thinking about what kind of anesthesia
they'll give me when I have my first baby."

The future expands, then contracts, like an eye's iris opening
        and closing,
walling me into a room where light and sound come and go,
first near, then far, as if I had vertigo.
It is easy, too easy, to imagine the world ending
on a day like today, the sun shining and the band playing,
the players dreamily moving now into Ellington's "Mood Indigo."
Easy to see the great gray plane hovering briefly overhead,
the gray metal belly opening and the bomb dropping,
a flash, a light "like a thousand suns,"
and then the long winter.
The white peacock. Erased. The goldfish in the fountain
swimming crazily as the water boils up around them, evaporates.
The children's castle. Gone. The children. The mothers and the fathers.
As if a hand had suddenly erased a huge blackboard.
Thank God you don't know what I'm thinking.
You press my hand as if to ask, "Am I here with you?
Do you want to go?" pulling me back to this moment,
to this music we are just coming to know, the crowd around us
growing denser, just wanting to live their lives,
each person a *nerve*, thinking and feeling
too much as sensation pours over them
in a ceaseless flow, the music, as we move to go,

jumping far back in time, the conductor oddly choosing
something devotional, a coronet solo
composed, and probably played here, by Purcell three centuries ago.
All is as it was as we make our way back along the Thames
to Putney Bridge, the old souls still sleeping unaware,
hands lightly touching, as the river bends in a gentle arc
around them. Mood indigo. The white peacock.
The walled garden and the low door.
As if, if it did happen, we could bow our heads
and ask, once more, to enter that innocent first world.

THE FIRST DAY

The ward is quiet, the mothers delivered,
except in one a woman labors still and calls,
with a sharp cry, that she is dying.
She is not dying but cannot know it now.
Trapped in the birthstorm, I did not cry,
but saw my body as the enemy
I could not accommodate, could not deny.
Morning arrived, and my daughter.
That's how it is in this world, birth, death,
matter-of-fact, happening like that.
The room was warm. The room was full of flowers,
her face all petals and leaves, a flower
resembling such as I had never seen.
All day she slept beside me, eyes darting
beneath bruised blue eyelids, retracing the journey,
dreaming the birth dream over and over
until it held no fear for her.
I dared not wake her. The hours passed.
I rested as her soul poured in her body,
the way clear water, poured from a height,
takes the shape of a flaring vase or glass, or light
fills a room's corners on a brilliant winter morning.
Slowly, she opened her eyes, a second waking,
taking me by surprise, a bright being
peering out from behind dark eyes,
as if she already knew what sights would be seen,
what marvels lay ahead of her, weariness and woe,
the joists and beams, the underpinnings of the world

shifting a little to make room for her.
The first day was over forever. Tranced,
I picked up the pen, the paper, and wrote:
I have had a child. Now I must live with death.

THE CELESTIAL

Korean Buddhists traditionally keep this breed of carp in temple ponds.

When God made the angels, a man made me,
turning my gaze heavenward for a purpose
I know and do not know. The world
is a sphere that mirrors my pond, all things
have order here: the sun rushes
across the sky, pulling the moon
on a pale fishing line, and I see myself
printed among the stars, a great fish
swimming in the night's black sea.
Weeks pass into months, the year going
from warm to cool, bright to dull,
ginkgo leaves drifting down,
down, to slowly settle on pondbottom,
like pieces of ragged gold foil. I, too,
am streaked with gold along my spine and tail
but am valued for my eyes, bulging
blue-green globes larger than my soul,
a small clear bubble wrapped around the purity
of nothing. It slips with each breath
from my astonished mouth and flies rapidly upward
— as prayers will sometimes —
but always catches on the pond's rough skin.
I twin until there are many of me.
I begin and begin.

O Ghosts of the Upper World,
don't we see you in your shimmering robes,
peering through seven watery veils
that, lifted, reveal nothing behind the curtain?
Don't we hear you chanting?
Bells call you to the temple and you hurry away,
orange robes streaming, as if
you were running headlong into a violent wind.

We do not hurry as we take the world in
through our mouths, as sensation
passes through us, unconcerned
to be swimming toward where we've already been.
To be, not do: that is the lesson
we try to teach you.
We have heard of an underworld where fire
is the transforming element and water burns
quickly away to vapor,
but will not see it ever.

Our gaze is upward and forever.

DOGWOOD

Whiter than paper, whiter than snow,
whiter than the moon in its fullness,
whiter than clouds passing over,

> *I close my eyes and see white stars*
> *hanging in the air of the backyard.*
> *For weeks they are out there.*

Whiter than music, whiter than bone,
whiter than ivory, whiter than hope,
whiter than prayer, whiter than a name,

> *Whitest of all white things in the world,*
> *I want to know what you know.*

Whiter than silence, whiter than thought,
whiter than interruption, whiter than frost,
whiter than the body's hollows,

> *Now, after too many white words,*
> *I stumble and touch branches heavy*
> *with ten thousand blurred white petals.*

Whiter than love or death,
whiter than my winter breath,
whiter than a white room's emptiness,

As if I could count them all, one
for each man, woman, and child.

Whiter than the blank white sky,
whiter than the white of an eye,
whiter than foam on the breaking black wave —

For weeks you have stood there,
arms raised like a priest
in silent ceremony, praising

creation in the only way you know,
now tell me why we have to die.

"IN HEAVEN IT IS ALWAYS AUTUMN"

John Donne

In heaven it is always autumn. The leaves are always near
to falling there but never fall, and pairs of souls out walking
heaven's paths no longer feel the weight of years upon them.
Safe in heaven's calm, they take each other's arm,
the light shining through them, all joy and terror gone.
But we are far from heaven here, in a garden ragged and unkept
as Eden would be with the walls knocked down, the paths littered
with the unswept leaves of many years, bright keepsakes
for children of the Fall. The light is gold, the sun pulling
the long shadow soul out of each thing, disclosing an outcome.
The last roses of the year nod their frail heads,
like listeners listening to all that's said, to ask,
What brought us here? What seed? What rain? What light?
What forced us upwards through dark earth? What made us bloom?
What wind shall take us soon, sweeping the garden bare?
Their voiceless voices hang there, as ours might,
if we were roses, too. Their beds are blanketed with leaves,
tended by an absent gardener whose life is elsewhere.
It is the last of many last days. Is it enough? To rest in this moment?
To turn our faces to the sun? To watch the lineaments of a world
        passing?
To feel the metal of a black iron chair, cool and eternal,
press against our skin? To apprehend a chill as clouds pass
overhead, turning us to shivering shade and shadow?

And then to be restored, small miracle, the sun shining brightly
as before? We go on, you leading the way, a figure
leaning on a cane that leaves its mark on the earth.
My friend, you have led me farther than I have ever been.
To a garden in autumn. To a heaven of impermanence
where the final falling off is slow, a slow and radiant happening.
The light is gold. And while we're here, I think it must be heaven.

CEMETERY REEF

Grand Cayman Island

Walking down the beach, I took your arm.
The treatments were over. Your hair was growing back.
For a week, time lay suspended. And yet, too fast,
too soon, everything was changing to memory.
But your arm was real when I touched it, real flesh and blood.
We were talking about doctors when I saw the blowfish,
green as the greenest apple, puffed-up and bobbing in the shallows.
But when I looked again, it was only a pair of bathing trunks,
ballooning out, aimlessly knocked back and forth by the tide.
Ahead, the cruise ships lay at anchor in the harbor.
At noon they'd slip away, like days we couldn't hold onto,
dropping over the blurred blue horizon to other ports of call.
The hotels we were passing all looked out to water,
a thousand beach chairs in the sand looked out to water,
but no one sat there early in the morning. And no one
slept in the empty hammock at the Governor's House,
where workmen in gray coveralls raked the seaweed into piles,
until the sand was white and smooth, like paper not yet written on.

All lies in retrospect now: how, each afternoon,
we put on masks and fins and swam to Cemetery Reef.
The coral looked like brains and flowers, like unreal cities
of melted peaks and towers, pointing up to where the sun,
flat and round as a host, lay dissolving on the water.
Schools of fish, bright as neon, ragged as flags,
drifted directionless with the tide, or swerved
and hid from our reaching hands in beds of waving kelp.
We breathed through snorkels, did the dead man's float,
the hollow rushing sound we heard inside our heads
our own frail breath going slowly *in* and *out*. Farther out,

the shallow reef dropped off to chasm, the waves
choppy and thick, the calm clear water darkening to ink.
How far could we swim before exhaustion took us,
before a shark or barracuda rounded a cornerless corner
to meet us eye to eye? My mind circled back to our dinner
in the Chinese restaurant: the waiter bringing six cookies
on a plate, alike in every way, except that one, just one,
contained a different fate. *Wealth, long life, happiness,*
the plate was passed around. Then your turn came.
You chose one, broke it open, read aloud,
Soon you will cross the great water, dropping it, as if stung.

And then, too quickly, it was the last day.
Dreaming, we call came to. We were back at Cemetery Reef,
walking a narrow path of broken shells toward the shining water.
Off to one side, a low stone wall squared off the cemetery,
the dead buried aboveground in white weathered slabs,
their plots neatly surrounded by smooth white stones.
Morning of all mornings, you swam out to the reef alone,
came back. Gathering our things to go, what made me say,
When we come back. . . . All lies unanswered now.
I remember how the flowers on the graves were red
and white plastic, the color of flesh and blood, of regret,
of paper not yet written on. Put there, *In Memory.*
In a colder place, we would soon — unwilling, stunned —
remember you with the kind that always die.

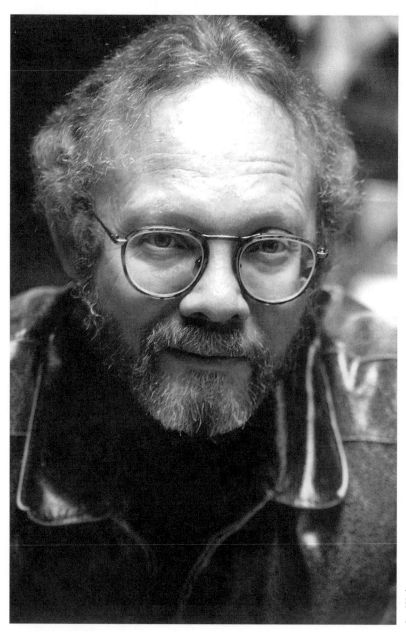

David St. John

GIN

There's a mystery
By the river, in one of the cabins
Shuttered with planks, its lock
Twisted; a bunch of magazines flipped open,
A body. A blanket stuffed with leaves
Or lengths of rope, an empty gin bottle.
Put down your newspaper. Look out
Beyond the bluffs, a coal barge is passing,
Its deck nearly
Level with the water, where it comes back riding
High. You start talking about nothing,
Or that famous party, where you went dressed
As a river. They listen,
The man beside you touching his odd face
In the countertop, the woman stirring tonic
In your glass. Down the bar the talk's divorce,
The docks, the nets
Filling with branches and sour fish. Listen,
I knew a woman who'd poke a hole in an egg, suck
It clean and fill the shell with gin,
Then walk around all day disgusting people
Until she was so drunk
The globe of gin broke in her hand. She'd stay
Alone at night on the boat, come back
Looking for another egg. That appeals to you, rocking
For hours carving at a hollow stone. Or finding
A trail by accident, walking the bluff's
Face. You know, your friends complain. They say
You give up only the vaguest news, and give a bakery
As your phone. Even your stories
Have no point, just lots of detail: The room
Was long and bright, small and close, angering Gaston;
They turned away to embrace him; She wore
The color out of season,
She wore hardly anything at all; Nobody died; Saturday.
These disguises of omission. Like forgetting
To say obtuse when you talk about the sun, leaving
Off the buttons as you're sewing up the coat. So,

People take the little
They know to make a marvelous stew;
Sometimes, it even resembles you. It's not so much
You cover your tracks, as that they bloom
In such false directions. This way friends who awaken
At night, beside you, awaken alone.

THE SWAN AT SHEFFIELD PARK

It is a dim April
Though perhaps no dimmer than any
London April my friend says
As we turn our backs
To the crooked Thames to the stark
London skyline
                    walking up the hill's
Mild slope to one of the paths
And prospects of Kew
He introduces
The various and gathered families
Of trees then every subtle
Shift of design along the grounds
The carefully laid views and pools
The chapel-sized orangery
Where citrus in their huge trolley tubs
Were wheeled behind the glass walls
And spared each winter
Fresh lime grapefruit and orange
That's what a queen wants
That's what the orangery says
Now April's skies grow a little
More forgiving
Breaking into these tall columns
Of white clouds
                    the kinds of elaborate
Shapes that children call God's Swans
Here in the country an hour
South of London
                    where Gibbon finished
Decline and Fall in Lord Sheffield's library
In the manor house I can see just there

In the trees
        as I walk with my friend along
The road that passes by his cottage
At the edge of the grounds of Sheffield Park
Once again
        the sky's high pillars collect
Into one flat unrelieved blanket
Above these shivering leaves
And bent blades
        a curtaining mist
Materializes out of the air
As we stop for a moment
On a stone bridge over the small falls
Between two of the lakes
And from the center of one of the lakes
A single swan glides toward us
Its wake a perfect spreading V
Widening along the water
        as each arm
Of the V begins to break against
The lake's shores
        the swan holds its head
And neck in a classical question mark
The crook of an old man's
Walking stick its eyes fixed on us
As it spreads its wings
In this exact feathery symmetry
Though it does not fly
        simply lifting
Its head until the orange beak
Almost touches the apex of the stone
Arch of the bridge
Waiting for whatever crumbs we might
Have thought to bring
For a swan
        that now turns from us
Gliding with those same effortless gestures
Away without a glance back over
Its smooth shoulder
        the mist
Thickens as the clouds drop lower
And the rain threading the branches and leaves
Grows darker and more dense
Until I can barely see the swan on the water

Moving slowly as smoke through this haze
Covering the surface of the lake
That white smudge sailing
To whatever shelter it can find and as
I look again there's nothing
                              only
The rain pocking the empty table
Of the lake
                    so even the swan knows
Better than I to get out of the rain
The way it curled white as breath and rose
To nothing along the wind
                                    tonight
By the wood stove of the cottage
Drinking and talking with my friend
I'll tell him about the two women
I saw last week in Chelsea
One of them wrapped in a jumpsuit of wet
Black plastic
                    her hair coal
Black greased and twirled into spikes
That fell like fingers onto her shoulders
But more alarming
                              those lines she'd drawn
Out from her mouth with an eyebrow pencil
Along her pale cheeks the perfect
Curved whiskers of a cat
And the other one
                              her friend dressed
In white canvas painter's pants white leather
Boots and a cellophane blouse
                                          who'd dyed
Her hair utterly white then teased it
So that it rose
Or fell in the breeze lightly and stiffly
As feathers who'd painted her mouth
The same hard rubbery orange as a swan's
And even to a person of no great humor
Or imagination they were
                                    these two
In the silent path they cut in the air
Along King's Road in every way
Beautiful
          and for the rest

Of the day I was so shaken I made
Myself stop for a drink in Soho
A strip joint called *The Blade*
I'd stumbled into and judging from my
Welcome not a place for the delicate
But I stuck it out through enough Scotch
To make me drunk fearless
And screaming through the first show
When at its end the final stripper
Stepped from the small stage right onto the bar top
Everyone clearing away the glasses and bottles
From the polished copper in front of them
As she threw off everything strutting
Down the narrow bar except
A white boa G-string
Shivering against her thighs as she
Kicked her silver high heels to either side
Then lay down in front of me
Her bare back and shoulders pressed flat
To the copper as it steamed and smudged beneath
Her body's heat
                the catcalls and hollers
Rising as she lifted each leg
Pointing her toes to the spotlights scattered
Across the ceiling
                  her legs held in a pale V
The silver sequins of her high heels
Glittering in the lights but
Then she stood abruptly
And stepped back onto the stage not
Waiting a moment before turning her back
To the hoarse cheers
                  disappearing
In the sheer misty gauze of the old curtains
And as the lights came up there was
Where she'd been
Just the trails and webs of cigarette smoke
Those long curlicues in a tattoo of light
Those ghosts and feathers of dust
Still drifting down onto the bare tables
The glistening bar
                onto the empty veiled stage
Of wood warped gently as waves

DAVID ST. JOHN

LUCIFER IN STARLIGHT

> *Tired of his dark dominion . . .*
> —George Meredith

It was something I'd overheard
One evening at a party; a man I liked enormously
        Saying to a mutual friend, a woman
Wearing a vest embroidered with scarlet and violet tulips
        That belled below each breast, "Well, I've always
Preferred Athens; Greece seems to me a country
        Of the day — Rome, I'm afraid, strikes me
As being a city of the night . . ."
        Of course, I knew instantly just what he meant —
        Not simply because I love
Standing on the terrace of my apartment on a clear evening
        As the constellations pulse low in the Roman sky,
The whole mind of night that I know so well
        Shimmering in its elaborate webs of infinite,
Almost divine irony. No, and it wasn't only that Rome
        Was *my* city of the night, that it was here I'd chosen
        To live when I grew tired of my ancient life
As the Underground Man. And it wasn't that Rome's darkness
        Was of the kind that consoles so many
        Vacancies of the soul; my Rome, with its endless history
Of falls . . . No, it was that this dark was the deep, sensual dark
        Of the dreamer; this dark was like the violet fur
Spread to reveal the illuminated nipples of
        The She-Wolf — all the sequins above in sequence,
The white buds lost in those fields of ever-deepening gentians,
        A dark like the polished back of a mirror,
        The pool of the night scalloped and hanging
Above me, the inverted reflection of a last,
                        Odd Narcissus . . .

                One night my friend Nico came by
Close to three A.M. — As we drank a little wine, I could see
        The black of her pupils blown wide,
The spread ripples of the opiate night . . . And Nico
        Pulled herself close to me, her mouth almost
        Touching my mouth, as she sighed, "Look . . . ,"
And deep within the pupil of her left eye,
        Almost like the mirage of a ship's distant, hanging

DAVID ST. JOHN

Lantern rocking with the waves,
I could see, at the most remote end of the receding,
      Circular hallway of her eye, there, at its doorway,
At the small aperture of the black telescope of the pupil,
      A tiny, dangling crucifix —
Silver, lit by the ragged shards of starlight, reflecting
      In her as quietly as pain, as simply as pain . . .
Some years later, I saw Nico on stage in New York, singing
      Inside loosed sheets of shattered light, a fluid
Kaleidoscope washing over her — the way any naked,
      Emerging Venus steps up along the scalloped lip
Of her shell, innocent and raw as fate, slowly
Obscured by a florescence that reveals her simple, deadly
      Love of sexual sincerity . . .
I didn't bother to say hello. I decided to remember
The way in Rome, out driving at night, she'd laugh as she let
      Her head fall back against the cracked, red leather
      Of my old Lancia's seats, the soft black wind
Fanning her pale, chalky hair out along its currents,
      Ivory waves of starlight breaking above us in the leaves;
The sad, lucent malevolence of the heavens, falling . . .
      Both of us racing silently as light. Nowhere,
Then forever . . .
      Into the mind of the Roman night.

LAST NIGHT WITH RAFAELLA

Last night, with Rafaella,

I sat at one of the outside tables
At *Rosati* watching the *ragazzi* on Vespas
Scream through the Piazza del Popolo

And talked again about changing my life,

Doing something meaningful — perhaps
Exploring a continent or discovering a vaccine,
Falling in love or over the white falls
Of a dramatic South American river! —
And Rafaella

DAVID ST. JOHN

Stroked the back of my wrist as I talked,

Smoothing the hairs until they lay as quietly
As wheat before the old authoritarian wind.

Rafaella had just returned from Milano
Where she'd supervised the Spring collection
Of a famous, even notorious, young designer —

A man whose name brought tears to the eyes
Of contessas, movie stars, and diplomats' wives
Along the Via Condotti or the Rue
Du Faubourg-St-Honoré.

So I felt comfortable there, with Rafaella,
Discussing these many important things, I mean
The spiritual life, and my own
Long disenchantment with the ordinary world.

Comfortable because I knew she was a sophisticated,
Well-traveled woman, so impossible
To shock. A friend who'd
Often rub the opal on her finger so slowly

It made your mouth water,

The whole while telling you what it would be like
To feel her tongue addressing your ear.

And how could I not trust the advice
Of a woman who, with the ball of her exquisite thumb,
Carefully flared rouge along the white cheekbones
Of the most beautiful women in the world?

Last night, as we lay in the dark,
The windows of her bedroom open to the cypress,
To the stars, to the wind knocking at those stiff
Umbrella pines along her garden's edge,
I noticed as she turned slowly in the moonlight

A small tattoo just above her hip bone —

It was a dove in flight or an angel with its
Head tucked beneath its wing,

DAVID ST. JOHN

I couldn't tell in the shadows . . .

And as I kissed this new illumination of her body
Rafaella said, *Do you know how to tell a model?*
In fashion, they wear tattoos like singular beads
Along their hips,
                    but artists' models
Wear them like badges against the daily nakedness,
The way Celestine has above one nipple that
Minute yellow bee and above
The other an elaborate, cupped poppy . . .

I thought about this,
Pouring myself a little wine and listening
To the owls marking the distances, the geometries
Of the dark.
              Rafaella's skin was
Slightly damp as I ran my fingertip
Along each delicate winged ridge of her
Collarbone, running the harp length of ribs
Before circling the shy angel . . .

And slowly, as the stars
Shifted in their rack of black complexities above,

Along my shoulder, Rafaella's hair fell in coils,

Like the frayed silk of some ancient tapestry,
Like the spun cocoons of the Orient —
Like a fragile ladder

To some whole other level of the breath.

(Rome)

William Stafford

HOW THE REAL BIBLE IS WRITTEN

Once we painted our house and went into it.
Today, after years, I remember that color
under the new paint now old.
I look out of the windows dangerously
and begin to know more. Now when I
walk through this town there are
too many turns before the turn
I need. Listen, birds and cicadas
still trying to tell me surface things:
I have learned how the paint goes on,
and then other things — how the real Bible is
written, downward through the pages,
carved, hacked, and molded, like the faces
of saints or the planks ripped aside
by steady centuries of weather, deeper than
dust, under the moles, caught by the
inspiration in an old badger's shoulder
that bores for grizzled secrets in the ground.

AT FOURTH AND MAIN IN LIBERAL, KANSAS, 1932

An instant sprang at me, a winter instant,
a thin gray panel of evening. Slanted
shadows leaned from a line of trees where rain
had slicked the sidewalk. No one was there —
it was only a quick flash of a scene,
unplanned, without connection to anything
that meant more than itself, but I carried it
onward like a gift from a child who knows
that the giving is what is important, the paper, the ribbon,
the holding of breath and surprise, the friends around,
and God holding it out to you, even a rock
or a slice of evening, and behind it the whole world.

513

WILLIAM STAFFORD

GROWING UP

One of my wings beat faster,
I couldn't help it —
the one away from the light.

It hurt to be told all the time
how I loved that terrible flame.

ASK ME

Some time when the river is ice ask me
mistakes I have made. Ask me whether
what I have done is my life. Others
have come in their slow way into
my thought, and some have tried to help
or to hurt: ask me what difference
their strongest love or hate has made.

I will listen to what you say.
You and I can turn and look
at the silent river and wait. We know
the current is there, hidden; and there
are comings and goings from miles away
that hold the stillness exactly before us.
What the river says, that is what I say.

CEREMONY

On the third finger of my left hand
under the bank of the Ninnescah
a muskrat whirled and bit to the bone.
The mangled hand made the water red.

That was something the ocean would remember:
I saw me in the current flowing through the land,
rolling, touching roots, the world incarnadined,
and the river richer by a kind of marriage.

While in the woods an owl started quavering
with drops like tears I raised my arm.
Under the bank a muskrat was trembling
with meaning my hand would wear forever.

In that river my blood flowed on.

TRAVELING THROUGH THE DARK

Traveling through the dark I found a deer
dead on the edge of the Wilson River road.
It is usually best to roll them into the canyon:
that road is narrow; to swerve might make more dead.

By glow of the tail-light I stumbled back of the car
and stood by the heap, a doe, a recent killing;
she had stiffened already, almost cold.
I dragged her off; she was large in the belly.

My fingers touching her side brought me the reason —
her side was warm; her fawn lay there waiting,
alive, still, never to be born.
Beside that mountain road I hesitated.

The car aimed ahead its lowered parking lights;
under the hood purred the steady engine.
I stood in the glare of the warm exhaust turning red;
around our group I could hear the wilderness listen.

I thought hard for us all — my only swerving — ,
then pushed her over the edge into the river.

VOCATION

This dream the world is having about itself
includes a trace on the plains of the Oregon trail,
a groove in the grass my father showed us all
one day while meadowlarks were trying to tell
something better about to happen.

WILLIAM STAFFORD

I dreamed the trace to the mountains, over the hills,
and there a girl who belonged wherever she was.
But then my mother called us back to the car:
she was afraid; she always blamed the place,
the time, anything my father planned.

Now both of my parents, the long line through the plain,
the meadowlarks, the sky, the world's whole dream
remain, and I hear him say while I stand between the two,
helpless, both of them part of me:
"Your job is to find what the world is trying to be."

ADULTS ONLY

Animals own a fur world;
people own worlds that are variously, pleasingly, bare.
And the way these worlds *are* once arrived for us kids with a jolt,
that night when the wild woman danced
in the giant cage we found we were all in
at the state fair.

Better women exist, no doubt, than that one,
and occasions more edifying, too, I suppose.
But we have to witness for ourselves what comes for us,
nor be distracted by barkers of irrelevant ware;
and a pretty good world, I say, arrived that night
when that woman came farming right out of her clothes,
by God,

At the state fair.

FIFTEEN

South of the bridge on Seventeenth
I found back of the willows one summer
day a motorcycle with engine running

as it lay on its side, ticking over
slowly in the high grass. I was fifteen.

I admired all that pulsing gleam, the
shiny flanks, the demure headlights
fringed where it lay; I led it gently
to the road and stood with that
companion, ready and friendly. I was fifteen.

We could find the end of a road, meet
the sky on out Seventeenth. I thought about
hills, and patting the handle got back a
confident opinion. On the bridge we indulged
a forward feeling, a tremble. I was fifteen.

Thinking, back farther in the grass I found
the owner, just coming to, where he had flipped
over the rail. He had blood on his hand, was pale —
I helped him walk to his machine. He ran his hand
over it, called me good man, roared away.

I stood there, fifteen.

WIDOW

On the first day when light came through the curtain
a mosquito thought was bothering her — what if
I am important? She wandered the house — the forgiving
table, the surprised-looking bed. Dishes
in the rack needed putting away, and she helped
them. But afterward she regretted — maybe nothing
should move, maybe this day the stillness begins.
She looked out a front window and held every
neighborhood shadow exactly where it was. Then
she carefully X'd out the calendar that had waited
all year for this date. She held out her hand
in a shaft of sun and flexed her fingers, in case
time had passed, in case her body was already gone.

WILLIAM STAFFORD

THE LIGHT BY THE BARN

The light by the barn that shines all night
pales at dawn when a little breeze comes.

A little breeze comes breathing the fields
from their sleep and waking the slow windmill.

The slow windmill sings the long day
about anguish and loss to the chickens at work.

The little breeze follows the slow windmill
and the chickens at work till the sun goes down —

Then the light by the barn again.

A WIND FROM A WING

Something outside my window in the dark
whispers a message. Maybe it is
a prayer sent by one of those friends
forgiving me the years when I sat out their war.
It flared, you know, generating
its own reasons for being, its heroes
anyone killed by an enemy. They looked up
and met fame on a bullet awarded so fast
their souls remained stuck in their bodies,
and then their names, caught on flypaper
citation, couldn't escape. Their families eat that
carrion, and like it. That is their punishment.

In a sky as distant and clear as Pascal's
nightmare, and immediate as our sweat
when God shakes us from sleep, my fate
shudders me awake. Little squeals
of the unborn fly past in the wind. It is midnight
and a motel, and nobody but me remembers
my mother, my father, and that hidden key
they left by our door when I was out late.

WILLIAM STAFFORD

WITH KIT, AGE 7, AT THE BEACH

We would climb the highest dune,
from there to gaze and come down:
the ocean was performing;
we contributed our climb.

Waves leapfrogged and came
straight out of the storm.
What should our gaze mean?
Kit waited for me to decide.

Standing on such a hill,
what would you tell your child?
That was an absolute vista.
Those waves raced far, and cold.

"How far could you swim, Daddy,
in such a storm?"
"As far as was needed," I said,
and as I talked, I swam.

NEAR

Walking along in this not quite prose way
we both know it is not quite prose we speak,
and it is time to notice this intolerable snow
innumerably touching, before we sink.

It is time to notice, I say, the freezing snow
hesitating toward us from its gray heaven;
listen — it is falling not quite silently
and under it still you and I are walking.

Maybe there are trumpets in the houses we pass
and a redbird watching from an evergreen —
but nothing will happen until we pause
to flame what we know, before any signal's given.

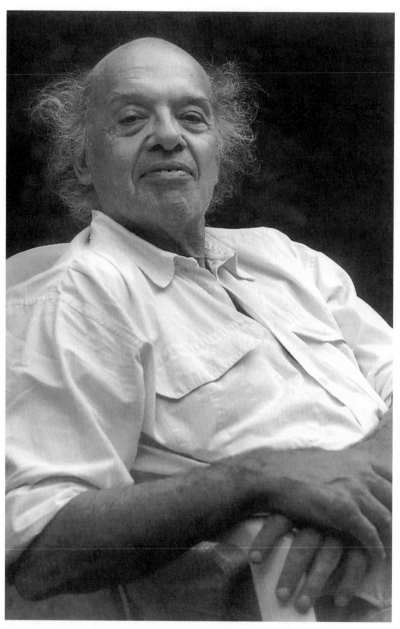

Gerald Stern

I REMEMBER GALILEO

I remember Galileo describing the mind
as a piece of paper blown around by the wind,
and I loved the sight of it sticking to a tree
or jumping into the backseat of a car,
and for years I watched paper leap through my cities;
but yesterday I saw the mind was a squirrel caught crossing
Route 80 between the wheels of a giant truck,
dancing back and forth like a thin leaf,
or a frightened string, for only two seconds living
on the white concrete before he got away,
his life shortened by all that terror, his head
jerking, his yellow teeth ground down to dust.

It was the speed of the squirrel and his lowness to the ground,
his great purpose and the alertness of his dancing,
that showed me the difference between him and paper.
Paper will do in theory, when there is time
to sit back in a metal chair and study shadows;
but for this life I need a squirrel,
his clawed feet spread, his whole soul quivering,
the hot wind rushing through his hair,
the loud noise shaking him from head to tail.
   O philosophical mind, O mind of paper, I need a squirrel
finishing his wild dash across the highway,
rushing up his green ungoverned hillside.

THE DANCING

In all these rotten shops, in all this broken furniture
and wrinkled ties and baseball trophies and coffee pots
I have never seen a postwar Philco
with the automatic eye
nor heard Ravel's "Bolero" the way I did
in 1945 in that tiny living room
on Beechwood Boulevard, nor danced as I did

521

then, my knives all flashing, my hair all streaming,
my mother red with laughter, my father cupping
his left hand under his armpit, doing the dance
of old Ukraine, the sound of his skin half drum,
half fart, the world at last a meadow
the three of us whirling and singing, the three of us
screaming and falling, as if we were dying,
as if we could never stop — in 1945 —
in Pittsburgh, beautiful filthy Pittsburgh, home
of the evil Mellons, 5,000 miles away
from the other dancing — in Poland and Germany —
oh God of mercy, oh wild God.

SOAP

Here is a green Jew
with thin black lips.
I stole him from the men's room
of the Amelia Earhart and wrapped him in toilet paper.
Up the street in *Parfumes*
are Austrian Jews and Hungarian,
without memories really,
holding their noses in the midst of that
paradise of theirs.
There is a woman outside
who hesitates because it is almost Christmas.
"I think I'll go in and buy a Jew," she says.
"I mean some soap, some nice new lilac or lily
to soothe me over the hard parts,
some Zest, some Fleur de Loo, some Wild Gardenia."

And here is a blue Jew.
It is his color, you know,
and he feels better buried in it, imprisoned
in all that sky, the land of death and plenty.
If he is an old one he dances,
or he sits stiffly,
listening to the meek words and admiring the vile actions
of first the Goths and then the Ostrogoths.
Inside is a lovely young girl,
a Dane, who gave good comfort

GERALD STERN

and sad support to soap of all kinds and sorts
during the war and during the occupation.
She touches my hand with unguents and salves.
She puts one under my nose all wrapped in tissue,
and squeezes his cheeks.

I buy a black Romanian for my shelf
I use him for hair and beard,
and even for teeth when things get bitter and sad.
He had one dream, this piece of soap,
if I'm getting it right,
he wanted to live in Wien
and sit behind a hedge on Sunday afternoon
listening to music and eating a tender schnitzel.
That was delirium. Other than that he'd dream
of America sometimes, but he was a kind of cynic,
and kind of lazy — conservative — even in his dream,
and for this he would pay, he paid for his lack of dream.
The Germans killed him because he didn't dream
enough, because he had no vision.

I buy a brush for my back, a simple plastic
handle with gentle bristles. I buy some dust
to sweeten my body. I buy a yellow cream
for my hairy face. From time to time I meet
a piece of soap on Broadway, a sliver really,
without much on him, sometimes I meet two friends
stuck together the way those slivers get
and bow a little, I bow to hide my horror,
my grief, sometimes the soap is so thin
the light goes through it, these are the thin old men
and thin old women the light goes through, these are
the Jews who were born in 1865
or 1870, for them I cringe, for them
I whimper a little, they are the ones who remember
the eighteenth century, they are the ones who listened
to heavenly voices, they were lied to and cheated.

My counterpart was born in 1925
in a city in Poland — I don't like to see him born
in a little village fifty miles from Kiev
and have to fight so wildly just for access
to books, I don't want to see him struggle
half his life to see a painting or just to

sit in one of the plush chairs listening to music.
He was dragged away in 1940
and turned to some use in 1941,
although he may have fought a little, piled
some bricks up or poured some dirty gasoline
over a German truck. His color was rose
and he floated for me for days and days; I love
the way he smelled the air, I love how he looked,
how his eyes lighted up, how his cheeks were almost pink
when he was happy. I love how he dreamed, how he almost
disappeared when he was in thought. For him
I write this poem, for my little brother, if I
should call him that — maybe he is the ghost
that lives in the place I have forgotten, that dear one
that died instead of me — oh ghost, forgive me! —
Maybe he stayed so I could leave, the *older* one
who stayed so I could leave — oh live forever!
forever! — Maybe he is a Being from the other
world, his left arm agate, his left eye crystal,
and he has come back again for the twentieth time,
this time to Poland, to Warsaw or Bialystok,
to see what hell is like. I think it's that,
he has come back to live in our hell, if he could
even prick his agate arm or even weep
with his crystal eye — oh weep with your crystal eye,
dear helpless Being, dear helpless Being. I'm writing this
in Iowa and Pennsylvania and New York City,
in time for Christmas, 1982,
the odor of Irish Spring, the stench of Ivory.

THE BULL-ROARER

I

I only saw my father's face in butchery
once — it was a horror — there were ten men
surrounding a calf, their faces were red, my father's
eyes were shining; there might have been fewer than ten,
some were farmers, some were my father's friends
down from the city. I was nine, maybe eight;
I remember we slept a few hours and left

at four in the morning, there were two cars, or three,
I think it was West Virginia. I remember
the pasture, the calf was screaming, his two eyes
where white with terror, there was blood and slaver
mixed, he was spread-eagled, there was a rope
still hanging from his neck, they all had knives
or ice picks — is that possible? — they were beery,
drunk, the blood was pouring from the throat
but they were stabbing him, one of them bellowed
as if he were a bull, he was the god
of the hunters, dressed in overalls and boots,
the king of animals; they seemed to know —
some of them seemed to know — the tendons and bones,
they were already cutting and slicing, pulling
the skin off, or maybe that was later, I stood there
staring at them, my father with a knife;
we didn't even have a dog — my mother froze
whenever she saw one — we were living in Beechview,
we had the newest car on the street, it was
an ugly suburb, everything was decent,
there was a little woods, but it was locust,
it would be covered with houses, we didn't even have
a parrot, my father left at eight in the morning
and drove his car downtown, he always wore
a suit and tie, his shoes were polished, he spent
the day with customers, he ate his lunch
at a little booth, I often sat with him,
with him and his friends, I had to show off, I drew
their likenesses, I drew the tables and chairs,
it was the Depression, none of them had brass rings
hanging from their ears, they all wore socks,
and long-sleeved shirts, they ate and drank with passion.

II

My mother is eighty-seven, she remembers
the visit to the farm, there was her brother,
my uncle Simon, and there was his friend, MacBride,
Lou MacBride, he was the connection, he was
a friend of the farmer's, maybe a cousin. I asked her
about the killing — "that is the way those farmers
got their meat, they lived like that, they butchered
whatever they needed." I asked if she could remember

anything strange, was she nervous or frightened?
"There was the tail, they cut the tail off
and chased each other; it was like pinning the tail
to the donkey." Both of us laughed. I didn't have the heart
to mention my father's face, or mention the knife —
and, most of all, my pain. What did I want?
That he should stay forever locked inside
his gold-flecked suits? That he should get up in the dark
and put his shoes on with a silver knife?
That he should unbutton his shirts and stuff the cardboard
into a chute? That he should always tie
his tie with three full loops, his own true version
of the Windsor knot? And what did I want for myself?
Some childish thing, that no one would ever leave me?
That there would always be logic — and loyalty?
— I think that tail goes back to the Paleolithic.
I think our game has gory roots — some cave,
or field, they chased each other — or they were grimmer,
pinning that tail, some power was amassed,
as well as something ludicrous, always that,
the tail was different from the horns, or paws,
it was the seat of shame — and there was envy,
not just contempt, but envy — horns a man has,
and he has furry hands and he has a mane,
but never a tail. I remember dimly
a toy we had, a kind of flattened stone,
curved at the sides, with a long rope at one end
we whirled around to make a thundering noise.
This was a "bull-roarer"; we made thunder
and felt the power in our shoulders and legs.
I saw this toy in southern Italy;
I saw children throwing it over their heads
as if they were in central Australia
or ancient Europe somewhere, in a meadow,
forcing the gods to roar. They call it Uranic,
a heavenly force, sometimes almost a voice,
locked up in that whirling stone, dear father.

GERALD STERN

ANOTHER INSANE DEVOTION

This was gruesome — fighting over a ham sandwich
with one of the tiny cats of Rome, he leaped
on my arm and half hung on to the food and half
hung on to my shirt and coat. I tore it apart
and let him have his portion, I think I lifted him
down, sandwich and all, on the sidewalk and sat
with my own sandwich beside him, maybe I petted
his bony head and felt him shiver. I have
told this story over and over; some things
root in the mind; his boldness, of course, was frightening
and unexpected — his stubbornness — though hunger
drove him mad. It was the breaking of boundaries,
the sudden invasion, but not only that, it was
the sharing of food and the sharing of space; he didn't
run into an alley or into a cellar,
he sat beside me, eating, and I didn't run
into a trattoria, say, shaking,
with food on my lips and blood on my cheek, sobbing;
but not only that, I had gone there to eat
and wait for someone. I had maybe an hour
before she would come and I was full of hope
and excitement. I have resisted for years
interpreting this, but now I think I was given
a clue, or I was giving myself a clue,
across the street from the glass sandwich shop.
That was my last night with her, the next day
I would leave on the train for Paris and she would
meet her husband. Thirty-five years ago
I ate my sandwich and moaned in her arms, we were
dying together; we never met again
although she was pregnant when I left her — I have
a daughter or son somewhere, darling grandchildren
in Norwich, Connecticut, or Canton, Ohio.
Every five years I think about her again
and plan on looking her up. The last time
I was sitting in New Brunswick, New Jersey,
and heard that her husband was teaching at Princeton,
if she was still married, or still alive, and tried
calling. I went that far. We lived
in Florence and Rome. We rowed in the bay of Naples
and floated, naked, on the boards. I started

to think of her again today. I still
am horrified by the cat's hunger. I still
am puzzled by the connection. This is another
insane devotion, there must be hundreds, although
it isn't just that, there is no pain, and the thought
is fleeting and sweet. I think it's my own dumb boyhood,
walking around with Slavic cheeks and burning
stupid eyes. I think I gave the cat
half of my sandwich to buy my life, I think
I broke it in half as a decent sacrifice.
It was this I bought, the red coleus,
the split rocking chair, the silk lampshade.
Happiness. I watched him with pleasure.
I bought memory. I could have lost it.
How crazy it sounds. His face twisted with cunning.
The wind blowing through his hair. His jaws working.

THE SWEETNESS OF LIFE

After the heavy rain we were able to tell about the mushrooms,
which ones made us sick, which ones had the dry bitterness,
which ones caused stomach pains and dizziness and hallucinations.

It was the beginning of religion again — on the river —
all the battles and ecstasies and persecutions
taking place beside the hackberries and the fallen locust.

I sat there like a lunatic,
weeping, raving, standing on my head, living
in three and four and five places at once.

I sat there letting the wild and domestic combine,
finally accepting the sweetness of life,
on my own mushy log,
in the white and spotted moonlight.

GERALD STERN

LILACS FOR GINSBERG

I was most interested in what they looked like dead
and I could learn to love them so I waited
for three or four days until the brown set in
and there was a certain reverse curl to the leaf by
which in putting my finger on the main artery
beside the throat I knew the blood had passed on
to someplace else and he was talking to two
demons from the afterlife although it was
just like the mountains in New York State since there was
smoke in the sky and they were yelping and he was
speaking in his telltale New Jersey English
and saying the same thing over and over the way he
did when he was on stage and his white shirt was
perfect and the lack of air and of light
aged the lilacs but he was sitting on a lily
in one or two seconds and he forgot about Eighth Street
and fame and cancer and bent down to pick a loose
diamond but more important than that he talked
to the demons in French and sang with his tinny voice
nor did he go on about his yellowing sickness
but counted the clusters and said they were only stars
and there were two universes intertwined, the
white and the purple, or they were just crumbs or specks
that he could sprinkle on his pie nor could he
exactly remember his sorrow except when he pressed
the lilacs to his face or when he stooped
to bury himself in the bush, then for a moment
he almost did, for lilacs clear the mind
and all the elaborations are possible in their
dear smell and even his death which was so
good and thoughtful became, for a moment, sorrowful.

Mark Strand

KEEPING THINGS WHOLE

In a field
I am the absence
of field.
This is
always the case.
Wherever I am
I am what is missing.

When I walk
I part the air
and always
the air moves in
to fill the spaces
where my body's been.

We all have reasons
for moving.
I move
to keep things whole.

THE DRESS

Lie down on the bright hill
with the moon's hand on your cheek,
your flesh deep in the white folds of your dress,
and you will not hear the passionate mole
extending the length of his darkness,
or the owl arranging all of the night,
which is his wisdom, or the poem
filling your pillow with its blue feathers.
But if you step out of your dress and move into the shade,
the mole will find you, so will the owl, and so will the poem,
and you will fall into another darkness, one you will find
yourself making and remaking until it is perfect.

MARK STRAND

THE PREDICTION

That night the moon drifted over the pond,
turning the water to milk, and under
the boughs of the trees, the blue trees,
a young woman walked, and for an instant

the future came to her:
rain falling on her husband's grave, rain falling
on the lawns of her children, her own mouth
filling with cold air, strangers moving into her house,

a man in her room writing a poem, the moon drifting into it,
a woman strolling under its trees, thinking of death,
thinking of him thinking of her, and the wind rising
and taking the moon and leaving the paper dark.

MY LIFE BY SOMEBODY ELSE

I have done what I could but you avoid me.
I left a bowl of milk on the desk to tempt you.
Nothing happened. I left my wallet there, full of money.
You must have hated me for that. You never came.

I sat at my typewriter naked, hoping you would wrestle me
to the floor. I played with myself just to arouse you.
Boredom drove me to sleep. I offered you my wife.
I sat her on the desk and spread her legs. I waited.

The days drag on. The exhausted light falls like a bandage
over my eyes. Is it because I am ugly? Was anyone
ever so sad? It is pointless to slash my wrists. My hands
would fall off. And then what hope would I have?

Why do you never come? Must I have you by being
somebody else? Must I write *My Life* by somebody else?
My Death by somebody else? Are you listening?
Somebody else has arrived. Somebody else is writing.

MARK STRAND

A MORNING

I have carried it with me each day: that morning I took
my uncle's boat from the brown water cove
and headed for Mosher Island.
Small waves splashed against the hull
and the hollow creek of oarlock and oar
rose into the woods of black pine crusted with lichen.
I moved like a dark star, drifting over the drowned
other half of the world until, by a distant prompting,
I looked over the gunwale and saw beneath the surface
a luminous room, a light-filled grave, saw for the first time
the one clear place given to us when we are alone.

THE IDEA

for Nolan Miller

For us, too, there was a wish to possess
Something beyond the world we knew, beyond ourselves,
Beyond our power to imagine, something nevertheless
In which we might see ourselves; and this desire
Came always in passing, in waning light, and in such cold
That ice on the valley's lakes cracked and rolled,
And blowing snow covered what earth we saw,
And scenes from the past, when they surfaced again,
Looked not as they had, but ghostly and white
Among false curves and hidden erasures;
And never once did we feel we were close
Until the night wind said, "Why do this,
Especially now? Go back to the place you belong;"
And there appeared, with its windows glowing, small,
In the distance, in the frozen reaches, a cabin;
And we stood before it, amazed at its being there,
And would have gone forward and opened the door,
And stepped into the glow and warmed ourselves there,
But that it was ours by not being ours,
And should remain empty. That was the idea.

A. M.

for Lee Rust Brown

. . . And here the dark infinitive to feel,
Which would endure and have the earth be still
And the star-strewn night pour down the mountains
Into the hissing fields and silent towns until the last
Insomniac turned in, must end, and early risers see
The scarlet clouds break up and golden plumes of smoke
From uniform dark homes turn white, and so on down
To the smallest blade of grass and fallen leaf
Touched by the arriving light. Another day has come,
Another fabulous escape from the damages of night,
So even the gulls, in the ragged circle of their flight,
Above the sea's long lanes that flash and fall, scream
Their approval. How well the sun's rays probe
The rotting carcass of a skate, how well
They show the worms and swarming flies at work,
How well they shine upon the fatal sprawl
Of everything on earth. How well they love us all.

from **DARK HARBOR**

XXX

There is a road through the canyon,
A river beside the road, a forest.
If there is more, I haven't seen it yet.

Still, it is possible to say this has been
An amazing century for fashion if for nothing else;
The way brave models held back their tears

When thinking of the millions of Jews and Serbs
That Hitler killed, and how the photographer
Steadied his hand when he considered

The Muzhiks that Stalin took care of.
The way skirts went up and down; how breasts
Were in, then out; and the long and the short of hair.

But the road that winds through the canyon
Is covered with snow, and the river flows
Under the ice. Cross-country skiers are moving

Like secrets between the trees of the glassed-in forest.
The day has made a fabulous cage of cold around
My face. Whenever I take a breath I hear cracking.

XXXIX

When after a long silence one picks up the pen
And leans over the paper and says to himself:
Today I shall consider Marsyas

Whose body was flayed to excess,
Who made no crime that would square
With what he was made to suffer.

Today I shall consider the shredded remains of Marsyas —
What do they mean as they gather the sunlight
That falls in pieces through the trees,

As in Titian's late painting? Poor Marsyas,
A body, a body of work as it turns and falls
Into suffering, becoming the flesh of light,

Which is fed to onlookers centuries later.
Can this be the cost of encompassing pain?
After a long silence, would I, whose body

Is whole, sheltered, kept in the dark by a mind
That prefers it that way, know what I'd done
And what its worth was? Or is a body scraped

From the bone of experience, the chart of suffering
To be read in such ways that all flesh might be redeemed,
At least for the moment, the moment it passes into song.

XLV

I am sure you would find it misty here,
With lots of stone cottages badly needing repair.
Groups of souls, wrapped in cloaks, sit in the fields

Or stroll the winding unpaved roads. They are polite,
And oblivious to their bodies, which the wind passes through,
Making a shushing sound. Not long ago,

I stopped to rest in a place where an especially
Thick mist swirled up from the river. Someone,
Who claimed to have known me years before,

Approached, saying there were many poets
Wandering around who wished to be alive again.
They were ready to say the words they had been unable to say —

Words whose absence had been the silence of love,
Of pain, and even of pleasure. Then he joined a small group,
Gathered beside a fire. I believe I recognized

Some of the faces, but as I approached they tucked
Their heads under their wings. I looked away to the hills
Above the river, where the golden lights of sunset

And sunrise are one and the same, and saw something flying
Back and forth, fluttering its wings. Then it stopped in mid-air.
It was an angel, one of the good ones, about to sing.

THE NIGHT, THE PORCH

To stare at nothing is to learn by heart
What all of us will be swept into, and baring oneself
To the wind is feeling the ungraspable somewhere close by.
Trees can sway or be still. Day or night can be what they wish.
What we desire, more than a season or weather, is the comfort
Of being strangers, at least to ourselves. This is the crux
Of the matter, which is why even now we seem to be waiting
For something whose appearance would be its vanishing —
The sound, say, of a few leaves falling, or just one leaf,
Or less. There is no end to what we can learn. The book out there
Tells us as much, and was never written with us in mind.

A PIECE OF THE STORM

for Sharon Horvath

From the shadow of domes in the city of domes,
A snowflake, a blizzard of one, weightless, entered your room
And made its way to the arm of the chair where you, looking up
From your book, saw it the moment it landed. That's all
There was to it. No more than a solemn waking
To brevity, to the lifting and falling away of attention, swiftly,

A time between times, a flowerless funeral. No more than that
Except for the feeling that this piece of the storm,
Which turned into nothing before your eyes, would come back,
That someone years hence, sitting as you are now, might say:
"It's time. The air is ready. The sky has an opening."

LEOPARDI

The night is warm and clear and without wind.
The stone-white moon waits above the rooftops
and above the nearby river. Every street is still
and the corner lights shine down only upon the hunched shapes of cars.
You are asleep. And sleep gathers in your room
and nothing at this moment bothers you. Jules,
an old wound has opened and I feel the pain of it again.
While you sleep I have gone outside to pay my late respects
to the sky that seems so gentle
and to the world that is not and that says to me:
"I do not give you any hope. Not even hope."
Down the street there is the voice of a drunk
singing an unrecognizable song
and a car a few blocks off.
Things pass and leave no trace,
and tomorrow will come and the day after,
and whatever our ancestors knew time has taken away.
They are gone and their children are gone
and the great nations are gone.
And the armies are gone that sent clouds of dust and smoke
rolling across Europe. The world is still and we do not hear them.
Once when I was a boy, and the birthday I had waited for
was over, I lay on my bed, awake and miserable, and very late
that night the sound of someone's voice singing down a side street,
dying little by little into the distance,
wounded me, as this does now.

Ellen Bryant Voigt

JANUARY

After days of putting down my poem
to wipe the chair, I see
the skin of the room is oozing pitch.
Steep as a church, a bishop's hat,
the roof is lined with spruce,
and this close to the stove
the heat has opened the sapline
at each dark flaw, as though it tapped
a living tree. Everyday, a pure emanation,
the syrup bleeds to the surface of the wood.

Now, a length of softwood in its craw,
the stove crackles with resin,
and the room itself
stretches and cracks with heat, cold,
the walls' mediation between them.
There are three pale coins of resin
in the usual place on the arm of the chair.
And the momentary flies,
hatched behind the wallboard
or in the pores of the old beams,
stagger down the window's white page.

If I think I am apart from this, I am a fool.
And if I think the black engine of the stove
can raise in me the same luminous waking,
I am still a fool,
since I am the one who keeps the fire.

THE HEN

The neck lodged under a stick,
the stick under her foot,
she held the full white breast
with both hands, yanked up and out,

and the head was delivered of the body.
Brain stuck like a lens; the profile
fringed with red feathers.
Deposed, abstracted,
the head lay on the ground like a coin.
But the rest, released into the yard,
language and direction wrung from it,
flapped the insufficient wings
and staggered forward, convulsed, instinctive —
I thought it was sobbing to see it hump the dust,
pulsing out those muddy juices,
as if something, deep in the gizzard,
in the sack of soft nuggets,
drove it toward the amputated member.
Even then, watching it litter the ground
with snowy refusals, I knew it was this
that held life, gave life,
and not the head with its hard contemplative eye.

THE TRUST

Something was killing sheep
but it was sheep this dog attended on the farm —
a black-and-white border collie, patrolling his fold
like a parish priest. The second time the neighbor came,
claiming to have spotted the dog at night, a crouched figure
slithering toward the pen on the far side of the county,
the farmer let him witness how the dog,
alert and steady, mended the frayed
edge of the flock, the clumped sheep calm
as they drifted together along the stony hill.
But still more sheep across the glen were slaughtered,
and the man returned more confident. This time,
the master called his dog forward,
and stroking the eager head, prized open the mouth to find,
wound around the base of the back teeth — squat molars
the paws can't reach to clean — small coils of wool,
fine and stiff, like threads from his own jacket.
So he took down the rifle from the rack
and shot the dog and buried him,
his best companion in the field for seven years.

Once satisfied, the appetite is never dulled again.
Night after night, its sweet insistent promise
drives the animal under the rail fence and miles away
for a fresh kill; and with guilty cunning brings him back
to his familiar charges, just now stirring in the early light,
brings him home to his proud husbandry.

FAIRY TALE

The wronged spirit brought the child
a basket of riches:
two parents, justice and mercy;
a beauty both stunning and organic;
fame beyond the wide walls of the castle;
and intelligence, lying like an asp
at the bottom of the basket.
With this last gift she could discern
the flaw in nature
and all of nature's fruits.

Thus she came to her
majority already skilled,
having pressed bright flowers
to a film, having memorized
the verses of the day.
For months, she did not eat,
she did not traffic with the agencies
of change: she had cast her will entirely

against decay. Even when
the wild tangle emerged
from the careful lawns, and ebony birds
came down from the woods
to roost in the chiseled turrets
and foul the court, she would not stir
nor in any way disturb
the triumph that would greet the shallow prince:
a soul unencumbered
in a neutral body.

ELLEN BRYANT VOIGT

WOMAN WHO WEEPS

Up from the valley, ten children working the fields
and three in the ground, plus four who'd slipped like fish
from a faulty seine, she wept to the priest:
    Father, I saw the Virgin on a hill,
    she was a lion, lying on her side,
    grooming her blond shoulders with her tongue.

Six months weeping as she hulled the corn,
gathered late fruit and milked the goats,
planted grain and watched the hillside blossom,
before she went to the Bishop, kissed his ring.
    Father, I saw Our Lady in a tree,
    swaddled in black, she was a raven,
    on one leg, on one bent claw
    she hunched in the tree but she was the tree,
    charred trunk in a thicket of green.

After seven years of weeping,
not as other stunned old women weep,
she baked flat bread, washed the cooking stones,
cut a staff from a sapling by the road.
The Holy Father sat in a gilded chair:
    Father, I saw Christ's Mother in a stream,
    she was a rock, the water
    parted on either side of her,
    from one stream she made two —
    two tresses loosened across her collarbone —
    until the pouring water met at her breast
    and made a single stream again —
Then from the marketplace, from the busiest stall
she stole five ripened figs
and carried her weeping back to the countryside,
with a cloth sack, with a beggar's cup,
village to village and into the smoky huts,
her soul a well, an eye, an open door.

ELLEN BRYANT VOIGT

THE LOTUS FLOWERS

The surface of the pond was mostly green —
bright green algae reaching out from the banks,
then the mass of waterlilies, their broad round leaves
rim to rim, each white flower spreading
from the center of a green saucer.
We teased and argued, choosing the largest,
the sweetest bloom, but when the rowboat
lumbered through and rearranged them,
we found the plants were anchored, the separate
muscular stems descending in the dense water —
only the most determined put her hand
into that frog-slimed pond
to wrestle with a flower. Back and forth
we pumped across the water, in twos and threes,
full of brave adventure. On the marshy shore,
the others hollered for their turns,
or at the hem of where we pitched the tents
gathered firewood —
                    this was wilderness,
although the pond was less than half an acre
and we could still see the grand magnolias
in the village cemetery, their waxy
white conical blossoms gleaming in the foliage.
A dozen girls, the oldest only twelve, two sisters
with their long braids, my shy neighbor,
someone squealing without interruption:
all we didn't know about the world buoyed us,
as the frightful water sustained and moved the flowers
tethered at a depth we couldn't see.

In the late afternoon, before they'd folded
into candles on the dark water,
I went to fill the bucket at the spring.
Deep in the pines, exposed tree roots
formed a natural arch, a cave of black loam.
I raked off the skin of leaves and needles,
leaving a pool so clear and shallow
I could count the pebbles
on the studded floor. The sudden cold
splashing up from the bucket to my hands
made me want to plunge my hand in —

and I held it under, feeling the shock that wakes
and deadens, watching first my fingers,
then the ledge beyond me,
the snake submerged and motionless,
the head propped on its coils the way a girl
crosses her arms before her on the sill
and rests her chin there.
                              Lugging the bucket
back to the noisy clearing, I found nothing changed,
the boat still rocked across the pond,
the fire straggled and cracked as we fed it
branches and debris into the night,
leaning back on our pallets —
spokes in a wheel — learning the names of the many
constellations, learning how each fixed
cluster took its name:
not from the strongest light, but from the pattern
made by stars of lesser magnitude,
so like the smaller stars we rowed among.

THE CUSP

So few birds — the ones that winter through
and the geese migrating through the empty fields,
fording the cropped, knuckled stalks of corn:
all around us, all that's green's suppressed,
and in the brooding wood, the bare trees,
shorn of leaves or else just shy of leaves,
make a dark estate beneath low clouds
that have the look of stubborn snow.

In a purely scientific exercise —
say you came from the moon, or returned
like Lazarus, blinking from the cave —
you wouldn't know if winter's passed or now beginning.
The bank slopes up, the bank slopes down to the ditch.
Would it help if I said grieving has an end?
Would it matter if I told you this is spring?

ELLEN BRYANT VOIGT

TWO TREES

At first, for the man and woman,
everything was beautiful.
Which is to say there was no beauty,
since there was not its opposite, its absence.
Every tree was "pleasant to the sight,"
the cattle also, and every creeping thing.

But at the center, foreground of the painting,
God put two trees, different from the others.
One was shrubby, spreading near the ground
lithe branches, like a fountain,
studded with fruit and thorns.
When the woman saw
this tree was good for food
and a tree to be desired to make one wise,
she ate,
            and also saw
the other, even more to be desired,
tallest in the garden, its leaves
a deeper green than all the others',
its boughs, shapely and proportionate,
hung with sweet fruit that never fell,
fruit that made the birds nesting there
graceful, brightly plumed and musical,
yet when they pecked it showed no scar.

To eat from both these trees was to be a god.
So God kept them from the second fruit,
and sent them into thistles and violent weather,
wearing the skins of lesser beasts —
let them garden dust and stony ground,
let them bear a child who was beautiful,
as they had been, and also bear a child
marked and hateful as they would become,
and bring these forth from the body's
stink and sorrow while the mind cried out
for that addictive tree it had tasted,
and for that other, crown still visible
over the wall.

Richard Wilbur

THE RIDE

The horse beneath me seemed
To know what course to steer
Through the horror of snow I dreamed,
And so I had no fear,

Nor was I chilled to death
By the wind's white shudders, thanks
To the veils of his patient breath
And the mist of sweat from his flanks.

It seemed that all night through,
Within my hand no rein
And nothing in my view
But the pillar of his mane,

I rode with magic ease
At a quick, unstumbling trot
Through shattering vacancies
On into what was not,

Till the weave of the storm grew thin,
With a threading of cedar-smoke,
And the ice-blind pane of an inn
Shimmered, and I awoke.

How shall I now get back
To the inn-yard where he stands,
Burdened with every lack,
And waken the stable-hands

To give him, before I think
That there was no horse at all,
Some hay, some water to drink,
A blanket and a stall?

RICHARD WILBUR

LOVE CALLS US TO THE THINGS OF THIS WORLD

The eyes open to a cry of pulleys,
And spirited from sleep, the astounded soul
Hangs for a moment bodiless and simple
As false dawn.
                    Outside the open window
The morning air is all awash with angels.

Some are in bed-sheets, some are in blouses,
Some are in smocks: but truly there they are.
Now they are rising together in calm swells
Of halcyon feeling, filling whatever they wear
With the deep joy of their impersonal breathing;

Now they are flying in place, conveying
The terrible speed of their omnipresence, moving
And staying like white water; and now of a sudden
They swoon down into so rapt a quiet
That nobody seems to be there.
                            The soul shrinks

From all that it is about to remember,
From the punctual rape of every blessèd day,
And cries,
                "Oh, let there be nothing on earth but laundry,
Nothing but rosy hands in the rising steam
And clear dances done in the sight of heaven."

Yet, as the sun acknowledges
With a warm look the world's hunks and colors,
The soul descends once more in bitter love
To accept the waking body, saying now
In a changed voice as the man yawns and rises,

"Bring them down from their ruddy gallows;
Let there be clean linen for the backs of thieves;
Let lovers go fresh and sweet to be undone,
And the heaviest nuns walk in a pure floating
Of dark habits,
                keeping their difficult balance."

RICHARD WILBUR

PLAYBOY

High on his stockroom ladder like a dunce
The stock-boy sits, and studies like a sage
The subject matter of one glossy page,
As lost in curves as Archimedes once.

Sometimes, without a glance, he feeds himself.
The left hand, like a mother-bird in flight,
Brings him a sandwich for a sidelong bite,
And then returns it to a dusty shelf.

What so engrosses him? The wild décor
Of this pink-papered alcove into which
A naked girl has stumbled, with its rich
Welter of pelts and pillows on the floor,

Amidst which, kneeling in a supple pose,
She lifts a goblet in her farther hand,
As if about to toast a flower-stand
Above which hovers an exploding rose

Fired from a long-necked crystal vase that rests
Upon a tasseled and vermillion cloth
One taste of which would shrivel up a moth?
Or is he pondering her perfect breasts?

Nothing escapes him of her body's grace
Or of her floodlit skin, so sleek and warm
And yet so strangely like a uniform,
But what now grips his fancy is her face,

And how the cunning picture holds her still
At just that smiling instant when her soul,
Grown sweetly faint, and swept beyond control,
Consents to his inexorable will.

COTTAGE STREET, 1953

Framed in her phoenix fire-screen, Edna Ward
Bends to the tray of Canton, pouring tea
For frightened Mrs. Plath; then, turning toward
The pale, slumped daughter, and my wife, and me,

Asks if we would prefer it weak or strong.
Will we have milk or lemon, she enquires?
The visit seems already strained and long.
Each in his turn, we tell her our desires.

It is my office to exemplify
The published poet in his happiness,
Thus cheering Sylvia, who has wished to die;
But half-ashamed, and impotent to bless,

I am a stupid life-guard who has found,
Swept to his shallows by the tide, a girl
Who, far from shore, has been immensely drowned,
And stares through water now with eyes of pearl.

How large is her refusal; and how slight
The genteel chat whereby we recommend
Life, of a summer afternoon, despite
The brewing dusk which hints that it may end.

And Edna Ward shall die in fifteen years,
After her eight-and-eighty summers of
Such grace and courage as permit no tears,
The thin hand reaching out, the last word *love*,

Outliving Sylvia who, condemned to live,
Shall study for a decade, as she must,
To state at last her brilliant negative
In poems free and helpless and unjust.

RICHARD WILBUR

THE WRITER

In her room at the prow of the house
Where light breaks, and the windows are tossed with linden,
My daughter is writing a story.

I pause in the stairwell, hearing
From her shut door a commotion of typewriter-keys
Like a chain hauled over a gunwale.

Young as she is, the stuff
Of her life is a great cargo, and some of it heavy:
I wish her a lucky passage.

But now it is she who pauses,
As if to reject my thought and its easy figure.
A stillness greatens, in which

The whole house seems to be thinking,
And then she is at it again with a bunched clamor
Of strokes, and again is silent.

I remember the dazed starling
Which was trapped in that very room, two years ago;
How we stole in, lifted a sash

And retreated, not to affright it;
And how for a helpless hour, through the crack of the door,
We watched the sleek, wild, dark

And iridescent creature
Batter against the brilliance, drop like a glove
To the hard floor, or the desk-top,

And wait then, humped and bloody,
For the wits to try it again; and how our spirits
Rose when, suddenly sure,

It lifted off from a chair-back,
Beating a smooth course for the right window
And clearing the sill of the world.

It is always a matter, my darling,
Of life or death, as I had forgotten. I wish
What I wished you before, but harder.

THE LILACS

Those laden lilacs
                   at the lawn's end
Came stark, spindly,
                     and in staggered file,
Like walking wounded
                       from the dead of winter.
We watched them waken
                      in the brusque weather
To rot and rootbreak,
                  to ripped branches,
And saw them shiver
                    as the memory swept them
Of night and numbness
                    and the taste of nothing.
Out of present pain
                 and from past terror
Their bullet-shaped buds
                    came quick and bursting,
As if they aimed
               to be open with us!
But the sun suddenly
                 settled about them,
And green and grateful
                 the lilacs grew,
Healed in that hush,
               that hospital quiet.
These lacquered leaves
                 where the light paddles
And the big blooms
                buzzing among them
Have kept their counsel,
                 conveying nothing
Of their mortal message,
                 unless one should measure

The depth and dumbness
                of death's kingdom
By the pure power
           of this perfume.

MAYFLIES

In sombre forest, when the sun was low,
I saw from unseen pools a mist of flies
     In their quadrillions rise
And animate a ragged patch of glow
With sudden glittering — as when a crowd
     Of stars appear
Through a brief gap in black and driven cloud,
One arc of their great round-dance showing clear.

It was no muddled swarm I witnessed, for
In entrechats each fluttering insect there
     Rose two steep yards in air,
Then slowly floated down to climb once more,
So that they all composed a manifold
     And figured scene,
And seemed the weavers of some cloth of gold,
Or the fine pistons of some bright machine.

Watching those lifelong dancers of a day
As night closed in, I felt myself alone
     In a life too much my own,
More mortal in my separateness than they —
Unless, I thought, I had been called to be
     Not fly or star
But one whose task is joyfully to see
How fair the fiats of the caller are.

C. K. Williams

BLADES

When I was about eight, I once stabbed somebody, another kid, a little
    girl.
I'd been hanging around in front of the supermarket near our house
and when she walked by, I let her have it, right in the gap between her
    shirt and her shorts
with a piece of broken-off car antenna I used to carry around in my
    pocket.
It happened so fast I still don't know how I did it: I was as shocked as she
    was
except she squealed and started yelling as though I'd plunged a knife in
    her
and everybody in the neighborhood gathered around us, then they called
    the cops,
then the girl's mother came running out of the store saying "What hap-
    pened? What happened?"
and the girl screamed, "He stabbed me!" and I screamed back, "I did
    not!" and she you did too
and me I didn't and we were both crying hysterically by that time.
Somebody pulled her shirt up and it was just a scratch but we went on
    and on
and the mother, standing between us, seemed to be absolutely terrified.
I still remember how she watched first one of us and then the other with
    a look of complete horror —
You did too! I did not! — as though we were both strangers, as though it
    was some natural disaster
she was beholding that was beyond any mode of comprehension so all
    she could do
was stare speechlessly at us, and then another expression came over her
    face,
one that I'd never seen before, that made me think she was going to cry
    herself
and sweep both of us, the girl and me, into her arms to hold us against
    her.
The police came just then, though, quieted everyone down, put the girl
    and the mother
into a squad-car to take to the hospital and me in another to take to jail
except they really only took me around the corner and let me go because
    the mother and daughter were black

and in those days you had to do something pretty terrible to get into
    trouble that way.

I don't understand how we twist these things or how we get them
    straight again
but I relived that day I don't know how many times before I realized I
    had it all wrong.
The boy wasn't me at all, he was another kid: I was just there.
And it wasn't the girl who was black, but him. The mother was real,
    though.
I really had thought she was going to embrace them both
and I had dreams about her for years afterwards: that I'd be being born
    again
and she'd be lifting me with that same wounded sorrow or she would
    suddenly appear out of nowhere,
blotting out everything but a single, blazing wing of holiness.
Who knows the rest? I can still remember how it felt the old way.
How I make my little thrust, how she crushes us against her, how I turn
    and snarl
at the cold circle of faces around us because something's torn in me,
some ancient cloak of terror we keep on ourselves because we'll do any-
    thing,
anything, not to know how silently we knell in the mouth of death
and not to obliterate the forgiveness and the lies we offer one another
    and call innocence.
This is innocence. I touch her, we kiss.
And this. I'm here or not here. I can't tell. I stab her. I stab her again. I
    still can't.

FROM MY WINDOW

Spring: the first morning when that one true block of sweet, laminar,
    complex scent arrives
from somewhere west and I keep coming to lean on the sill, glorying in
    the end of the wretched winter.
The scabby-barked sycamores ringing the empty lot across the way are
    budded — I hadn't noticed —
and the thick spikes of the unlikely urban crocuses have already broken
    the gritty soil.
Up the street, some surveyors with tripods are waving each other left and
    right the way they do.

C. K. WILLIAMS

A girl in a gym suit jogged by a while ago, some kids passed, playing hooky, I imagine,
and now the paraplegic Vietnam vet who lives in a half-converted warehouse down the block
and the friend who stays with him and seems to help him out come weaving towards me,
their battered wheelchair lurching uncertainly from one edge of the sidewalk to the other.
I know where they're going — to the "Legion": once, when I was putting something out, they stopped,
both drunk that time, too, both reeking — it wasn't ten o'clock — and we chatted for a bit.
I don't know how they stay alive — on benefits most likely. I wonder if they're lovers?
They don't look it. Right now, in fact, they look a wreck, careening haphazardly along,
contriving, as they reach beneath me, to dip a wheel from the curb so that the chair skewers, teeters,
tips, and they both tumble, the one slowly, almost gracefully sliding in stages from his seat,
his expression hardly marking it, the other staggering over him, spinning heavily down,
to lie on the asphalt, his mouth working, his feet shoving weakly and fruitlessly against the curb.
In the storefront office on the corner, Reed and Son, Real Estate, have come to see the show.
Gazing through the golden letters of their name, they're not, at least, thank god, laughing.
Now the buddy, grabbing at a hydrant, gets himself erect and stands there for a moment, panting.
Now he has to lift the other one, who lies utterly still, a forearm shielding his eyes from the sun.
He hauls him partly upright, then hefts him almost all the way into the chair, but a dangling foot
catches a support-plate, jerking everything around so that he has to put him down,
set the chair to rights, and hoist him again and as he does he jerks the grimy jeans right off him.
No drawers, shrunken, blotchy thighs: under the thick, white coils of belly blubber,
the poor, blunt pud, tiny, terrified, retracted, is almost invisible in the sparse genital hair,
then his friend pulls his pants up, he slumps wholly back as though he were, at last, to be let be,

and the friend leans against the cyclone fence, suddenly staring up at me
     as though he'd known,
all along, that I was watching and I can't help wondering if he knows that
     in the winter, too,
I watched, the night he went out to the lot and walked, paced rather,
     almost ran, for how many hours.
It was snowing, the city in that holy silence, the last we have, when the
     storm takes hold,
and he was making patterns that I thought at first were circles, then real-
     ized made a figure eight,
what must have been to him a perfect symmetry but which, from where
     I was, shivered, bent,
and lay on its side: a warped, unclear infinity, slowly, as the snow came
     faster, going out.
Over and over again, his head lowered to the task, he slogged the path
     he'd blazed,
but the race was lost, his prints were filling faster than he made them
     now and I looked away,
up across the skeletal trees to the tall center city buildings, some, though
     it was midnight,
with all their offices still gleaming, their scarlet warning beacons signal-
     ing erratically
against the thickening flakes, their smoldering auras softening portions
     of the dim, milky sky.
In the morning, nothing: every trace of him effaced, all the field pure
     white,
its surface glittering, the dawn, glancing from its glaze, oblique, relent-
     less, unadorned.

THE GAS STATION

This is before I'd read Nietzsche. Before Kant or Kierkegaard, even
     before Whitman and Yeats.
I don't think there were three words in my head yet. I knew, perhaps, that
     I should suffer,
I can remember I almost cried for this or for that, nothing special, noth-
     ing to speak of.
Probably I was mad with grief for the loss of my childhood, but I would-
     n't have known that.
It's dawn. A gas station. Route twenty-two. I remember exactly: route
     twenty-two curved,

there was a squat, striped concrete divider they'd put in after a plague of
collisions.

The gas station? Texaco, Esso — I don't know. They were just words anyway then, just what their signs said.

I wouldn't have understood the first thing about monopoly or imperial-
ist or oppression.

It's dawn. It's so late. Even then, when I was never tired, I'm just holding on.

Slumped on my friend's shoulder, I watch the relentless, wordless misery
of the route twenty-two sky

that seems to be filming my face with a grainy oil I keep trying to rub off
or in.

Why are we here? Because one of my friends, in the men's room over
there, has blue balls.

He has to jerk off. I don't know what that means, "blue balls," or why he
has to do that —

it must be important to have to stop here after this long night, but I
don't ask.

I'm just trying, I think, to keep my head as empty as I can for as long as
I can.

One of my other friends is asleep. He's so ugly, his mouth hanging, slack
and wet.

Another — I'll never see this one again — stares from the window as
though he were frightened.

Here's what we've done. We were in Times Square, a pimp found us, cor-
ralled us, led us somewhere,

down a dark street, another dark street, up dark stairs, dark hall, dark
apartment,

where his whore, his girl or his wife or his mother for all I know dragged
herself from her sleep,

propped herself on an elbow, gazed into the dark hall, and agreed, for two
dollars each, to take care of us.

Take care of us. Some of the words that come through me now seem to
stay, to hook in.

My friend in the bathroom is taking so long. The filthy sky must be starting to lighten.

It took me a long time, too, with the woman, I mean. Did I mention that
she, the woman, the whore or mother,

was having her time and all she would deign do was to blow us? Did I say
that? Deign? Blow?

What a joy, though, the idea was in those days. Blown! What a thing to
tell the next day.

She only deigned, though, no more. She was like a machine. When I lift
her back to me now,

there's nothing there but that dark, curly head, working, a machine, up
    and down, and now,
Freud, Marx, Fathers, tell me, what am I, doing this, telling this, on her,
    on myself,
hammering it down, cementing it, sealing it in, but a machine, too? *Why
    am I doing this?*
I still haven't read Augustine. I don't understand Chomsky that well.
    Should I?
My friend at last comes back. Maybe the right words were there all along.
    Complicity. Wonder.
How pure we were then, before Rimbaud, before Blake. *Grace. Love. Take
    care of us. Please.*

NORMALITY

"Sometimes I feel as though all I really want is to take his little whizzer
    in my mouth . . .
Didn't you ever feel anything like that? I mean, I'll be changing him, and
    he's smiling,
kicking his legs like crazy, and I can tell he's really excited and I know *I'm*
    excited
and I think how clean and pure and soft he is down there, and that won-
    derful *smell*, you know,
at first you think it's the powder you put on them but then you realize
    it's them, *him*,
it's his goddamned intrinsic odor, I could eat it up, and what would be
    so wrong with it?
I'm not trying to shock you; I mean, maybe if you let yourself, you'd feel
    things like that . . .
Maybe it's you who's fucked up and repressed; I'll bet what I feel for my
    baby's *normal*."

THE NEIGHBOR

Her five horrid, deformed little dogs, who incessantly yap on the roof
    under my window;
her cats, god knows how many, who must piss on her rugs — her land-
    ing's a sickening reek;

her shadow, once, fumbling the chain on her door, then the door slam-
ming fearfully shut:
only the barking, and the music, jazz, filtering as it does day and night
into the hall.

The time it was Chris Conner singing "Lush Life," how it brought back
my college sweetheart,
my first real love, who, till I left her, played the same record, and, head
on my shoulder,
hand on my thigh, sang sweetly along, of regrets and depletions she was
too young for,
as I was too young, later, to believe in her pain: it startled, then bored,
then repelled me.

My starting to fancy she'd ended up in this firetrap in the Village, that
my neighbor was her;
my thinking we'd meet, recognize one another, become friends, that I'd
accomplish a penance;
my seeing her — it wasn't her — at the mailbox, grey-yellow hair, army
pants under a nightgown:
her turning away, hiding her ravaged face in her hands, muttering an
inappropriate "Hi."

Sometimes, there are frightening goings-on in the stairwell, a man
shouting *Shut up!*
the dogs frantically snarling, claws scrabbling, then her, her voice, hoarse,
harsh, hollow,
almost only a tone, incoherent, a note, a squawk, bone on metal, metal
gone molten,
calling them back, Come back, darlings; come back, dear ones, my sweet
angels, come back.

Medea she was, next time I saw her, sorceress, tranced, ecstatic, stock-
still on the sidewalk,
ragged coat hanging agape, passersby flowing around her, her mouth
torn suddenly open,
as though in a scream, silently though, as though only in her brain or
breast had it erupted:
a cry so pure, practiced, detached, it had no need of a voice or could no
longer bear one.

These invisible links that allure, these transfigurations even of anguish
that hold us:
the girl, my old love, the last, lost time I saw her, when she came to find
me at a party:

her drunkenly stumbling, falling, sprawling, skirt hiked, eyes veined red,
    swollen with tears;
her shame, her dishonor; my ignorant, arrogant coarseness; my secret
    pride, my turning away.

Still life on a roof top: dead trees in barrels, a bench, broken; dogs, excre-
    ment, sky.
What pathways through pain, what junctures of vulnerability, what
    crossings and counterings?
Too many lives in our lives already, too many chances for sorrow, too
    many unaccounted-for pasts.
Behold me, the god of frenzied, inexhaustible love says, rising in bloody
    splendor: *Behold me!*

Her making her way down the littered vestibule stairs, one agonized step
    at a time;
my holding the door, her crossing the fragmented tiles, faltering at the
    step to the street,
droning, not looking at me, "Can you help me?" taking my arm, leaning
    lightly against me;
her wavering step into the world, her whispering, "Thanks, love," light-
    ly, lightly against me.

DEPTHS

I'm on a parapet looking down
into a deep cleft in the earth
at minuscule people and cars
moving along its narrow bottom.
Though my father's arms are around me
I feel how far it would be to fall,
how perilous: I cringe back,
my father holds me more tightly.
Was there ever such a crevice?
No, I realized much, much later
we were on an ordinary building
looking down into a city street.

A picture book: desert sunlight,
a man and woman clad in sandals,
pastel robes, loose burnooses,

plying a material like dough,
the man kneading in a trough,
the woman throwing at a wheel.
Somehow I come to think they're angels,
in heaven, fashioning human beings.
Was there ever such a story?
No, the book, at Sunday school,
showed daily life in the Bible,
the people were just making jars.

Just jars, and yet those coils of clay,
tinted light to dark like skin,
swelled beneath the woman's hands
as I knew already flesh should swell,
and as I'd know it later, when,
alone with someone in the dark,
I'd close my eyes, move my hands
across her, and my mouth across her,
trying to experience an ideal,
to participate in radiances
I passionately believed existed,
and not only in imagination.

Or, with love itself, the love
that came to me so readily, so
intensely, so convincingly each time,
and each time ravaged me
when it spoiled and failed, and left
me only memories of its promise.
Could real love ever come to me?
Would I distort it if it did?
Even now I feel a frost of fear
to think I might not have found you,
my love, or not believed in you,
and still be reeling on another roof.

Charles Wright

REUNION

Already one day has detached itself from all the rest up ahead.
It has my photograph in its soft pocket.
It wants to carry my breath into the past in its bag of wind.

I write poems to untie myself, to do penance and disappear
Through the upper right-hand corner of things, to say grace.

GRACE

Its hair is a fine weed,
Matted, where something has lain,
Or fallen repeatedly:

Its arms are rivers that sink
Suddenly under the earth,
Elbow and wristbone: cold sleeve:

Its face is a long soliloquy,
A language of numerals,
Impossible to erase.

VIRGO DESCENDING

Through the viridian (and black of the burnt match),
Through ox-blood and ochre, the ham-colored clay,
Through plate after plate, down
Where the worm and the mole will not go,
Through ore-seam and fire-seam,
My grandmother, senile and 89, crimpbacked, stands
Like a door ajar on her soft bed,
The open beams and bare studs of the hall

Pink as an infant's skin in the floating dark;
Shavings and curls swing down like snowflakes across her face.

My aunt and I walk past. As always, my father
Is planning rooms, dragging his lame leg,
Stroke-straightened and foreign, behind him,
An aberrant 2-by-4 he can't fit snug.
I lay my head on my aunt's shoulder, feeling
At home, and walk on.
Through arches and door jambs, the spidery wires
And coiled cables, the blueprint takes shape:
My mother's room to the left, the door closed;
My father's room to the left, the door closed —

Ahead, my brother's room, unfinished;
Behind, my sister's room, also unfinished.
Buttresses, winches, block-and-tackle: the scale of everything
Is enormous. We keep on walking. And pass
My aunt's room, almost complete, the curtains up,
The lamp and the medicine arranged
In their proper places, in arm's reach of where the bed will go . . .
The next one is mine, now more than half done,
Cloyed by the scent of jasmine,
White-gummed and anxious, their mouths sucking the air dry.

Home is what you lie in, or hang above, the house
Your father made, or keeps on making,
The dirt you moisten, the sap you push up and nourish . . .
I enter the living room, it, too, unfinished, its far wall
Not there, opening on to a radiance
I can't begin to imagine, a light
My father walks from, approaching me,
Dragging his right leg, rolling his plans into a perfect curl.
That light, he mutters, that damned light.
We can't keep it out. It keeps on filling your room.

CHARLES WRIGHT

HIM

His sorrow hangs like a heart in the star-flowered boundary tree.
It mirrors the endless wind.

He feeds on the lunar differences and flies up at the dawn.

When he lies down, the waters will lie down with him,
And all that walks and all that stands still, and sleep through the
     thunder.

It's for him that the willow bleeds.

Look for him high in the flat black of the northern Pacific sky,
Released in his suit of lights,
               lifted and laid clear.

SNOW

If we, as we are, are dust, and dust, as it will, rises,
Then we will rise, and recongregate
In the wind, in the cloud, and be their issue,

Things in a fall in a world of fall, and slip
Through the spiked branches and snapped joints of the evergreens,
White ants, white ants and the little ribs.

CALIFORNIA DREAMING

We are not born yet, and everything's crystal under our feet.
We are not brethren, we are not underlings.
We are another nation,
              living by voices that you will never hear,
Caught in the net of splendor
                 of time-to-come on the earth.
We shine in our distant chambers, we are golden.

Midmorning, and Darvon dustfall off the Pacific
Stuns us to ecstasy,
                              October sun
Stuck like a tack on the eastern drift of the sky,
The idea of God on the other,
                              body by body
Rinsed in the Sunday prayer-light, draining away
Into the undercoating and slow sparks of the west,
                              which is our solitude and our joy.

I've looked at this ridge of lights for six years now
                              and still don't like it,
Strung out like Good Friday along a cliff
That Easters down to the ocean,
A dark wing with ruffled feathers as far out as Catalina
Fallen from some sky,
                              ruffled and laid back by the wind,
Santa Ana that lisps its hot breath
                              on the neck of everything.

What if the soul indeed is outside the body,
                              a little rainfall of light
Moistening our every step, prismatic, apotheosizic?
What if inside the body another shape is waiting to come out,
White as a quilt, loose as a fever,
                              and sways in the easy tides there?
What other anagoge in this life but the self?
What other ladder to Paradise
                              but the smooth handholds of the rib cage?
High in the palm tree the orioles twitter and grieve.
We twitter and grieve, the spider twirls the honey bee,
Who twitters and grieves, around in her net,
                              then draws it by one leg
Up to the fishbone fern leaves inside the pepper tree
                              swaddled in silk
And turns it again and again until it is shining.

Some nights, when the rock-and-roll band next door has quit playing,
And the last helicopter has thwonked back to the Marine base,
And the dark lets all its weight down
                              to within a half inch of the ground,
I sit outside in the gold lamé of the moon
                              as the town sleeps and the country sleeps

Like flung confetti around me,
And wonder just what in the hell I'm doing out here
So many thousands of miles away from what I know best.
And what I know best
                      has nothing to do with Point Conception
And Avalon and the long erasure of ocean
Out there where the landscape ends.
What I know best is a little thing.
It sits on the far side of the simile,
                      the like that's like the like.

————————

Today is sweet stuff on the tongue.
The question of how we should live our lives in this world
Will find no answer from us
                      this morning,
Sunflick, the ocean humping its back
Beneath us, shivering out
                      wave after wave we fall from
And cut through in a white scar of healed waters,
Our wet suits glossed slick as seals,
                      our boards grown sharp as cries.
We rise and fall like the sun.

————————

Ghost of the Muse and her dogsbody
Suspended above the beach, November 25,
Sun like a Valium disc, smog like rust in the trees.
White-hooded and friar-backed,
                      a gull choir eyeballs the wave reach.
Invisibly pistoned, the sea keeps it up,
                      plunges and draws back, plunges and draws back,
Yesterday hung like a porcelain cup behind the eyes,
Sonorous valves, insistent extremities,
                      the worm creeping out of the heart . . .

————————

Who are these people we pretend to be,
                      untouched by the setting sun?
They stand less stiffly than we do, and handsomer,
First on the left foot, and then the right.
Just for a moment we see ourselves inside them,
                      peering out,
And then they go their own way and we go ours,
Back to the window seat above the driveway,

Christmas lights in the pepper tree,
> black Madonna

Gazing out from the alicanthus.
Chalk eyes downcast, heavy with weeping and bitterness,
Her time has come round again.

Piece by small piece the world falls away from us like spores
From a milkweed pod,
> and everything we have known,

And everyone we have known,
Is taken away by the wind to forgetfulness,
Somebody always humming,
> California dreaming . . .

NIGHT JOURNAL

— I think of Issa, a man of few words:
The world of dew
Is the world of dew.
And yet . . .
And yet . . .

— Three words contain
> all that we know for sure of the next life

Or the last one: Close your eyes.
Everything else is gossip,
> false mirrors, trick windows

Flashing like Dutch glass
In the undiminishable sun.

— I write it down in visible ink,
Black words that disappear when held up to the light —
I write it down
> not to remember but to forget,

Words like thousands of pieces of shot film
> exposed to the sun.

I never see anything but the ground.

— Everyone wants to tell his story.
The Chinese say we live in the world of the 10,000 things,

Each of the 10,000 things
                             crying out to us
Precisely nothing,
A silence whose tune we've come to understand,
Words like birthmarks,
                             embolic sunsets drying behind the tongue.
If we were as eloquent,
If what we say could spread the good news the way that dogwood does,
Its votive candles
                        phosphorous and articulate in the green haze
Of spring, surely something would hear us.

— Even a chip of beauty
                             is beauty intractable in the mind,
Words the color of wind
Moving across the fields there
                                  wind-addled and wind-sprung,
Abstracted as water glints,
The fields lion-colored and rope-colored,
As in a picture of Paradise,
                             the bodies languishing over the sky
Trailing their dark identities
That drift off and sieve away to the nothingness
Behind them
                    moving across the fields there
As words move, slowly, trailing their dark identities.

— Our words, like blown kisses, are swallowed by ghosts
Along the way,
                        their destinations bereft
In a rub of brightness unending:
How distant everything always is,
                                      and yet how close,
Music starting to rise like smoke from under the trees.

— Birds sing an atonal row
                                unsyncopated
From tree to tree,
                        dew chants
Whose songs have no words
                                from tree to tree
When night puts her dark lens in,
One on this limb, two others back there.

— Words, like all things, are caught in their finitude.
They start here, they finish here
No matter how high they rise —
                                    my judgment is that I know this
And never love anything hard enough
That would stamp me
                    and sink me suddenly into bliss.

POEM HALF IN THE MANNER OF LI HO

All things aspire to weightlessness,
                    some place beyond the lip of language,
Some silence, some zone of grace,

Sky white as raw silk,
                    opening mirror cold-sprung in the west,
Sunset like dead grass.

If God hurt the way we hurt,
                    he, too, would be heart-sore,
Disconsolate, unappeasable.

                    ————————

Li Ho, the story goes, would leave home
Each day at dawn, riding a colt, a servant boy
                    walking behind him,
An antique tapestry bag
Strapped to his back.
                    When inspiration struck, Ho would write
The lines down and drop them in the bag.
At night he'd go home and work the lines up into a poem,
No matter how disconnected and loose-leafed they were.
His mother once said,
"He won't stop until he has vomited out his heart."

And so he did.
            Like John Keats,
He died believing his name would never be written among the
      Characters.
Without hope, he thought himself — that worst curse — unlucky.
At twenty-seven, at death's line, he saw a man come
In purple, driving a red dragon,

CHARLES WRIGHT

A tablet in one hand, who said,
                    "I'm here to summon Li Ho."
Ho got from his bed and wept.
Far from the sick room's dragon-dark, snow stormed the passes,
Monkeys surfed the bo trees
                    and foolish men ate white jade.

How mournful the southern hills are,
                              how white their despair
Under December's T'ang blue blank page.

What's the use of words — there are no words
For December's chill redaction,
                        for the way it makes us feel.

We hang like clouds between heaven and earth,
                          between something and nothing,
Sometimes with shadows, sometimes without.

Gerald Malanga

James Wright

AUTUMN BEGINS IN MARTINS FERRY, OHIO

In the Shreve High football stadium,
I think of Polacks nursing long beers in Tiltonsville,
And gray faces of Negroes in the blast furnace at Benwood,
And the ruptured night watchman of Wheeling Steel,
Dreaming of heroes.

All the proud fathers are ashamed to go home.
Their women cluck like starved pullets,
Dying for love.

Therefore,
Their sons grow suicidally beautiful
At the beginning of October,
And gallop terribly against each other's bodies.

LYING IN A HAMMOCK AT WILLIAM DUFFY'S FARM
IN PINE ISLAND, MINNESOTA

Over my head, I see the bronze butterfly,
Asleep on the black trunk,
Blowing like a leaf in green shadow.
Down the ravine behind the empty house,
The cowbells follow one another
Into the distances of the afternoon.
To my right,
In a field of sunlight between two pines,
The droppings of last year's horses
Blaze up into golden stones.
I lean back, as the evening darkens and comes on.
A chicken hawk floats over, looking for home.
I have wasted my life.

JAMES WRIGHT

THE JEWEL

There is this cave
In the air behind my body
That nobody is going to touch:
A cloister, a silence
Closing around a blossom of fire.
When I stand upright in the wind,
My bones turn to dark emeralds.

THE MINNEAPOLIS POEM

to John Logan

1

I wonder how many old men last winter
Hungry and frightened by namelessness prowled
The Mississippi shore
Lashed blind by the wind, dreaming
Of suicide in the river.
The police remove their cadavers by daybreak
And turn them in somewhere.
Where?
How does the city keep lists of its fathers
Who have no names?
By Nicollet Island I gaze down at the dark water
So beautifully slow.
And I wish my brothers good luck
And a warm grave.

2

The Chippewa young men
Stab one another shrieking
Jesus Christ.
Split-lipped homosexuals limp in terror of assault.
High school backfields search under benches
Near the Post Office. Their faces are the rich

Raw bacon without eyes.
The Walker Art Center crowd stare
At the Guthrie Theater.

3

Tall Negro girls from Chicago
Listen to light songs.
They know when the supposed patron
Is a plainclothesman.
A cop's palm
Is a roach dangling down the scorched fangs
Of a light bulb.
The soul of a cop's eyes
Is an eternity of Sunday daybreak in the suburbs
Of Juárez, Mexico.

4

The legless beggars are gone, carried away
By white birds.
The Artificial Limbs Exchange is gutted
And sown with lime.
The whalebone crutches and hand-me-down trusses
Huddle together dreaming in a desolation
Of dry groins.
I think of poor men astonished to waken
Exposed in broad daylight by the blade
Of a strange plough.

5

All over the walls of comb cells
Automobiles perfumed and blindered
Consent with a mutter of high good humor
To take their two naps a day.
Without sound windows glide back
Into dusk.
The sockets of a thousand blind bee graves tier upon tier
Tower not quite toppling.
There are men in this city who labor dawn after dawn
To sell me my death.

6

But I could not bear
To allow my poor brother my body to die
In Minneapolis.
The old man Walt Whitman our countryman
Is now in America our country
Dead.
But he was not buried in Minneapolis
At least.
And no more may I be
Please God.

7

I want to be lifted up
By some great white bird unknown to the police,
And soar for a thousand miles and be carefully hidden
Modest and golden as one last corn grain,
Stored with the secrets of the wheat and the mysterious lives
Of the unnamed poor.

IN RESPONSE TO A RUMOR THAT THE OLDEST WHOREHOUSE IN WHEELING, WEST VIRGINIA, HAS BEEN CONDEMNED

I will grieve alone,
As I strolled alone, years ago, down along
The Ohio shore.
I hid in the hobo jungle weeds
Upstream from the sewer main,
Pondering, gazing.

I saw, down river,
At Twenty-third and Water Streets
By the vinegar works,
The doors open in early evening.
Swinging their purses, the women
Poured down the long street to the river
And into the river.

I do not know how it was
They could drown every evening.
What time near dawn did they climb up the other shore,
Drying their wings?

For the river at Wheeling, West Virginia,
Has only two shores:
The one in hell, the other
In Bridgeport, Ohio.

And nobody would commit suicide, only
To find beyond death
Bridgeport, Ohio.

THE YOUNG GOOD MAN

1

The young good man walked out savoring
His own tongue instead of the lips
Of the wild crab apple.
You will believe this,

But there used to be places just on the other side
Of Cadiz, Ohio, where you could slip in
Without anybody knowing,
And find them sweet.

Everybody I knew, loved, and respected,
Like Charlie Duff, my cousin Dave,
George Ellis, Gene Turner from Bellaire
Who tackled me twice, and even I swear to Christ
John Shunk, the one man all the way from Pittsburgh
To Cincinnati who knew how to use
A diving suit and who got his name
In the newspapers all the time for
Dragging up the drowned boys,

Said leave them crab apples alone,
They taste so bitter you pucker
Two days at least. You bite one,
You'll be sorry.

JAMES WRIGHT

2

I don't know why,
One evening in August something illuminated my body
And I got sick of laying my cold
Hands on myself.
I lied to my family I was going for a walk uptown.
When I got to that hill,
Which now, I hear, Bluehart has sold to the Hanna
Strip Mine Company, it was no trouble at all to me.
Within fifteen yards of his charged fence I found me
A wild crab apple.

I licked it all over.
You are going to believe this.
It tasted sweet.

I know what would have happened to my tongue
If I had bitten. The people who love me
Are sure as hell no fools.

3

You and I could not have been simple married lovers.
There are so many reasons I can't count them,
But here are some few:
You are much more intelligent and learned than I am.
I have a very quick felicity of tongue.
Sooner or later I would have bitten your heart
With some snide witty remark or other.
And you wouldn't stand for it.
Our lives being what we are,
We didn't have a chance.

I wish we had had.
I have written this poem to you before I die.
And I don't mean to die
For some good time yet.

JAMES WRIGHT

THE OLD WPA SWIMMING POOL
IN MARTINS FERRY, OHIO

I am almost afraid to write down
This thing. I must have been,
Say, seven years old. That afternoon,
The families of the WPA had come out
To have a good time celebrating
A long gouge in the ground,
That the fierce husbands
Had filled with concrete.

We knew even then the Ohio
River was dying.
Most of the good men who lived along that shore
Wanted to be in love and give good love
To beautiful women, who weren't pretty,
And to small children like me who wondered,
What the hell is this?

When people don't have quite enough to eat
In August, and the river,
That is supposed to be some holiness,
Starts dying,

They swim in the earth. Uncle Sherman,
Uncle Willie, Uncle Emerson, and my father
Helped dig that hole in the ground.

I had seen by that time two or three
Holes in the ground,
And you know what they were.

But this one was not the usual, cheap
Economics, it was not the solitary
Scar on a poor man's face, that respectable
Hole in the ground you used to be able to buy
After you died for seventy-five dollars and
Your wages tached for six months by the Heslop
Brothers.

Brothers, dear God.

No, this hole was filled with water,
And suddenly I flung myself into the water.
All I had on was a jockstrap my brother stole
From a miserable football team.

Oh never mind, Jesus Christ, my father
And my uncles dug a hole in the ground,
No grave for once. It is going to be hard
For you to believe; when I rose from that water,

A little girl who belonged to somebody else,
A face thin and haunted appeared
Over my left shoulder, and whispered, Take care now,
Be patient, and live.

I have loved you all this time,
And didn't even know
I am alive.

BEAUTIFUL OHIO

Those old Winnebago men
Knew what they were singing.
All summer long and all alone,
I had found a way
To sit on a railroad tie
Above the sewer main.
It spilled a shining waterfall out of a pipe
Somebody had gouged through the slanted earth.
Sixteen thousand and five hundred more or less people
In Martins Ferry, my home, my native country,
Quickened the river
With the speed of light.
And the light caught there
The solid speed of their lives
In the instant of that waterfall.
I know what we call it
Most of the time.
But I have my own song for it,
And sometimes, even today,
I call it beauty.

JAMES WRIGHT

THE JOURNEY

Anghiari is medieval, a sleeve sloping down
A steep hill, suddenly sweeping out
To the edge of a cliff, and dwindling.
But far up the mountain, behind the town,
We too were swept out, out by the wind,
Alone with the Tuscan grass.

Wind had been blowing across the hills
For days, and everything now was graying gold
With dust, everything we saw, even
Some small children scampering along a road,
Twittering Italian to a small caged bird.
We sat beside them to rest in some brushwood,
And I leaned down to rinse the dust from my face.

I found the spider web there, whose hinges
Reeled heavily and crazily with the dust,
Whole mounds and cemeteries of it, sagging
And scattering shadows among shells and wings.
And then she stepped into the center of air
Slender and fastidious, the golden hair
Of daylight along her shoulders, she poised there,
While ruins crumbled on every side of her.
Free of the dust, as though a moment before
She had stepped inside the earth, to bathe herself.

I gazed, close to her, till at last she stepped
Away in her own good time.

Many men
Have searched all over Tuscany and never found
What I found there, the heart of the light
Itself shelled and leaved, balancing
On filaments themselves falling. The secret
Of this journey is to let the wind
Blow its dust all over your body,
To let it go on blowing, to step lightly, lightly
All the way through your ruins, and not to lose
Any sleep over the dead, who surely
Will bury their own, don't worry.

Notes on the Poets

This section offers information on the life and work of the poets in *Contemporary American Poetry*. Each note includes a selected bibliography.

AI (1947)

Born Florence Anthony in Albany, Texas, Ai attended the University of Arizona and the University of California at Irvine. "One-half Japanese, one-eighth Choctaw, one-fourth Black, and one-sixteenth Irish," she has said that "the history of my family is itself a history of America." Her chosen name, Ai, means "love" in Japanese. The recipient of Guggenheim and Radcliffe Fellowships, she received the Lamont Poetry Award from the Academy of American Poets for *Killing Floor* (1978), the American Book Award for *Sin* (1987), and the National Book Award for *Vice: New and Selected Poems* (1999). She teaches at Oklahoma State University in Stillwater.

Ai's early, compressed dramatic monologues give voice to characters whose lives have been stripped to their bare essentials: hunger, sex, and survival. Murderers, wife-beaters, prostitutes, and molesters of the dead and the living inhabit these poems, enacting principles of social Darwinism against barren desert landscapes. Like Stephen Crane's *Maggie*, Ai's poems attempt "to show that environment is a tremendous thing in this world, and often shapes lives regardless." In graphic, unadorned language, her narrators relate their stories matter-of-factly, their struggle for existence characterized by its fundamental condition: violence. The titles of her books emphasize the oppressive nature of the fallen state: *Cruelty, Sin, Fate, Greed, Vice*. Though her poems refuse consolation, their confrontational stance suggests an attempt at exorcism.

Her recent work implies the inexorable movement of violence from private lives to the public realm. Monologues by cultural icons such as Marilyn Monroe and James Dean and by political figures such as John Kennedy and J. Edgar Hoover, as well as by anonymous journalists and paparazzi, extend the range of her concerns by demonstrating again and again how personal tragedy can transform itself into national, even global, malaise. No one escapes complicity, and the violence of our age, witnessed not only in the Los Angeles riots of 1992 but in Vietnam and Rwanda, begins its blossoming in the hardscrabble lives of individuals eking out their existence on the ragged edges of any republic.

Poetry: *Cruelty* (1973). *Killing Floor* (1979). *Sin* (1986). *Fate* (1991). *Greed* (1993). *Vice: New and Selected Poems* (1999).

A. R. AMMONS (1926)

Born in Whiteville, North Carolina, A. R. Ammons was educated at Wake Forest College and at Berkeley. He has worked as an executive for a biological glass company and since 1964 has taught at Cornell, where he is Goldwin Smith Professor of Poetry. The recipient of several prestigious fellowships, Ammons has also received two National Book Awards, the National Book Critics Circle Award, and the Bollingen Prize in Poetry.

Ammons has been called an American Romantic. So he is — in more ways than one. To begin with, the surface of his poems bristles and blooms primarily with the flora of the natural world observed by a well-trained and informed sensibility. At times one senses that this poet has observed the ever-shifting vagaries of the natural world with the zeal of a professional bird-watcher. At the same time, the world that Ammons perceives seems remarkably devoid of other humans and — perhaps as a consequence — devoid of that darker, painful, and seamier side of human life we've come to expect in the work of contemporary poets. Even when he turns his attention to an urban existence quite removed from nature, as in "Marginals," or to the possibility that "the sun will burst," as in "Open," Ammons has a distinctive capacity for reaffirming the "worm supreme, / transformer of bloated, breaking flesh," and the manner in which even ruinage transforms "into the wills of sex and song, leaving / . . . the scent / of pinestraw / rising dominant from the striking sun!"

At the heart of Ammons's poetry and vision seems to be a profound philosophical belief that the radiant energy at the heart of the natural world — as perceived by the seer-poet — becomes the inward and organic energy of the poem itself, which in turn is transformed from within into an emblematic and musical affirmation of the cosmic energy at the heart of all life. In the presence of this radiance, even a pot "prays, crack my enamel: / let the rust in." And the more we hear Ammons's philosophical music, the more we see those "pillars of ice wet-bright in melt, / warm / with always-yielding joy: yes"; as we move further into the world of Ammons's poetry, the better we can understand his moral and aesthetic conviction: "I in the night standing saying oaksongs / entertaining my soul to me."

Poetry: *Ommateum, with Doxology* (1955). *Expressions of Sea Level* (1964). *Corsons Inlet* (1965). *Tape for the Turn of the Year* (1965). *Northfield Poems* (1966). *Selected Poems* (1968). *Uplands* (1970). *Briefings: Poems Small and Easy* (1971). *Collected Poems 1951–1971* (1972). *Sphere: The Form of a Motion* (1974). *Diversifications* (1975). *The Snow Poems* (1977). *The Selected Poems 1951–1977* (1977). *Selected Longer Poems* (1980). *A Coast of Trees* (1981). *Worldly Hopes* (1982). *Lake Effect Country* (1983). *Selected Poems: Expanded Edition* (1986).

Sumerian Vistas (1987). *The Really Short Poems of* A. R. Ammons (1991). *Garbage* (1993). *Brink Road* (1996). *Glare* (1997).

Prose: *Set in Motion: Essays, Interviews, & Dialogues*, edited by Z. Burr (1999).

JOHN ASHBERY (1927)

John Ashbery was born in Rochester, New York. A graduate of Harvard and Columbia, he lived in France for many years, and he was editor of *Art News*. He currently teaches at Brooklyn College. The recipient of MacArthur and Fulbright fellowships (among many other honors), in 1975 Ashbery's book *Self-Portrait in a Convex Mirror* won the Pulitzer Prize, the National Book Award, and the National Book Critics Circle Award.

With the publication of *The Tennis Court Oath*, Ashbery was recognized as one of the most experimental and, at times, one of the most exasperating poets of his generation: his montages of words and unrelated, juxtaposed images threatened the reader to attention, but then these fragments slipped away like verbal hallucinations, leaving the atmosphere charged with an emotional haze. Critics recognized the possible influences of Wallace Stevens, the French symbolists, and New York action painters; however, even the most unorthodox tools of criticism were blunted by this enigmatic poetry whose syntax refused to yield a recognizable sense of development or sustained meaning. While Ashbery's recent poems have become ostensibly more accessible and translucent, most critics continue to be baffled and to venture complex interpretations that, by comparison, make Ashbery's poems sound utterly transparent.

One critic has observed that Ashbery's largest aesthetic principle is the discovery that the world consents, every day, to being shaped into a poem. Ashbery himself has modified this view by asserting that there are no traditional subjects or themes in his poetry: "Most of my poems," he has said in an interview, "are about the experience of experience . . . and the particular experience is of lesser interest to me than the way it filters through to me. I believe this is the way in which it happens with most people, and I'm trying to record a kind of generalized transcript of what's really going on in our minds all day long."

Before the publication of *Three Poems* — long prose poems that may be viewed, at least in part, as an extended statement of poetics — Ashbery offered a somewhat minimal key to his enigmatic poetics when he wrote, "the carnivorous / Way of these lines is to devour their own nature, leaving / Nothing but a bitter impression of absence, which as we know involves presence, but still, / Nevertheless these are fundamental absences, struggling to get up and be off themselves." And the more one reads Ashbery's work, the more it is clear that these "absences" in his poetry — as in the work of Rilke — are the consequences of the innocent eye confronting experience: the lingering pain of loss.

Poetry: *Turandot and Other Poems* (1953). *Some Trees* (1956). *The Tennis Court Oath* (1962). *Rivers and Mountains* (1966). *The Double Dream of Spring* (1970). *Three Poems* (1972). *The Vermont Notebook* (1975). *Self-Portrait in a Convex Mirror* (1975). *Houseboat Days* (1977). *As We Know* (1979). *Shadow Train* (1981). *A Wave* (1984). *Selected Poems* (1985). *April Galleons* (1987). *Flow Chart* (1991). *Three Books: Houseboat Days, Shadow Train, A Wave* (1993). *Hotel Lautramont* (1994). *And the Stars Were Shining* (1994). *Can You Hear, Bird* (1995). *The Mooring of Starting Out* (1998). *Wakefulness* (1998). *Girls on the Run* (1999).

Prose: *A Nest of Ninnies*, a novel, with James Schuyler (1969). *Three Plays* (1978). *Reported Sightings: Art Chronicles 1957–1987*, edited by D. Bergman (1989).

MARVIN BELL (1937)

Born in New York City, Marvin Bell attended Alfred University, Syracuse University, the University of Chicago, and the University of Iowa, where he has been teaching in the Writers' Workshop since 1965. His book *A Probable Volume of Dreams* was the 1969 Lamont Poetry Selection of the Academy of American Poets, and he has been awarded fellowships by the National Endowment for the Arts and the Guggenheim Foundation.

Because Bell is committed to enlarging the experiment of American free verse, the surface quality of his poems can be deceptively laconic. But they amply demonstrate the fact that the "freer" poetry seems to be, the more carefully crafted it is. (Of course, the obverse is equally true: the more carefully crafted a poem is, the freer it seems.) The effectiveness of his seemingly straightforward but somewhat strange love poem "To Dorothy," for example, is highly controlled by Bell's drawing on the centuries-old tradition of love lyrics using gardens and flowers as metaphors for the loved one. The power of "To an Adolescent Weeping Willow," on the other hand, depends in part on a careful blending of concentric and intraconnecting images, rhythms, and syntactical repetitions.

On a philosophical level, Bell's subjects include love; desire; the nature of reality, knowledge, and belief; the existential nature of truth and of the human condition; courage; and a pursuit of truths behind appearances that is peculiarly American. Those philosophical subjects, however, are rooted in the day-to-day human experiences of a father and lover, remembering World War II or clover in moonlight, discovering a potter's sponge in a foreign country, and especially, trying to understand the inner nature of his vocation and his craft and to capture the ecstasy at the heart of metaphor — or the metaphor at the heart of ecstasy.

What is also remarkable about much of Bell's work is that, by fully *doing* what it *says*, a poem is not only "about" the immediate subject at hand but also is its own statement of poetics — just as Robert Frost's "Birches" is as much a poem about the nature of poetic craft as it is a poem about trees. A few other poets of this generation have written poems that are their own statement of poetics: Heyen's "The Return," Creeley's "The Language," and Kunitz's "The Layers" come to mind. However, perhaps no poet has pursued the philosophical and ecstatic dimensions of aesthetics in so many individual poems as rigorously as Bell has. The rewards of that quest have been abundant and rich, as much for his readers as for Bell.

Although it isn't possible to devise a full-fledged system of aesthetics from Bell's poetry (that isn't what poetry does), it is possible to suggest a few of the touchstones that inform Marvin Bell's vibrant vision: a vigorous life of the imagination leads to much the same depth of knowledge as that offered by the pursuit of history, mathematics, and physics and the exploration of unknown frontiers ("Sevens (Version 3): In the Closed Iris of Creation"); commitment to one's art demands the same painful, self-effacing mortification and loneliness as any other quest for genuine excellence ("The Self and the Mulberry"); and human beings, born to be makers and lovers, realize that the ultimate source of meaningful loving and making is that ever-endless chain of honorable human labor — "because men and women had sown green grass, / and flowered to my eye in man-made light, / and to some would be as fire in the body / and to others a light in the mind. . . ."

Poetry: *Things We Dreamt We Died For* (1966). *A Probable Volume of Dreams* (1969). *The Escape into You: A Sequence* (1971). *Residue of Song* (1974). *Stars Which See, Stars Which Do Not See* (1977). *These Green-Going-to-Yellow* (1981). *Segues: A Correspondence in Poetry*, with William Stafford (1983). *Drawn by Stones, by Earth, by Things That Have Been in the Fire* (1984). *New and Selected Poems* (1987). *Iris of Creation* (1990). *The Book of the Dead Man* (1994). *Ardor: The Book of the Dead Man, Vol. II* (1997). *Wednesday: Selected Poems* (1998).

Prose and Poetry: *Old Snow Just Melting: Essays and Interviews* (1983). *A Marvin Bell Reader: Selected Poetry and Prose* (1994).

JOHN BERRYMAN (1914–1972)

John Berryman graduated from Columbia and Clare College (Cambridge). He taught at Brown, Harvard, Princeton, and at the University of Minnesota. A recipient of Rockefeller and Guggenheim fellowships and of a special grant from the National Arts Council, he also won the Pulitzer Prize and the National Book Award. On January 7, 1972, John Berryman committed suicide.

In the course of his career, Berryman wrote not only a distinguished long poem in homage to Anne Bradstreet but also an equally notable sonnet sequence. However, his major work is his sequence of 385 *Dream Songs*, for which he may well be recognized as one of the truly great poets of the century. The scope, depth, daring, and craftsmanship of these poems have caused critics to compare Berryman with Homer, Dante, and Whitman.

The Dream Songs constitutes a loose narrative about a multidimensional figure most often called Henry Pussycat. Berryman wrote that Henry is "an imaginary character (not the poet . . .), a white American in early middle age, sometimes in blackface, who has suffered an irreversible loss and talks to himself sometimes in the first person, sometimes in the third, sometimes even in the second; he has a friend, never named, who addresses him as Mr Bones and variants thereof." There are moments in *The Dream Songs* when Henry, Mr Bones, and the poet are barely distinguishable from one another — and are not meant to be distinguishable. Thus Berryman attempts and achieves a linear-multidimensional vision — maneuvered by a dazzling shift of pronouns — which is a verbal equivalent to what Picasso achieved in his Cubist period.

Like Odysseus, Henry Pussycat undergoes a fantastic range of experience. He even dies and comes back to life. His emotions shift from incredible panic, horror, and self-pity to sheer joy and self-deprecating slapstick. If Henry gets out of hand, his friend and conscience, his sidekick and minstrel chorus are always there either to cut him down to size or to support him through despair. At the end of his journey, which takes him across spiritual as well as spatial and historical boundaries, Henry, the schizophrenic Odysseus of the atomic age, returns to his wife and child, scarred but bearing that most ancient and essential knowledge: to be human is to suffer.

Poetry: *Poems* (1942). *The Dispossessed* (1948). *Homage to Mistress Bradstreet* (1956). *His Thoughts Made Pockets & The Plane Buckt* (1958). *Short Poems* (1964). *77 Dream Songs* (1967). *His Toy, His Dream, His Rest* (1968). *The Dream Songs* (1969). *Love & Fame* (1970, revised 1972). *Delusions, Etc.* (1972). *Henry's Fate & Other Poems, 1967–1972* (1977). *Collected Poems 1937–1971*, edited by C. Thornbury (1989).

Prose: *Stephen Crane*, a biography (1950). *Recovery*, a novel (1973). *The Freedom of the Poet*, essays and stories (1976). *We Dream of Honour: John Berryman's Letters to His Mother* (1987).

ELIZABETH BISHOP (1911–1979)

A native of Worcester, Massachusetts, Elizabeth Bishop received her formal education at Vassar. She lived in Brazil for many years but also taught in the United States at Harvard and elsewhere and was Consultant in Poetry at the Library of Congress. Her many awards included the Pulitzer Prize, the National Book Award, and the Order of Rio Branco (Brazil).

Although Bishop was far less prolific than most poets of her generation, she was one of the few poets about whom it could be said that each new book — indeed each new poem — was an "event." One reason may be that she was far less predictable than many of her contemporaries; that is, readers of poetry did not come to expect a particular kind of poem from Bishop the way that they had come to expect a certain kind of poem from Anne Sexton or Robert Lowell.

Another reason why Bishop's poems are rare moments of delight and epiphany stems from her stunning perceptions and reconstruction of the details of physical reality. As Randall Jarrell says in *Poetry and the Age*, "all her poems have written underneath, *I have seen it.*" Whether the matter at hand is the exotic rainbow glow of a tremendous fish or the commonplace sheen of oil in a dingy filling station, Bishop knows that poetry and vision are rooted, first of all, in what Archibald MacLeish has called "the shine of the world." In her better poems, Bishop amply demonstrates that the perception of sensible objects and moral vision, for the poet, may be one and the same experience.

Ralph J. Mills, Jr. has rightfully noted another, more ambitious dimension of Bishop's achievement. In addition to her graceful use of fairly strict forms — and the unmistakable presence of a formalist approach even in the freer verse — Bishop's poems are distinguished by what Mills calls a "total accomplishment of language, technique, music, and imagery working simultaneously, or (in T. S. Eliot's phrase) 'the complete consort dancing together.'"

Poetry: *North and South* (1946). *Poems: North and South — A Cold Spring* (1955). *Questions of Travel* (1965). *Selected Poems* (1967). *The Ballad of the Burglar of Babylon* (1968). *The Complete Poems* (1969/1979). *Geography III* (1976). *The Complete Poems 1927–1979* (1983). *Edgar Allan Poe & the Juke Box* (2001).

Prose: *The Collected Prose*, edited by R. Giroux (1984).

Translations: *The Diary of Helena Morley* (1957). *Anthology of Contemporary Brazilian Poetry*, editor and translator, with others (1972).

ROBERT BLY (1923)

For the 1975 edition of *Contemporary Poets*, Robert Bly wrote, "I earn my living giving readings at American colleges and universities, and by translating." More than twenty-five years later, to a large extent, he still does, with the hiatus of the phenomenal success of his book for and about the men's movement, *Iron John*. Bly graduated from Harvard and — though he hates to admit it — the University of Iowa Writers' Workshop. The founder of the influential journal and small press called *The Fifties, The Sixties . . . to The Nineties*, Bly has received fellowships from several foundations and won the National Book Award.

Because of his considerable impact as a poet, translator, editor, and publisher, as well as a student of and commentator on America's psychic life since at least 1962, Robert Bly may well be the most influential poet of the second half of the twentieth century.

Influenced by the thought of the seventeenth-century German theosophist Jacob Boehme, and the techniques of such twentieth-century Spanish surrealists as Lorca and Neruda, Bly's poems tend to be almost purely phenomenological. Revolting against the rationalism and empiricism of his century, Boehme emphasized an intuitive perception of the outer tangible world of humans and things as a symbol of the corresponding and truer inner spiritual world. The outward man is asleep, Boehme wrote; he is only the husk of the real inner man. Like the American Romantic Transcendentalist Emerson, Boehme insisted that men neither see nor respond to that inner spiritual world: "The wise of this world . . . have shut and locked us up in their art and rationality, so that we have had to see with their eyes."

Bly himself has written that American poetry took a wrong turn, moving in "a destructive motion outward" rather than a "plunge inward, trying for a great (spiritual and imaginative) intensity." In his revolt against Eliot's theory of the "objective correlative" and against Pound's practice in the *Cantos* of "eating up more and more of the outer world, with less and less life at the center," Bly has fashioned his poems after the work of Rilke, Trakl, and twentieth-century Spanish surrealists. In them, he seems to have found a poetics that corresponds to Boehme's mysticism, enabling him to plunge beneath the phenomenology of surfaces and find images and words to suggest the inner reality and spiritual intensity of experience. Moreover, many of Bly's poems continue to be implicit reaffirmations of a statement that appeared on the flyleaf of *The Lion's Tail and Eyes* in which he suggests that his poems come from "the part of the personality which is nourished by notice of things that are growing" and simultaneously that they "resist the Puritan insistence on being busy, the need to think of everything in terms of work."

Poetry: *The Lion's Tail and Eyes: Poems Written Out of Laziness and Silence,* with James Wright and William Duffy (1962). *Silence in the Snowy Fields* (1962). *The Light Around the Body* (1967). *The Morning Glory* (1969; expanded edition, 1975). *The Teeth Mother Naked at Last* (1970). *Jumping Out of Bed* (1973; revised and expanded edition, 1988). *Sleepers Joining Hands* (1973). *Point Reyes Poems* (1974/1989). *Old Man Rubbing His Eyes* (1975). *This Body Is Made of Camphor and Gopherwood* (1977). *This Tree Will Be Here for a Thousand Years* (1979). *The Man in the Black Coat Turns* (1981). *Loving a Woman in Two Worlds* (1985). *Selected Poems* (1986). *Angels of Pompeii* (1991). *What Have I Ever Lost by Dying* (1992). *Meditations on the Insatiable Soul* (1994). *Morning Poems* (1997). *Eating the Honey of Words: New and Selected Poems* (1999).

Prose: *Leaping Poetry: An Idea with Poems and Translations* (1975). *Talking All Morning: Collected Interviews and Conversations* (1979). *The Eight Stages of Translation* (1983). *A Little Book on the Human Shadow,* edited by W. Booth (1988). *American Poetry: Wildness and Domesticity,* critical essays (1990). *Remembering James Wright* (1991). *Iron John* (1992). *The Sibling Society* (1996).

Translations and Versions: POETRY: *Twenty Poems of Georg Trakl,* with J. Wright (1961). *Twenty Poems of César Vallejo,* with J. Knoepfle and J. Wright (1962). *Juan Ramon Jiménez: Forty Poems* (1967). *Late Arrival on Earth: Selected Poems of Gunnar Ekelöf,* with C. Paulston (1967). *Pablo Neruda: Twenty Poems,* with J. Wright (1967). *Tomas Tranströmer: Twenty Poems* (1970). *Neruda and Vallejo: Selected Poems,* with J. Knoepfle and J. Wright (1971). *Night Visions,* poems by Tomas Tranströmer (1971). *Bashó* (1972). *Lorca and Jiménez: Selected Poems* (1973). *Blase de Otero and Miguel Hernandez: Selected Poems* (1974). *Friends, You Drank Some Darkness: Three Swedish Poets: Martinson, Ekelöf and Tranströmer* (1976). *The Kabir Book: 44 of the Ecstatic Poems of Kabir* (1977). *Vicente Alexandre: Twenty Poems,* with L. Hyde (1977). *Rolf Jacobsen: Twenty Poems* (1977). *Rainer Maria Rilke: The Voices* (1977). *I Never Wanted Fame: Ten Poems and Proverbs,* by Antonio Machado (1979). *Mirabai: Six Versions* (1980). *Rumi: Night and Sleep,* with C. Barks (1980). *Canciones,* by Antonio Machado (1980). *Truth Barriers: Poems by Tomas Tranströmer* (1980). *Selected Poems of Rainer Maria Rilke* (1981). *When Grapes Turn to Wine: Versions of Rumi* (1983). *Time Alone: Selected Poems of Antonio Machado* (1983). *Twenty Poems of Olav Hauge* (1987). *Ten Poems of Francis Ponge Translated by Robert Bly and Ten Poems of Robert Bly Inspired by Francis Ponge* (1990).

Anthologies: *A Poetry Reading Against the Vietnam War,* with D. Ray (1966). *Forty Poems Touching on Recent American History* (1966/1970). *The Sea and the Honeycomb: A Book of Tiny Poems* (1966/1971). *News of the Universe: Poems of Twofold Consciousness* (1980). *The Rag and Bone Shop of the Heart: Poetry for Men* (1992).

GWENDOLYN BROOKS (1917)

A graduate of Wilson Junior College in Chicago, Gwendolyn Brooks began her professional career in 1941 with Inez Boulton's poetry workshop at the South Side Community Art Center in Chicago. She was awarded two Guggenheim fellowships, a grant from the National Institute of Arts and Letters, and the Pulitzer Prize for her second book of poems, *Annie Allen*. In 1969 Brooks was named Poet Laureate of the State of Illinois, an honor formerly held by Carl Sandburg. Among her more recent honors is the National Book Foundation's medal for Distinguished Contribution to American Letters (1994).

Brooks's poems are often marked by direct and bold social observation and by language that precedes — indeed foreshadows — much of the poetry written by younger African American poets today. Her African American hero's assertion, "I helped to save them . . . / Even if I had to kick their law into their teeth in order to do that for them," might well have been written in the 1960s or 1970s rather than in the 1940s. In those poems addressed specifically to the horror of the African American experience in America, she is also capable of a range of emotions: brutal anger, wry satire, and visionary serenity.

Informed by the spectrum of the African American experience and her own emotional objectivity, some of her poems are also marked by the simplicity, quiet, and gentility of a woman's sensibilities. Yet in a poem like "the mother," she also demonstrates the kind of fierce emotion that other women poets like Anne Sexton and Adrienne Rich have displayed in more consciously personal or political poems. Gentle or fierce, personal or social, her poems consistently affirm the common denominator of human experience in poetry and in the human community.

Poetry: *A Street in Bronzeville* (1945). *Annie Allen* (1949). *Bronzeville Boys and Girls* (1956). *Selected Poems* (1963). *In the Time of Detachment, in the Time of Cold* (1965). *In the Mecca: Poems* (1968). *Riot* (1969). *The Wall* (nd). *Family Pictures* (1970). *Aloneness* (1971). *Beckonings* (1975). *To Disembark* (1981). *The Near-Johannesburg Boy and Other Poems* (1986). *Blacks* [collected poems], (1987). *Gottschalk and the Grande Tarantelle* (1988). *Children Coming Home* (1991).

Prose: *Maud Martha*, a novel (1953). *Report from Part One: An Autobiography* (1972). *The World of Gwendolyn Brooks* (1972). *Primer for Blacks* (1980).

OLGA BROUMAS (1949)

Born in Syros, Greece, Olga Broumas published her first book there in 1967. That same year she came to the United States to study architecture and dance at the University of Pennsylvania, then creative writing at the University of Oregon. Her first book in English, *Beginning with O* (1977), received the Yale Younger Poets Award. A licensed bodywork therapist, she has received fellowships from the Guggenheim Foundation and the National Endowment for the Arts, and the Witter Bynner Award of the American Academy and Institute of Arts and

Letters. She has taught at Boston University and is currently Poet-in-Residence at Brandeis University.

The sensuous lyrics of Olga Broumas have their source in the Sapphic tradition of her native country, and her poems celebrate lust while exploring the politics of desire. Her subject is the body in its various configurations — omphalos, sanctuary, and muse — and her conflation of flesh and landscape, their common salts, gives an ecstatic, feminist slant to "the eyes of fire, the nostrils of air, the mouth of water, the beard of earth" drawn by William Blake. Broumas populates her land- and seascapes with goddesses ancient — perhaps ancestral — and contemporary; they bathe in the visionary light of her gaze.

Unabashedly explicit, Broumas's poems reenact versions of mythology and fable to extend (and return) their provenance to the communal body: "We came together / like months / in a lunar year, measured in nights, dividing / perfectly into female phases. Like women anywhere / living in groups we had synchronous menses. And had / no need of a wound, a puncture, to seal our bond." Broumas's fascination with linguistic roots, her compulsive tracings of words to their Greek and Latin sources, reaffirms the classical role of the poet for our time. She renders her alphabet in the service of praise.

Poetry: *Beginning with O* (1977). *Soie Sauvage* (1979). *Pastoral Jazz* (1983). *Perpetua* (1989). *The Choir* (1989–1991). *Rave: Poems 1975–1999* (1999).

Collaborations: *Black Holes, Black Stockings*, with Jane Miller (1985). *Sappho's Gymnasium*, with T Begley (1994). *Ithaca: Little Summer in Winter*, with T Begley (1996).

Translations: *What I Love: Poems*, by Odysseas Elytis (1986). *The Little Mariner*, by Odysseas Elytis (1988). *Open Papers*, by Odysseas Elytis, trans. with T Begley (1995). *Eros, Eros, Eros: Selected & Last Poems*, by Odysseas Elytis (1998).

LUCILLE CLIFTON (1936)

Lucille Clifton was born in Depew, New York, and educated at the State University of New York at Fredonia. Currently teaching at St. Mary's College in Maryland, she has also held distinguished posts at a number of other colleges and universities. Clifton's awards and distinctions as a poet, fiction writer, and screenplay writer include creative writing fellowships from the National Endowment for the Arts, an Emmy, and two nominations for the Pulitzer Prize for poetry.

Clifton's entire comment on her work in the third edition of *Contemporary Poets* (1980) consists of one brief sentence: "I am a Black woman poet, and I sound like one." And yet, after reading even a short selection of her poems, we quickly realize that Clifton's description of herself does not explain why she is one of the most unique voices of her generation. Of course, like numerous other women writers, she explores the dimensions of her sexual identity and her role as daughter, as mother, as lover, as woman; like many other African American poets (men and women), she too addresses herself to the quality of the African American experience in America, just as she too makes full use of the African American idiom. But no other poet of her generation (regardless of gender or race) *sounds* quite like Clifton. Why that is, however, is rather difficult to identify in the standard language of literary criticism.

Clifton's subjects and themes run the gamut of human experience. She laments the loss of an aborted child, and she celebrates her own mature body and sexuality with wonderful verve. She admonishes children to "come home from the movies" and face the responsibilities of everyday life, but she also recalls the pain and terror of her own growth into adult responsibility. She engages in social criticism and in criticism of individual human beings, but she also affirms "the bond of live things everywhere." She feels religious doubts, but she is nonetheless a profoundly religious spirit whose sensibility encompasses both the Judeo-Christian tradition and a primal sense of spiritualism and magic. Despite the high seriousness of many of her poems, she also obviously revels in a vibrant sense of humor that she directs not only at others, but also at herself and her craft. She can poke gentle fun at herself because "she is a poet / she don't have no sense," but after the joy and celebration, after the anguish and despair, after the doubt and struggle to believe, she also can assert, "I am left with plain hands and / nothing to give you but poems."

One of the striking characteristics of Clifton's poems is their distilled brevity. Like Emily Dickinson, Clifton rarely offers any but the most essential elaborations on experience. However, for a clue to the sound of Clifton's poems, we have to turn elsewhere: African-American spirituals and secular folksongs; the rich history of rhythm and blues; the rhythms and sounds of an African American fundamentalist revival meeting and of magical incantations; the phrasing and timing of classic African American humorists; an utterly physical sense of language (somehow we can *see* how these poems incorporate a range of bodily movements); a belief in the power of idiom to give voice to the human heart as much by transcending individual race and culture as by affirming it; a belief in the language of poetry, not as a threat of further social and human alienation but as a bridge of reconciliation; a belief in the power of song and in the impotency of slogans; a belief in tongues.

Poetry: *Good Times* (1969). *Good News About the Earth* (1972). *An Ordinary Woman* (1974). *Two-Headed Woman* (1980). *Good Woman: Poems and a Memoir 1969–1980* (1987). *Next: New Poems* (1987). *Quilting: Poems 1987–1990* (1991).

The Book of Light (1993). *The Terrible Stories* (1996). *Blessing the Boats: New and Selected Poems 1988–2000* (2000).

Prose: *Generations of Americans: A Memoir* (1976).

ROBERT CREELEY (1926)

A New Englander by birth and sensibility, Robert Creeley was born in Arlington, Massachusetts, and was educated at Harvard, Black Mountain College, and the University of New Mexico. He has traveled widely and has taught at the University of New Mexico and at Black Mountain College where he also edited the influential journal *Black Mountain Review.* He is currently David Gray Professor of Poetry and Letters at the State University of New York at Buffalo.

Generally associated with the "Projectivists" and poets of the Black Mountain School, Creeley nevertheless is a Puritan at heart — Emily Dickinson's cool, hip, one-eyed, and unvirginal nephew. Like all good Puritans, Creeley is "hung up": "I think I grow tensions / like flowers . . ." ("The Flower"). Pain is central to his work — a sharp, stinging pain evoked in such images as "Each wound is perfect, / encloses itself in a tiny / imperceptible blossom, / making pain." In other poems, such as "Something" and "The Lover," a Puritan sensibility surfaces more explicitly, as it does in the very structure and substance of collections such as *A Day Book* and *Hello* — sustained attempts at recording and discovering the "meaning" of diurnal events, an implicit quest for signs of salvation, especially love. "I love you. / Do you love me. / What to say / when you see me" ("A Form of Women") might be a summary of one of Creeley's central concerns.

No critical essay or explanatory statement reveals Creeley's poetics as precisely as his own poems, especially "The Language" in which he states simply, "Locate *I* . . . ." The position of the *I* — as locus, as viewer, and as speaker — largely determines the form and the direction of the poem. The position of words on the page results from the location of this I, who, by arranging the poem as it is, speaks not only in grammatical units but also in linear units. In other words, Creeley's poems evolve on both a sequential grammatical level and on a cumulative linear level, with each individual line reaffirming or modifying the sense of the sentence and of the poem. And such contrapuntal tension in the very structure of Creeley's poems — perhaps more than the sparse, occasionally hesistant language — reflects the contemporary struggle with those forces that would make us all inarticulate.

Poetry: *Le Fou* (1952). *The Kind of Act of* (1953). *The Immoral Proposition* (1953). *All That Is Lovely in Men* (1955). *A Form of Women* (1959). *For Love:*

Poems 1950–1960 (1962). *Words* (1967). *The Charm: Early and Uncollected Poems* (1967/1969). *Pieces* (1968). *A Day Book* (1972). *Presences,* with Marisol (1976). *Selected Poems* (1976). *Hello: A Journal* (1978). *Later* (1979). *The Collected Poems of Robert Creeley 1945–1975* (1983). *Mirrors* (1983). *Memory Gardens* (1986). *Windows* (1990). *Selected Poems* (1991). *Echoes* (1994). *So There: Poems 1976–83* (1998). *Day Book of a Virtual Poet* (1998).

Prose: ESSAYS AND CRITICISM: A *Quick Graph: Collected Notes and Essays* (1970). *Contexts of Poetry: Interviews 1961–1971,* edited by D. M. Allen (1973). *Was That a Real Poem & Other Essays,* edited by D. M. Allen (1979). *Charles Olson & Robert Creeley: The Complete Correspondence,* edited by G. F. Butterick (1983). *Collected Essays* (1989). *Autobiography* (1990). *Tales Out of School: Selected Interviews* (1994). FICTION: *The Island* (1963). *The Gold Diggers and Other Stories* (1965). *Mabel: A Story* (1976). *The Collected Prose of Robert Creeley* (1984).

JAMES DICKEY (1923–1997)

James Dickey received his bachelor's and master's degrees from Vanderbilt University. He was a night fighter pilot during both World War II and the Korean War; as a civilian, he worked as an advertising executive; and he taught at a variety of universities, including the University of South Carolina. In 1966 Dickey received the National Book Award for poetry and was appointed Consultant in Poetry at the Library of Congress.

One of the less ostensibly "academic" poets of his generation, Dickey, in poems that are often disarmingly frank in subject matter and in "moral tone," has refused to assume those moral postures often expected of today's poets: during Vietnam, he did not write antiwar poetry but rather, as in "The Firebombing," he confronted his own understanding of and sympathy with the pilot whose mission was to drop napalm on enemy villages without the luxury of questioning the morality of such an act. In several other poems, he has explored varieties of sexual experiences, including implicit and explicit sexual encounters between humans and animals, as in "The Sheep Child."

Dickey's poems are marked by an exuberant language and by a primal energy, passion, and ritual. Probing the most elemental in humankind, his poems often trace a human's mythic subconscious and paradoxical evolution to a primitive level where humans and animals become companions and mates in the same irrational but holy species. Moreover, at the heart of Dickey's vision, poetry is the tongue articulating the consciousness of all creation on this planet, from the mute stone up the earthly chain of being to humankind. And in this way, his poems often recall Whitman's poetry and vision.

Simultaneously, many of Dickey's poems are also marked by a Southern Puritanism similar to that found in the work of William Faulkner and Flannery O'Connor. His characters are grotesque — physically and spiritually wounded. They are violent creatures; their brutal sexuality is immersed in pain and death. And they move about in a world churning with violence and profound evil that is as much inherent in the human condition as it is man-made. Dickey's vision, then, includes the polarities of light and grace, darkness and sin. The total impact of his poems is often the drama of Adam, shimmering with primal light, awakening to guilt, and finding it magical.

Poetry: *Into the Stone and Other Poems*, in *Poets of Today* VII (1960). *Drowning with Others* (1962). *Helmets* (1964). *Buckdancer's Choice* (1965). *Poems 1957–1967* (1967). *The Eye-Beaters, Blood, Victory, Madness, Buckhead and Mercy* (1970). *The Zodiac* (1976). *The Enemy from Eden* (1978). *The Strength of Fields* (1979). *The Early Motion: Drowning with Others and Helmets* (1981). *Falling, May Day Sermon, and Other Poems* (1981). *Puella* (1982). *The Central Motion: Poems 1968–1979* (1983). *The Eagle's Mile* (1990). *The Whole Motion: Collected Poems 1945–1992* (1992). *The Selected Poems* (1998). *The James Dickey Reader*, edited by Henry Hart (1999).

Prose: ESSAYS, CRITICISM AND LETTERS: *The Suspect in Poetry* (1964). *Babel to Byzantium: Poets & Poetry Now* (1968). *Self-Interviews*, edited by B. and J. Reiss (1970/1984). *Sorties: Journals and New Essays* (1971). *Crux: The Letters of James Dickey*, edited by Matthew J. Bruccoli and Judith S. Baughman (1999). FICTION AND OTHER PROSE: *Deliverance* (1970). *The Poet Turns on Himself* (1982). *Night Hurdling* (1983). *Alnilam* (1988). *To the White Sea* (1994).

STEPHEN DOBYNS (1941)

Born in East Orange, New Jersey, Stephen Dobyns was raised in several states, moving every year or two. He never graduated from high school, but attended Shimer College, Wayne State University, and the University of Iowa. He has taught at several universities and in the MFA Program at Warren Wilson College, and has worked as a reporter for the Detroit *News*. Dobyns's first book, *Concurring Beasts* (1972), was the Lamont Poetry Selection of the Academy of American Poets. *Black Dog, Red Dog* (1984) was the winner of the National Poetry Series competition, and *Cemetery Nights* (1987) was chosen for the Poetry Society of America's Melville Cane Award. The author of twenty novels in addition to his books of poetry, Dobyns has been the recipient of fellowships from the Guggenheim Foundation and the National Endowment for the Arts.

"How hard to love the world; we must love the world," Dobyns has written, and this dichotomy, its terse imperative, informs his work. In muscular lines and insistent rhythms, his narratives function as metaphysical monologues, darkly comic in their bleak and sometimes absurd vision of the human condition. The humorous veneer, however, barely conceals the desperation of his characters. Violence, spiritual destitution, and a contagious impotence — sexual, political, psychological — ravage their suburban landscape. "The speaker in Dobyns's poems," critic Peter Stitt has noted, "is obsessed by the futility of human life, by its meaninglessness; obsessed by our inability to know what is going on, our inability to control it; obsessed by our frail and imperfect bodies, by the certainty that they will die and turn to dust."

Dobyns's consolation is the creative act, any gesture of communication that dispels tension between individuals, that expresses tenderness: "A poem is a window that hangs between two or more human beings who otherwise live in darkened rooms." Underlying his existential fables (his recent books of poems are titled *Common Carnage* and *Pallbearers Envying the One Who Rides*, respectively) is the desire to grasp anything, "fragments of language, / fragments of blue sky," that might kindle compassion.

Poetry: *Concurring Beasts* (1972). *Griffon* (1976). *Heat Death* (1980). *The Balthus Poems* (1982). *Black Dog, Red Dog* (1984). *Cemetery Nights* (1987). *Body Traffic* (1990). *Velocities: New and Selected Poems, 1966–1992* (1994). *Common Carnage* (1996). *Pallbearers Envying the One Who Rides* (1999).

Prose: ESSAYS: *Best Words, Best Order* (1996). NOVELS: *A Man of Little Evils* (1973). *Saratoga Longshot* (1976). *Saratoga Swimmer* (1981). *Dancer with One Leg* (1983). *Saratoga Headhunter* (1985). *Cold Dog Soup* (1985). *Saratoga Snapper* (1986). *A Boat Off the Coast* (1987). *Two Deaths of Senora Puccini* (1988). *Saratoga Bestiary* (1988). *The House on Alexandrine* (1990). *Saratoga Hexameter* (1990). *After Shocks/Near Escapes* (1991). *Saratoga Haunting* (1993). *The Wrestler's Cruel Study* (1993). *Saratoga Backtalk* (1994). *Saratoga Fleshpot* (1995). *The Church of Dead Girls* (1997). *Saratoga Strongbox* (1998). *Boy in the Water* (1999). SHORT FICTION: *Eating Naked* (2000).

RITA DOVE (1952)

Rita Dove was born in Akron, Ohio. She received a B.A. from Miami University, studied modern European literature at the University of Tübingen, and received an M.F.A. from the University of Iowa. A professor of English at the University of Virginia, Dove's literary honors include grants and fellowships from the National Endowment for the Arts, and the General Electric Foundation. In 1987 she was awarded the Pulitzer Prize for poetry.

Many of Dove's poems are deeply rooted in moments of intimate personal experience: a child marvels at the power of language; an adolescent girl fantasizes the arrival of a dreamed-of lover; a young mother teaches her daughter the truth and mystery of her vagina. And many of her poems — most notably the book-length sequence, *Thomas and Beulah* — find their source in extended family history.

Unlike such predecessors as Sylvia Plath and W. D. Snodgrass, Dove is not a personal-confessional poet. No doubt there is suffering and anguish in her poems, often revealed in haunting images (as in "Crab-Boil," where the crabs suffocating in the pot, "the scratch, / shell on tin, of their distress," underscore the African-American narrator's discomfort on the whites-only beach in Ft. Myers, Florida, in 1962); but there is no sense of personal evil to confess or to exorcise. Rather, Dove is what might be called a "fictive" poet, in whose work autobiography and family history are transformed into a lyrical fiction, into a larger drama in which the reader participates. This communal drama does not borrow from established myth for its resonance; instead, it strives to become archetype, to be its own myth.

Even when she uses traditional myth, Dove seems compelled to retell it from her own perspective — the terrifying rediscovery of the garden of Eden in Mississippi — thereby implicitly reaffirming her assertion that "each god is empty / without us. . . ." But whether focusing on personal experience, family history, or communal archetype, Dove's poems not only erect verbal silos — "the ribs of the modern world" — at the heart of the American myth, they are also carefully structured circles of images, layers of metaphors that re-create an epiphanal moment irrevocably sculpted in words.

Poetry: *Ten Poems* (1977). *The Yellow House on the Corner* (1980). *Museum* (1983). *Thomas and Beulah* (1986). *Grace Notes* (1989). *Selected Poems* (1993). *The Darker Face of the Earth* (verse play) (1994). *Mother Love* (1995). *On the Bus with Rosa Parks* (1999).

Prose: *Fifth Sunday,* short stories (1985). *Through the Ivory Gate,* a novel (1991). *The Poet's World* (1995).

ALAN DUGAN (1923)

Alan Dugan was born in Brooklyn and graduated from Mexico City College. His first book of poems won the Yale Series of Younger Poets award, the Pulitzer Prize, and the National Book Award. He subsequently received the Shelley Memorial Award from the Poetry Society of America and an Award in Literature from the American Academy and Institute of Arts and Letters.

Although Dugan's most effective poems can be humorous, lyrical, or cerebral, his work also can be tough, brutal, and "ugly." For William J. Martz's *The Distinctive Voice* (1966), Dugan wrote about his voice as a poet: "I am trying to say what is hardest to say; that is, words wrung out of intense experience and not constructed." Moreover, as Richard Howard has observed, in Dugan's poetry one senses that "the act of writing poetry is, precisely, an invocation of destruction, a luring of language to its wreck. . . . He is too honest . . . for the consolation of some visionary transcendence of language."

In many of his poems, Dugan talks about the least public of experiences in a language still generally considered the least public — perhaps "unpoetic." Moreover, he refuses to burden his subject and language with any obviously stated mystical, magical, or "great social" impact. He tells it "like it is" and, rather than being offensive — as one might vaguely and uneasily wish they were — his poems emerge as the product of a fierce and fully American honesty and of a craftsmanship generating words that burn through all pretense like acid.

Poetry: *Poems* (1961). *Poems 2* (1963). *Poems 3* (1967). *Collected Poems* (1969). *Poems 4* (1974). *Sequence* (1976). *New and Collected Poems 1961–1983* [includes *Poems 5*] (1983). *Poems 6* (1989).

CAROL FROST (1948)

Born in Lowell, Massachusetts, Carol Frost was educated at the Sorbonne, the State University College at Oneonta, New York, and Syracuse University. She has been Distinguished Writer-in-residence at Wichita State University and Visiting Writer at Washington University in St. Louis. Currently Writer-in-residence at Hartwick College, she has directed the Catskill Poetry Workshop since 1988. Among her awards are fellowships from the National Endowment for the Arts and two Pushcart Prizes.

Frost's lyrics are distinguished by their meditative tone, rigorous intellect, and erotic appetite. Often short, her poems achieve density through their use of Yeats's "passionate syntax," idiosyncratic punctuation, and casual abstraction. In *Pure* (1994), she developed a free-verse form, a truncated sonnet of eleven lines, that makes use of traditional method — the singular focus, the quick turn — while subverting traditional structure. Unsentimental, her poems emphasize the vicissitudes of love and lust, reveling in the sensual pleasure of their language and the integrity of their lines.

Drawn toward purity, particularly in an age that celebrates Whitman's "urge and urge and urge" and favors Darwinian principle, Frost's poems examine the impossibility of divesting oneself of the philosophical import and moral underpinnings of language and gesture. The epigraph to *Day of the Body* (1986), ". . . *thou among the wastes of time must go,*" with its biblical injunction and implicit call to purpose, informs her reverent meditations on the nature of the soul's passage through the physical world, "a little in awe of everything." Her poems reach back to the glimmerings of consciousness in early man — the origins of desire "where / the beauty of relation begins" — and focus, through Time, on "people and animals / ripening in dark / green garden where the world is / made." Her lyrics explore myth and archetype to consider "the difference between . . . early ideals — / a garden where plums and peaches grew well and tasted wild / and they were unembarrassed by genitals — and what had become of them." Domestic tension and muted humor infuse such lines. Carol Frost, unlike so many of her contemporaries, deemphasizes the Self to assume her place within "the harmony and breaking down / of such harmony that is the passing world."

Poetry: *Liar's Dice* (1978). *The Fearful Child* (1983). *Day of the Body* (1986). *Chimera* (1990). *Pure* (1994). *Venus and Don Juan* (1996). *Love and Scorn: New and Selected Poems* (2000).

ALLEN GINSBERG (1926–1997)

Born in Newark, New Jersey, Allen Ginsberg attended Columbia University and was dismissed, but returned later to receive his B.A. in 1948. A leader of the Beat Movement and the San Francisco Renaissance, in 1954 he married Peter Orlovsky. He was the recipient of grants from the Guggenheim Foundation, the National Endowment for the Arts, and the National Institute of Arts and Letters. In 1974, with Adrienne Rich, he was cowinner of the National Book Award.

In his poem "Ego Confession," Ginsberg asserts, "I want to be known as the most brilliant man in America . . . / I want to be the spectacle of Poesy triumphant over trickery of the world. . . ." Poet, guru, world traveler, prophet, and visionary Uncle Sam of the Flower-Acid-Rock Generation, Ginsberg may well have been the planet's most renowned poet. And if Ginsberg's notoriety as a sociocultural *enfant terrible* obscured his power as a poet, he is nevertheless recognized by his contemporaries as one of the most influential post-1945 poets. His first major poem, "Howl," is a milestone, perhaps as significant a poem and document for his generation as "The Waste Land" was for Eliot's. It is conceivable that Ginsberg's entire work may eventually achieve the stature of *Leaves of Grass.*

At once intimate and prophetic, hilarious and terrifying, profoundly religious and, at times, commensurately outrageous, Ginsberg's poetry encompasses a myriad of experiences, ranges over the full spectrum of human life on this planet, and — like the poetry of Whitman — is a combination of incredible power and drivel. Clearly, in technique, scope, and intent, Whitman is Ginsberg's model and mentor; like him, Ginsberg is attempting to re-create not only the world but also the full dimensions of a human's physical and spiritual odyssey through a given moment in history — with the crucial difference that Whitman's poems were hefty songs and Ginsberg's are often reverberating lamentations.

Part of Ginsberg's impact results from his prophetic stance as a man and as a poet, sustained by the vital spirit of William Blake and the prophets of the Old Testament. A modern-day Isaiah, whose public personality often betrayed the depth and range of his erudition, Ginsberg was the public conscience of the nation — if not of the species — lamenting the imponderable evil humankind has perpetrated against life. But like Isaiah, Blake, and Whitman, he was also moved by a profound belief in the holiness of life and by a vision of a new Jerusalem, a new world.

Poetry: *Howl and Other Poems* (1956). *Empty Mirror: Early Poems* (1961). *Kaddish and Other Poems* (1961). *Reality Sandwiches* (1963). *Airplane Dreams: Compositions from Journals* (1968/1969). *Ankor-Wat* (1968). *Planet News, 1961–1967* (1968). *The Gates of Wrath: Rhymed Poems, 1948–1952* (1972). *The Fall of America: Poems of These States, 1965–1971* (1973). *Iron Horse* (1973). *First Blues* (1975). *Mind Breaths: Poems 1972–1977* (1978). *Plutonium Ode: Poems 1977–1980* (1982). *Collected Poems: 1947–1980* (1984). *White Shroud: Poems 1980–1985* (1986). *Cosmopolitan Greetings: Poems 1986-1992* (1994). *Selected Poems: 1947–1995* (1997). *Death and Fame: Last Poems 1993–1997* (1999). *Poems for the Nation* (2000).

Prose: *The Yage Letters*, with William Burroughs (1963). *Indian Journals* (1970). *Improvised Poetics*, edited by M. Robinson (1971). *Allen Verbatim: Lectures on Poetry, Politics, Consciousness*, edited by G. Ball (1974). *To Eberhart from Ginsberg: A Letter About Howl 1956* (1976). *As Ever: The Collected Correspondence of Allen Ginsberg & Neal Cassady*, edited by B. Gifford (1977). *Journals: Early Fifties Early Sixties*, edited by G. Ball (1977). *Composed on the Tongue*, edited by D. Allen (1980). *Straight Hearts Delight: Love Poems and Selected Letters 1974–1980*, with Peter Orlovsky, edited by W. Layland (1980). *Your Reason and Blake's System* (1988). *Deliberate Prose: Selected Essays, 1952–1995*, edited by B. Morgan (2000).

LOUISE GLÜCK (1943)

Born in New York City and raised on Long Island, Louise Glück attended Sarah Lawrence and Columbia, where she studied with Stanley Kunitz. She has taught at many colleges and universities and has been awarded fellowships from the National Endowment for the Arts and the Guggenheim Foundation. Her books of poetry also have won the National Book Critics Circle Award and the Pulitzer Prize.

"I have always been too at ease with extremes," writes Louise Glück. Whether those extremes are life and death, love and pain, possession and release, or illusion and reality, it is from the tension between them that many of her most moving poems draw their force. But because of her skill with the striking image, the canny tonal shift, and the poetic line, the weight of her themes never overwhelms the poem. Whether writing in her early dense, near-surrealistic mode ("Fish bones walked the waves off Hatteras") or in the looser, more conversational style of her later work ("I have a friend who still believes in heaven") she controls the rhythm of the poetic line the way a skilled rider handles the reins, alternately tightening and loosening to keep the desired momentum.

Though aspects of autobiography are present in Glück's poems, they rarely serve an expiational purpose. Rather, her self-scrutiny is linked to a wider search for meaning and value, and above all for what it means to be human. It is that exploration of human existence — the "hard loss" of birth, the "thrust and ache" of male/female relations — that may account for the frequent presence in her poems of ancient Greek characters, themes, and images. Taking to heart the Sophoclean edict that "Man is the measure of all things," she seems to forswear both a specifically Christian redemption and a generically spiritual transcendence. In "Celestial Music," a friend who believes in God tells her to look up: "When I look up, nothing. / Only clouds, snow, a white business in the trees."

If the gods long ago "sank down to human shape with longing" — if there is no supernatural world — Glück's poetry seems all the more urgent regarding the question of what makes us human: the part that loves or the part that is mortal? That is the common denominator in her poetry: to be human is to love, to long, to suffer, and to know you will die. Not that Glück would seem to want it otherwise, for "There is always something to be made of pain."

Poetry: *Firstborn* (1968/1981). *The House on Marshland* (1975). *Descending Figure* (1980). *The Triumph of Achilles* (1985). *Ararat* (1990). *The Wild Iris* (1992). *The First Four Books of Poems* (1996). *Meadowlands* (1996). *Vita Nova* (1999).

Prose: *Proofs and Theories: Essays on Poetry* (1994).

ALBERT GOLDBARTH (1948)

Born in Chicago, Albert Goldbarth was educated at the University of Illinois-Chicago, the University of Iowa, and the University of Utah. He has taught at Cornell, Syracuse, the University of Texas, and Wichita

State University, where he is Distinguished Professor of the Humanities. Among his numerous awards are fellowships from the Guggenheim Foundation and the National Endowment for the Arts, the National Book Critics Circle Award for *Heaven and Earth: A Cosmology* (1991), and The Center for the Study of Science Fiction Theodore Sturgeon Memorial Award.

Wildly prolific and unabashedly enthusiastic, Albert Goldbarth is, according to David Barber in *Poetry*, "American poetry's consummate showman . . . whose sensibility conceivably owes as much to Barnum as to Whitman." Like Barnum, Goldbarth is an impresario of the wonders of the New World, an entrepreneur of American culture, boyish, breathless, and awestruck. Like Whitman, he renders his bustling scenarios in "the blab of the pave," tossing slang, vulgarity, jargon, prayer, Yiddish phrases, and neologisms, the whole potpourri of American language, into a mixed stew, a linguistic melting pot of overbrimming abundance. Nothing is ever wasted. His poems respond to the barrage of stimulation, the technological overkill that forces the mind to shuffle detail upon detail toward significance. His purpose, in Joseph Conrad's phrase, is "to render the highest possible justice to the visible world," and perhaps more than any other contemporary poet, Goldbarth conveys the sense of what it means to live in America at the turn of the millennium.

A hip, comic, self-styled Adam whose incumbent task is to name everything, Goldbarth layers the surfaces of his poems with talk-show dross and junk mail salesmanship as well as scholarly erudition. Underneath his voracious appetite for knowledge and full-throttle narrative momentum, however, lies an abiding tenderness, a concern for the consolations of faith in an age that has come to rely on technology. His poems draw on family, his Jewish heritage, and the common aspects of love as much as they draw on ancient history, archeology, and popular culture. He recognizes that the comic books, mechanical toys, and bric-a-brac of one century will provide the detritus through which future generations might sift for meaning, and that personal relationships exist against the backdrop of a historic and cosmological continuum. His ambitious and seemingly inexhaustible catalogs, his manic, Pentecostal sermonizing, and his vast generosity of spirit allow him to view our world, and those who inhabit it, "wholly, culture-wide, cross-time."

Poetry: *Coprolites* (1973). *Jan. 31* (1974). *Opticks* (1974). *Keeping* (1975). *A Year of Happy* (1976). *Comings Back* (1976). *Different Fleshes* (1979). *Who Gathered and Whispered Behind Me* (1981). *Faith* (1982). *Original Light: New & Selected Poems 1973–1983* (1983). *Arts & Sciences* (1986). *Popular Culture* (1989). *Heaven and Earth: A Cosmology* (1991). *The Gods* (1993). *Across the Layers: poems old and new* (1993). *Marriage, and Other Science Fiction* (1994). *A Lineage of Ragpickers* (1996). *Adventures in Ancient Egypt* (1996). *Beyond* (1998). *Troubled Lovers in History* (1999).

Prose: A *Sympathy of Souls* (1990). *Great Topics of the World* (1995). *Dark Waves and Light Matter* (1999).

KIMIKO HAHN (1955)

Born in Mt. Kisco, New York, Kimiko Hahn, the daughter of two artists, attended the University of Iowa and Columbia University. She has taught at the Poetry Project at St. Mark's Church, the Parsons School of Design, Sarah Lawrence College, and Yale University, and currently teaches at Queens College/CUNY. Among her awards are The Theodore Roethke Memorial Poetry Prize and an Association of Asian American Studies Literature Award for *Earshot* (1992), an American Book Award for *The Unbearable Heart* (1995), a Lila Wallace–Readers Digest Writers Award, and fellowships from the New York Foundation for the Arts and the National Endowment for the Arts. In 1995, she wrote ten "portraits" of women for the HBO special, "Ain't Nuthin' but a She Thing."

Asian as well as American literary traditions inform the poems of Kimiko Hahn. A poet of exile even on her familiar New York streets, she relies on storytelling to center herself and to ward off grief, fully realized and/or potential — the loss of her mother who was "broadsided by an Arab kid fleeing a car of white kids with baseball bats," the violence intimated in the consonantal harshness "of boys in the empty lot" that penetrates her daughters' bedroom. For Hahn, the creative act, the engaged *process*, often becomes a means of attaining solace as the poem extends itself organically, finding its true subject through shifts of consciousness and verbal improvisation. In "The Izu Dancer," her attempt to recall Japanese, to "resume the journey inside words / I had begun as a child," by reading the Kawabata tale, is undercut by unbidden and intrusive recollections of lust for an American professor who drove a red Volkswagen: "Perhaps I did not want the language enough." Yet that hint of betrayal, as well as the play of the mind across such disparate and cross-cultural elements, allows the poet to translate the past and interpret desire, "flesh / and emblem," with fluency. "I can only speak for myself," she realizes.

Kimiko Hahn's poems portray "someone tearing the past apart," Adrienne Rich has written, "and rebuilding with naked raw hands." Her elegiac and passionate voice, sustained by "the unbearable heart" that gives her work its human measure, unfurls in a New World of its own making.

Poetry: *We Stand Our Ground* with Susan Sherman and Gale Jackson (1988). *Air Pocket* (1989). *Earshot* (1992). *The Unbearable Heart* (1995). *Volatile* (1999). *Mosquito and Ant* (1999).

DONALD HALL (1928)

Born in New Haven, Connecticut, Donald Hall is a graduate of Harvard and Oxford. In a way, he is also a "graduate" of the University of Michigan, where he taught for several years before returning to his family's farm in New Hampshire, where he now lives and writes. In 1954, his book *Exiles and Marriages* was the Academy of American Poets' Lamont Poetry Selection. His other literary awards include the Lenore Marshall Prize, the National Book Critics Circle Award, and appointment as Poet Laureate of New Hampshire.

Hall's many other accomplishments include monographs on Marianne Moore and Henry Moore and such noted textbooks as *Writing Well* and *To Read Literature*. He also has edited many anthologies, including *Contemporary American Poetry* (1962).

In a variety of statements — and especially in his dazzling essay "Goatfoot, Milktongue, Twinbird: The Psychic Origins of Poetic Form" — Hall has repeatedly affirmed that the essential beauty of poetry lies in the sensual body of the poem — the sheer physical pleasure that a poem offers. That physical pleasure, Hall observes, "reaches us through our mouths (Milktongue) . . . in the muscles of our legs (Goatfoot) . . . in the resolution of dance and noise (Twinbird)." Hall's quest for the sensual body of his own poems was originally in more traditional forms; later, his poems became less formal, more expansive, and more sensual — without losing the control and discipline learned in the atelier of formalism.

Moreover, Hall's quest for the sensual body of poetry hasn't been the aesthete's pursuit of pleasure found in the notions of Walter Pater or in the work of some of Hall's own contemporaries. For Hall knows all too well: "Milktongue also remembers hunger, and the cry without answer. Goatfoot remembers falling, and the ache that bent the night. Twinbird remembers the loss of the brother, so long he believed in abandonment forever." At the heart of Hall's own poetry are the ever-present ache and modulated cry of abandonment, of grief over loss that is also at the heart of human experience.

More recently the sense of loss in Hall's poems has been complemented and perhaps surpassed by a large measure of a joyous reconciliation with personal history, a discovery of the redemptive power inherent in all cycles of existence. Thus twenty-five years after the grandfather's body has slid into the ground like snow melting on the roof of the saphouse, his grandchildren dip their fingers in the maple syrup the dead man preserved in his cellar. Thus Hall himself can exclaim, "Oh, this delicious falling into the arms of leaves, / into the soft laps of leaves! . . . / Now I leap and fall, exultant, recovering / from death, on account of death, in accord with the dead. . . ." And thus he evokes still another ancient image of the sensual pleasure of poetry in the myth of Philomel, magically transformed into a nightingale whose torn tongue makes song, makes music, out of grief.

Poetry: *Exiles and Marriages* (1955). *The Dark Houses* (1958). *A Roof of Tiger Lilies* (1964). *The Alligator Bride: Poems New and Selected* (1969). *The Yellow Room: Love Poems* (1971). *The Town of Hill* (1975). *Kicking the Leaves* (1978). *The Happy Man* (1986). *The One Day: A Poem in Three Parts* (1988). *Old and New Poems, 1947–1990* (1990). *The Museum of Clear Ideas: New Poems* (1993). *The Old Life* (1996). *Without* (1998).

Prose: FICTION: *The Ideal Bakery* (1987). CRITICISM: *Goatfoot Milktongue Twinbird: Interviews, Essays, and Notes on Poetry 1970–76* (1978). *To Keep Moving: Essays 1959–69* (1980). *The Weather for Poetry: Essays, Reviews, and Notes on Poetry 1977–81* (1983). *Poetry and Ambition: Essays 1982–1988* (1990). MEMOIRS AND OTHER: *String Too Short To Be Saved: Childhood Reminiscences* (1961/1979). *Dock Ellis in the Country of Baseball* (1976). *Remembering Poets: Reminiscences and Opinions* (1978). *Fathers Playing Catch with Sons: Essays on Sports* (1985). *Seasons at Eagle Pond* (1987). *Daylilies at Eagle Pond* (1990). *Here at Eagle Pond* (1990). *Their Ancient Glittering Eyes: Remembering Poets and More Poets* (1992). *Life Work* (1993).

MICHAEL S. HARPER (1938)

Michael Harper was born in Brooklyn and educated at California State in Los Angeles and at the University of Iowa. He has taught at various universities, including Brown, where he is I. J. Kapstein Professor of English. In addition to fellowships and grants from the National Endowment for the Arts, and the National Institute of Arts and Letters, Harper also has received the Black Academy of Arts and Letters Award.

The titles of Michael Harper's books are genuine flags of his substantive and sustained concerns. Many of his poems are indeed "images of kin": the woman to whom he is married, their living children, their children who died as infants, his own parents and grandparents. But in Harper's poems kinship also expands in time and space to include historical figures, ranging from Frederick Douglass to Martin Luther King and Malcolm X, as well as members of the artistic community — jazz musicians such as John Coltrane, Charlie Parker, Bessie Smith, and Billie Holiday and writers such as Richard Wright and, especially among his contemporaries, Robert Hayden.

Moreover, the focus of Harper's concern is a powerful sense of kinship as shared history. Such a vision, then, begins by asserting that "history is your own heartbeat," but it necessarily expands in ever-widening circles of kinship, generated by the pulse that is at the heart of the human family. Full and active participation in those human bonds, Harper knows, may often result in considerable pain and anguish, for to be fully human often necessitates recognizing the nightmare of our condition and accepting its necessary consequence: "nightmare begins responsibility."

Harper is also one of the poets of his generation whose poetry and sensibility have been influenced by the work and presence of the classic American jazz musicians. In his poems they assume the dimensions and implications of larger figures from ancient myths. But they are more than just mythical presences, for in their work Harper has searched for and learned what he calls "the cadence of street talk in the inner car of the great musicians, the great blues singers." And as Ralph J. Mills, Jr., has noted, Harper's poetry is infused with "a complex jazz of sudden leaps, silences, long rides." No less important, Harper reflects that rich tradition of making music out of fundamental human suffering, whether it be personal, racial, or historical. The conscious transmutation of suffering into song is at once an assertion of our humanity and an affirmation of our freedom. But in one of his essays Harper also tells the story of how John Coltrane tried to find an especially soft reed that would alleviate his pain as he played his horn in search of a particular tone. Coltrane eventually gave up looking for such a reed, regardless of how painful it was for him to make music. "There was no easy way to get that sound," Harper concludes: "play through the pain to *a love supreme*" — the phrase that appears most frequently in Harper's work. No wonder Michael Harper's poems are such "healing songs."

Poetry: *Dear John, Dear Coltrane* (1970). *History Is Your Own Heartbeat* (1971). *Photographs: Negatives: History as Apple Tree* (1972). *Song: I Want a Witness* (1972). *Debridement* (1973). *Nightmare Begins Responsibility* (1974). *Images of Kin: New and Selected Poems* (1977). *Healing Song for the Inner Ear* (1985). *Spiritual Warfare* (1984). *Rhode Island: Eight Poems* (1985). *Honorable Amendments* (1995). *Songlines in Michaeltree* (2000).

ROBERT HASS (1941)

Born in San Francisco and raised in San Rafael, California, Robert Hass received a B.A. from St. Mary's College and a Ph.D. from Stanford University. He has taught at the State University of New York at Buffalo, St. Mary's College, and since 1989, at the University of California at Berkeley. The recipient of a Guggenheim Fellowship, Hass also won the Yale Series of Younger Poets award, the National Book Critics Circle Award for criticism, and a distinguished John D. and Catherine T. Mac-Arthur Fellowship. In 1995 he was appointed Poet Laureate of the United States.

Representing the second generation of poets since 1945, Hass is both heir to and active participant in the restlessness and eclectic spirit of contemporary American poetry. In his early work there is the unmistakable and vibrant influence of the previous generation of poets who helped shape the aesthetics of the late sixties and early seventies. In many poems the Chinese and Japanese aesthetics that so influenced Gary Snyder are present. By contrast, the imagery, tone, structure, and closure of other poems vividly call to mind Robert Bly's and Louis Simpson's earlier experiments in North American neosurrealism. A poem like "Bookbuying in the Tenderloin," meanwhile, reflects the aesthetic and thematic sensibilities of poets such as Robert Lowell and John Logan: the deterioration of Judeo-Christian spiritual values, commensurate with commerce in sex, and the deterioration of sexual mores and values, foreshadows the death of western civilization — expressed in rhymed, occasional couplets: "The sky glowers. My God, it is a test, / this riding out the dying of the West."

Peculiar to Hass's poetry is the obsession with the relationship between language and the physical world — between word and thing. This tension, never fully resolved, is explored both explicitly ("a word is elegy to what it signifies") and implicitly through the joy Hass takes in simply naming things ("Tall Buttercup. Wild Vetch"; "*silver* or *moonlight* or *wet grass*"). If images of decay ("The dead with their black lips are heaped / on one another, intimate as lovers") are central to Hass's early poems, so too is the belief in "the magic of names and poems" and in the vision that "our words are clear / and our movements give off light." And it is a sustained belief in such magic that enables Hass in later poems — most of them written in long, lyrical lines — to wrestle with "All the new thinking . . . about loss," to affirm "moments when the body is as numinous as words, days that are the good flesh continuing" and to celebrate the physical, sensual, and transcendent pleasures of this world (not the least of which is food): "Such tenderness, these afternoons and evenings, / saying *blackberry, blackberry, blackberry*."

Poetry: *Field Guide* (1973). *Praise* (1979). *Human Wishes* (1989). *Sun Under Wood* (1996).

Prose: *Twentieth Century Pleasures: Prose on Poetry*, essays (1984). *An Unnamed Flowing: The Cultures of American Poetry* (2000).

Translations: *The Separate Notebooks*, poems by Czeslaw Milosz, with R. Gorcynski and R. Pinsky (1984). *Unattainable Earth*, poems by Czeslaw Milosz, with the author (1986). *Collected Poems*, by Czeslaw Milosz, with the author and others (1989). *Provinces: Poems 1987–1991*, by Czeslaw Milosz, with the author (1991). *The Essential Haiku* (1994). *Facing the River*, by Czeslaw Milosz, with the author (1995). *Road-Side Dog*, by Czeslaw Milosz, with the author (1998).

ROBERT HAYDEN (1913–1980)

A native of Detroit, Robert Hayden received a B.A. from Wayne State University and an M.A. from the University of Michigan. He taught at Fisk, Louisville, and Washington, and he was professor of English at the

University of Michigan. He was a staff member of the Breadloaf Writers Conference, and from 1976 to 1978 he served as Consultant in Poetry at the Library of Congress. His honors and awards included a Rosenwald Fellowship, a Ford Foundation grant, and the First World Festival of Negro Arts Prize for Poetry, Dakar, Senegal, in 1966.

From the publication of his first book in 1940, Hayden's poetry consistently reflected a sensibility informed by a vital awareness of and participation in the broad spectrum of the African-American experience. He explored dimensions of his own childhood and personal life; he focused on central historical and cultural figures and events; and he re-created such immeasurable horrors as an African-American man's castration at the hands of the Ku Klux Klan. No less important, while eschewing political rhetoric, he recognized that much the same moral poison infected the air of both Selma and Saigon, that the ashes in the pits at Dachau resulted from a fire not unlike that which burned on lawns in innumerable American towns.

Hayden's moral vision is all the more powerful because his work reveals that he is equally conscious of the broader aesthetic traditions in the art of poetry and of the obvious — but often overlooked — fact that the wellsprings of poetry run more deeply and serendipitously than even the most active pools of political or racial experience. The impact of a poem like "Monet's 'Waterlilies'" emerges out of the fact that Hayden's vision is rooted specifically in such a seemingly apolitical and nonmoral work of art. The depths of horror in "Night, Death, Mississippi" are intensified by the delicate and exquisite lyrical qualities of "The Night-Blooming Cereus."

In short, whether about Frederick Douglass or Rilke or a diver, Robert Hayden's poems are themselves vibrant "lives grown out of his life, the lives / fleshing his dream of *the beautiful, needful thing.*"

Poetry: *Heart-Shape in the Dust* (1940). *The Lion and the Archer*, with Myron O'Higgins (1948). *Figures of Time: Poems* (1955). *A Ballad of Remembrance* (1962). *Selected Poems* (1966). *Words in the Mourning Time* (1970). *The Night-Blooming Cereus* (1975). *Angle of Ascent: New and Selected Poems* (1975). *American Journal* (1978/1982). *Robert Hayden: Collected Poems* (1985).

Prose: *The Collected Prose of Robert Hayden* (1984).

WILLIAM HEYEN (1940)

Born in Brooklyn, New York, William Heyen grew up on then-rural Long Island. He attended the State University of New York at Brockport and Ohio University, and taught at the former from 1967 until his recent retirement. He has been a Senior Fulbright Lecturer in American

Literature at Hannover University in Germany, and the recipient of fellowships from the National Endowment for the Arts, the Guggenheim Foundation, and the New York Foundation for the Arts. In 1982 he was awarded the Witter Bynner Prize from the American Academy and Institute of Arts and Letters. His *Crazy Horse in Stillness* (1996) received the National Small Press Book Award.

Prolific, obsessive, and fiercely intelligent, Heyen has managed an impressive body of work in both traditional and unconventional, even unique, modes. Finding it impossible, it would seem, to write only a single poem on a particular topic, Heyen instead exhausts his vast knowledge of the subject by composing long sequences of poems that provide multiple perspectives, that attempt to see "from all sides at once." He has written such sequences on the rural Long Island of his boyhood; the Holocaust; the history of the American chestnut tree; the Gulf War; Crazy Horse and Custer; even the Royal Family. This latter sequence, *Diana, Charles, & the Queen* (1998), consists of 324 separate poems, each "two quatrains, / usually rhymed." Yet his narrowly focused though wildly diverse topics allow him an ambitious, inclusive range. The poems in *Crazy Horse in Stillness*, for example, circle widely enough around their subject to draw upon pop culture and cyberspace. Despite such eccentric gestures, Heyen's visionary lyricism remains constant, rooted in the Emersonian transcendentalism of the nineteenth century.

Heyen's poetry remains aware of its moral function as it confronts history — as it confronts, in fact, up-to-the-minute events, as recent poems on Woodstock '99 and the death of Wilt "The Stilt" Chamberlain attest — and serves as the conscience of a still-developing democracy. His poems on Nature extend their tradition by evincing ecological and environmental concerns, sometimes uncomfortably so. Whatever the object of attention, Heyen wields a formidable intellect and lyric intensity upon his sometimes deceptively simple surfaces. "Prune for shade," reads his shortest poem, and that epigrammatic imperative could serve as a description of this poet's particular craft.

Poetry: *Depth of Field* (1970). *Noise in the Trees: Poems and a Memoir* (1974). *The Swastika Poems* (1977). *Long Island Light: Poems and a Memoir* (1979). *The City Parables* (1980). *Lord Dragonfly: Five Sequences* (1981). *Erika: Poems of the Holocaust* (1984). *The Chestnut Rain: A Poem* (1986). *Brockport, New York: Beginning with 'And'* (1988). *Falling from Heaven: Holocaust Poems* with Louis Daniel Brodsky (1991). *Pterodactyl Rose: Poems of Ecology* (1991). *Ribbons: The Gulf War — A Poem* (1991). *The Host: Selected Poems 1965–1990* (1994). *Crazy Horse in Stillness: Poems* (1996). *Diana, Charles, & the Queen: Poems* (1998).

Prose: FICTION: *Vic Holyfield and the Class of 1957: A Romance* (1986). ESSAYS: *With Me Far Away: A Memoir* (1994). *Pig Notes & Dumb Music: Prose on Poetry* (1998).

ANDREW HUDGINS (1951)

Born in Killeen, Texas, Andrew Hudgins attended Sidney Lanier High School in Montgomery, Alabama, where the football team was named the Poets. He attended Huntingdon College, the University of Alabama, Syracuse University, and the University of Iowa, and in 1984 was a Wallace Stegner Fellow at Stanford University. He has taught at Baylor University and, since 1985, the University of Cincinnati. In 1989–1990 he held the Alfred Hodder Fellowship at Princeton. His honors include the Witter Bynner Award of the American Academy and Institute of Arts and Letters, the Poets' Prize for *After the Lost War* (1988), and fellowships from the Ingram Merrill Foundation and the National Endowment for the Arts.

Rooted in his Southern Baptist upbringing, the poems of Andrew Hudgins, though not religious in the conventional sense, focus on fundamentalism as a backdrop for human behavior to illustrate the disparity between biblical injunction and Darwinian imperative. In *Saints and Strangers* (1985), naked adolescents cavort in a baptismal font and one boy sings "Amazing Grace" in the cartoon voice of Donald Duck. Such irreverence, however, doesn't mitigate the overarching presence of "God's clear flesh beneath / its human dying." The poems admit the oppression as well as the ecstasy inherent in religious (and Southern) iconography, and reflect this duality in their comic desperation, their repetitious rituals of absolution and violence, and their plainspoken, at times scatological, language arranged within the formal cadences of blank verse.

Hudgins's second volume, the ambitious, book-length narrative *After the Lost War* (1988), has been described by the poet as "a historical novel in verse that masquerades as a biography of the Civil War veteran and poet Sidney Lanier." The sequence questions the validity and power of the romantic imagination confronted by the landscape of the defeated South, and anticipates Hudgins's later work in which his characters, often unwillingly, test their faith — in themselves, in God — against commonplace horrors. "I wish my soul were larger than it is," prays one narrator, as racism, sexual violence, and death course through these poems. "This world, / this world is home," insists another. "But it / will never feel like home."

Poetry: *Saints and Strangers* (1985). *After the Lost War: A Narrative* (1988). *The Never-Ending* (1991). *The Glass Hammer: A Southern Childhood* (1994). *Babylon in a Jar* (1998).

Prose: *The Glass Anvil* (1997).

RICHARD HUGO (1923–1982)

Richard Hugo was born in Seattle and educated at the University of Washington. He was a bombardier in the U.S. Army Air Corps during World War II and subsequently worked for the Boeing Company for twelve years. He later was director of the creative writing program at the University of Montana (Missoula) and served as editor of the Yale Series of Younger Poets. His awards included the Theodore Roethke Memorial Poetry Prize and fellowships from the Rockefeller and Guggenheim foundations.

Perhaps more than the work of any other poet of his generation, Hugo's poetry is rooted in and mines a specific, identifiable landscape — the American Far West. However, Hugo's landscape isn't the breathtaking panorama of a Grand Canyon or spectacular hills and plains against a blazing sunset of romantic American western movies. The landscape in his poetry is suggested in Hugo's comment: "Usually I find a poem is triggered by something, a small town or an abandoned house, that I feel others would ignore." Thus the geographic, human, and moral landscape in Hugo's poems is a bleak and threatening panorama in which one finds those small, dry, and blistered towns where all life and human constructs decay too soon — and where perhaps nothing dies soon enough.

If, like Wallace Stevens, Hugo understands the extent to which "the soil is man's intelligence," he nevertheless does not succumb to easy fatalism. In poems whose language and texture assert their own organic shapes and rhythms, as if in defiance of the odds of lunar dust, Hugo affirms the things of this earth and of his poetic landscape. Just as Rilke could assert, "Maybe we're here only to say: *house, / bridge, well, gate, jug, olive tree, window* — / at most, *pillar, tower* . . . but to say them, remember, / oh, to say them in a way that the things themselves / never dreamed of existing so intensely," so Hugo can assert, "To live good, keep your life and the scene. / Cow, brook, hay; these are names of coins."

"A part of the West belongs to Hugo," William Stafford has written. "By telling over and over again its places and people, he reclaims it from the very bleakness he confronts; and it all begins to loom as a great intense abode that we can't neglect, that we can't bear to let go." Thus Richard Hugo's intense love of the things of *his* earth keeps them and us alive at a level of intensity and joy we could not know without the melancholy and redemptive beauty of his poems.

Poetry: *A Run of Jacks* (1961). *Five Poets of the Pacific Northwest*, with Kenneth Hanson, Carolyn Kizer, William Stafford, and David Wagoner (1964). *Death of the Kapowsin Tavern* (1985). *Good Luck in Cracked Italian* (1969). *The Lady in Kicking Horse Reservoir* (1973). *Rain Five Days and I Love It* (1975). *What Thou Lovest Well, Remains American* (1975). *Duwamish Head* (1976). *31 Letters and 13 Dreams* (1977). *Road Ends at Tahola* (1978). *Selected Poems* (1979). *White*

Center (1980). *The Right Madness of Skye* (1980). *Making Certain It Goes On: The Collected Poems of Richard Hugo* (1983). *Sea Lanes Out* (1983).

Prose: *The Triggering Town: Lectures and Essays on Poetry and Writing* (1979). *Death and the Good Life,* a novel (1981). *The Real West Marginal Way: A Poet's Autobiography* (1986).

DAVID IGNATOW (1914–1997)

A native of Brooklyn, David Ignatow worked as a salesman, public relations writer, shipyard handyman, and treasurer and president of a bindery firm. He taught at the New School for Social Research, Vassar, and Columbia and subsequently as poet-in-residence at York College. In addition to awards from the National Institute of Arts and Letters and the National Endowment for the Arts, he received fellowships from the Rockefeller and Guggenheim foundations. In 1975 he was awarded the Bollingen Prize in Poetry.

An avowed disciple of William Carlos Williams, who focuses primarily on the urban experience, Ignatow wrote in his *Notebooks* that his role is to remind other poets — and, by implication, all readers of poetry — that "there is a world outside, the more decisive world that yet must be treated tragically by us in the highest intensity and sensuousness, though while it ignores us we must not run off into separate worlds of our own." Admitting that he is "antipoetic," he affirms that experience must be looked at and accepted just as it is and that "nothing should be taken for more than it says to you on its surface."

Ranging from comedy, through rage, to tragedy — and addressing himself to both his personal experiences as well as to our communal life — Ignatow constantly attempts to see life as it really is, without illusion or self-deception of any kind. And in so doing, he views himself as being at the opposite pole of Whitman's affirmative optimism. "My idea of being a moral leader," he wrote, "is to point out the terrible deficiencies in man. Whitman spent his life boosting the good side. My life will be spent pointing out the bad." But he adds a most crucial phrase: if he is intent on pointing to human deficiencies, he says that he will do so "from the standpoint of forgiveness and peace."

In his book-length sequence, *Shadowing the Ground,* Ignatow brought the same tragic sense of human existence to bear on aging and death — but with humor and unmatched serenity. By so doing he became the first poet of his generation, as Yeats did, to mine a new mother-lode of gorgeous and lively poetry in old age and the prospect of death. A singular and powerful voice in contemporary poetry, eschewing all current modes of language to be himself first of all, David Ignatow crafted poems marked by a certain nontheatrical directness and charged with a unique strength of spirit, humanity, and wisdom.

Poetry: *Poems* (1948). *The Gentle Weight Lifter* (1955). *Say Pardon* (1961). *Figures of the Human* (1964). *Rescue the Dead* (1968). *Poems 1934–1969* (1970). *Facing the Tree: New Poems* (1975). *Selected Poems*, chosen by R. Bly (1975). *Tread the Dark: New Poems* (1978). *Whisper to the Earth* (1981). *Leaving the Door Open* (1984). *New and Collected Poems: 1970–1985* (1986). *Despite the Plainness of the Day: Love Poems* (1990). *Shadowing the Ground* (1991). *Against the Evidence: Selected Poems 1934–1994* (1993). *At My Ease: Uncollected Poems of the Fifties and Sixties*, edited by V. R. Terris (1998). *Living Is What I Wanted: Last Poems*, edited by V. R. Terris (1999).

Prose: *The Notebooks of David Ignatow*, edited by R. J. Mills, Jr. (1983). *Open Between Us: Essays, Reviews, and Interviews*, edited by R. J. Mills, Jr. (1980). *The One in Many: A Poet's Memoirs* (1988).

DONALD JUSTICE (1925)

Donald Justice was born in Miami, Florida. He attended the University of Miami, the University of North Carolina at Chapel Hill, Stanford University, and the University of Iowa. He has taught at the University of Missouri, Syracuse University, the University of California, and the University of Iowa. Justice has been the recipient of grants, awards, and fellowships from the Ford and Guggenheim foundations, the National Endowment for the Arts, and the National Institute of Arts and Letters. In 1980 he was awarded the Pulitzer Prize for his *Selected Poems*.

Many of Justice's poems generate much the same kind of emotional center and aura as Edward Hopper's well-known paintings (such as *Nighthawks*): the figures, landscapes, the dramatic situations reflect the depth of loneliness, the isolation, and the spiritual desolation at the heart of twentieth-century experience. Any number of these people or situations could suddenly turn up in our own nightmares or in our living rooms. However, while Hopper achieves his effects by means of bold colors, thick strokes, and stark contrasts, the surface texture of Justice's poems is far more delicate and subtle — the restrained turn of a phrase (as in "Men at Forty"), the carefully controlled but haunting repetitions of lines (as in the villanelle "In Memory of the Unknown Poet, Robert Boardman Vaughn").

Given a list of some of Justice's subjects — loneliness, isolation, madness, despair, terror — he might be wrongfully associated with some of the personal-confessional poets. His poems, however, do not suggest any of the verbal or emotional sensationalism that occasionally may be ascribed to some of those other poets. Rightfully celebrated for his formal qualities, as a craftsman, Justice is a master of sparse elegance, with none of the pejorative connotations that may be clustered around those words. Justice's poems are not the result of emotional or technical self-indulgence; rather, they are moving because of his consummate linguistic, tonal, and formal exactitude.

If Justice's commitment to the "well-made poem" suggests his formal schooling among the New Critics, he is also one of the obvious emotional-spiritual heirs of T. S. Eliot — that is, the vision found in Eliot's earlier poems, before his conversion to Christianity. Like the work of other poets of his generation, Justice's poems flesh out in more intimate and sustained detail the figures and states of being that Eliot only sketched in poems like "The Love Song of J. Alfred Prufrock," "Preludes," and "The Waste Land." What further distinguishes Justice's work is not only his unrelieved sense of loss ("But the years are gone. There are no more years."), but also his profound acceptance of (*not* resignation to) the human condition as he finds it. But if Donald Justice's poems are elegies of loss, they are also unswerving and powerful affirmations that to be human is to make poetry of "the boredom, and the horror, and the glory."

Poetry: *The Summer Anniversaries* (1960). *A Local Storm* (1963). *Four Poets*, with others (1963). *Night Light* (1967). *Sixteen Poems* (1970). *From a Notebook* (1972). *Departures* (1973). *New and Selected Poems* (1995).

Prose and Poetry: *Platonic Scripts*, essays (1984). *Selected Poems* (1979). *The Sunset Maker: Poems/Stories/A Memoir* (1987). *A Donald Justice Reader: Selected Poetry and Prose* (1991). *Oblivion: On Writers & Writing* (1999).

Translations: *The Man Closing Up*, poems by Guillevic (1973).

GALWAY KINNELL (1927)

Galway Kinnell is a graduate of Princeton and the University of Rochester. He was a Fulbright Fellow in Paris, served in the U.S. Navy, and was a field worker for the Congress of Racial Equality. He has traveled widely in the Middle East and in Europe, where he taught at the universities of Grenoble and Nice (France). Presently Erich Maria Remarque Professor of Creative Writing at New York University, Kinnell has received several awards and fellowships, including the Brandeis University Creative Arts Award, the American Book Award, and the Pulitzer Prize.

Kinnell's earlier poems were both traditionally formal and informed by a traditional Christian sensibility. However, while retaining an essentially religious and sacramental dimension, his later work — as he has said in an interview — has become an increasing "struggle against the desire for heaven," as well as a movement away from competent poetry that risks being ornamental and toward a freer verse that takes more risks and in which "there is the chance of finding that great thing you might be after, of finding glory."

Confronted by a constant threat of extinction, in his poetry Kinnell accepts all forms of death as part of the rhythm that produces life, but he is capable of witnessing even the most elemental energy as an affirmation of life. Perhaps human life is a participation in the ultimate madness of a universe flinging itself into emptiness; the image of fire often reappearing in his poems may not be the flame of the phoenix. Thus Kinnell insists that for man, "as he goes up in flames, his own work / is / to open himself, to *be* / the flames."

In their language and substance, Kinnell's poems achieve that rhythm and solemnity often found in a shaman's chant. And yet his poems are also intensely personal, reflecting an attempt to strip away personality, to go deeper into the self "until," he says, "you're just a person. If you could keep going deeper and deeper, you'd finally not be a person either; you'd be an animal; and if you kept going deeper and deeper, you'd be a blade of grass or ultimately perhaps a stone. And if a stone could read, [poetry] would speak for it." For Kinnell, then, poetry is primal experience and myth, the most elemental kind of prayer, or a "paradigm of what people might wish to say in addressing the cosmos."

Poetry: *What a Kingdom It Was* (1960). *Flower Herding on Mount Monadnock* (1964). *Body Rags* (1968). *First Poems: 1946–54* (1971). *The Book of Nightmares* (1971). *The Avenue Bearing the Initial of Christ into the New World: Poems 1946–64* (1974). *Mortal Acts, Mortal Words* (1980). *Selected Poems* (1982). *The Past* (1985). *When One Has Lived a Long Time Alone* (1990). *Three Books: Body Rags, Mortal Acts, Mortal Words, The Past* (1993). *Imperfect Thirst* (1994). *A New Selected Poems* (2000).

Prose: *Black Light*, novel (1966; revised edition, 1981). *Walking Down the Stairs: Selections from Interviews* (1978).

Translations: POETRY: *The Poems of François Villon* (1965; revised version, 1977; new edition, 1982). *On the Motion and Immobility of Douve*, by Yves Bonnefoy (1968). *Lackawanna Elegy*, by Yvan Goll (1970). *Early Poems 1947–1959*, by Yvan Goll; with R. Pevear (1990). FICTION: *Bitter Victory*, by Rene Hardy (1965).

CAROLYN KIZER (1925)

Born in Spokane, Washington, Carolyn Kizer graduated from Sarah Lawrence College and was a fellow of the Chinese government in comparative literature at Columbia University, followed by a year of study in Nationalist China. The founder of the quarterly *Poetry Northwest*, in 1964–1965 she was a Specialist in Literature for the U.S. State Department in Pakistan, and from 1966 to 1970 she served as the first director of the Literature Program for the newly established National Endowment for the Arts. Since 1970 she has been professor, visiting professor, or poet-in-residence at universities throughout the United States. She currently lives in Berkeley, California.

With the publication of her first book-length collection of poems Carolyn Kizer staked out the diverse technical and thematic territories of her art. Whether she is working with free verse, with more formal verse, or with combinations of free verse and occasional slant rhymes, Kizer's poetry is always remarkable for its consummate grace and control. (She is one member of her generation who continues to explore the possibilities and power of strict form.) The intellectual credibility and emotional impact of her poems are further enhanced by her unique intellectual wit and hearty, often stinging, sense of humor. Indeed, Kizer was one of the first poets to approach feminist subjects and themes with a measure of healthy humor and sophisticated wit, which are an integral part of her sensibility rather than merely the device of poetic irony.

Kizer's concern for the cause of feminism has been at the heart of her poetry from the very start of her career — for the most fundamental of reasons: ". . . we are the custodians of the world's best-kept secret: / Merely the private lives of one-half of humanity." And it's important to note that the composition of "Pro Femina" dates back to the mid-1950s, before feminism was an issue of general consciousness. But Kizer's interest isn't limited to feminism as a sociopolitical cause; rather, what generally rivets her attention is the quality of representative women's diurnal experiences. "The Great Blue Heron," for example, is a meditation on the "invisible wires" that connect mother and daughter; "A Widow in Wintertime" is a portrait of repressed sexuality, disciplined loneliness, and "metaphysic famines."

However, Kizer doesn't limit herself to the "famines" of experience either, for also at the heart of her poetry is her vision of the profound patterns of physical and metaphysical life: change, transformation, and transubstantiation in nature and in the spirit, for good or ill; birth, death, and rebirth of love, the self, the soul, as in "Semele Recycled" where "the inner parts remember . . . / the comfortable odor of dung, the animal incense, / and passion, its bloody labor, / its birth and rebirth and decay." In short, without sacrificing their feminist edge, Kizer's poems are powerful, mythmaking hymns in celebration of "we who invented dying / And the whole alchemy of resurrection."

Poetry: *Poems* (1959). *The Ungrateful Garden* (1961/1999). *Five Poets of the Pacific Northwest*, with Kenneth Hanson, Richard Hugo, William Stafford, and David Wagoner; edited by R. Skelton (1964). *Knock Upon Silence* (1965/1966). *Midnight Was My Cry: New and Selected Poems* (1971). *Mermaids in the Basement: Poems for Women* (1984). *Yin: New Poems* (1984). *The Nearness of You* (1986). *Harping On: Poems 1985–1995* (1996). *Cool, Calm and Collected* (2001).

Prose: *Proses: On Poems & Poets* (1993). *Picking and Choosing: Essays on Prose* (1996).

Translations: *Carrying Over: Poems from the Chinese, Urdu, Macedonian, Yiddish, and French African* (1988). *A Splintered Mirror: Contemporary Chinese Poets*, with D. Finkel (1990).

BILL KNOTT (1940)

Bill Knott was born in Michigan and grew up in an orphanage. He attended John Logan's seminal Poetry Seminar in Chicago during 1960–1963. In 1966, under an assumed name, he sent a mimeographed letter to poets and editors, claiming that Bill Knott, an orphan and a virgin, had committed suicide, unable to endure any longer without love. His first book, *The Naomi Poems: Corpse and Beans* (1968) appeared under the pseudonym Saint Geraud (1940–1966). Several subsequent books published under his own name retained those dates. "I thought people should declare themselves dead, declare themselves casualties of the [Vietnam] war," Knott told an interviewer. He declined the Discovery Award of the Poetry Center of New York, but has been the recipient of the Elliston Poetry Prize for *Selected and Collected Poems* (1977) and a fellowship from the National Endowment for the Arts. He teaches at Emerson College in Boston.

"The most original poet of my generation, Bill Knott, is also the greatest outsider," Stephen Dobyns has written. His startlingly inventive poems remain untouched by current fashion, and exhibit the intrinsic isolation — the excruciating loneliness and goofy saintliness — of being human. He is a master of the brief lyric and fragmentary love poem, and at times expresses, consciously or otherwise, the sensibility of the enlightened Zenist in his death poems and their emphasis on the void. Knott often puns on his name: the *not*, the nothing, negative space, the distances between lovers. His deceptive, sometimes deadpan humor moves beyond self-deprecatory wit to confront the absence of love and to learn, if possible, how to live with it.

His quirky thought, surreal imagery, compressed language, and unyielding intensity reveal an eccentric and private personality attuned to and in correspondence with other wounded souls. His intuitive, Magritte-like juxtapositions are oddly affecting. Although some of Knott's more recent poems have become formidably dense, even obscure, in their pursuit of the rigorous purity of the sonnet, his work is "likely to endure," James Wright claimed, because his lyrics remain "among the most beautiful poems I have ever read in any language." John Logan was more succinct: "These poems give asylum to the orphan in each of us."

Poetry: *The Naomi Poems: Corpse and Beans* (1968). *Aurealism: A Study* (1970). *Are You Ready Mary Baker Eddy???*, with James Tate (1971). *Nights of Naomi* (1971). *Auto-Necrophilia* (1971). *Love Poems to Myself* (1974). *Rome in Rome* (1976). *Selected and Collected Poems* (1977). *For Anne and Other Poems* (1977). *Becos* (1983). *Poems: 1963–1983* (1989). *Outremer* (1989). *The Quicken Tree* (1995). *Laugh at the End of the World: Collected Comic Poems 1969–1999* (2000).

Prose: NOVEL: *Lucky Darryl*, with James Tate (1977).

YUSEF KOMUNYAKAA (1947)

Yusef Komunyakaa was born and raised in Bogalusa, Louisiana. After graduating from the University of Colorado, Colorado State University, and the University of California at Irvine, he held a fellowship in poetry at the Provincetown Fine Arts Work Center. Since 1985, he has taught creative writing and literature at Indiana University. His awards and distinctions include fellowships from the National Endowment for the Arts, the Thomas Forcade Award for Literature and Art Dedicated to the Healing of Vietnam in America, and the Pulitzer Prize.

From the primal experience of the African veldts where he speaks of having "eaten handfuls of fire / back to the bright sea / of my first breath . . ." to the German Third Reich that produced the "Nazi Doll" with a heart that hums "the song of dust / like a sweet beehive," from his childhood experiences as one of the boys wearing their mothers' clothes in afternoons that live in the republic of their bones, to the horror of the war in Vietnam where the cry "from the hills / belongs to a girl still burning / inside my head . . ." — history courses through the poetry of Yusef Komunyakaa like a great Nile of the imagination.

The aesthetics at work in Komunyakaa's poetry are not so much that of the Harlem Renaissance as that of the European Renaissance, which influenced American poetry down into the twentieth century. And this poet's strength in large part is his ability to couple a near mystical African-American superstition with a glimpse of a Wallace Stevens image of eleven black birds on a power line, "a luminous / message. . . ." He knows that poetry and its music are "a bridge, / more than a ledger of bones," that links Villon and Leadbelly. And he knows that the Muse with whom he sleeps is silence, "my impossible white wife." Thus, "the tongue even lies to itself, / gathering wildfire for songs of gibe."

Poetry: *Dedications and Other Darkhorses* (1977). *Lost in the Bonewheel Factory* (1979). *Copacetic* (1984). *Toys in a Field* (1986). *I Apologize for the Eyes in My Head* (1986). *February in Sydney* (1989). *Magic City* (1992). *Neon Vernacular: New and Selected Poems* (1993). *Thieves of Paradise* (1998). *Pleasure Dome: New and Collected Poems, 1975–1999* (1999).

Prose: *Blue Notes: Essays, Interviews, and Commentaries*, edited by Radiclani Clytus (2000).

MAXINE KUMIN (1925)

Maxine Kumin was born in Philadelphia and educated at Radcliffe. The author of several children's books (three of them written with Anne Sexton), she has taught at Tufts, the University of Massachusetts, and Princeton. An officer of the Radcliffe Institute's Society of Fellows, Kumin was awarded the Pulitzer Prize in 1973 for *Up Country*, and the Ruth Lilly Prize in 1999. She lives in rural New Hampshire, where she raises horses.

One of Kumin's critics has faulted her work for often being "the poetry of a special world, unmistakably upper middle-class, comfortable, urbane, safe in its place at the center of things." To suggest that such arenas of experience may not be legitimate or "worthy" concerns of poetry in this century and country is nonsense, of course. Besides, when Eliot posited his dictum, "Redeem the time," he didn't specify that it had to be an urban and industrial time fraught with its unique sets of psychic and physical terrors. Moreover, if Kumin's poetry does focus on the middle-class experience, like Louis Simpson she too is "taking part in a great experiment — / whether writers can live peacefully in the sub-urbs / and not be bored to death."

Kumin's personal experiment as a poet also has an edge of intensity that goes considerably beyond mere survival of boredom. Because of her powerful sense of observation and her masterful handling of technique, the objects and experiences of suburban life in Kumin's poetry assume a greater hum and buzz of emblematic implication of the direction of the human soul.

Consequently, the ordinary task of ridding one's garden of wood-chucks suggests a greater kind of historical extermination. Beneath the ostensible safety of suburban life lies the nightmare of a cleansing fire all inhabitants must pass through. No less important, one senses in Kumin's poetry a conscious urgency to discover in the natural world not only emblems of endurance, survival, and continuity but also momentary symbols of that more human longing for the possibility of transcendence. With remarkable grace and wit, the poems of Maxine Kumin do indeed redeem the personal and communal time and space in which she lives, in which most of us measure the worth of our lives.

Poetry: *Halfway* (1961). *The Privilege* (1965). *The Nightmare Factory* (1970). *Up Country* (1972). *House, Bridge, Fountain, Gate* (1975). *The Retrieval System* (1978). *Our Ground Time Here Will Be Brief: New and Selected Poems* (1982).

The Long Approach (1985). *Nurture: Poems* (1989). *Looking for Luck* (1992). *Connecting the Dots* (1996). *Selected Poems, 1960–1990* (1997).

Prose: ESSAYS: *To Make a Prairie: Essays on Poets, Poetry, and Country Living* (1979). *In Deep: Country Essays* (1988). *Always Beginning* (2000). FICTION: *Through Dooms of Love* (1965). *The Passions of Uxport* (1968). *The Abduction* (1971). *The Designated Heir* (1974). *Why Can't We Live Together Like Civilized Human Beings?* (1982). *Women, Animals, and Vegetables* (1994). *Quit Monks or Die!* (1999). MEMOIR: *Inside the Halo and Beyond* (2000).

STANLEY KUNITZ (1905)

Born in Worcester, Massachusetts, and educated at Harvard, Stanley Kunitz has taught at Bennington, Brandeis, Columbia, and Yale. He also has been a Cultural Exchange Scholar in the Soviet Union and Poland. From 1969 to 1976, he was editor of the Yale Series of Younger Poets; from 1974 to 1976, he served as Consultant in Poetry at the Library of Congress. The recipient of grants from the Guggenheim and Ford foundations, the Academy of American Poets, and the National Institute of Arts and Letters, he was awarded the Pulitzer Prize in 1959 and the National Book Award in 1995.

In addition to his moving translations of the poetry of Anna Akhmatova, Kunitz has been a major contributor to the many collections of translations of the poetry of Andrei Voznesensky and Yevgeny Yevtushenko that have appeared in this country. Moreover, since 1931, he has been one of the editors of eight major dictionaries of literary biographies.

After the publication of *The Testing-Tree* in 1971, Stanley Kunitz wrote, "I am no more reconciled than I ever was to the world's wrongs and the injustice of time." Among the wrongs and injustices present in Kunitz's poetry are the memories of a painful childhood that seemingly cannot be redeemed or reshaped; inevitable participation in the outrageous scientific and technological violence against the human spirit; and — despite the moments of beauty's hope — the inescapable promise of "a dusty finger on my lip."

Throughout his career, Kunitz's measure of emotional and moral energy has been further intensified by his equally passionate reverence for and use of form. In his poems, more than in the work of most poets of his generation, one senses that any experience or vision — regardless of how intense it might have been in itself — has consistently been forged by the white heat of a metaphysical sensibility. Thus Kunitz's poems have a physical presence and quality that are verbal equivalents of graceful sculptures forged out of the toughest metal — just as the works of certain contemporary metalsmiths are intricate sculptures of iron and steel that seem to be leaping toward pure sound.

Poetry: *Intellectual Things* (1930). *Passport to the War: A Selection of Poems* (1944). *Selected Poems 1928–1958* (1958). *The Testing-Tree: Poems* (1971). *The Lincoln Relics: A Poem* (1979). *The Poems of Stanley Kunitz 1928–1978* (1979). *The Wellfleet Whale and Companion Poems* (1983). *Next-to-Last Things: New Poems and Essays* (1985). *Passing Through: The Later Poems, New and Selected* (1995).

Prose: *A Kind of Order, a Kind of Folly: Essays and Conversations* (1975). *The Art of Poetry: Interviews with Stanley Kunitz* (1989).

Translations: *Poems of Akhmatova*, with M. Hayward (1973).

LI-YOUNG LEE (1957)

Li-Young Lee was born in Jakarta, Indonesia, of Chinese parents. In 1959, his father, after spending a year as a political prisoner in President Sukarno's jails, fled Indonesia with his family. Between 1959 and 1964 they traveled in Hong Kong, Macau, and Japan, until arriving in America. Li-Young Lee has studied at the University of Pittsburgh, the University of Arizona, and the State University of New York, College at Brockport. His many awards include fellowships from the Guggenheim and Whiting Foundations, and the National Endowment for the Arts, as well as awards from the Academy of American Poets and the Lannan Foundation.

Clearly one of the most gripping voices to have emerged in American poetry since the late 1980s, Li-Young Lee is also a master of modulation. While maintaining his unmistakable voice, he is capable of being lyrical ("My Indigo"), elegaic ("Eating Alone"), as well as meditative and religious ("This Room and Everything in It"); moreover, in a poem like "Persimmons," he becomes almost operatic in much the same way as Whitman. Lee can be gentle, reverential, passionate, and musical. And although he is first and foremost an American poet, his rich Asian experience and upbringing weave through his voice and poetry like a contrapuntal thread generating extraordinary harmony.

Family is at the heart of much of Lee's poetry: his mother and grandmother singing together "like young girls" and conjuring vivid images of Peking or the Summer Palace; his brother, "in heavy boots . . . walking / through bare rooms over my head . . . / what could he possibly need there in heaven?" And finally, his father, who is both the source of pain and his greatest inspiration; the father, who pulls "the metal splinter from my palm," which, seen from another viewpoint, "you would have thought you saw a man / planting something in a boy's palm, / a silver tear, a tiny flame." It is that tear and it is that flame which serve as tangible epiphanies of pain and light that lead him to affirm "you must sing to be found; when found, you must sing."

Poetry: *Rose* (1986). *The City in Which I Love You* (1990). *Book of My Nights* (2001).

Prose: *The Winged Seed* (1995).

DENISE LEVERTOV (1923–1997)

Born in Essex, England, Denise Levertov was privately educated, served as a nurse during World War II, and emigrated to the United States in 1948. She taught at Vassar, Drew, City College of New York, MIT, and at Tufts University. A scholar at the Radcliffe Institute for Independent Study, Levertov also received the Morton Dauwen Zabel Award, a fellowship from the Guggenheim Foundation, an award from the National Institute of Arts and Letters, and a distinguished Senior Fellowship from the National Endowment for the Arts.

Influenced by William Carlos Williams and the Black Mountain School — or simply their natural aesthetic compatriot — Denise Levertov wrote poems that are nevertheless charged by an unmistakably distinctive voice, capable of ranging from a tough to a tender lyricism that is proportionately intense. Her poems are not simply spoken by a woman; they fully explore and — with assurance, pleasure, or grief — celebrate the multifaceted experience of the contemporary woman. By so doing, they invite all of us into a celebration of the full range of human experience.

In an early interview Levertov said, "I believe in writing about what lies under the hand, in a sense. . . . Not necessarily in the visual world — the external world — it can be an inner experience — but it must be something true." And in one of her poems Levertov wrote, "The best work is made / from hard, strong materials, / obstinately precise. . . ." Her own poems repeatedly assert that the most obstinate and hard materials — even in that kind of natural lyrical poem she mastered — are not onyx and steel, but rather the small, at times elusive, materials of daily human life.

An antiwar poem such as "Life at War" affirms the inestimable power of the simple but sacred human gesture over "the gray filth" that can coat our dreams and drab the imagination. But so much of her work also reminds us that each new poem is that difficult and laborious Jacob's ladder between the facts of the diurnal and the bid for the eternal; each poem carves the physical details and quality of our daily communal experience in the unyielding onyx and steel of a cosmic history that would obliterate us.

Poetry: *The Double Image* (1946). *Here and Now* (1957). *Overland to the Islands* (1958). *With Eyes at the Back of Our Heads* (1959). *The Jacob's Ladder*

(1961). *O Taste and See: New Poems* (1964). *The Sorrow Dance* (1967). *A Tree Telling of Orpheus* (1968). *Relearning the Alphabet* (1970). *To Stay Alive* (1971). *Footprints* (1972). *The Freeing of the Dust* (1975). *Life in the Forest* (1978). *Collected Earlier Poems 1940–1960* (1979). *Candles in Babylon* (1982). *Denise Levertov: Poems 1960–1967* (1983). *Oblique Prayers* (1984). *Denise Levertov: Poems 1968–1972* (1987). *Breathing the Water* (1988). *A Door in the Hive* (1989). *Evening Train* (1992). *Sands of the Well* (1996). *The Life Around Us: Selected Poems on Ecological Themes* (1997). *The Stream and the Sapphire: Selected Poems on Religious Themes* (1999). *This Great Unknowing: Last Poems* (1999).

Prose: *The Poet in the World*, essays (1973). *Light Up the Cave*, essays (1981). *New & Selected Essays* (1992). *Denise Levertov: Selected Criticism* (1993). *Tesserae: Memories and Suppositions* (1995). *Conversations with Denise Levertov*, edited by J. S. Brooker (1998). *The Letters of Denise Levertov and William Carlos Williams* (1998).

Translations: *In Praise of Krishna: Songs from the Bengali*, with E. R. Dimmock, Jr. (1968). *Selected Poems of Guillevic* (1969). *Black Iris*, poems by Jean Joubert (1988).

PHILIP LEVINE (1928)

Philip Levine was born in Detroit. He received a B.A. and an M.A. from Wayne State University and an M.F.A. from the University of Iowa. Subsequently, he held a fellowship in poetry at Stanford University. From 1958 until his retirement he taught at California State University, Fresno. He has received grants from the National Endowment for the Arts, the National Institute of Arts and Letters, and the Guggenheim Foundation, and he has been awarded the National Book Award and the Pulitzer Prize.

Critics can't seem to agree on what Levine's central theme is. One says it's a "rogue's gallery of drunks, draft-dodgers, boxers, Hell's Angels, midgets, poor neighbors." Another asserts that his themes include "Hiroshima, the torture of Algerian prisoners, soldiers in eye-to-eye combat, generalized and brutal bigotry . . . man's cruelty to man." Still another critic argues that Levine's "fields of exploration" include "experiences which manifest themselves in irrational, dreamlike, fantastic or visionary forms." In fact, all these observations are true, for what is consistently striking about Levine's poetry is precisely his wide range of themes.

Levine himself has written, "I try to pay homage to the people who taught me my life was a holy thing, who convinced me that my formal education was a lie. . . . These people, both Black and white, were mainly rural people, and the horror of the modern world was clearer to them than to me, and the beauty and value of the world was something they knew in a way I did not, first hand." No less important in his poetry is the vital role of Levine's own sense of place — especially the bleak, dirty, and threatening industrial cityscape of Levine's childhood in Detroit; more recently one notes references to Levine's own personal life and background, especially members of his family.

Equally striking — although not immediately noticeable to the more casual reader — is Levine's mastery of a range of forms, from the most ostensible manipulation of tighter forms, through the freer lyric, to the more surrealistic and incantatory poems. Levine displays a seemingly contradictory range of emotional, moral, and often profoundly religious responses to the horror and beauty in the world around him — and inside us all.

Reading the body of Levine's work, one senses a fiercely honest exploration of the totality of a complex human life and a particular personality moving about the crucial arenas of our common experience. One also senses a complex, intense, and disciplined sensibility's response — in pity and in condemnation, in anger and in awe, in lamentation and in song — to the conflicting phenomena of contemporary life that offer us these choices: to sit on the father's shoulders and awaken in another world, to pray to become all we'll never be, or to offer ourselves as sacrificial animals in the slaughterhouse of a blasphemous industrial liturgy of annihilation. Philip Levine's answer to the last alternative continues to be a resounding "No. Not this pig."

Poetry: *On the Edge* (1963). *Silent in America: Vivas for Those Who Failed* (1965). *Not This Pig* (1968). *Five Detroits* (1970). *Pili's Wall* (1971). *Red Dust* (1971). *They Feed They Lion* (1972). *1933* (1974). *The Names of the Lost* (1976). *Ashes: Poems Old and New* (1979). *7 Years from Somewhere* (1979). *One for the Rose* (1981). *Selected Poems* (1984). *Sweet Will* (1985). *A Walk with Tom Jefferson* (1988). *What Work Is* (1991). *New Selected Poems* (1992). *The Simple Truth* (1994). *They Feed They Lion and The Names of the Lost* (1999). *The Mercy* (1999).

Prose: *Don't Ask*, essays (1981). *The Bread of Time: Toward an Autobiography* (1994).

Translations: *Tarumba: The Selected Poems of Jaime Sabines*, with E. Trejo (1979). *Off the Map: The Selected Poems of Gloria Fuertes*, with A. Long (1984).

JOHN LOGAN (1923–1987)

Born in Red Oak, Iowa, John Logan received a B.A. in zoology from Coe College, an M.A. in English from the University of Iowa, and did graduate work in philosophy at Georgetown, Notre Dame, and Berkeley. He taught at Notre Dame, San Francisco State, the University of Hawaii, and the State University of New York at Buffalo. Logan served as poetry editor for *The Nation*; he also founded and, with Aaron Siskind, edited *Choice* — a magazine of poetry and photography. He was the recipient of a Rockefeller grant, a Morton Dauwen Zabel Award from the National Institute of Arts and Letters, a Guggenheim Fellowship, a fellowship from the National Endowment for the Arts, and the Lenore Marshall Poetry Prize.

Perhaps because he began his career as a scientist, Logan's poems are constructed out of the most minute details observed from the world around him. Such lines as "I let the rain / move its audible little hands / gently on my skin" suggest the sensuousness of his language in response to the physical world. He lingers on things and the words for things, delighting in their sound and texture. In Logan's poetry, suffering neither negates the fact of beauty nor the possibility of celebration. Pain and guilt do not negate the alternatives of joy and grace. His poems repeatedly affirm that "there is a freshness / nothing can destroy in us / not even we ourselves."

Logan's work is distinguished from that of most personal-confessional poets by its lack of any self-flagellation. He spares us the leprous details of individual incidents of failure, deterioration, and guilt. If he asks his readers to be confessors, as he openly does in "Three Moves," he doesn't seek absolution for any given act or general Manichean sense of sin. Rather, he offers an exchange of that more human and grace-giving embrace of an accepting forgiveness of the guilt that is in each of us. And thus each of us readers becomes, as it were, Logan's anonymous lover.

The full organic development and structure of his poems, as well as the careful orchestration of tone, further distinguish Logan's work. At his best, his poems are utterly personal and natural, determined neither by structural, thematic, nor tonal formula. His poems succeed in sounding as natural as breathing; they begin simply and grow in intensity out of their own emotional necessity, as the breath of a man in battle or in love. Through a harmonious counterpoint of tones that reflect the varied inner strains of a total personality, these poems rise to — and are themselves — epiphanies. Rich mosaics of an integrated personality's experience of the human, illuminations of that range of music rising from the total self, the poems of John Logan are at once "unpredictable as grace" and "a ballet for the ear."

Poetry: *Cycle for Mother Cabrini* (1955; revised edition 1971). *Ghosts of the Heart* (1960). *Spring of the Thief: Poems 1960–1962* (1963). *The Thirty-three Ring Circus* (1964). *The Zig-Zag Walk: Poems 1963–1968* (1969). *The Anonymous Lover* (1973). *Poem in Progress* (1975). *John Logan / Poems / Aaron Siskind / Photographs* (1976). *The Bridge of Change: Poems 1974–1979* (1980). *Only the Dreamer Can Change the Dream: Selected Poems* (1981). *The Transformation:*

Poems January to March 1981 (1983). *John Logan: The Collected Poems* (1989). *The Poem as Relic* [uncollected poems], edited by M. Basinski (1989).

Prose: *The House That Jack Built; or, A Portrait of the Artist as a Sad Sensualist* (1974; revised edition, 1984). *A Ballet for the Ear: Interviews, Essays, and Reviews*, edited by A. Poulin, Jr. (1983). *John Logan: The Collected Fiction* (1991).

ROBERT LOWELL (1917–1977)

Born in Boston, Robert Lowell attended Harvard and graduated from Kenyon College. A conscientious objector during World War II, he spent several months in prison. He taught at various universities, including Harvard and the University of Iowa, and he served as Consultant in Poetry at the Library of Congress. His many awards included the Pulitzer Prize, the National Book Award, the Copernicus Award, and the Bollingen Poetry Translation Award.

Lowell's career seems to have evolved in three stages. His early poems, written under the tutelage of John Crowe Ransom and Allen Tate, were intricately wrought and complex, clearly reflecting the dictates of the New Criticism. Emerging out of a Christian spiritual tradition, an English poetic tradition influenced by the French symbolists, and a New England historical and ethical tradition, they were poems written by a young man whose sensibilities and talent began to mature at a time when T. S. Eliot was an overpowering presence in American poetry.

In *Life Studies* — perhaps his most brilliant and significant book, and the result of an encounter with W. D. Snodgrass — Lowell implicitly renounced many of the New Critics' formal demands and Eliot's cultural and spiritual vision. These poems were less consciously wrought and extremely intimate. As M. L. Rosenthal has observed, the orchestration of *Life Studies* traced the deterioration of Western civilization, the U.S. republic, Lowell's own family, and his very self. In the powerful concluding poem, "Skunk Hour," Lowell asserted, "The season's ill . . . / My mind's not right." And in this cultural and personal wasteland, he found no kingfisher, no Christ diving in fire.

"I am tired. Everyone's tired of my turmoil," Lowell wrote in *For the Union Dead*, and this realization marked the start of a third phase in his career. The poems grew more serenely formal, less intricate, and surely less hysterical. In *Near the Ocean*, he turned to muted couplets; his *Notebook* and *History*, though tracing intimate aspects of his life, were sonnet sequences. Although their central theme of the desolation and deterioration of humans and their world remained, Lowell was able to view that drama with a measure of objectivity, distance, and — at times — a detachment that bordered on ennui. In his last book, *Day by Day*,

Lowell returned once again to the lyrical and personal modes; however, despite the intimacy of subject matter, the poems continued to be marked by a kind of intellectual detachment.

Poetry: *Land of Unlikeness* (1944). *Lord Weary's Castle* (1946). *The Mills of the Kavanaughs* (1951). *Life Studies* (1959). *Imitations* (1961). *For the Union Dead* (1964). *The Old Glory,* verse drama (1965; expanded edition, 1968). *Near the Ocean* (1967). *Notebook 1967–1968* (1969). *Notebook* (augmented edition 1970). *For Lizzie and Harriet* (1973). *History* (1973). *The Dolphin* (1973). *Selected Poems* (1976). *Day by Day* (1977). *Collected Poems* (2000).

Prose: *Robert Lowell: Interviews and Memoirs,* edited by J. Myers (1987). *Collected Prose,* edited by Robert Giroux (1990).

Translations: POETRY: *The Voyage and Other Versions of Poems by Baudelaire* (1968). VERSE DRAMA: *Phaedra,* by Racine (1961). *Prometheus,* by Aeschylus (1969). *The Oresteia of Aeschylus* (1979).

WILLIAM MATTHEWS (1942–1997)

Born in Cincinnati, Ohio, William Matthews was a graduate of Yale University and the University of North Carolina at Chapel Hill. He began his teaching career at Wells College and subsequently taught at Cornell, the University of Colorado, the University of Washington, Columbia University, and City College of New York. Cofounding editor of Lillabulero Press and its magazine from 1966–1974, Matthews received grants and fellowships from the National Endowment for the Arts and the Guggenheim and Ingram Merrill foundations. In 1996 he was the recipient of the National Book Critics Circle Award, and in 1997 received the Modern Poetry Association's Ruth Lilly Award.

The fertile turmoil of the radical tradition in contemporary American poetry is fully alive in William Matthews's poems. Like the work of other poets whose first books appeared in the late 1960s and early 1970s, his early poems reflect both a direct and indirect involvement in the continuing aesthetic ferment of the time, wrestling with fundamental assumptions regarding the use of symbol, irony, and artistic detachment. Matthews's range of subjects and themes is as broad and challenging as the aesthetic and cultural strands that shaped his work. But whether the ostensible subject is basketball, onions, or hiking with his sons, a Matthews poem is always "about" much more. If "Men at My Father's Funeral" and "Grief" probe the source of the creative impulse, "the flesh made word," "Moving Again" and "The Cloister" question its purpose, its "fierce privacy." In the latter poem, Matthews quarrels with his muse and accepts the rigorous self-discipline and essential loneliness imposed upon any serious practitioner of the craft. "Pissing off the Back of the Boat in the Nivernais Canal" begins as a funny take on the drunken poet's penis, but draws the reader into a meditation on the relationship between penis and tongue as they concern sex and the artistic process; it is a poem about flesh and the imagination, and, ultimately, it is a poem about poetry itself.

If "Pissing off the Back of a Boat" affirms the inseparability of desire and linguistic creation in Matthews's poetry, it also signals his abiding search for profundity within humor and lightness at the core of the profound. Indeed, his poems consistently seek to unite perceived dualities. "Each emotion lusts for its opposite," Matthews wrote. Thus there is truth at the heart of fiction; excellence uncoils with a "sweet ferocity"; and, despite "death's old sweet song . . . / [a] relentless joy infests the blues all day."

Poetry: *Ruining the New Road* (1970). *Sleek for the Long Flight* (1972). *Sticks and Stones* (1975). *Rising and Falling* (1979). *Flood* (1982). *A Happy Childhood* (1984). *Foreseeable Futures* (1987). *Blues If You Want* (1989). *Selected Poems and Translations* (1992). *Time & Money* (1995). *After All: Last Poems* (1998).

Prose: *Curiosities*, essays (1989).

Translations: *A World Rich in Anniversaries*, prose poems by Jean Follain, with M. Feeney (1979). *The Mortal City: 100 Epigrams of Martial* (1995).

JAMES MERRILL (1926–1995)

James Merrill was born in New York City, the son of Charles Merrill, the founder of the Wall Street brokerage firm of Merrill Lynch. He attended Lawrenceville School, graduated from Amherst College, and served in the U.S. Army. Unlike most of his contemporaries, James Merrill did not seek a professional teaching career. His many awards and distinctions included the Pulitzer Prize, the National Book Award, and the Rebekah Bobbitt National Prize for Poetry awarded by the Library of Congress.

Most critics would agree that James Merrill's poetry has consistently reflected the influence of New Criticism and that his mentor is more likely W. H. Auden than William Carlos Williams. Indeed, in Merrill's long trilogy *The Changing Light at Sandover*, Auden's spirit is Merrill's "guide." Clearly, Merrill was a masterful formalist whose manipulation of metrics and of sound — especially end rhymes — revealed the range of startling and subtle nuances in language in much the same way as Rothko unveils the nuances of color in painting. Even in what seem to be more personal poems, one is never quite sure whether the speaker is Merrill or a persona. Most of his poems are marked by a tone edged with a measure of ironic detachment that, in some literary circles — where irony is blasphemy and guts rule — might be considered indicative of high, albeit elegant, decadence.

When so many poets of his generation lead their readers into the bedlam of their tortured souls and the bedrooms of their monstrous marriages — and, indeed, into their very own and much-used beds — one emerges from the surroundings of Merrill's poetry with the heady sense of having lingered in a rather rarefied atmosphere. (Indeed, as a son of Charles Merrill, the cofounder of the Merrill Lynch stock brokerage house, James Merrill was born into enormous wealth and privilege.) This is the physical, moral, and aesthetic world as perceived by Proust rather than by Baudelaire, by Henry James rather than by Walt Whitman. This is the world where, in Merrill's words, "Light into the olive entered / And was oil," an arena of human experience where it does seem that "the world beneath the world is brightening."

And yet, despite the seeming orderliness of his poems, Merrill's Weltanschauung and aesthetic often lead him — and us — to the very edge of chaos. Merrill's persona in "Laboratory Poem" knows that the heart must climb "through violence into exquisite disciplines." And whatever entrances into immortality that art may offer, it leaves us *and* the artist with that unnerving realization that "the life it asks of us is a dog's life." Thus, if poetry, if speech "is but a mouth pressed / Lightly and humbly against the angel's hand," in a Rilkean attempt to impress the angel with the things of this world, it's distinctly possible that this very angel "does not want even these few lines written." In short, in a society where "Art, Public Spirit / Ignorance, Economics, Love of Self / Hatred of Self" are earnestly dedicated to "*sparing* us the worst" and just as earnestly *inspire* the worst, Merrill's poems stand on the edge of chaos, radiant attempts to survive its meanings — and our own.

Poetry: *The Black Swan* (1946). *First Poems* (1951). *The Country of a Thousand Years of Peace and Other Poems* (1959; revised edition, 1970). *Water Street* (1962). *Nights and Days* (1966). *The Fire Screen* (1969). *Braving the Elements* (1972). *The Yellow Pages* (1974). *Divine Comedies* (1976). *Mirabell: Book of Numbers* (1978). *Scripts for a Pageant* (1980). *From the First Nine: Poems 1946–1976* (1982). *The Changing Light at Sandover* (1982). *Late Settings* (1985). *The Inner Room* (1988). *Selected Poems* (1992). *A Scattering of Salts* (1995).

Prose: FICTION: *The Seraglio* (1957). *The (Diblos) Notebook* (1965). ESSAYS: *Recitative: Prose*, edited and with an introduction by J. D. McClatchy (1986). AUTOBIOGRAPHY: *A Different Person: A Memoir* (1993).

W. S. MERWIN (1927)

W. S. Merwin was born in New York City and educated at Princeton. He was tutor to Robert Graves's son for a year, but — unlike most of his contemporaries — he has not had a teaching career. Since 1951 he has devoted most of his time to writing, to giving poetry readings, and to translating French, Spanish, Latin, Portuguese, Greek, Chinese, and Japanese writers. He has lived in the United States, England, Mexico, southern France, and currently resides in Hawaii. In addition to the Pulitzer Prize and the Shelley Memorial Award, he has received grants from the National Endowment for the Arts, the Rockefeller Foundation, the Academy of American Poets, the National Institute of Arts and Letters, and the Arts Council of Great Britain.

One of the most prolific poets and translators of his generation, Merwin is among those contemporary poets (others include James Wright and John Logan) whose talents were originally shaped by New Criticism and whose style underwent a radical change in the course of their career. His early poems were elegant, controlled, symmetrical, and often concerned with myth and archetype. However, the appearance of *The Drunk in the Furnace* suggested a dissatisfaction with old techniques: his forms were looser; his language appeared less contrived and closer to the spoken word. Like other poets of the period, he turned to family history and individual human suffering in search of larger, more immediate patterns of human experience.

Merwin's most radical departure — and most exciting style — appeared still later in *The Moving Target*. Open and terse, these surrealistic poems — and most of the poems that Merwin has published since — are controlled not as much by a craftsman's delicate hand as by a powerful imagination. And they rise out of the depths of a more personal, sometimes enigmatic necessity. Merwin's aesthetics are clear in the statement that he wrote for *Naked Poetry* (edited by Stephen Berg and Robert Mezey): "In an age when time and technique encroach hourly, or appear to, on the source itself of poetry, it seems as though what is needed for any particular nebulous hope that may become a poem is not a manipulable, more or less predictably recurring pattern, but an unduplicatable resonance, something that would be like an echo except that it is repeating no sound. Something that always belonged to it: its sense and its conformation before it entered words."

Throughout his career, one of Merwin's dominant concerns has been death — or perhaps more specifically, extinction. The journey motif that critics have recognized in Merwin's poetry is emblematic of all life's motion toward death. However, in later poems, this concern doesn't necessarily focus on any sudden or cataclysmic end of life — although many of his later poems are clearly laments for the destruction of our ecology and, thus, our society and culture. Rather, it is more manifest in powerful and menacing shadows surrounding frail light, in sound struggling against the tyranny of silence, in the slow but seemingly inevitable transformation of all organic life into inert matter. And if Merwin agrees with Berryman that the individual has undertaken the biggest job of all — *son fin* — Merwin has also erected a powerful emblem of his vision in his prose piece, "Tergvinder's Stone." In the presence of a mysterious, almost mystical stone in the middle of his living room and his life, Merwin's central character kneels in the darkness of the stone, converses with the stone, and even in the silence of the stone "knows that it is peace."

Poetry: *A Mask for Janus* (1952). *The Dancing Bears* (1954). *Green with Beasts* (1956). *The Drunk in the Furnace* (1960). *The Moving Target* (1963). *The Lice* (1967). *Animae: Poems* (1969). *The Carrier of Ladders* (1970). *Writings to an Unfinished Accompaniment* (1973). *The First Four Books of Poems* (1975). *The Compass Flower* (1977). *Finding the Islands* (1982). *Opening the Hand* (1983). *Selected Poems* (1988). *The Rain in the Trees* (1988). *Travels* (1993). *The Second Four Books of Poems* (1993). *The Vixen* (1995). *Flower & Hand: Poems 1977–1983: The Compass Flower: Opening the Hand: Feathers from the Hill* (1997). *Folding Cliffs: A Narrative* (1998). *The River Sound* (1999).

Prose: FICTION: *A New Right Arm* (1969). *The Miner's Pale Children* (1970). *Houses and Travellers* (1977). AUTOBIOGRAPHY: *Unframed Originals* (1982). ESSAYS: *Regions of Memory: Uncollected Prose 1949–1982*, edited by E. Folsom and C. Nelson (1987). *The Lost Upland* (1992).

Translations: POETRY: *The Poem of the Cid* (1959). *Spanish Ballads* (1961). *The Song of Roland* (1963). *Selected Translations 1948–1968* (1968). *Transparence of the World*, poems by Jean Follain (1969). *Voices*, poems by Antonio Porchia (1969/1988). *Twenty Love Poems and a Song of Despair*, by Pablo Neruda (1969). *Chinese Figures: Second Series* (1971). *Japanese Figures* (1971). *Asian Figures* (1973). *Selected Poems of Osip Mandelstam*, with C. Brown (1974). *Vertical Poetry*, by Roberto Juarroz (1977/1988). *Selected Translations 1968–1978* (1979). *The Peacock's Egg: Love Poems from Ancient India*, with J. M. Masson (1981). *From the Spanish Morning* (1985). *Sun at Midnight*, poems by Muso Soseki (1989). *Pieces of Shadow: Selected Poems of Jaime Sabines* (1996). *East Window: The Asian Translations* (1999). PROSE: *The Satires of Perseus* (1960). *The Life of Lazarillo de Tormes: His Fortunes and Adversities* (1962). *Products of the Perfected Civilization*, by Sebastian Chamfort (1969). DRAMA: *Iphigenia at Aulis*, by Euripides; with G. E. Dimmock, Jr. (1977). *Four French Plays* (1985).

MARILYN NELSON (1946)

Born in Cleveland, Ohio, Marilyn Nelson was educated at the University of California, Davis, the University of Pennsylvania, and the University of Minnesota. She has taught at Lane Comunity College (Oregon), the Norre Nissum Seminary Fellowship in Denmark, Saint Olaf College (Minnesota), and since 1978, the University of Connecticut. She has been the recipient of the Annisfield-Wolf Award and a fellowship from the National Endowment for the Arts.

A poet of domestic plenitude and spiritual bounty, Marilyn Nelson writes from the African-American literary tradition that acknowledges, without much bitterness, "the fact of oppression," and tempers rage with intergenerational love, humor, and religious sensibility. To her, "the body" represents community rather than the individual, and the self remains only an extension of that hub, that central "homeplace" from which the poet engages social and theological issues. Biblical allusions, family history, and folk wisdom intertwine in affirmative sequences that honor the past while deepening the present. "I had originally intended 'Mama' of my second book, *Mama's Promises* [1985], to be not only myself, my mother, and other mothers whose stories I snitched for the poems, but also the Divine Mother, the feminine face of God," she has stated. This movement outward from a central source toward communal imagination becomes a redemptive element not only in the lives of those embraced, but in the process that re-creates those lives. Nelson's third book, *The Homeplace* (1990), gives play to this idea of *elevation*, serving as an homage to her father and his comrades, the black World War II aviators known as the Tuskegee Airmen.

The "Abba Jacob" poems of *Magnificat* (1994) and *The Fields of Praise: New and Selected Poems* (1997) "imitate the format of the apothegms of the Desert Fathers, the earlier Christian monks," Nelson has noted, and their subject, the discipline required to approach spiritual wisdom, had been anticipated by the taut lines and nods to traditional forms — sonnets, villanelles, and ballads — that began to appear in her work in *The Homeplace*. Such discipline has its own requirements, though, and in poems that confront racial violence at home ("Boys in the Park" and "Minor Miracle") and abroad ("As Simple as That"), Nelson reconfigures her terms of affirmation in the light of "the atrocities we commit and bear," placing faith in the power of language, its incantatory and restorative spell: "*Justice* I willed myself *peace* to unknow / *conscience* the evil I saw *dignity* / pinpricked in her *faith* blue *humanity* eyes."

Poetry: *For the Body* (1978). *Mama's Promises* (1985). *The Homeplace* (1990). *Magnificat* (1994). *The Fields of Praise: New and Selected Poems* (1997). *Carver: A Life in Poems* (2000).

Other: *Hundreds of Hens and Other Poems for Children by Halfdan Rasmussed*, translated from the Danish with Pamela Espeland (1982). *The Cat Walked Through the Casserole and Other Poems for Children*, with Pamela Espeland (1984).

NAOMI SHIHAB NYE (1952)

Naomi Shihab Nye, born of a Palestinian father and an American mother, grew up in St. Louis, Missouri, Jerusalem, and San Antonio, Texas, graduating from Trinity University in 1974. Nye has worked as a writer-in-the-schools for the past twenty-six years across the country and also has been a visiting writer at a wide variety of universities, including Berkeley and Hawaii. She has participated in three Arts America tours in the Middle East and Asia, and her awards include the I. B. Lavin Award from the Academy of American Poets and a Guggenheim Fellowship.

A friend and informal student of William Stafford, Naomi Nye probes that vein of poetry unearthed by Stafford. Hers is a quiet, gentle voice that can celebrate the beauty of such simple items as melons, bananas, and peppers through which she can learn the "secrets of dying, / how to do it gracefully . . . softening in silence . . . / finely tuned to its own skin." Nye understands that even in the life of the imagination and deeper into the life of memories, therefore history, the dust-covered things of this and other worlds "have only to be touched lightly / to shine."

Her middle-eastern heritage is also vibrant in her poems. It is the texture of experience: her father balancing a tray of coffee which becomes the center of the flower of guests. It is the source of anguish and her understanding of it, "the man with laughing eyes" who reminds her, "until you speak Arabic — / you will not understand pain." And what seems to be a somewhat simplified view of experience turns into epiphany when she goes out into the slick street to hail a cab "by shouting *Pain!* and it stopped / in every language." Her faith in such consolation, the "Vocabulary of Dearness," remains evident throughout her work. In "Steps," the "thick swoops and curls of [newly painted] Arabic letters stay moist / and glistening till tomorrow when the children show up," and it's "One of these children [who] will tell a story that keeps her people / alive."

Poetry: *Different Ways to Pray* (1980). *Hugging the Jukebox* (1982). *The Yellow Glove* (1986). *Red Suitcase* (1994). *Words Under the Words: Selected Poems* (1995). *Fuel* (1998).

Prose: PARAGRAPHS: *Mint* (1991). ESSAYS: *Never in a Hurry* (1996).

FRANK O'HARA (1926–1966)

Before his untimely, accidental death on Fire Island, Frank O'Hara was associate curator and then curator of the international program at the Museum of Modern Art in New York and an editorial associate for *Art News*. Born in Baltimore, O'Hara was educated at the New England Conservatory of Music, Harvard, and the University of Michigan. He collaborated in various projects involving poetry and the visual arts, and in 1956 was awarded a Ford Fellowship for drama.

Before the publication of his *Collected Poems* (and the companion volume, *Poems Retrieved*), O'Hara was almost a closet poet, the product and hero of a pop-camp imagination whose seeming antipoems were often light and chatty, marked by a spontaneity, exuberance, and wit that were characteristic of his contemporaries in the visual arts. His most memorable poems, like the paintings of Oldenburg and Warhol, focused on the all-too-obvious things of our urban and suburban world: hamburgers, malts, cigarettes, instant coffee. Looming above that world were its own godly artifacts: Lichtenstein's suprahuman heroes of the comic strips and Warhol's movie stars. Their mythic proportions were — and continue to be — the dimensions of contemporary human fantasies and dreams of redemption. Moreover, in O'Hara's poems there is the stinging, if somewhat hysterical, crackle of a melancholy comment on the absurdity of such hollow rites.

It now seems clear that O'Hara's scope and power as a poet extend far beyond the circumscribed world of a merely campy and gay subculture. One leaves the body of O'Hara's poetry — and his sense of what constitutes the identifiable substance and quality of our communal experience — with a verbal-emotional equivalent of Kandinsky's acute perception of "the particular spiritual perfume of the triangle." One also leaves the existential world of O'Hara's poems with a fuller understanding of the truth of Cocteau's rejection of history: "*J'ai une tres mauvaise memoire de l'avenir.*"

Poetry: *A City Winter and Other Poems* (1952). *Meditations in an Emergency* (1957). *Hartigan and Rivers with O'Hara: An Exhibition of Pictures, with Poems* (1959). *Second Avenue* (1960). *Odes* (1960). *Lunch Poems* (1964). *Love Poems: Tentative Title* (1965). *In Memory of My Feelings: A Selection of Poems*, edited by B. Berkson (1967). *Odes* (1969). *The Collected Poems of Frank O'Hara*, edited by D. Allen (1971). *The Selected Poems of Frank O'Hara*, edited by D. Allen (1974). *Hymns of St. Bridget*, with Bill Berkson (1974). *Early Poems 1946–1951*, edited by D. Allen (1976). *Poems Retrieved*, edited by D. Allen (1977). *To Be True to a City*, edited by Jim Elledge (1990).

Prose: *Jackson Pollock* (1959). *A Frank O'Hara Miscellany* (1974). *Art Chronicles 1954–1966* (1975). *Standing Still and Walking in New York*, notes and essays, edited by D. Allen (1975). *Early Writing*, edited by D. Allen (1977). *Selected Plays* (1978).

SHARON OLDS (1942)

Born in San Francisco in 1942, Sharon Olds was educated at Stanford University and Columbia University. Her first book, *Satan Says* (1980), was the recipient of the inaugural San Francisco Poetry Center Award, and her second, *The Dead and the Living* (1984), received both the Lamont Prize from the Academy of American Poets and the National Book Critics Circle Award. She has received fellowships from the

Guggenheim Foundation and the National Endowment for the Arts. Olds teaches at New York University and at Goldwater Hospital on Roosevelt Island in New York.

Critics have commented on the influence of Sylvia Plath's poems on Olds's work, and certainly Olds has written in the Confessional mode, though the author and her narrators should not be confused. Whoever speaks them, her poems have a startling power and urgency, even a breathlessness, as if any momentary hesitation on the speaker's part, any self-censorship, would inhibit the work and disallow its existence. Her narrative thrust seems unable to restrain itself and often suits the brutal revelations of the poems. Richard Wilbur has described Plath's work, her "brilliant negative," as "free and helpless and unjust," suggesting that Plath writes out of only one aspect of personality, and such description might apply to some of Olds's work as well. Yet Olds's insistence on formerly taboo subjects, her intensely personal emphases and erotic self-absorption, convey a politics, sexual and otherwise, that opens her poems to a more inclusive perspective.

Her subject is the body and the space it inhabits, as well as the violations of that space. For Olds, the body offers a defining sense of self against the father's psychological abuse, and becomes, like language, a source of cathartic pleasure, a means of escape from domestic dysfunction. Her sexual imagery and blunt, at times vulgar, vocabulary preserve an essential privacy by claiming selfhood, and allow love to evolve despite its history of lack. Her poems for her children, especially, display a disarming vulnerability that extends from the "egg in my side before I was born" to the larger, communal body of frailty and ceaseless regeneration.

Poetry: *Satan Says* (1980). *The Dead and the Living* (1984). *The Gold Cell* (1987). *The Father* (1992). *The Wellspring* (1995). *Blood, Tin, Straw* (1999).

CARL PHILLIPS (1959)

Born in Everett, Washington, Carl Phillips attended Harvard, the University of Massachusetts at Amherst, and Harvard again to study classical philology, before pursuing an advanced degree in creative writing at Boston University. "I consider the study of Classics to have been the most significant influence on my writing," he has stated. "I believe I learned most about poetry from reading — in the original Latin and Greek — the political speeches of Cicero and those that occur in the historical writings of Thucydides, respectively." He has been the recipient of the Morse Poetry Prize for his first volume, *In the Blood* (1992), an Academy of American Poets Prize, and fellowships from the Library of

Congress and Guggenheim Foundation. Phillips taught high school Latin for eight years and, more recently, has taught at Harvard and at Washington University in St. Louis.

In an interview with Charles H. Rowell in *Callaloo*, Carl Phillips names his subjects: "hunger, loss, devotion" and "the nature of desire." Avoiding traditional narrative and conventional syntax, he trusts instead intuition and its associative imagery, combined with densely textured phrases, to convey an erotic and spiritual intellect in the flux of ceaseless self-examination. Oddly Puritan in measure and restraint, austere enough in language so that each word bears its particular weight, his poems seem hushed and reverential, barely spoken, the hesitant shifts of the mind given utterance and eloquence. "I think of writing as prayer," Phillips told Rowell, then added, "And sex is also prayer." This sexual element in his work, homoerotic and coolly passionate, infuses his philosophical musings with moral urgency: "the yearnings of the body," Phillips told David Dykes in *Excerpt*, "can serve as metaphors or parallels for the yearnings of the soul." In unassuming yet profoundly moving meditations on hunger for man and God, loss of human love and heavenly dispensation, and devotion to the sacraments of desire, Phillips delineates those planes where the profane and sacred intersect in numinous coupling.

Poetry: *In the Blood* (1992). *Cortege* (1995). *From the Devotions* (1998). *Pastoral* (2000). *The Tether* (2001).

SYLVIA PLATH (1932–1963)

A native of Boston and a graduate of Smith College, in 1955 Sylvia Plath won a Fulbright Scholarship to Newnham College, Cambridge. While in England, she met and married the British poet Ted Hughes. After she taught for a year at Smith (1957–1958), the couple returned to England where in 1960 she published her first book of poems and subsequently completed her novel, *The Bell Jar.* On February 11, 1963, Sylvia Plath committed suicide.

A friend of Anne Sexton and student of Robert Lowell, Sylvia Plath wrote poems that were intended to sound and to feel brutally personal, almost unbearably painful. Her poems are not merely *about* acute mental and emotional suffering; their very structure — the controlled flow of images, the insistent appositives — draws the reader fully into that suffering. Indeed, her later poems are so well crafted that some critics have argued, wrongheadedly, that she seemed engaged in "a murderous art" — that after writing such frighteningly honest and painfully personal poems, her suicide was virtually inevitable. As a *critical premise,* such an argument is utter nonsense, its absurdity manifestly clear when transferred to another artist and to his or her work. If Plath virtually had no choice but to commit suicide after writing the poems in *Ariel*, then what inevitable choice did Melville have after writing *Moby Dick*?

What makes Plath interesting as a poet is not primarily her ostensible subject matter and tone; rather, the success of the poems depends largely on her precision of observation, imagination, and language — as well as on the mastery of her craftsmanship. For example, the onion simile in "Cut" not only accurately describes the swirls of a thumb print but also serves as the entire poem's controlling metaphor. Moreover, in such poems as "Cut" and "Lady Lazarus," or even in a celebrated poem such as "Daddy," there is also a strong measure of wit and humor — albeit black — often conveyed through resuscitated clichés that manage to rescue the poems from pathos.

On more than one occasion, Plath insisted that even the most personal poetry cannot be merely a *cri de coeur*; it must be informed by and participate in a greater historical drama. Her own poems participate fully in the vibrant Puritan tradition, not only through her preoccupation with evil (which is utterly distinct from personal suffering) but also through her metaphysical and emblematic technique. They also occur against a constant historical drama, especially the contemporary phenomenon of Nazi Germany out of which she fabricates a modern myth. In short, the pain, the suffering, the fine edge of madness — all are ultimately crafted and controlled by the poet's reasoned and careful hand flashing a measure of genius.

Poetry: *The Colossus* (1962). *Uncollected Poems* (1965). *Ariel* (1966). *Crossing the Water: Transitional Poems* (1971). *Crystal Gazer and Other Poems* (1971). *Lyonesse: Poems* (1971). *Winter Trees* (1972). *The Collected Poems of Sylvia Plath*, edited by T. Hughes (1981). *Stings*, original drafts of the poem in facsimile, with an essay by S. R. Van Dyne (1982). *The Voice of the Poet*, edited by J. D. McClatchy (1999).

Prose: *The Bell Jar*, novel (under the pseudonym Victoria Lucas, 1963; under the name Sylvia Plath, 1971). *Letters Home*, edited by A. Plath (1975). *Johnny Panic and the Bible of Dreams: Short Stories, Prose, and Diary Excerpts*, edited by T. Hughes (1979). *The Journals of Sylvia Plath*, edited by T. Hughes and F. McCullough (1982).

ADRIENNE RICH (1929)

Adrienne Rich's first book of poems won the Yale Series of Younger Poets award while she was an undergraduate at Radcliffe. She has taught at Brandeis, Swarthmore, Harvard, and Columbia, and her many honors include the Dorothea Tanning Prize for "mastery in the art of poetry" from the Academy of American Poets, the MacArthur Fellowship, the Ruth Lilly Poetry Prize, and the Poets' Prize. In 1974 Rich and Allen Ginsberg were cowinners of the National Book Award for poetry. Rich rejected her share as a personal award, but in a statement she wrote with the two other women nominated that year, she accepted the award in the name of all women. In 1997 she declined the National Medal for the Arts. Rich's letter, reprinted in the *New York Times*, stated: "I could not accept such an award from President Clinton or this White House because the very meaning of art, as I understand it, is incompatible with the cynical politics of this administration. . . . [A]rt means nothing if it simply decorates the dinner-table of power which holds it hostage. The radical disparities of wealth and power in America are widening at a devastating rate. A President cannot meaningfully honor certain token artists while the people at large are so dishonored."

Adrienne Rich has described her poems written since the late 1970s as "a coming-home to the darkest and richest source of my poetry: sex, sexuality, sexual wounds, sexual identity, sexual politics: many names for pieces of one whole. I feel [this poetry] continues the work I've been trying to do — breaking down the artificial barriers between private and public, between Vietnam and the lovers' bed, between the deepest images we carry out of our dreams and the most daylight events 'out in the world.' This is the intention and longing behind everything I write."

Sexual identity and its profound political implications are indeed among the substantial sources of Rich's more recent work, especially in her courageous and beautiful sequence of love poems addressed to another woman — a theme that reappears in *The Dream of a Common Language*. Moreover, even as she speaks about and for women, her poetry is informed by a vigorous intelligence that transcends any unilateral sense of sexuality and politics; her poetry reaches beyond the limited periphery of any "movement" to become at once a profoundly personal statement forged into a powerful description of our common condition.

If some of Rich's poems can be read as a "diving into the wreck," it is crucial to realize that her purpose is not only "to see the damage that was done" but also to catch a glimpse of "the treasures that prevail." Like the astronomer in "Planetarium," she is "a woman trying to translate pulsations / into images," not only for their own sake, not only for her own sake, but "for the relief of the body / and the reconstruction of the mind." Meanwhile, having found the courage to utter, "I choose to love this time for once / with all my intelligence," she also can assert and demonstrate *"a whole new poetry beginning here."*

Poetry: *A Change of World* (1951). *The Diamond Cutters* (1955). *Snapshots of a Daughter-in-Law: Poems 1954–1962* (1963; revised edition, 1967). *Necessities of Life: Poems 1962–1965* (1966). *Leaflets: Poems 1965–1968* (1969). *The Will to Change: Poems 1968–1970* (1971). *Diving into the Wreck: Poems 1971–1972*

(1973). *Poems: Selected and New, 1950–1974* (1975). *Twenty-one Love Poems* (1976). *The Dream of a Common Language: Poems 1974–1977* (1978). *A Wild Patience Has Taken Me This Far: Poems 1978–1981* (1981). *Sources* (1983). *The Fact of a Doorframe: Poems Selected and New 1950–1984* (1985). *Your Native Land, Your Life* (1986). *Time's Power: Poems 1985–1988* (1989). *An Atlas of the Difficult World: Poems 1988–1991* (1991). *Collected Early Poems* (1993). *Dark Fields of the Republic: Poems 1991–1995* (1995). *Midnight Salvage: Poems 1995–1998* (1999).

Prose: *Of Woman Born: Motherhood as Experience and Institution* (1976). *On Lies, Secrets and Silence: Selected Prose 1966–1978* (1979). *Compulsory Heterosexuality and Lesbian Experience* (1982). *Women and Honor: Some Notes on Lying* (1982). *Blood, Bread, and Poetry: Selected Prose 1979–1985* (1986). *What Is Found There* (1993).

ANNE SEXTON (1928–1974)

Anne Sexton was born in Newton, Massachusetts. According to the short autobiographical note she wrote for *A Controversy of Poets* (1965), Anne Sexton received "no visible education." However, with Sylvia Plath and George Starbuck, she did attend seminars by Robert Lowell at Boston University; she participated in a summer seminar taught by W. D. Snodgrass at Antioch College; and she was a scholar at the Radcliffe Institute. In addition to her several books of poetry, she wrote three children's books with Maxine Kumin. Her many awards included fellowships from the American Academy of Arts and Letters, the Radcliffe Institute, and the Ford Foundation; she was awarded the Pulitzer Prize; and was elected a fellow of the Royal Society of Literature in London. On October 4, 1974, Anne Sexton committed suicide.

Possibly the most famous of the personal-confessional poets, Anne Sexton also probably confessed to more than any of her contemporaries, re-creating experiences with unabashed, almost embarrassing honesty. Indeed, it is also probable that she "confessed" to a number of events that she simply invented. In "With Mercy for the Greedy" she wrote, "I was born / doing reference work in sin, and born / confessing it." Like other confessional Puritans, she did just that. But in various interviews, she also insisted that poetry is as much fabrication as it is confession — that even the most brutal truth is shaped by imagination's energy and the artisan's hand. Moreover, doing research in sin, by necessity, must involve a commensurate search for grace, for God. That combination, for Sexton, was absolute — and as risky as Russian roulette.

When it wasn't yet fashionable for women to write poems about being a woman, Sexton wrote them — openly, unashamedly, and without resorting to political rhetoric. She knew all along that the victimized woman is "misunderstood" and "not a woman, quite." But, like Hester

Prynne, the first liberated woman in American literature, Sexton also knew that a relationship between a man and woman could make them gods. And she knew that she could be the ultimate survivor: "A woman like that is not ashamed to die."

Like Sylvia Plath and John Berryman, Anne Sexton chose the moment of her death. But before doing so — as Maxine Kumin has reported — she found the signs of grace and hope spelled out on her typewriter keys. Sexton knew full well that, regardless of how painful it might seem, each poem is an affirmation and celebration of life — as is all poetry.

Poetry: *To Bedlam and Part Way Back* (1960). *All My Pretty Ones* (1962). *Live or Die* (1966). *Love Poems* (1969). *Transformations* (1971). *The Book of Folly* (1972). *The Death Notebooks* (1974). *The Awful Rowing Toward God* (1975). *45 Mercy Street*, edited by L. G. Sexton (1976). *Words for Dr. Y: Uncollected Poems with Three Stories*, edited by L. G. Sexton (1978). *Anne Sexton: The Complete Poems*, edited by L. G. Sexton, with a foreword by M. Kumin (1981). *Selected Poems of Anne Sexton*, edited with an introduction by D. W. Middlebrook and D. H. George (1988).

Prose: *Anne Sexton: A Self-Portrait in Letters*, edited by L. G. Sexton and L. Ames (1977). *No Evil Star: Selected Essays, Interviews, Prose*, edited by S. E. Colburn (1985).

CHARLES SIMIC (1938)

Charles Simic was born in Belgrade, Yugoslavia, raised in Paris, Chicago, and New York City, and received a B.A. from New York University. He has worked as a bookkeeper, accountant, house painter, and shirt salesman; he served in the U.S. Army from 1961 to 1963; and he has taught at California State University at Hayward. Since 1973 he has been teaching at the University of New Hampshire. He has received several PEN Translation Awards, fellowships from the National Endowment for the Arts and the Guggenheim, Ingram Merrill, and MacArthur foundations, and the Pulitzer Prize for Poetry.

Charles Simic has described himself as "a realist *and* a surrealist, always drawn between the two." Thus, for some readers, reading Simic's poetry for the first time may be a little like walking into a landscape designed by Salvador Dali ("a meadow / Where the grass was silence / And the flowers / Words") and populated by Hieronymous Bosch ("Grandmothers who wring the necks / Of chickens; old nuns . . . / Who pull schoolboys by the ear"). This rare combination may be partly accounted for by Simic's childhood and early adolescence in wartime Yugoslavia — where, in his own words, "Hitler and Stalin fought over my soul, my destiny . . ." and his essential imagination was shaped — and by his education in the United States, where he learned the first literature he knew, American literature. Whatever the reasons, clearly this is not the realism of high seriousness found in the poetry of someone like Robert Lowell; neither is it the kind of stark and dark surrealism found in the work of poets like Mark Strand. Rather, throughout Simic's poetry, even in scenes that are emotionally devastating, there are almost always threads of humor, ranging from ironic, sophisticated wit to cunning peasant wit.

Moreover, in Simic's world, where old women sniff the air for snow and silence is some enormous animal to be dismantled, the real and the surreal coexist and have value primarily as image and substance and not as idea and abstraction. In "A Letter," a friend insists, "'We reach the real by overcoming the seduction of images.'" Simic answers, "Such abstinence will never be possible for me," because "trees with an infinity of tragic shapes / ... make thinking difficult." Perhaps that accounts for the seemingly total absence of the pursuit of transcendence in his work. For Simic, salvation, as it were, is "To breakfast on slices of watermelon / In the company of naked gods and goddesses / On a patch of last night's snow."

Simic's persistent humor (which may suggest a sense of the absurdity of human existence, as in Beckett's play, *Waiting for Godot*) and the absence of traditional transcendence (which might suggest the commensurate absence of spirituality) do not preclude a profound moral commitment. In "Poem Without a Title," he laments the consequences of industrial technology: "I say to the lead / Why did you let yourself / Be cast into a bullet?" "Fear" speaks of the nameless dread inherent in the human condition. "I believe in the soul," Simic insists in "The Old World"; "so far / It hasn't made much difference."

The great themes of literature are all present in Charles Simic's work, but they are incarnate in the images of the simple and the small. It is the drama of a life found in a bit of thread; it is the sudden discovery of a poem not when the poet looks up at the sky, but when he bends over to tie his shoes and looks into the earth. It is to stare steadily into the small pieces of this fractured world, "So that briefly, in that one spell, / Your heartache hushes at the beauty of it."

Poetry: *What the Grass Says* (1967). *Somewhere Among Us a Stone Is Taking Notes* (1969). *Dismantling the Silence* (1971). *Return to a Place Lit by a Glass of Milk* (1974). *Charon's Cosmology* (1977). *Classic Ballroom Dances* (1980). *Austerities* (1982). *Weather Forecast for Utopia and Vicinity* (1983). *Selected Poems 1963–1983* (1985). *Unending Blues* (1986). *The World Doesn't End* (1989). *Selected Poems 1963–1983* (revised and expanded edition, 1990). *The Book of Gods and Devils* (1990). *Hotel Insomnia* (1992). *A Wedding in Hell* (1994). *Walking the Black Cat* (1996). *Jackstraws* (1999). *Selected Early Poems* (1999).

Prose: *The Uncertain Certainty,* essays (1986). *Wonderful Words, Silent Truth,* essays (1990). *Dimestore Alchemy (The Art of Joseph Cornell)* (1992). *The Unemployed Fortune-Teller: Essays & Memoirs* (1994). *Orphan Factory: Essays and Memoirs* (1998).

Translations: POETRY: *Fire Gardens,* by Ivan V. Lalic, with C. W. Truesdale (1970). *The Little Box,* by Vasko Popa (1970). *Four Modern Yugoslav Poets* (1970). *Homage to the Lame Wolf,* by Vasko Popa (1979; expanded edition, 1987). *Atlantis,* by Salvko Mihalic, with P. Kastmiler (1987). *Selected Poems of Tomaz Salamun* (1988). *Roll Call of Mirrors,* selected poems of Ivan V. Lalic (1987). *Some Other Wine and Light,* by Aleksandar Ristovic (1989). *The Bandit Wind,* by Slavko Janevski (1991). *Night Mail: Selected Poems,* by Nicola Tadic (1992). *Devil's Lunch: Selected Poems,* by Aleksandar Ristovic (2000).

LOUIS SIMPSON (1923)

Educated at Munro College (Jamaica, West Indies) and at Columbia, where he received his doctorate, Louis Simpson has taught at Columbia, the University of California at Berkeley, and at the State University of New York at Stony Brook. With Donald Hall and Robert Pack, he edited the celebrated anthology *New Poets of England and America* (1957) and he is the author and editor of the textbook *An Introduction to Poetry* (1968). He has received the Rome Fellowship of the American Academy of Arts and Letters, a *Hudson Review* Fellowship, a Guggenheim Foundation fellowship, and the Pulitzer Prize.

Like many other poets of his generation, Simpson began his poetic career as a formalist and gradually worked toward a verse in which content primarily determines form. In the process, his own language has become increasingly natural and closer to the colloquial idiom of American speech — a language "closely related to the language in which men actually think and speak." At the same time, both his language and his view of the American experience — the root source of much of his poetry — have retained an educated and literate edge that inform his poems with a fully conscious sense of history and tradition.

Reading Simpson's poetry, one might be reminded of Robert Frost's famous aphorism about his lover's-quarrel with the world. No less a lover, Simpson quarrels, more specifically, with America. It is an ongoing struggle to come to grips with the pathetic or tragic failure of the American dream and myth — especially as announced by Whitman. "Where are you, Walt? / The Open Road goes to the used-car lot," he says in "Walt Whitman at Bear Mountain." The open road also leads to the suburbs where, it seems, "You were born to waste your life." Yet it is in the daily routines of suburban living — driving to the mall, walking the dog, taking out the trash — that Simpson insists on looking for some semblance of a peculiarly American spiritual and intellectual life.

Poetry: *The Arrivistes: Poems 1940–1949* (1949). *Good News of Death and Other Poems*, in *Poets of Today II*, with Norma Faber and Robert Pack (1955). *A Dream of Governors* (1959). *At the End of the Open Road* (1963). *Selected Poems* (1965). *Adventures of the Letter I* (1971). *Searching for the Ox* (1976). *Armidale* (1980). *Caviare at the Funeral* (1980). *The Best Hour of the Night* (1983). *People Live Here: Selected Poems 1949–1983* (1983). *Collected Poems* (1988). *In the Room We Share* (1990). *There You Are* (1995).

Prose: *James Hogg: A Critical Study* (1962). *Riverside Drive*, a novel (1962). *North of Jamaica*, autobiography (1972). *Three on the Tower: The Lives and Works of Ezra Pound, T. S. Eliot and William Carlos Williams* (1975). *A Revolution in Taste: Studies of Dylan Thomas, Allen Ginsberg, Sylvia Plath and Robert Lowell* (1978). *A Company of Poets* (1981). *The Character of the Poet* (1986). *Selected Prose*, autobiography, fiction, literary criticism (1989). *The King My Father's Wreck*, autobiography (1994). *Ships Going into the Blue* (1995).

Translation: *Modern Poets of France* (1997).

W. D. SNODGRASS (1926)

Born in Wilkinsburg, Pennsylvania, and educated at Geneva College and at the University of Iowa, W. D. Snodgrass has taught at the University of Rochester, Wayne State, Syracuse, Old Dominion, and the University of Delaware. He has received fellowships from the Guggenheim and Ingram Merrill foundations, the Academy of American Poets, the National Institute of Arts and Letters, and the National Endowment for the Arts. His first book of poems won the Pulitzer Prize in 1960.

Until the late 1970s, Snodgrass was known primarily as a personal-confessional poet; indeed, he, rather than Robert Lowell, was probably responsible for the emergence of that mode of poetry in the late 1950s and early 1960s. Unlike Lowell, Plath, and Sexton, Snodgrass made poetry not out of madness and sensationally violent suffering but rather out of the daily neuroses and everyday failures of a man — a husband, father, and teacher. Snodgrass also saw such domestic suffering as occurring against a backdrop of a more universal suffering inherent in the whole of human experience. In *Heart's Needle*, he stated *and* demonstrated, "We need the landscape to repeat us." Snodgrass also shared that fundamental concern of his generation announced by Albert Camus: "There is but one truly serious philosophical problem, and that is suicide." In "April Inventory," he wrote, "I have not learned how often I / Can win, can love, but choose to die."

Although noted for their candor, Snodgrass's early poems were also controlled by an unmistakable sense of irony, directed by a highly literate imagination shaped by the New Critics, and organized by a consciously formal craftsmanship. Consequently, Snodgrass achieves a good measure of distance between himself as subject and himself as poem;

thus the speaker of a "personal" Snodgrass poem often sounds more like a personal-confessional "persona."

In any case, little in Snodgrass's early poetry foreshadowed the appearance of *The Führer Bunker*. A cycle of dramatic monologues, these poems are spoken by leading figures of the Nazi regime during the last days of the Third Reich — including Albert Speer, Martin Bormann, Joseph Goebbels, Magda Goebbels, Eva Braun, and Adolf Hitler. Displaying an even more powerful range of dazzling craftsmanship in *The Führer Bunker* — which unfolds like a modern-day *Inferno* — Snodgrass zeros in on the historical and moral landscape that modern humankind seems intent or fated to repeat. The power and the horror of this cycle do not depend on what Snodgrass has to say about the historical figures and events *per se*; he knows all too well that there is little that can be said. Rather, the emotional and moral impact of this cycle emerges out of the fact that, like the dark and suffering creatures Dante encountered in hell, the personages in this Nazi *Götterdämmerung* are not the monsters we have met in the history books. They are all too recognizable, all too human.

Poetry: *Heart's Needle* (1959). *After Experience* (1967). *Remains* (under the pseudonym S. S. Gardons, 1970; revised edition under the name W. D. Snodgrass, with a foreword by A. Poulin, Jr., 1985). *The Führer Bunker: A Cycle of Poems in Progress* (1977). *If Birds Build with Your Hair* (1979). *The Boy Made of Meat* (1983). *A Locked House* (1986). *Selected Poems: 1957–1987* (1987). *W. D.'s Midnight Carnival*, in collaboration with the painter DeLoss McGraw (1988). *The Death of Cock Robin*, in collaboration with the painter DeLoss McGraw (1989). *Each in His Own Season* (1993). *The Führer Bunker: The Complete Cycle* (1995). *De-Compositions* (2000).

Prose: *In Radical Pursuit: Critical Essays and Lectures* (1975). *After-Images: Autobiographical Sketches* (1999).

Translations: *Gallows Songs*, poems by Christian Morgenstern, translated with L. Segal (1967). *Six Troubadour Songs* (1977). *Traditional Hungarian Songs* (1978). *Six Minnesinger Songs* (1983). *Antonio Vivaldi: The Four Seasons* (1984). *Star and Other Poems*, by Mihai Eminescu (1990). *Selected Translations* (1998).

GARY SNYDER (1930)

Born in San Francisco, Gary Snyder received a bachelor's degree in literature and anthropology from Reed College. He did further study in languages at Berkeley and later studied Zen Buddhism in a monastery in Kyoto, Japan. He has worked as a seaman, logger, and forester, and he has taught at Berkeley and the University of California at Davis. The recipient of a Bollingen Foundation grant for Buddhist Studies, a grant from the National Institute of Arts and Letters, and a Guggenheim Foundation fellowship, he was awarded the Pulitzer Prize in 1975.

In *Six San Francisco Poets* (1969), David Kherdian quotes Snyder as saying, "As much as the books I've read, the jobs I've had have been significant in shaping me. My sense of body and language and the knowledge that intelligence and insight, sensitivity, awareness, and brilliance are not limited to educated people, or anything like it." Many of Snyder's poems are direct and simple, marked by an elemental reverence for life and salvaging poetry from the most basic human experience.

The simplicity, however, is not simplistic, for it reflects the profound influence of Zen on Snyder's sensibility and thought. As Snyder has said, "A poet faces two directions: one is the world of people and language and society, and the other is the nonhuman, nonverbal world, which is nature. . . ." For Snyder, "nature" refers to the natural world and "the inner world . . . before language, before custom, before culture. There's no words in that realm."

Snyder's response to both the inner and outer worlds has resulted in the quest for a primitive identification with nature and a contemporary concern for the ecological consequences of progress and civilization. "As a poet," Snyder has said, "I hold the most archaic values on earth. They go back to the late Paleolithic: the fertility of the soil, the magic of animals, the power-vision in solitude, the terrifying initiation and rebirth, the love and ecstasy of the dance, the common work of the tribe. I try to hold history and wilderness in mind, that my poems may approach the true measure of things and stand against the unbalance and ignorance of our times."

Among the "archaic values" that Snyder has attempted to erect "against the unbalance and ignorance of our times" are a vital and sacred reintegration of human sexuality and a full celebration of the whole sexual self. Few poets of his generation have celebrated heterosexual love as vividly as Snyder has. "The Bath," for example, extols the pleasurable glory of the male and female bodies with unabashed and reverential joy.

Poetry: *Riprap* (1959/1990). *Myths and Texts* (1960/1978). *Riprap and Cold Mountain Poems* (1965). *Six Sections from Mountains and Rivers Without End* (1965). *Three Worlds. Three Realms. Six Roads* (1966). *A Range of Poems* (1966). *The Back Country* (1968). *The Blue Sky* (1969). *Regarding Wave* (1970). *Manzanita* (1972). *Fudo Trilogy* (1973). *Turtle Island* (1974). *Axe Handles* (1983). *Left Out in the Rain: Poems 1947–1984* (1986). *No Nature: New and Selected Poems* (1992). *Mountains and Rivers Without End* (1996). *The Gary Snyder Reader: Prose, Poetry, and Translations 1952–1998* (1999).

Prose: ESSAYS AND INTERVIEWS: *Earth House Hold: Technical Notes and Queries to Fellow Dharma Revolutionaries* (1969). *The Old Ways* (1977). *He Who Hunted Birds in His Father's Village: Dimensions of a Haida Myth* (1979). *The Real Work: Interviews & Talks 1964–1979*, edited by S. McLean (1980). *Good Wild Sacred*

(1984). *A Passage Through India* (1984). *The Practice of the Wild* (1990). *A Place in Space: Ethics, Aesthetics, and Watersheds* (1996).

GARY SOTO (1952)

Born and raised in Fresno, California, Gary Soto received a B.A. from California State University (Fresno) and an M.F.A. from the University of California at Irvine. While in college, he worked at a number of odd jobs, such as chopping beets or cotton, and picking grapes. The author of numerous books for children and young adults, he has taught at Wayne State University and the University of Cincinnati, and currently teaches at the University of California, Riverside. He is the recipient of fellowships from the Guggenheim Foundation and The National Endowment for the Arts, in addition to the American Book Award from the Before Columbus Foundation.

The stuff of Gary's Soto's poems — especially his early lyrics — is the stuff that makes up the life of the migrant worker, the tenant farmer, the men and women who are hired on a day-to-day basis to work the fields of California: sweat, dust, and more dust. "And next summer . . . ?" Soto asks. The answer is obvious: "Boredom, / in early June, will settle / on the eyelash shading your pupil from dust. . . ." Soto's poems also give us brief glances of life in the barrio. In "Mexicans Begin Jogging," the factory boss insists he flee the border patrol despite Soto's telling him there's no need: "I was American."

His journey, then, in poems that are perhaps less lyrical and closer to the gritty, American speech found in the poetry of Philip Levine, is in the pursuit of the American dream, sometimes by ridiculing it, sometimes by sneering at the values it propagates in such television role models as Donna Reed and Ozzie and Harriet. Sometimes, it is in the recognition of having been envious of "the children of San Francisco [who] are blond, / shiny, and careful at the lights. . . ." This journey is a spiritual one; it is that quest for identity which is at the heart of the American melting pot experience, and it is undertaken at some cost: many people, whole countries," Soto tells his daughter, "May go under because we desire TV / And chilled drinks. . . ." It is also the pilgrimage that we all must make: "We are [those] passengers, the old and the young alike. / Who will know us when we breathe through the grass?"

Poetry: *The Elements of San Joaquin* (1977). *The Tale of Sunlight* (1978). *Where Sparrows Work Hard* (1981). *Black Hair* (1985). *Who Will Know Us?* (1990). *A Fire in My Hands* (1990). *Home Course in Religion* (1991). *Neighborhood Odes* (1992). *Canto Familiar* (1995). *New and Selected Poems* (1995). *Junior College: Poems* (1997). *A Natural Man* (1999).

Prose: ESSAYS: *Living Up the Street* (1992).

ELIZABETH SPIRES (1952)

Born in Lancaster, Ohio, and raised in nearby Circleville where, she told interviewer A. V. Christie in 1993, she "had indiscriminately read the books in the Children's Room of the Circleville Public Library, including about three hundred sappy biographies," Elizabeth Spires was educated at Vassar College and The Johns Hopkins University. The Amy Lowell Travelling Poetry Scholar in 1986–1987, she has received fellowships from the Ingram Merrill, Guggenheim and Whiting Foundations, and from the National Endowment for the Arts. The author of several books for children, she has taught at Washington College in Chestertown, Maryland, in the Writing Seminars at Johns Hopkins, and at Goucher College in Baltimore.

Like Elizabeth Bishop, whom she interviewed for *The Paris Review* in 1977 and to whom she has been compared for her austere vocabulary, elegant diction, imaginative play, and meditative decorum, Elizabeth Spires has built an impressive body of work poem by poem, focusing, according to Christie, on the "tension . . . between the immediate and the visionary." Her attraction to the themes of the Metaphysical Poets has been evident since her first volume, *Globe* (1981), and has deepened in subsequent volumes. "I suppose the poems I care about the most," she has stated, "are the ones that see the pattern and the connections between people, between the living and the dead, how the past, the present, and the future connect with each other."

Her subject, then, is Time, its circularity rather than its linear progression, birth as much as death, and images of circles fill her poems: globes, islands, sundials, coins, eggs, the mouths of goldfish "frozen over O-shaped syllables of air." The poems themselves engage in circular patterns, often using repetition, strict stanzaic structure, and slant rhyme, as ghosts and souls drift through her fluid lines. Her circular imagery also suggests isolation and the need for self-sufficiency, so the poems become self-reflexive, as much about artistic discipline and the act of creation as about their ostensible subjects. Her purpose as a poet (and, more recently, as a mother) is to challenge the inevitable: "Only when we are 'in the process' do we lose our sense of time rapidly passing and, for a little while, escape death."

Poetry: *Globe* (1981). *Swan's Island* (1985). *Annonciade* (1989). *Worldling* (1995).

Other: FOR CHILDREN: *With One White Wing* (1995). *The Mouse of Amherst* (1999). *I Am Arachne* (2001).

DAVID ST. JOHN (1949)

Born in Fresno, California, David St. John was educated at California State University, Fresno, and the University of Iowa Writers' Workshop. He has taught at Oberlin College and The Johns Hopkins University. Presently he is Professor of English and Director of Creative Writing at the University of Southern California. St. John has received grants and fellowships from the Guggenheim and Ingram Merrill Foundations and the National Endowment for the Arts. In 1984, he received the Prix de Rome Fellowship awarded by the American Academy and Institute of Arts and Letters, and he has been Visiting Scholar at the Getty Research Institute for the History of Art and the Humanities.

In his early poem, "Gin," St. John writes: "You know, your friends complain. They say / you give up only the vaguest news, and give a bakery / As your phone. Even your stories / Have no point, just lots of detail." His work is characterized by such "disguises of omission," and his method often makes use of elision, fragmentation, collage, and fierce understatement. His elegant, precisely detailed surfaces, such gorgeous veneer, belie an undercurrent of decadence, an atmospheric *noir* that slowly surfaces to reveal decay at the heart of glamour. Love, alienation, and degradation commingle as his characters waver between nihilism and the muted promises of desire.

Critics have commented upon St. John's European influences, especially Baudelaire and Mallarmé, and Floyd Collins has noted that St. John, "like Poe and the French Symbolists before him, deliberately debases the corporeal in a fervent desire for the spiritual." In their assumption that transcendence, if possible, may be approached through unconventional measures, his poems resist moralizing. Like the photographic stills from nonexistent films created by Cindy Sherman, or the scores to nonexistent films composed by Brian Eno, St. John's poems suggest larger narratives, those abandoned novels populated with the ghosts of romance whose lives touched upon momentary grandeur before flaring into oblivion.

Poetry: *Hush* (1976). *The Shore* (1980). *No Heaven* (1985). *Terraces of Rain: An Italian Sketchbook* (1991). *Study for the World's Body: New and Selected Poems* (1994). *In the Pines: Lost Poems, 1972–1997* (1999). *The Red Leaves of Night* (1999).

Prose: *Where the Angels Come Toward Us: Selected Essays, Reviews, and Interviews* (1995).

WILLIAM STAFFORD (1914–1993)

William Stafford received his B.A. and M.A. from the University of Kansas and his Ph.D. from the University of Iowa, where he was also a member of the Writers' Workshop. A conscientious objector during World War II and active in pacifist organizations, he taught at Manchester College, San Jose State College, and Lewis and Clark College, where he was professor emeritus. From 1970 to 1971, he was Consultant in Poetry at the Library of Congress. In addition to a fellowship from the Guggenheim Foundation, a grant from the National Endowment for the Arts, the Shelley Memorial Award, and the Melville Cane Award, he also received the National Book Award.

In a statement for William J. Martz's *The Distinctive Voice* (1966), William Stafford wrote, "When you make a poem you merely speak or write the language of every day, capturing as many bonuses as possible and economizing on the losses; that is, you come awake to what always goes on in the language, and you use it to the limit of your ability and your power of attention at the moment." Part of what is truly distinctive about Stafford's poetry is his sustained ability to make each poem sound as though it were, in fact, the language of everyday. But it's clear that his power as a poet arises equally out of his ability to capture an extraordinary number of bonuses — the intensity of feeling that daily speech cannot maintain. By so doing, he achieves what he considered to be the meaningful opportunity in the social process of language: "to become more aware of what being alive means."

To a large extent, this awareness also may be the primary thematic focus of Stafford's work: "Your job is to find out what the world is trying to be," he writes in his poem "Vocation." Thus his poetry reflects his attempt not only to capture the possibilities of everyday language but also to maintain "the worth of local things": the plains and small towns of the midwestern and western landscape, the often overlooked experiences of everyday life, and his relationship with his family. Stafford's is also a highly personal poetry, but one which is neither self-torturing nor confessional; rather, it is calm and gentle while remaining honest and firm. Moreover, while neither ostensibly religious nor trailing remnants of the kind of Puritanism inherent in the work of many of his contemporaries, Stafford's poems — as Richard Howard notes in *Alone with America* (1980) — occur within a *paysage moralise* and are informed by an equally powerful moral vision.

Poetry: *West of Your City* (1961). *Traveling Through the Dark* (1961). *Five Poets of the Pacific Northwest*, with Kenneth Hanson, Richard Hugo, Carolyn Kizer, and David Wagoner; edited by R. Skelton (1964). *The Rescued Year* (1966). *Eleven Untitled Poems* (1968). *Weather* (1969). *Allegiances* (1970). *Temporary Facts* (1970). *In the Clock of Reason* (1973). *Someday, Maybe* (1973). *That Other Alone, Poems* (1973). *Going Places* (1974). *North by West* (1975). *Braided Apart*, with Kim Stafford (1976). *Late, Passing Prairie Farm* (1976). *Stories That Could Be True: New and Collected Poems* (1977). *The Design on the Oriole* (1977). *All About Light* (1978). *Tuft by Puff* (1978). *Smoke's Way* (1978). *Tuned in Late One Night* (1978). *Two About Music* (1978). *A Meeting with Disma Tumminello and William Stafford*, poems by William Stafford, photographs of Disma Tumminello's sculptures (1978). *The Quiet of the Land* (1979). *Around You, Your*

House & A Catechism (1979). *Things That Happen Where There Aren't Any People* (1980). *Wyoming Circuit* (1980). *Sometimes a Legend: Puget Sound Country* (1981). *A Glass Face in the Rain* (1982). *Segues: A Conversation in Poetry*, with Marvin Bell (1983). *Smoke's Way: Poems from Limited Editions 1968–1981* (1983). *Roving Across Fields: A Conversation and Uncollected Poems 1942–1982* (1983). *Stories and Storms and Strangers* (1984). *Listening Deep* (1984). *Wyoming* (1985). *Brother Wind* (1986). *An Oregon Message* (1987). *You and Some Other Character* (1987). *Annie Over*, with Marvin Bell (1988). *Fin, Feather, Fur* (1989). *How to Hold Your Arms When It Rains* (1990). *Passwords* (1991). *My Name Is William Tell* (1992). *The Darkness Around Us Is Deep*, ed. by Robert Bly (1993). *The Way It Is: New and Selected Poems* (1998).

Prose: *Down in My Heart*, a memoir (1947/1971/1985). *The Achievement of Brother Antoninus* (1967). *Leftovers, a Care Package: Two Lectures* (1973). *Writing the Australian Crawl: Views of the Writer's Vocation* (1978). *You Must Revise Your Life*, essays (1986).

GERALD STERN (1925)

Born in Pittsburgh, Gerald Stern was educated at the University of Pittsburgh and at Columbia. He served in the U.S. Army Air Corps and subsequently traveled widely and taught high school English in Europe. In this country he has taught at several colleges and universities, including Pittsburgh and Iowa. Stern's book *Lucky Life* was the Academy of American Poets' Lamont Poetry selection for 1977. He also has been recipient of the Poetry Society of America's Melville Cane Award, creative writing fellowships from the National Endowment for the Arts, and the National Book Award.

Compared with many of today's poets, who publish their first books when they are in their early twenties, Gerald Stern came to poetry relatively late in life; he was forty-six when his first book was published. The wait, the years of seeming silence, the apprenticeship proved to be worthwhile, for Stern has grown into a unique presence in contemporary poetry.

Reading Stern's poems and being moved by the persuasive rhythms of their exhilaration or by the resonating cadences of their sorrow, one may exclaim quite spontaneously, "Wonderful! Wonderful!" (At their best, Stern's poems warrant a *physical* response.) But the specific reasons for the poems' effectiveness or for our response may not be identified quite so spontaneously. Clearly, the cultural and literary "influences" are all there: the biblical prophets and psalmists, William Blake and Walt Whitman, Allen Ginsberg and Frank O'Hara. Those influences, however, are more like translucent flags or crystalline signals, rather than prescriptive aesthetic or moral imperatives. Enigmatically, Stern seems to combine Ginsberg's visionary moral stance and O'Hara's chatty urban sophistication, but in the process sounds entirely unique. In an interview published in *American Poetry Review* in early 1984, Stern offered a more personal explanation for his voice: "Everything depends on your signature, your breath, your person. Maybe your rhythm. Your peculiarity, your uniqueness. Your crankiness. That thumb print of yours."

Perhaps the seeming enigma lies more deeply in the expansiveness of Stern's imagination, for he is a poet whose work not only includes, but also attempts to reconcile, the emotional, moral, and existential polarities of experience into a more integrally human whole. Thus his poems encompass the urban experience as much as the rural experience; Cavafy's Alexandria as much as O'Hara's Bickford's; Dionysian joy as much as Judaic anguish. The poem "Lilacs for Ginsberg" begins on a level of straightforward realism and suddenly blooms into a lovely surrealistic lyric, while the poem "The Dancing" begins with reminiscence and celebration, then suddenly shifts from "whirling and singing" to the darker "screaming and falling" that connects the family, safe in Pittsburgh in 1945, with victims of the Holocaust. In the same interview, Stern said, "Poets are witnesses, living proof of the uniqueness of the individual soul, of the unforgivable sadness of its perishing, of its immortality. . . . The more living the poet, the more unbearable the death; the greater the poem, the more it ransoms." To that end this poet understands the essential need for the reconciliation of polarities: "stretching my body and turning on my left side / for music, / humming to myself and turning on my right side / for words."

Poetry: *The Pineys* (1971). *The Name of Beasts and Other Poems* (1972). *Rejoicings* (1973; reprinted as *Rejoicings: Poems 1966–1972*, 1984). *Lucky Life* (1977). *The Red Coal* (1981). *Paradise Poems* (1984). *Lovesick* (1987). *Two Long Poems* (1990). *Leaving Another Kingdom: Selected Poems* (1990). *Bread Without Sugar* (1992). *Odd Mercy* (1995). *This Time: New and Selected Poems* (1998). *Last Blue* (2000).

MARK STRAND (1934)

Mark Strand was born of American parents in Summerside, Prince Edward Island, Canada. He holds degrees from Antioch, Yale, and Iowa and was a Fulbright fellow in Florence, Italy. Strand has taught at many universities, including Iowa, Yale, Wesleyan, Utah, and Johns Hopkins, and currently teaches in the Committee on Social Thought at the University of Chicago. A former Poet Laureate of the United States, he has received fellowships from the National Endowment for the Arts and the MacArthur Foundation, and his prizes include the National Institute of Arts and Letters award and the Pulitzer Prize.

The development and impact of Mark Strand's poems, like those of Elizabeth Bishop, depend in large part on the straightforward technique of reportage: a seemingly simple presentation of surface facts. What differentiates Strand's poetry from that of others who employ this technique, however, is that Strand doesn't report only the factual images of the perceived physical world, but especially the figures, contours, and dramatic configurations of dreams and of nonconscious states — what Jung termed the archetypal symbols of the collective unconscious. Even when they address themselves to recognizable figures and situations of the tangible world, Strand's poems continue to generate an aura of the dream world.

Strand's work is further differentiated — not only from other poets who use the technique of reportage but also from those who, like Robert Bly, use the unconscious as a source of imagery — by the measure of irony that suffuses so many of his poems. Given the dramatic situation of a Strand poem, the speaker seems to bring a very conscious intelligence to bear on his reporting; that conscious intelligence directs the development of the action and choreographs the emotional impact of the images, thereby harnessing the full surge of the subconscious — occasionally with an edge of humor. Thus, one of Strand's unique characteristics is that many of his poems reflect a controlling sensibility that might be termed *ironic surrealism*.

Another characteristic that is almost entirely unique to the poetry of Mark Strand is the extent to which the personality of the speaker of his poems seems to be the result of a conscious obliteration of all traces of the surface texture of personality. In other words, these poems offer us a personality of absence rather than of presence. This personality suggests, "Wherever I am / I am what is missing." But such absence — the fact of absence, the threat of absence, the longing for absence — is also one of Strand's central themes. And so there's a startling but also wonderful irony at work when Strand asserts, "More is less. / I long for more." Should some readers fault Strand's poems for the personality of its speakers and theme of absence, it is important to note Strand's own realization that, confronted by such absence, it is possible to see "the blaze of promise everywhere."

Poetry: *Sleeping with One Eye Open* (1964). *Reasons for Moving* (1968). *Darker* (1970). *The Sargentville Notebook* (1973). *The Story of Our Lives* (1973). *The Late Hour* (1978). *Elegy for My Father* (1973). *Selected Poems* (1980/1990). *The Continuous Life* (1990). *Reasons for Moving, Darker, & The Sargentville Notebook* (1992). *Dark Harbor* (1993). *Blizzard of One* (1998).

Prose: *The Monument*, poetic prose (1978). *Art of the Real* (1983). *Mr. & Mrs. Baby*, fiction (1985). *William Bailey* (1987). *Hopper* (1994). *Weather of Words: Poetic Invention* (2000).

Translations: POETRY: *18 Poems from the Quechua* (1971). *The Owl's Insomnia: Selected Poems of Rafael Alberti* (1973). *Souvenir of the Ancient World*, by Carlos Drummond de Andrade (1976). *Travelling in the Family*, by Carlos Drummond de Andrade, with Thomas Colchie (1986). PROSE: *Texas*, by Jorge Luis Borges (1975).

ELLEN BRYANT VOIGT (1943)

Born in Danville, Virginia, Ellen Bryant Voigt attended Converse College in South Carolina and the University of Iowa. A former faculty member at Goddard College and the Massachusets Institute of Technology, she teaches in the Warren Wilson College low-residency M.F.A. Program for Writers. Currently the Vermont State Poet, she has received fellowships from the Guggenheim and Lila Wallace Foundations and the National Endowment for the Arts.

Landscape has played a formative role in the poetic development of Ellen Bryant Voigt. As a child in the rural South and as an adult in New England, she learned to accept the world on its own terms, not turning away from its natural violence or ignoring its lessons of trust and betrayal. In poems of quiet, celebratory power, she addresses family bonds and domestic struggles, "summer and winter, youth and age, / as though the forces of plenty and of loss / played equally on the human soul." Darkness inhabits many of these poems — the deaths of children and parents, marital tension, mastectomy, suicide — yet Voigt always attempts to strike a balance, "to fix / some truth beyond all change." In "At the Movie: Virginia, 1956," the narrator remembers the segregated theater of her adolescence, the "sullen glamor" of the balcony, and the drawn lines and "stringent rule" that limited the future of both races, one "that would try to be invisible" and the other, "not knowing how to see," that owned "everything / but easy passage out of there." For these children, the only "lit horizon" is the movie screen where images of suffocation — *King Solomon's Mines* and the undersea continent of Atlantis — flicker and beckon.

Critics have praised the linguistic density of Voigt's poems and commented upon their lucid and unsentimental evocations of the past. In *Kyrie* (1995), Voigt has written a book-length sequence on the influenza pandemic of 1918–1919. Its loose sonnets with their overlapping voices, grief-stricken yet at times mordantly funny, create a swelling *chorale* of the living that serves both as elegy for those lost and as thanksgiving for their own survival. Set against the backdrop of World War I, the book speaks to incomprehensible devastation at a time when AIDS ravages the globe, and remains more powerful for its muted metaphor. Such restraint characterizes Voigt's passionate eloquence.

Poetry: *Claiming Kin* (1976). *The Forces of Plenty* (1983). *The Lotus Flowers* (1987). *Two Trees* (1992). *Kyrie* (1995).

Prose: *The Flexible Lyric* (1999).

RICHARD WILBUR (1921)

A graduate of Amherst and Harvard, Richard Wilbur has taught at Harvard, Wellesley, Wesleyan, and Smith. In addition to having served as Poet Laureate, he has been awarded Guggenheim and Ford Foundation fellowships, the Prix de Rome, the National Book Award and, twice, the Pulitzer Prize.

Among poets whose sensibilities were shaped by the New Critics, Wilbur continues to be the consummate artist. His poetry is marked by grace, wit, and a kind of masterful craftsmanship equaled by few of his contemporaries. In his statement for John Ciardi's *Mid-Century American Poets* (1950), Wilbur affirmed the poet's need for form, for "artistry," saying that "limitation makes for power: the strength of the genie comes of his being confined in a bottle." Elsewhere he has stated that the poet must move "to attempt a maximum range" and to do so "without apparent strain." At his best, Wilbur's mastery of language and form is not merely without strain — it is dazzling and breathtaking.

The precision of sensuous detail and the verbal entrechats in Wilbur's poems are formal affirmations of his profound humanism, his belief in humankind's potential natural grace in this "world of sensible objects." In an era when many other poets have loitered around the deterioration of social, psychic, and personal fabrics and have proclaimed us and our world absurd, Wilbur has consistently sought for "a reconciliation between joy and pleasure, between acceptance and transcendence" — often against strenuous odds. And he has succeeded. By so doing, his poems have found and continue to offer the possibility of human beauty and grace.

Poetry: *The Beautiful Changes and Other Poems* (1947). *Ceremony and Other Poems* (1950). *Things of This World: Poems* (1956). *Advice to a Prophet and Other Poems* (1961). *The Poems of Richard Wilbur* (1963). *Walking to Sleep: New Poems and Translations* (1969). *The Mind-Reader: New Poems* (1976). *Opposites: Poems and Drawings* (1979). *Seven Poems* (1981). *New and Collected Poems* (1988). *More Opposites: Poems and Drawings* (1991). *Mayflies: New Poems and Translations* (2000).

Prose: *Responses: Prose Pieces 1953–1976*, essays (1976, expanded edition, 2000).

Translations: POETRY: *The Whale and Other Uncollected Translations* (1982). VERSE DRAMA: *The Misanthrope*, by Molière (1955). *Tartuffe*, by Molière (1963). *The School for Wives*, by Molière (1971). *The Learned Ladies*, by Molière (1978).

Andromache, by Racine (1982). *Four Comedies,* by Molière (1982). *Phaedra,* by Racine (1986).

C. K. WILLIAMS (1936)

Born in Newark, New Jersey, and educated at Bucknell and the University of Pennsylvania, C. K. Williams has engaged in a wide range of professional activities. He established a program of poetry-therapy for the emotionally disturbed in Philadelphia, where he was also a group therapist for disturbed adolescents. He has been an editor and ghost-writer of articles, booklets, and speeches in the fields of psychiatry and architecture. And he has taught creative writing at Drexel, Irvine, Columbia, George Mason, and Princeton. In addition to a Guggenheim fellowship, Williams has been awarded the *Paris Review's* Bernard F. Connor Prize and the National Book Critics Circle Award. In 2000, he received the Pulitzer Prize for *Repair.*

Reading the poems of C. K. Williams, we are quickly struck by how much pain and grief are harbored in their stark lines. Perhaps no other postwar poet in the United States has confronted so unswervingly and relentlessly the levels and dimensions of anguish as the fulcrum of human experience. Moreover, unlike many of his contemporaries, Williams has explored human suffering without the seeming intellectual comfort of a formal philosophical system such as existentialism (W. D. Snodgrass), without even a precarious solace of faith or of a theological framework (John Berryman), and certainly without the emotional-aesthetic buffer of a strong ironic sense in the service of sustained artifice (Sylvia Plath). Whether confronting inner states of psychic pain in earlier poems or more external constructs of human anguish in later poems, Williams's poetry has as its heart the fundamental and essentially unconsoled vision announced in "It Is This Way with Men": "They are pounded into the earth / like nails; move an inch, / they are driven down again. / The earth is sore with them."

The anguish of our common condition, in an age that threatens annihilation on all sides, also seems to have rendered Williams commensurately unsympathetic to the kinds of artifices we have come to expect from poetry. Thus, in his earlier poems he seemed intent on stripping language down to its most essential syntax and then stripping it even further of most signs of syntax's own formal artifice. Consider the intense aesthetic and syntactical starkness of these lines: "if you told him god lived in his own penis / he'd bite into it / and tear like a carnivore / this is how men renounce / this is how we obliterate." Clearly, the visual aesthetic equivalent of such lines would be found more in Käthe Kollwitz's hauntingly sparse but blunt depictions of pain than in the more complex, inventive, and often witty depictions by Hieronymous Bosch.

In his fifth book, *Tar*, Williams introduced a long tonal line that may well be unique in postwar American poetry. Williams's lines may look like Ginsberg's, but they are not marked by the incantatory quality in many of Ginsberg's poems. And while their tone is very conversational, like many of Simpson's recent poems, Williams's tone isn't marked by the crackling terseness found in Simpson's. Approaching the quality of a highly refined, sparse prose, Williams's new tonal lines continue to accommodate his dark vision but also enable him to be more experiential-ly, intellectually, and aesthetically expansive, allowing the reader to participate in the poet's own thought processes. These new poems also reflect a maturation of Williams's vision: the pain, the anguish, the anni-hilation are still present and unconsoled, but that vision is also counter-pointed by the recognition of the possibility of beauty: "all the field pure white, / its surface glittering, the dawn, glancing from its glaze, oblique, relentless, unadorned."

Poetry: *A Day for Anne Frank* (1968). *Lies* (1969). *I Am the Bitter Name* (1972). *With Ignorance* (1977). *Tar* (1983). *Flesh and Blood* (1987). *Poems 1963–1983* (1988). *A Dream of Mind* (1992). *Selected Poems* (1994). *The Vigil* (1997). *Repair* (1999).

Prose: *Poetry and Consciousness: Selected Essays* (1998). *Misgivings*, memoir (2000).

Translations: POETRY: *The Lark. The Thrush. The Starling*, by Issa (1983). VERSE DRAMA: *Women of Trachis*, by Sophocles; with G. Dickerson (1978). *The Bacchae*, by Euripides (1990).

CHARLES WRIGHT (1935)

Born in Pickwick Dam, Tennessee, Charles Wright was educated at Davidson College, the University of Iowa, and the University of Rome, where he was a Fulbright fellow. He served in the U.S. Army Intelligence Service and has taught in Italy as well as at Iowa, Princeton, Columbia, and the University of Virginia. Wright has received fellowships and awards from the National Endowment for the Arts, the Ingram Merrill Foundation, and the Academy of American Poets. The recipient of the PEN Translation Prize, in 1983 he was cowinner of the American Book Award, and in 1997 received the National Book Critics Circle Award and the Pulitzer Prize.

THE NEW POEM
It will not resemble the sea.
It will not have dirt on its thick hands.
It will not be part of the weather.

It will not reveal its name.
It will not have dreams you can count on.
It will not be photogenic.

It will not attend our sorrow.
It will not console our children.
It will not be able to help us.

If Charles Wright's "The New Poem" were read as a statement of his poetics (in the way that Marvin Bell's "White Clover" or William Heyen's "The Return" may be read), we might rightfully conclude that Wright's sense of poetics — and the implicit broader vision from which it might issue — is desolate to the brink of barbarism. For the "new poem" would have nothing to do with the physical world, would reflect no characteristic inherent in the art of poetry, and would address no human concerns. It's no wonder that one critic has asserted that Wright's poetry struggles to render the connections between his life and his poems "tenuous, often invisible" and characterized Wright's poems as being "unanchored to incident," thus "resisting description" and "defying exposition."

In light of Wright's full body of poetry, however, "The New Poem" is more rightly read as a statement of antipoetics, perhaps even as a parody of a certain modish aesthetic. That is, it is a poem suggesting what Wright hopes his own poems will *not* be, a nine-commandment tablet listing what poetry in general ought *not* to do, and, indeed, perhaps a kind of oxymoron repudiating the view in some literary circles that finds quality and worth in poetry that is seemingly not rooted in any recognizable human reality.

Because they are carefully, delicately crafted, and because, as other critics have noted, they often rely more on links of the imagination than on narrative and other surface connections, some of Wright's poems may seem less immediately accessible than the work of other poets. However, on closer examination it is clear that the range of Wright's concerns is fully rooted in the range of recognizable and shared human experience. His work includes poems of place energized by the spirit of that place, Blackwater Mountain in Tennessee, for example; it includes poems emerging out of childhood, adolescent, and mature experience and the states of emotional feeling inherent in those stages of human development; and it includes poems of the natural, physical world with its splendors and horrors.

What is also striking about the work of Charles Wright is its strong and consistent religious nature; Wright is one of the few poets of his generation who continues to wrestle openly with the traditional values (if not the working tenets) of the Judeo-Christian tradition and to use the symbols, saints, and metaphors of that tradition as an integral part of his sensibility and vocabulary. The poem "Snow" uses as its launching point the biblical phrase "Dust thou art, and unto dust shalt thou return"; "California Dreaming," whose very tone resonates with biblical rhythms and whose language incorporates traditional religious phrases and concepts, is a profound exploration of the possibility of a tradition-oriented spirituality within the boundaries and texture of contemporary experience. What if, in his quest for transcendence, Wright recognizes that "The ache for anything is a thick dust in the heart," that transcendence may be no more than being "Released as a glint, as a flash, as a spark?" Of the people and places in his world, past and present, he asserts, "I am their music"; of his music, he ventures, "I write poems to untie myself, to do penance and disappear / Through the upper right-hand corner of things, to say grace."

Poetry: *The Voyage* (1963). *6 Poems* (1965). *The Dream Animal* (1968). *Private Madrigals* (1969). *The Grave of the Right Hand* (1970). *The Venice Notebook* (1971). *Backwater* (1973). *Hard Freight* (1973). *Bloodlines* (1975). *China Trace* (1977). *Colophons* (1977). *The Southern Cross* (1981). *Country Music: Selected Early Poems* (1982). *The Other Side of the River* (1984). *Zone Journals* (1988). *Xionia* (1990). *The World of the Ten Thousand Things: Poems 1980–1990* (1990). *Chickamauga* (1995). *Black Zodiac* (1997). *Appalachia* (1999). *Negative Blue: Selected Later Poems* (2000).

Prose: *Halflife: Improvisations and Interviews* (1988). *Quarter Notes: Improvisations and Interviews* (1995).

Translations: *The Storm and Other Poems*, by Eugenio Montale (1978). *The Motets*, poems by Eugenio Montale (1981). *Orphic Songs*, poems by Dino Campana (1984).

JAMES WRIGHT (1927–1980)

James Wright was born in the steel town of Martin's Ferry, Ohio — a place he subsequently transformed into a literary landmark in the contemporary imagination. He received his B.A. from Kenyon College, his M.A. and Ph.D. from the University of Washington, and attended the University of Vienna as a Fulbright Scholar. The recipient of several awards for poetry — including the Pulitzer Prize — he taught at Macalester College, the University of Minnesota, and Hunter College.

Like the styles of many other poets of his generation, James Wright's underwent significant changes in the course of his career. With the publication of his first book, Wright stated that he "wanted to make [his] poems say something humanly important" and pointed to Robert Frost and E. A. Robinson as his models. Thus his early poems are often concerned with his response to the life and suffering of others. After his second book, however, he asserted, "Whatever I write from now on will be entirely different."

According to Robert Bly, Wright's decision was largely the result of his having read — and translated — the work of the German poet Georg Trakl, a contemporary of Rilke. "In Trakl," Bly writes, "a series of images makes a series of events. Because these events appear out of their 'natural' order, without the connection we have learned to expect from reading newspapers, doors silently open to unused parts of the brain." In Wright's poems such as "The Jewel," "Lying in a Hammock . . . ," and "A Blessing" — generally written between 1960 and 1970 — the doors open to startling images, strange but emotionally precise. More personal than his earlier poems, these discover in his own subconscious and imagination the secret pools of human fear and joy. Moreover, the poems themselves seem to evolve quietly through layers of images until they surface with the quick thrust of a striking final image and epiphany.

In poems written after the publication of his *Collected Poems* in 1971, Wright sought a vital integration of his earlier concern with others — "those old Winnebago men" — and the image of epiphany — "the instant of that waterfall." The results enable us to join Wright in his assertion: "I know what we call it / Most of the time. / But I have my own song for it, / And sometimes, even today, / I call it beauty."

Poetry: *The Green Wall* (1957). *Saint Judas* (1959). *The Lion's Tail and Eyes: Poems Written Out of Laziness and Silence*, with Robert Bly and William Duffy (1962). *The Branch Will Not Break* (1963). *Shall We Gather at the River* (1968). *Collected Poems* (1971). *Two Citizens* (1973). *Moments of the Italian Summer* (1976). *To a Blossoming Pear Tree* (1977). *Leave It to the Sunlight*, edited by A. Wright (1981). *A Reply to Matthew Arnold*, edited by A. Wright (1981). *This Journey*, edited by A. Wright (1981). *The Shape of Light*, edited by A. Wright (1986). *Above the River: The Complete Poems*, edited by A. Wright (1990).

Prose: *Collected Prose*, essays, edited by A. Wright (1982). *The Delicacy and Strength of Lace*, letters between James Wright and Leslie Marmon Silko, edited by A. Wright (1985). *A Secret Field: Selections from the Final Journals*, edited by A. Wright (1985). *Against the Exile*, letters to Wayne Burns, edited by J. R. Doheny (1985).

Translations: *Twenty Poems of Georg Trakl*, with R. Bly (1961). *Twenty Poems of César Vallejo*, with R. Bly (1962). *The Rider on the White Horse: Selected Short Fiction of Theodor Storm* (1964). *Pablo Neruda: Twenty Poems*, with R. Bly (1967). *Poems by Hermann Hesse* (1970). *Neruda and Vallejo: Selected Poems*, with R. Bly and J. Knoepfle (1971). *Wandering: Notes and Sketches by Hermann Hesse*, with F. Wright (1972).

Criticism: A Selected Bibliography

Most of the following books and pamphlets contain substantial discussions of the work of individual poets, especially those represented in this book; some also include critical essays or statements of poetics by these poets. A few books in this bibliography, however, are primarily concerned with poetry in the United States before 1960; still others focus on various aspects of the art of poetry in the twentieth century.

Advanced students of poetry will want to turn to book-length bibliographies devoted to individual poets, as well as to such standard bibliographical sources as *Contemporary Poets* (St. Martin's Press); *Contemporary Authors* (Gale Research Company); *Dictionary of Literary Biography* (Gale Research Company); the annual bibliographies published in *PMLA*, *American Literature*, and *Journal of Modern Literature*; the regular bibliographies in *Twentieth Century Literature*; and *Contemporary Literary Criticism* (Gale Research Company), an annual volume of critical excerpts. Of course, many of the books listed here also include their own individual bibliographies.

Readers should be aware that several of the earlier, seminal books of criticism devoted to post-1960 U.S. poetry are now out of print and available only in larger libraries.

Lastly, books of criticism by poets represented in this volume are listed in the Notes on the Poets.

D. M. Allen and W. Tallman, eds., *The Poetics of the New American Poetry* (1973).

C. Altieri, *Enlarging the Temple: New Directions in American Poetry During the 1960's* (1979).

C. Altieri, *Painterly Abstraction in Modernist American Poetry: Infinite Incantations of Ourselves* (1990).

D. Baker, *Heresy and the Ideal: On Contemporary Poetry* (2000).

H. A. Baker, Jr., *Afro-American Poets* (1988).

J. D. Bellamy, ed., *American Poetry Observed: Poets on Their Work* (1984).

R. Berke, *Bounds Out of Bounds: A Compass for Recent American and British Poetry* (1981).

M. K. Blasing, *American Poetry: The Rhetoric of Its Forms* (1988).

H. Bloom, *The Anxiety of Influence: A Theory of Poetry* (1973).

H. Bloom, *A Map of Misreading* (1975).

R. Boyers, ed., *Excursions: Selected Literary Essays* (1977).

J. E. B. Breslin, *From Modern to Contemporary: American Poetry 1945–1965* (1984).

N. Bunge, ed., *Finding the Words: Interviews with Writers Who Teach* (1984).

G. Cambon, *Recent American Poetry* (1962).

P. Carroll, *The Poem in Its Skin* (1968).

S. Charters, *Some Poems/Poets: Poets and Poetry* (1971).

C. Clausen, *The Place of Poetry: Two Centuries of an Art in Crisis* (1981).

J. Clausen, *A Movement of Poets: Thoughts on Poetry & Feminism* (1983).

M. Davidson, *The San Francisco Renaissance: Poetics and Community at Mid-Century* (1989).

T. M. Disch, *The Castle of Indolence* (1995).

W. Dodd, *Toward the End of the Century: Essays into Poetry* (1992).

M. Duberman, *Black Mountain: An Experiment in Community* (1972).

CRITICISM: A SELECTED BIBLIOGRAPHY

I. Ehrenpreis, *American Poetry* (1965).

E. Faas, ed., *Towards a New American Poetics: Essays and Interviews* (1978).

R. Frank and H. Sayre, eds., *The Line in Postmodern Poetry* (1989).

S. Fredman, *Poet's Prose: The Crisis in American Verse* (1983).

S. Friebert and D. Young, eds., *A Field Guide to Contemporary Poetry and Poetics* (1980).

T. Gardner, *Discovering Ourselves in Whitman: The Contemporary American Long Poem* (1988).

A. Gayle, *The Black Aesthetic* (1971).

D. Gioia, *Can Poetry Matter? Essays on Poetry and American Culture* (1992)

P. Goodman, *Speaking and Language: A Defense of Poetry* (1971).

J. Gould, *Modern American Women Poets* (1984).

J. Grahn, *The Highest Apple: Sappho and the Lesbian Poetic Tradition* (1985).

D. Hall, ed., *Claims for Poetry* (1982).

M. Harris and K. Aguero, eds., *A Gift of Tongues: Critical Challenges in Contemporary Poetry* (1988).

S. Henderson, ed., *Understanding the New Black Poetry: Black Speech and Black Music as Poetic Reference* (1973).

W. Heyen, ed., *American Poets in 1976* (1975).

J. Holden, *The Rhetoric of the Contemporary Lyric* (1980).

J. Holden, *The Old Formalism: Character in Contemporary American Poetry* (2000).

R. Howard, *Alone with America: Essays on the Art of Poetry in the United States Since 1950* (1969; enlarged edition, 1980).

E. B. Hungerford, *Poets in Progress: Critical Prefaces to Thirteen Modern American Poets* (1967).

R. Jackson, *Acts of Mind: Conversations with Contemporary Poets* (1983).

R. Jackson, *The Dismantling of Time in Contemporary Poetry* (1988).

M. Jarman and R. McDowell, *The Reaper Essays* (1996).

D. Kalstone, *Five Temperaments: Elizabeth Bishop, Robert Lowell, James Merrill, Adrienne Rich, John Ashbery* (1977).

L. Keller, *Remaking It New: Contemporary Poetry and the Modern Feminist* (1989).

L. Keller and C. Miller, eds., *Feminist Measures: Soundings in Poetry and Theory* (1994).

D. Kherdian, *Six San Francisco Poets* (1969).

H. Kohl, *A Grain of Poetry* (1999).

R. Kostelanetz, *The Old Poetries and the New* (1981).

R. Kostelanetz, ed., *On Contemporary Literature* (1964).

G. Kuzma, ed., *A Book of Rereadings in Recent American Poetry* (1980).

H. Lazer, *What Is a Poet?* (1987).

D. Lehman, ed., *Ecstatic Occasions, Expedient Forms: Sixty-Five Leading Contemporary Poets Select and Comment on Their Poems* (1988).

G. Lensing and R. Moran, *Four Poets and the Emotive Imagination: Robert Bly, James Wright, Louis Simpson and William Stafford* (1976).

L. Lieberman, *Unassigned Frequencies: American Poetry in Review* (1977).

H. R. Madhubuti (Don L. Lee), *Dynamite Voices* (1971).

K. Malkoff, *Crowell's Handbook of Contemporary American Poetry: A Critical Handbook of American Poetry Since 1940* (1973).

K. Malkoff, *Escape from the Self* (1977).

P. Mariani, *A Useable Past: Essays on Modern and Contemporary Poetry* (1984).

R. K. Martin, *The Homosexual Tradition in American Poetry* (1979).

D. Mason, *The Poetry of Life and the Life of Poetry* (2000).

J. Mazzaro, *Postmodern American Poetry* (1980).

J. Mazzaro, ed., *Modern American Poetry: Essays in Criticism* (1970).

J. D. McClatchy, *White Paper: On Contemporary American Poetry* (1987).

M. McQuade, *Stealing Glimpses* (1999).

D. Meltzer, *The San Francisco Poets* (1971).

J. F. Mersmann, *Out of the Vietnam Vortex: A Study of Poets and Poetry Against the War* (1974).

D. M. Middlebrook and M. Yalom, eds., *Coming to Light: American Women Poets in the Twentieth Century* (1985).

B. Miller, ed., *Black American Poets Between Worlds 1940–1960* (1987).

R. J. Mills, Jr., *Creation's Very Self: On the Personal Element in Recent American Poetry* (1969).

R. J. Mills, Jr., *Cry of the Human: Essays on Contemporary American Poetry* (1974).

C. Molesworth, *The Fierce Embrace: A Study of Contemporary American Poetry* (1979).

C. Nelson, *Our Last First Poets: Vision and History in Contemporary American Poetry* (1984).

H. Nemerov, *Reflections on Poetry & Poets* (1972).

H. Nemerov, ed., *Poets on Poetry* (1961).

A. Oberg, *Modern American Lyric* (1978).

D. Ossman, *The Sullen Art: Interviews by David Ossman with Modern American Poets* (1963).

A. Ostriker, *Stealing the Language: The Emergence of Women's Poetry in America* (1986).

A. Ostroff, ed., *The Contemporary Poet as Artist and Critic* (1964).

G. Owen, ed., *Modern American Poetry: Essays in Criticism* (1972).

W. Packard, ed., *The Craft of Poetry: Interviews from the New York Quarterly* (1974).

J. Parini, *The Columbia History of American Poetry* (1994).

T. Parkinson, *Poets, Poems, Movements* (1988).

T. Parkinson, ed., *A Casebook on the Beat* (1961).

R. Philips, *The Confessional Poets* (1973).

R. H. Pierce, *The Continuity of American Poetry* (1973).

R. Pinsky, *The Situation of Poetry: Contemporary Poetry and Its Traditions* (1977).

G. Plimpton, ed., *Poets at Work* (1989).

W. Prunty, *Fallen from the Symboled World: Precedents for the New Formalism* (1990).

K. Rexroth, *American Poetry in the Twentieth Century* (1973).

S. Rodman, *Tongues of Fallen Angels*, interviews (1984).

M. L. Rosenthal, *The Modern Poetic Sequence: The Genius of Modern Poetry* (1983).

M. L. Rosenthal, *The Modern Poets: A Critical Introduction* (1962).

M. L. Rosenthal, *The New Poets: American and British Poetry Since World War II* (1967).

M. L. Rosenthal, *Poetry and the Common Life* (1974; revised edition, 1984).

M. L. Rosenthal, *The Poet's Art* (1989).

S. Santos, *A Poetry of Two Minds* (2000).

R. B. Shaw, ed., *American Poetry Since 1960: Some Critical Perspectives* (1974).

M. Sienicka, *The Making of a New American Poem: Some Tendencies in the Post-World War II American Poetry* (1972).

E. Simpson, *Poets in Their Youth: A Memoir* (1982).

D. Smith, *Local Assays: On Contemporary American Poetry* (1985).

T. Steele, *Missing Measures: Modern Poetry and the Revolt Against Meter* (1990).

S. Stepanchev, *American Poetry Since 1945: A Critical Survey* (1965).

J. Sternberg, ed., *The Writer on Her Work* (1980).

P. Stitt, *The World's Hieroglyphic Beauty: Five American Poets* (1987).

P. Stitt, *Uncertainty & Plenitude: Five Contemporary Poets* (1997)

G. Thurley, *The American Moment: American Poetry in the Mid-Century* (1977).

C. Tomlinson, *Some Americans: A Personal Record* (1981).

L. P. Turco, *Visions and Revisions in American Poetry* (1986).

H. Vendler, *The Music of What Happens: Poems, Poets, Critics* (1989).

H. Vendler, *Part of Nature, Part of Us* (1980).

H. Vendler, *Soul Says: On Recent Poetry* (1995).

J. Vinson, ed., *Contemporary Poets* (1985).

R. Von Hallberg, *American Poetry and Culture: 1945–1980* (1988).

H. H. Waggoner, *American Poetry from the Puritans to the Present* (1968; revised edition, 1984).

A. Williamson, *Eloquence and Mere Life: Essays on the Art of Poetry* (1994).

A. Williamson, *Introspection and Contemporary Poetry* (1984).

Writers at Work: The Paris Review Interviews (First Series, 1958; Second Series, 1963; Third Series, 1967; Fourth Series, 1976; Fifth Series, 1981).

Notes on the Editors

A. POULIN, JR. (1938–1996)

A. Poulin, Jr., was born of immigrant Québécois parents in Lisbon, Maine. He received a B.A. from St. Francis College, an M.A. from Loyola University (Chicago), and an M.F.A. from the University of Iowa. He taught for the European Division of the University of Maryland, at the University of New Hampshire, and at St. Francis College, where he was chairman of the Division of Humanities. In 1971 Poulin joined the faculty at the State University of New York, College at Brockport, where he was Professor of English. In 1980 he was Visiting Fulbright Lecturer in Contemporary American Poetry at the universities of Athens and Thessaloniki in Greece.

Poulin also was Director of the Brockport Writers Forum and recorded videotaped interviews with more than twenty contemporary poets, including John Ashbery, Robert Bly, Robert Creeley, Allen Ginsberg, Robert Hayden, David Ignatow, Galway Kinnell, Carolyn Kizer, Stanley Kunitz, John Logan, William Matthews, Adrienne Rich, Anne Sexton, Louis Simpson, Gary Snyder, William Stafford, and Mark Strand — some of the poets represented in *Contemporary American Poetry*.

A poet, translator, and editor, Poulin wrote a number of books and chapbooks of poetry including: *In Advent* (1972), *The Widow's Taboo: Poems After the Catawba* (1977), *The Nameless Garden* (1978), *A Nest of Sonnets* (1986), *A Momentary Order* (1987), and *Cave Dwellers* (1991). His books of translations include *Anne Hébert: Selected Poems* (1987) and *Day Has No Equal but Night* (1994), also by the Québécois poet Anne Hébert, Rainer Maria Rilke's *Duino Elegies and The Sonnets to Orpheus* (1977) and *The Complete French Poems of Rainer Maria Rilke* (1986). Poulin also edited *A Ballet for the Ear: Interviews, Essays, and Reviews* by John Logan (1983) and, with David A. DeTurk, coedited *The American Folk Scene: Dimensions of the Folksong Revival* (1967).

For his poetry and translations, Poulin received both a creative writing fellowship and translator's grant from the National Endowment for the Arts, as well as a poetry fellowship from the New York Foundation for the Arts, two translation awards from Columbia University's Translation Center, and a Faculty Enrichment Programme grant for research and translation from the Embassy of Canada. In 1989 Poulin was awarded an honorary Doctorate of Humane Letters by the University of New England.

A. Poulin, Jr. was also the founding editor and publisher of BOA Editions, Ltd., now in its third decade, a nonprofit publishing house devoted to the publication of poetry and of poetry in translation.

MICHAEL WATERS (1949)

Michael Waters was born in New York City. He attended the State University of New York at Brockport (B.A., M.A.), the University of Nottingham (England), the University of Iowa (M.F.A.), and Ohio University where he received the Ph.D. degree in American Literature and Creative Writing. He has taught in the Creative Writing Programs at Ohio University and the University of Maryland, and has been Visiting Professor of American Literature at the University of Athens, Greece (1981–1982) and Banister Writer-in-Residence at Sweet Briar College in Virginia (1987–1989). He teaches for several summer programs, including the Catskill Poetry Workshop at Hartwick College and the Writers' Center at the Chautauqua Institute, and since 1978 has been on the faculty at Salisbury University in Maryland where he is Professor of English.

Waters's books of poems include *Fish Light* (1975), *Not Just Any Death* (1979), *Anniversary of the Air* (1985), *The Burden Lifters* (1989), *Bountiful* (1992), *Green Ash, Red Maple, Black Gum* (1997), and *Parthenopi: New and Selected Poems* (2001). He has edited *Dissolve to Island: On the Poetry of John Logan* (1984).

For his poetry, Waters has received a fellowship in creative writing from the National Endowment for the Arts, several Individual Artist Awards from the Maryland State Arts Council, and two Pushcart Prizes. He has been a resident fellow at Yaddo, the MacDowell Colony, the Virginia Center for the Creative Arts, the Anderson Center for Interdisciplinary Studies, and the Tyrone Guthrie Centre at Annaghmakerrig (Ireland). Waters has read his poems at universities and other venues in the United States and abroad, including the Al-Merbid Poetry Festival in Baghdad (1986), the Conference on Contemporary Greek and American Poetry in Athens (1991), and the Summer Seminars in Prague (2000). In 1998 he read in Bucharest and Iasi under the auspices of the Museum for Romanian Literature.

Michael Waters currently resides in Salisbury, on the Eastern Shore of Maryland, with his wife, the translator Mihaela Moscaliuc, and his daughter, Kiernan.

Acknowledgments

Ai: "The Mortician's Twelve-Year-Old Son" by Ai from *Killing Floor*, 1979. Reprinted with the permission of the poet. "Twenty-Year Marriage." Copyright © 1973 by Ai, "Riot Act, April 29, 1992," "Finished," "I Have Got To Stop Loving You So I Have Killed My Black Goat," "The Mother's Tale," "Why I Can't Leave You" from *Vice: New and Selected Poems* by Ai. Copyright © 1999 by Ai. Used by permission of W. W. Norton & Company, Inc.

A. R. Ammons: "With Ropes of Hemp," "Open," "Catalyst," "Grace Abounding," "Triphammer Bridge," and "Epiphany" all from *Collected Poems 1951–1971* by A. R. Ammons. Copyright © 1972 by A. R. Ammons. "The Only Way Around Is Through" from *Lake Effect Country* by A. R. Ammons. Copyright © 1983 by A. R. Ammons. "Marginals" and "The Clenched-Jaw School" from *Brink Road* by A. R. Ammons. Copyright © 1996 by A. R. Ammons. Used by permission of W. W. Norton & Company, Inc.

John Ashbery: "Self Portrait in a Convex Mirror," copyright © 1974 by John Ashbery, from *Self-Portrait in a Convex Mirror* by John Ashbery. Used by permission of Viking Penguin, a division of Penguin Putnam Inc.

Marvin Bell: "Sevens (Version 3): In the Closed Iris of Creation," "The Self and the Mulberry," "The Mystery of Emily Dickinson," "Treetops," "To an Adolescent Weeping Willow," "White Clover," and "Drawn by Stones, by Earth, by Things That Have Been in the Fire" from *Nightwork* © 2000 by Marvin Bell. Reprinted by permission of Copper Canyon Press, Post Office Box 271, Port Townsend, WA 98368.

John Berryman: Dream Songs #4, #14, #26, #29, #47, #89, #91, #129, #172, #366, #382, and #384 from *The Dream Songs* by John Berryman. Copyright © 1969 by John Berryman. Copyright renewed © 1997 by Kate Donahue Berryman. Reprinted by permission of Farrar, Straus and Giroux, LLC.

Elizabeth Bishop: "At the Fishhouses," "Cape Breton," "The Fish," "In the Waiting Room," and "One Art" from *The Complete Poems 1927–1979* by Elizabeth Bishop. Reprinted by permission of Farrar, Straus and Giroux, LLC.

Robert Bly: "Warning to the Reader," "The Dead Seal" from *What Have I Ever Lost by Dying* by Robert Bly. Copyright © 1992 by Robert Bly. "On the Oregon Coast" from *Meditations on the Insatiable Soul* by Robert Bly. Copyright © 1994 by Robert Bly. "An Empty Place," "Six Winter Privacy Poems" from *Selected Poems* by Robert Bly. Copyright © 1986 by Robert Bly. "The Resemblance Between Your Life and a Dog," "The Yellow Dot," "The Russian" from *Morning Poems* by Robert Bly. Copyright © 1997 by Robert Bly. "Snowbanks North of the House" by Robert Bly, copyright © 1987 by Robert Bly from *The Man in the Black Coat Turns*. Reprinted by permission of Doubleday, a Division of Random House, Inc. "Looking into a Tidal Pool" from *The Morning Glory* and "Driving to Town Late to Mail a Letter" from *Silence in the Snowy Fields* are reprinted by permission of Robert Bly.

Gwendolyn Brooks: "the mother," "a song in the front yard," "The Lovers of the Poor," "We Real Cool," "An Aspect of Love, Alive in the Fire and Ice," "The Bean Eaters" from *Blacks*, by Gwendolyn Brooks © 1991. "The Coora Flower" from *Children Coming Home* by Gwendolyn Brooks. Reprinted by permission of the poet in honor of A. Poulin, Jr.

Olga Broumas: "The Choir," "Caritas," "Perpetua," "Soothsaying," "Calypso," "Mercy" from *Rave: Poems 1975–1999* © 1999 by Olga Broumas. Reprinted by permission of Cooper Canyon Press, Post Office Box 271, Port Townsend, WA 98368.

Lucille Clifton: "scar," copyright © 1996 by Lucille Clifton. "at the cemetery, walnut grove plantation, south carolina, 1989," copyright © 1991 by Lucille Clifton. Reprinted from *Quilting* by Lucille Clifton. "the lost baby poem," "at last we killed the roaches," copyright © 1987 by Lucille Clifton. Reprinted from *Good Woman: Poems and a Memoir 1969–1980*, by Lucille Clifton. "poem to my uterus," "lumpectomy eve," "lorena," "moonchild," "the birth of language," "wishes for sons" copyright © 2000, by Lucille Clifton. Reprinted from *Blessing the Boats*, by Lucille Clifton. All are reprinted with the permission of BOA Editions, Ltd. "i was born with twelve fingers" and "homage to my hips" copyright © 1980 by The University of Massachusetts Press. First appeared in *two-headed woman*, published by The University of Massachusetts Press. Reprinted by permission of Curtis Brown, Ltd.

   Robert Creeley: "I Know a Man," "After Lorcas," "The Figures," "The Language," "The Flower," "Something," "The Warning," "The Act of Love" — all from *The Collected Poems 1945–1975*. Reprinted with the permission of University of California Press.

   James Dickey: "The Heaven of Animals," "The Sheep Child," "The Poisoned Man," "At Darien Bridge" and "Adultery" from *Poems 1957–1967* © 1978 by James Dickey, Wesleyan University Press, reprinted by permission of University Press of New England.

   Stephen Dobyns: "Tenderly," "How Could You Ever Be Fine," "Beauty," "Bowlers Anonymous," "How To Like It," "Fragments" from *Velocities* by Stephen Dobyns, copyright © 1994 by Stephen Dobyns. "Cemetery Nights" by Stephen Dobyns from *Cemetery Nights* by Stephen Dobyns, copyright © 1987 by Stephen Dobyns. Used by permission of Penguin, a division of Penguin Putnam Inc.

   Rita Dove: "Parsley" from *Museum*, Carnegie-Mellon University Press, © 1983 by Rita Dove. "Daystar," "Wingfoot Lake," from *Thomas and Beulah*, Carnegie-Mellon University Press, © 1986 by Rita Dove. Reprinted by permission of the author. "Crab-Boil," "The Breathing, and Endless News," "After Reading *'Mickey in the Night Kitchen'* for the Third Time Before Bed" from *Grace Notes* by Rita Dove. Copyright © 1989 by Rita Dove. "Testimonial" from *On the Bus with Rosa Parks* by Rita Dove. Copyright © 1999 by Rita Dove. Used by permission of W. W. Norton & Company, Inc.

   Alan Dugan: "Closing Time at the Second Avenue Deli," "Elegy," "Morning Song," "Love Song: I and Thou," "Untitled Poem," "To an Ex-Student" from *New and Collected Poems, 1961–1983* and "Criticism of Bergson and Darwin," "Surviving the Hurricane," and "Lament for Cellists and Jacqueline DuPré" from *Poems Six*, 1989. "Rising in Fall" by Alan Dugan from *New and Collected Poems* (Ecco, 1983). Reprinted with permission of the poet.

   Carol Frost: "Sin," "Chimera," "Homo Sapiens," "Sexual Jealousy," "Harm," "Laws," "Nothing," Fury," "Scorn," "To Kill a Deer," "Papilio," "Apple Rind," "The St. Louis Zoo," and "The Undressing" — all from *Love and Scorn: New and Selected Poems*, 2000, from *Triquarterly*. Reprinted by permission of Northwestern University Press.

   Allen Ginsberg: All lines from "Howl" from *Collected Poems: 1947–1980* by Allen Ginsberg. Copyright © 1955 by Allen Ginsberg. "Ode to Failure" from *Collected Poems: 1947–1980* by Allen Ginsberg. Copyright © 1984 by Allen Ginsberg. Reprinted by permission of HarperCollins Publishers, Inc.

   Louise Glück: "Nostros," "Midnight," "Parable of Flight," "Parable of the Gift" from *Meadowlands* by Louise Glück. Copyright © 1996 by Louise Glück. "The Mirror" fr. *Descending Figure* and "Mock Orange" fr. *The Triumph of Achilles* from *The First Four Books of Poems* by Louise Glück. Copyright 1968, 1971, 1972, 1973, 1974, 1975, 1976, 1977, 1978, 1079, 1980, 1985, 1995 by Louise Glück. "The White Rose," "Matins," and "Vespers" from *The Wild Iris* by Louise Glück. Copyright © 1993 by Louise Glück. "Celestial Music" from *Ararat* by Louise Glück. Copyright © 1990 by Louise Glück. Reprinted by permission of Harper Collins, Inc.

   Albert Goldbarth: "The Talk Show," "Reality Organization," and "The Whole Earth Catalogue" from *Heaven and Earth: A Cosmology*, copyright © 1991. Reprinted by permission of The University of Georgia Press. "*Ancestored-Back* Is the Overpresiding Spirit of this Poem" from *Troubled Lovers in History*, 1999. "Arguing Bartusiak" from *Marriage, and Other Science Fiction*, 1994. Reprinted with permission from Ohio State University Press.

   Kimiko Hahn: "The Shower" and "The Glass Bracelets" from *Volatile* © 1999. "When You Leave" from *Air Pocket* © 1989. "The Izu Dancer" and "The Older Child" from *Earshot* © 1992. Reprinted by permission of Hanging Loose Press.

ACKNOWLEDGMENTS

Donald Hall: "Maple Syrup," "In the Kitchen of the Old House," and "Digging" from *Old and New Poems* by Donald Hall. Copyright © 1990 by Donald Hall. "The Porcelain Couple" and "The Ship Pounding" from *Without* by Donald Hall. Copyright © 1998 by Donald Hall. "When the Young Husband" from *The Museums of Clear Ideas* by Donald Hall. Copyright © 1993 by Donald Hall. Reprinted by permission of Houghton Mifflin Company. All rights reserved.

Michael S. Harper: "We Assume: On the Death of Our Son, Reuben Masai Harper," "Reuben, Reuben," "Dear John, Dear Coltrane," "Love Medley: Patrice Cuchulain," "This Is My Son's Song: 'Ungie, Hi Ungie'" from *Images of Kin*, 1977. "My Father at 75" and "Studs" from *Honorable Amendments*, 1995. Reprinted by permission of the University of Illinois Press and Michael S. Harper. "Here Where Coltrane Is" by Michael Harper from *Images of Kin.* Copyright 1977 by Michael S. Harper. Used with permission of the poet and the University of Illinois Press.

Robert Hass: "The Image," and "Meditation at Lagunitas" from *Praise* by Robert Hass. Copyright © 1979 by Robert Hass. "Late Spring," "A Story About the Body," "Privilege of Being," "Dragonflies Mating," and "Spring Drawing" from *Human Wishes* by Robert Hass. Copyright © 1989 by Robert Hass. "6 (This morning in the early sun)," "Happiness," "Our Lady of the Snows," and "Faint Music" from *Sun Under Wood* by Robert Hass. Copyright © 1996 by Robert Hass. Reprinted by permission of Harper Collins, Inc. Ecco Press.

Robert Hayden: "Those Winter Sundays." Copyright © 1966 by Robert Hayden, "Night, Death, Mississippi" by Frederick Glaysher, editor. Copyright © 1962, 1966 by Robert Hayden, "Monet's 'Waterlilies'" by Frederick Glaysher, editor. Copyright © 1970 by Robert Hayden, "Soledad"; "The Night-Blooming Cereus"; "Free Fantasia: Tiger Flowers." Copyright © 1972 by Robert Hayden, "A Plague of Starlings." Copyright © 1975 by Robert Hayden, from *Collected Poems of Robert Hayden* by Robert Hayden, edited by Frederick Glaysher. Used by permission of Liveright Publishing Corporation.

William Heyen: "The Return," "The Pigeons," "Witness," "Simple Truths," and "Redwings" are from *The Host: Selected Poems 1965–1990* by William Heyen. Reprinted by permission of Time Being Books. Copyright © 1994 by Time Being Press. All rights reserved. "Yellowthroats" first appeared in *Georgia Review*; "Blackbird Spring" and "Yellowjackets" in *Ontario Review*; © William Heyen. Reprinted by permission of the author.

Andrew Hudgins: "The Chinaberry," "One Threw a Dirt Clod and It Ran," "Ashes," and "Supper" from *Babylon in a Jar.* Copyright © 1998 by Andrew Hudgins. "Heat Lightning in a Time of Drought" from *The Never-Ending.* Copyright © 1991 by Andrew Hudgins. Previously published in *The Georgia Review.* "Mary Magdalene's Left Foot" from *Saints and Strangers.* Copyright © 1985 by Andrew Hudgins. Previously published in *Ploughshares.* "Grandmother's Spit" from *The Glass Hammer.* Copyright © 1994 by Andrew Hudgins. Previously published in *The Atlantic.* All are reprinted by permission of Houghton Mifflin Company. All rights reserved.

Richard Hugo: "Degrees of Gray in Philipsburg." Copyright © 1973 by Richard Hugo. "The Lady in Kicking Horse Reservoir." Copyright © 1973 by Richard Hugo, "Death in the Aquarium," "Living Alone," "A Map of Montana in Italy," and "Langaig" from *Making Certain It Goes On: The Collected Poems of Richard Hugo* by Richard Hugo. Copyright © 1984 by The Estate of Richard Hugo. Used by permission of W. W. Norton & Company, Inc.

David Ignatow: "1905," "Each Day," and "88 [Hello, drug addict, can you become a poem]" from *New and Collected Poems, 1970–1985* © 1986 by David Ignatow, Wesleyan University Press. "No Theory," "Communion," "The Dream," "For One Moment," "The Inheritance," "Self-Employed," "Moving Picture," "My Native Land," and "Notes for a Lecture" from *Poems 1934–1969,* © 1970 by David Ignatow, Wesleyan University Press. All are reprinted by permission of University Press of New England.

Donald Justice: "Early Poems," "First Death," "Children Walking Home from School Through Good Neighborhood," "Psalm and Lament," "Absences," "Men at Forty," "Variations on a Text by Vallejo," and "In Memory of the Unknown Poet, Robert Boardman Vaughn" from *New and Selected Poems* by Donald Justice. Copyright © 1995 by Donald Justice. Reprinted by permission of Alfred A. Knopf, a Division of Random House Inc.

Galway Kinnell: "Blackberry Eating," "The Bear," and "The Fundamental Project of Technology" from *Three Books* by Galway Kinnell. Copyright © 1993 by Galway Kinnell. "Telephoning in Mexican Sunlight" from *Imperfect Thirst* by Galway Kinnell. Copyright © 1994 by Galway Kinnell. Reprinted by permission of Houghton Mifflin Company. All rights reserved. "Flower of Five Blossoms" from *When One Has Lived a Long Time Alone* by Galway Kinnell. Copyright © 1990 by Galway Kinnell. Reprinted by permission of Alfred A. Knopf, a Division of Random House, Inc.

Carolyn Kizer: "Thrall," "A Widow in Wintertime," "Pro Femina: One," and "The Intruder," from *Calm, Cool, and Collected* © 2000 by Carolyn Kizer. Reprinted by permission of Copper Canyon Press, Post Office Box 271, Port Townsend, WA 98368. "Semele Recycled," copyright © 1984, by Carolyn Kizer. Reprinted from *Yin*, by Carolyn Kizer, with the permission of BOA Editions, Ltd.

Bill Knott: "Poem to Poetry," "Sleep," "At the Crossroads" (previously titled "Poem"), "Death, "Rigor Vitus," and "Goodbye," copyright © 2000 by Bill Knott. Reprinted from *Laugh at the End of the World: Collected Comic Poems 1969–1999*, by Bill Knott. "Another First Kiss: To —" from *The Quicken Tree* copyright © 1995 by Bill Knott. All are reprinted with the permission of BOA Editions, Ltd. "Poem [I am one man, worshipping silk knees]," "Poem (The Starfish One)," "The Sculpture," "Poem [Once I had to leave you so]," "Poem [The way the world is not]," "Poem [I am the only one who can say]," "Death [Perfume opens its eyes of you]," "Hair Poem," "The Closet," "Poem [Night, in whose death did your ennui take refuge]." Reprinted by permission of the poet.

Yusef Komunyakaa: "Audacity of the Lower Gods," "Blackberries," "Work," "In the Background of Silence," "Tu Do Street," and "Thanks" from *Neon Vernacular*, 1993. "Boys in Dresses" from *Magic City*, © 1992 by Yusef Komunyakaa, Wesleyan University Press, reprinted by permission of University Press of New England.

Maxine Kumin: "Heaven as Anus," "The Grace of Geldings in Ripe Pastures," and "In the Park" reprinted from Maxine Kumin's *Our Ground Time Here Will Be Brief*. Reprinted by permission of the author. "Morning Swim." Copyright © 1965 by Maxine Kumin, "To Swim, to Believe," "The Excrement Poem." Copyright © 1978 by Maxine Kumin, "Woodchucks." Copyright © 1972 by Maxine Kumin, "In the Pea Patch" and "Nurture." Copyright © 1989 by Maxine Kumin, from *Selected Poems 1960–1990* by Maxine Kumin. Copyright © 1996 by Maxine Kumin. Used by permission of W. W. Norton & Company, Inc.

Stanley Kunitz: "The Layers." Copyright © 1978 by Stanley Kunitz, "Robin Redbreast." Copyright © 1969 by Stanley Kunitz, "The Wellfleet Whale." Copyright © 1985 by Stanley Kunitz, "Touch Me" and "The Long Boat." Copyright © 1985 by Stanley Kunitz, "The Abduction." Copyright © 1985 by Stanley Kunitz, from *Passing Through: The Later Poems New and Selected* by Stanley Kunitz. Copyright © 1995 by Stanley Kunitz. Used by permission of W. W. Norton & Company, Inc.

Li-Young Lee: "The Gift," "Persimmons," "Eating Alone," "Eating Together," and "My Indigo," copyright © 1986, by Li-Young Lee. Reprinted from *Rose*, by Li-Young Lee. "This Room and Everything in it," and "You Must Sing," copyright © 1990, by Li-Young Lee. Reprinted from *The City in Which I Love You*, by Li-Young Lee. All are reprinted with the permission of BOA Editions, Ltd.

Denise Levertov: "Where is the Angel?" by Denise Levertov from *A Door in the Hive*, copyright © 1989 by Denise Levertov. "The Acolyte" by Denise Levertov from *Candles in Babylon*, copyright © 1982 by Denise Levertov. "Wedding Ring" by Denise Levertov from *Life in the Forest*, copyright © 1978 by Denise Levertov. "Our Bodies," "The

ACKNOWLEDGMENTS

Mutes," and "Life at War" by Denise Levertov from *Poems 1960–1967*, copyright © 1996 by Denise Levertov. "The Poem Unwritten" by Denise Levertov from *Poems 1968–1972*, copyright © 1970 by Denise Levertov. All are reprinted by permission of New Directions Publishing Corp.

Philip Levine: "The Simple Truth" from *The Simple Truth* by Philip Levine. Copyright © 1994 by Philip Levine. "On the Birth of Good and Evil During the Long Winter of '28," "I Was Born in Lucerne," "They Feed They Lion," "On My Own," "Animals Are Passing from Our Lives," and "You Can Have It" from *New Selected Poems* by Philip Levine. Copyright © 1991 by Philip Levine. "What Work Is" from *What Work Is* by Philip Levine. Copyright © 1991 by Philip Levine. Reprinted by permission of Alfred A. Knopf, a Division of Random House Inc.

John Logan: "Three Moves," "Spring of the Thief," "Middle-Aged Midwesterner at Waikiki Again," and "Poem for My Brother," copyright © 1989 by John Logan. Reprinted from *John Logan: The Collected Poems*, by John Logan, with the permission of BOA Editions, Ltd.

Robert Lowell: "Eye and Tooth," "For the Union Dead," "Memories of West Street and Lepke," "Skunk Hour," and "'To Speak of Woe That Is in Marriage'" from *Selected Poems* by Robert Lowell. Copyright © 1976 by Robert Lowell. Reprinted by permission of Farrar, Straus and Giroux, LLC.

William Matthews: "Men at My Father's Funeral" from *Time and Money*. Copyright © 1995 by William Matthews. Previously published in *The Ohio Review*. "Grief" from *Time and Money*. Copyright © 1995 by William Matthews. Previously published in *The New Yorker*. "Housework," "In Memory of the Utah Stars," "Pissing Off the Back of the Boat into the Nivernais Canal," "Moving Again," and "Onions" from *Selected Poems & Translations* by William Matthews. Copyright © 1992 by William Matthews. "The Cloister" from *After All: Last Poems* by William Matthews. Copyright © 1998 by the Estate of William Matthews. All are reprinted by permission of Houghton Mifflin Company. All rights reserved.

James Merrill: "The Octopus," "Charles on Fire," "The Mad Scene," "The Kimono," and "Laboratory Poem" from *Selected Poems 1946–1985* by James Merrill. Copyright © 1992 by James Merrill. "My Father's Irish Setters," "A Downward Look," "b o d y," and "An Upward Look" from *A Scattering of Salts* by James Merrill. Copyright © 1995 by James Merrill. Reprinted by permission of Alfred A. Knopf, a Division of Random House Inc.

W. S. Merwin: "Field Mushrooms" from *Travels* by W. S. Merwin. Copyright © 1992 by W. S. Merwin. "The Rose Beetle" from *The Rain in the Trees* by W. S. Merwin. Copyright © 1998 by W. S. Merwin. Reprinted by permission of Alfred A. Knopf, a Division of Random House Inc. "The Poem," "How We Are Spared," "For the Anniversary of My Death," "Dead Hand," "The Chaff," "Remembering a Boatman," "Fog-Horn," and "St Vincent's" from *Selected Poems* (Atheneum, 1988). "The Free" from *The Carrier of Ladders* (Atheneum, 1970). "When You Go Away" from *The Lice* (Atheneum, 1967.) Copyright © 1968, 1970, 1988 by W. S. Merwin. No changes shall be made to the text of the above work without the express consent of The Wylie Agency, Inc.

Marilyn Nelson: "I Decide Not to Have Children," "Mama's Murders," "Women's Locker Room," "As Simple As That," "Boys in the Park," and "Minor Miracle." Reprinted by permission of Louisiana State University Press from *The Fields of Praise: New and Selected Poems*, by Marilyn Nelson. Copyright © 1997 by Marilyn Nelson.

Naomi Shihab Nye: "Vocabulary of Dearness," "Steps," "The Small Vases from Hebron," and "The Last Day of August," copyright © 1998 by Naomi Shihab Nye. Reprinted from *Fuel*, by Naomi Shihab Nye. "Arabic," "Morning Paper, Society Page," and "What Brings Us Out," copyright © 1994, by Naomi Shihab Nye. Reprinted from *Red Suitcase*, by Naomi Shihab Nye, with the permission of BOA Editions, Ltd. "The Shapes of Mouths at Parties" from *Hugging the JukeBox* (Dutton, 1982). Reprinted with the per-

ACKNOWLEDGMENTS

mission of the poet. "The Traveling Onion" from *Words Under the Words: Selected Poems* by Naomi Shihab Nye, copyright © 1995. Used by permission of Far Corner Books.

Frank O'Hara: "Why I Am Not a Painter," "Poem [I don't know as I get what D. H. Lawrence is driving at]," "For Grace, After a Party," and "Getting Up Ahead of Someone (Sun)" from *Collected Poems* by Frank O'Hara. Copyright © 1971 by Maureen Granville-Smith, Administratrix of the Estate of Frank O'Hara. Reprinted by permission of Alfred A. Knopf, a Division of Random House Inc. "Poem [Lana Turner has collapsed]," "Steps," "The Day Lady Died," and "Personal Poem" from *Lunch Poems*. © Copyright 1964 by Frank O'Hara. Reprinted by permission of City Lights.

Sharon Olds: "Monarchs" from *Satan Says*, by Sharon Olds, © 1980. Reprinted by permission of the University of Pittsburgh Press. "A Woman in Heat Wiping Herself" and "The Pope's Penis" from *The Gold Cell* by Sharon Olds. Copyright © 1987 by Sharon Olds. "Early Images of Heaven," "May 1968," and "Good Will" from *The Wellspring* by Sharon Olds. Copyright © 1996 by Sharon Olds. "The Elder Sister" from *The Dead and the Living* by Sharon Olds. Copyright © 1983 by Sharon Olds. "The Lifting" and "The Glass" from *The Father* by Sharon Olds. Copyright © 1992 by Sharon Olds. Reprinted by permission of Alfred A. Knopf, a Division of Random House Inc.

Carl Phillips: "Glads," "Toys," and "Our Lady" copyright 1995 by Carl Phillips. Reprinted from *Cortege*. "As from a Quiver of Arrows" and "Luna Moth" copyright © 1998 by Carl Phillips. Reprinted from *From The Devotions*, "Parable" by Carl Phillips. Reprinted from *Pastoral*. All are reprinted with the permission of Graywolf Press, Saint Paul, Minnesota. "Luck" by Carl Phillips originally appeared in *The Nation*. Copyright © 1999 by Carl Phillips. Reprinted by permission of the author. "Blue" from *In the Blood* by Carl Phillips. Copyright © 1992 by Carl Phillips. Reprinted with the permission of Northeastern University Press.

Sylvia Plath: "Stillborn" from *The Collected Poems of Sylvia Plath* edited by Ted Hughes. Copyright © 1960, 1965, 1971, 1981 by the Estate of Sylvia Plath. Editorial material copyright © 1981 by Ted Hughes. All lines from "Crossing the Water" from *Crossing the Water* by Sylvia Plath. Copyright © 1962 by Ted Hughes. Copyright renewed. All lines from "Daddy," "Cut," and "Lady Lazarus" from *Ariel* by Sylvia Plath. Copyright © 1963 by Ted Hughes. All are reprinted by permission of HarperCollins Publishers, Inc.

Adrienne Rich: "Power," "Planetarium" "Diving into the Wreck," and "Splittings" from *The Fact of a Doorframe: Poems Selected and New 1950–1984* by Adrienne Rich. Copyright © 1984 by Adrienne Rich. Copyright © 1975, 1978 by W. W. Norton & Company, Inc. Copyright © 1981 by Adrienne Rich. "Part XIII (Dedications)" from *An Atlas of the Difficult World: Poems 1988–1991* by Adrienne Rich. Copyright © 1991 by Adrienne Rich. "The Novel" and "One Life" from *Time's Power: Poems 1985–1988* by Adrienne Rich. Copyright © 1989 by Adrienne Rich. Used by permission of the author and W. W. Norton & Company, Inc.

Anne Sexton: "With Mercy for the Greedy," "To a Friend Whose Work Has Cometo Triumph," and "The Abortion" from *All My Pretty Ones* by Anne Sexton. Copyright © 1962 by Anne Sexton, renewed 1990 by Linda G. Sexton. "Her Kind" from *To Bedlam and Part Way Back* by Anne Sexton. Copyright © 1960 by Anne Sexton, renewed 1988 by Linda G. Sexton. "The Fury of Cocks" from *The Death of Notebooks*. Copyright © 1974 by Anne Sexton. "In Celebration of My Uterus" from *Love Poems*, Copyright © 1967, 1968, 1969 by Anne Sexton. "Man and Wife" from *Live or Die*. Copyright © 1966 by Anne Sexton. All are reprinted by permission of Houghton Mifflin Company. All rights reserved.

Charles Simic: "The Old World" from *Hotel Insomnia*, copyright © 1992 by Charles Simic. "The Little Pins of Memory" from *The Book of Gods and Devils*, copyright © 1990 by Charles Simic. "Entertaining the Canary" from *Walking the Black Cat: Poems*, copyright © 1992 by Charles Simic. All are reprinted by permission of Harcourt, Inc. "Charles Simic," "Poem Without a Title," "February," "Poem," "Stone," "Fork,"

"Solitude," "Fear," "Classic Ballroom Dances," and *"errata"* from *Selected Poems 1963–1993*, 1990. Reprinted by permission of George Braziller, Inc. Publishers.

Louis Simpson: "Dinner at the Sea-View Inn," "Quiet Desperation," "In the Suburbs," and "Physical Universe" from *Collected Poems* (Paragon House, 1990). "Working Late" and "Riverside Drive" from *In the Room That We Share* (Paragon House, 1990). Poems by Louis Simpson reprinted by permission of the author. Copyright © Louis Simpson. "The Cabin" by Louis Simpson from *There You Are*, Copyright © 1994. Reprinted by permission of Story Line Press.

W. D. Snodgrass: "Viewing the Body," "from *Heart's Needle:* 9 [I get numb and go in]," "After Experience Taught Me . . . ," and "Old Apple Trees" from *Selected Poems: 1957–1987* (Soho, 1987). Reprinted by permission of Soho Press. "Love Lamp," copyright © 1993 by W. D. Snodgrass. Reprinted from *Each In His Own Season*, by W. D. Snodgrass with the permission of BOA Editions, Inc.

Gary Snyder: "Bubbs Creek Haircut" from *Mountains and Rivers Without End* by Gary Snyder. Copyright © 1996 by Gary Snyder. Reprinted by permission of Counterpoint Press, a member of Perseus Books, LLC. Reprinted by permission of North Point Press, a division of Farrar, Straus and Giroux, LLC: "Axe Handles" from *Axe Handles* by Gary Snyder. Copyright © 1983 by Gary Snyder. "Hay for the Horses" from *Riprap and Cold Mountain Poems* by Gary Snyder. Copyright © 1990 by Gary Snyder. "'One Should Not Talk to a Skilled Hunter About What Is Forbidden by the Buddha'" and "The Bath" by Gary Snyder from *Turtle Island*, copyright © 1974 by Gary Snyder. Reprinted by permission of New Directions Publishing Corp.

Gary Soto: "Black Hair," "Envying the Children of San Francisco," "Oranges," "Failing in the Presence of Ants," "Mexicans Begin Jogging," and "The Tale of Sunlight" from *New and Selected Poems* by Gary Soto © 1995. Published by Chronicle Books, San Francisco. Used with permission.

Elizabeth Spires: "Sunday Afternoon at Fulham Palace," "The Celestial," and "The Beds" from *Annonciade* by Elizabeth Spires, copyright © 1985, 1986, 1987, 1988, 1989 by Elizabeth Spires. Used by permission of Viking Penguin, a division of Penguin Putnam Inc. "The First Day" from *Worldling* by Elizabeth Spires. Copyright © 1995 by Elizabeth Spires. Used by permission of W. W. Norton & Company, Inc. "'In Heaven It Is Always Autumn'" and "Dogwood" copyright 1996, 2000 by Elizabeth Spires. "Cemetery Reef." Copyright © 2000 by Elizabeth Spires. Reprinted by permission of the poet.

David St. John: "Gin," "The Swan at Sheffield Park," "Lucifer in Starlight," and "Last Night with Rafaella" from *Study for the World's Body: New and Selected Poems* (HarperCollins, 1994), © 1994, David St. John. Reprinted by permission of the author.

William Stafford: "How the Real Bible Is Written," "At Fourth and Main in Liberal, Kansas, 1932," "Growing Up," "Ask Me," "Ceremony," "Traveling Through the Dark," "Vocation," "Adults Only," "Fifteen," "The Light by the Barn," "With Kit, Age 7, at the Beach," and "Near," copyright 1960, 1962, 1966, 1970, 1977, 1978, 1991, 1998 by the Estate of William Stafford. Reprinted from *The Way It Is: New & Selected Poems* with the permission of Graywolf Press, Saint Paul, Minnesota. "Widow" and "A Wind from a Wing" are reprinted with the permission of Confluence Press from *My Name is William Tell*, copyright 1992 by William Stafford.

Gerald Stern: "The Bull-Roarer" from *Bread Without Sugar* by Gerald Stern. Copyright © 1992 by Gerald Stern. "I Remember Galileo," "The Dancing," "Soap," "Another Insane Devotion," "The Sweetness of Life," and "Lilacs for Ginsberg" from *This Time: New and Selected Poems* by Gerald Stern. Copyright © 1998 by Gerald Stern. Used by permission of W. W. Norton & Company, Inc.

Mark Strand: "Keeping Things Whole," "The Dress," "The Prediction," "My Life by Somebody Else," "A Morning," and "Leopardi" from *Selected Poems* by Mark Strand. Copyright © 1979, 1980 by Mark Strand. "The Idea" and "A.M." from *The Continuous Life* by Mark Strand. Copyright © 1990 by Mark Strand. "XXX," "XXXIX," and "XLV," from

Dark Harbor by Mark Strand. Copyright © 1993 by Mark Strand. "The Night, The Porch" and "A Piece of the Storm" from *Blizzard of One* by Mark Strand. Copyright © 1998 by Mark Strand. Reprinted by permission of Alfred A. Knopf, a Division of Random House Inc.

Ellen Bryant Voigt: "The Hen" from *Claiming Kin.* © 1978 by Ellen Bryant Voigt, Wesleyan University Press, reprinted by permission of University Press of New England. "January" from *The Forces of Plenty* by Ellen Bryant Voigt (Norton, 1983). "The Trust," "Fairy Tale," "The Lotus Flowers," and "The Cusp" from *The Lotus Flowers* by Ellen Bryant Voigt (Norton, 1987). Reprinted with the permission of the poet. "Two Trees," "Woman Who Weeps" from *Two Trees* by Ellen Bryant Voigt. Copyright © 1992 by Ellen Bryant Voigt. Used by permission of W. W. Norton & Company, Inc.

Richard Wilbur: "Love Calls Us to the Things of This World" from *Things of This World*, copyright © 1956 and renewed 1984 by Richard Wilbur. "The Ride" from *New and Collected Poems*, copyright © 1982 by Richard Wilbur. "The Lilacs" from *Walking to Sleep: New Poems and Translations*, copyright © 1963, 1991 by Richard Wilbur. "Playboy" from *Walking to Sleep: New Poems and Translations*, copyright © 1968 and renewed 1996 by Richard Wilbur. "Cottage Street, 1953" from *The Mind-Reader*, copyright © 1972 by Richard Wilbur. "The Writer" from *The Mind-Reader*, copyright © 1971 by Richard Wilbur. All are reprinted by permission of Harcourt, Inc. "Mayflies" from *Mayflies: New Poems and Translations*, copyright © 2000 by Richard Wilbur, reprinted by permission of Harcourt, Inc. First appeared in *The New Yorker.*

C. K. Williams: "Normality" from *Flesh and Blood* by C. K. Williams. Copyright © 1987 by C. K. Williams. "Blades," "From My Window," and "The Gas Station" from *Poems 1963–1983* by C. K. Williams. Copyright © 1988 by C. K. Williams. "Depths" from *Repair* by C. K. Williams. Copyright © 1999 by C. K. Williams. "The Neighbor" from *The Vigil* by C. K. Williams. Copyright © 1997 by C. K. Williams. Reprinted by permission of Farrar, Straus and Giroux, LLC.

Charles Wright: "Reunion," "Grace," "Virgo Descending," "Him," and "Snow" from *Country Music: Selected Early Poems*, 1982 and "California Dreaming" from *The Other Side of the River*, 1984 by Charles Wright. Reprinted with permission from Charles Wright. "Poem Half in the Manner of Li Ho" from *Black Zodiac* by Charles Wright. Copyright © 1997 by Charles Wright. "Night Journal" from *Zone Journals* by Charles Wright. Copyright © 1988 by Charles Wright. Reprinted by permission of Farrar, Straus and Giroux, LLC.

James Wright: "Autumn Begins in Martins Ferry, Ohio," "Lying in a Hammock at William Duffy's Farm in Pine Island, Minnesota," "The Jewel," "The Minneapolis Poem," and "In Response to a Rumor That the Oldest Whorehouse in Wheeling, West Virginia, Has Been Condemned" from *Above the River: The Complete Poems*, © 1990 by James Wright, Wesleyan University Press, reprinted by permission of University Press of New England. "The Journey" from *This Journey* by James Wright. Copyright © 1977, 1978, 1980, 1981, 1982 by Anne Wright, Executrix of the Estate of James Wright. Reprinted by permission of Random House, Inc. "Beautiful Ohio" from *Above the River: The Complete Poems* by James Wright, introduction by Donald Hall. Copyright © 1990 by Anne Wright, introduction © 1990 by Donald Hall. Reprinted by permission of Farrar, Straus and Giroux, LLC. "The Good Young Man" and "The Old WPA Swimming Pool in Martins Ferry, Ohio" from *Above the River: The Complete Poems* by James Wright. Copyright © 1990 by James Wright. Reprinted by permission of Anne Wright.

To the Student

Will you take the time to write your reactions to *Contemporary American Poetry?* Your comments will help us to plan future editions of the work. Please fill out the questionnaire and mail it to:

Marketing Services
College Division
Houghton Mifflin Company
222 Berkeley Street
Boston, MA 02116-3764

1. Please give the name and number of the course for which you used this textbook. Indicate whether the course is one or two semesters.

_____

Name of your college or university

_____

Which year did you take the course?
___ Freshman ___ Sophomore ___ Junior ___ Senior

2. Please check the name of each poet below whose works you read for the course.

__ Ai	__ Glück	__ Kunitz	__ Simic
__ Ammons	__ Goldbarth	__ Lee	__ Simpson
__ Ashbery	__ Hahn	__ Levertov	__ Snodgrass
__ Bell	__ Hall	__ Levine	__ Snyder
__ Berryman	__ Harper	__ Logan	__ Soto
__ Bishop	__ Hass	__ Lowell	__ Spires
__ Bly	__ Hayden	__ Matthews	__ St. John
__ Brooks	__ Heyen	__ Merrill	__ Stafford
__ Broumas	__ Hudgins	__ Merwin	__ Stern
__ Clifton	__ Hugo	__ Nelson	__ Strand
__ Creeley	__ Ignatow	__ Nye	__ Voigt
__ Dickey	__ Justice	__ O'Hara	__ Wilbur
__ Dobyns	__ Kinnell	__ Olds	__ Williams
__ Dove	__ Kizer	__ Phillips	__ C. Wright
__ Dugan	__ Knott	__ Plath	__ J. Wright
__ Frost	__ Komunyakaa	__ Rich	
__ Ginsberg	__ Kumin	__ Sexton	

3. Of the poets you read, please list the five or so who made the strongest impression on you. _____

_____

4. Of the poets you read, please list any whose works you feel you did not understand or appreciate. _____

_____

5. When you studied a given poet, did you read all of his or her works in the anthology? ___ Usually ___ Sometimes ___ Rarely

6. Did your course include poets who are not represented in this text-book? ___ Yes ___ No If you read additional poets, please list as many as you can recall. _____

_____

7. Do you plan to keep this textbook for your own library?
   ___ Yes ___ No

8. How much did you use the Notes on the Poets at the back of the book?
   ___ Very often ___ Often ___ Occasionally __ Rarely ___Never

9. Did you use the selected bibliography of critical works?
   ___ Yes ___ No

10. Please make any additional comments that you care to about the anthology.

_____

_____

_____

_____

_____

_____

_____

_____

_____

_____

_____

_____

_____

_____

_____

_____

_____

_____

Thank you for your help.